Webster's

English/Spanish Dictionary

® Landoll, Inc.
© 1997 Landoll, Inc.
Ashland, Ohio 44805

a *prep.* at; to
a-ba-ce-ría *f.* grocery
a-ba-ce-ro *m.* grocer
á-ba-co *m.* abacus
a-bad *m.* abbot
a-ba-de-sa *f.* abbess
a-ba-di-a *f.* abbey
a-ba-jo *adv.* beneath; down; below; *prep.* down
a-ban-de-ra-mien-to *m.* registration (nautical)
a-ban-de-rar *v.* to register
a-ban-do-na-do, -da *adj.* derelict; careless
a-ban-do-nar *v.* to desert; forsake; abandon; give up
a-ban-do-no *m.* abandonment; neglect
a-ba-ni-car *v.* to fan
a-ba-ni-co *m.* fan
a-ba-ra-jar *v.* to catch
a-ba-ra-tar *v.* to lower; become cheaper
a-bar-car *v.* to embrace; comprise; encompass
a-ba-ti-do, -da *adj.* downcast; dejected; despondently; glum
a-ba-ti-mien-to *m.* dejection
a-ba-tir(se) *v.* to knock down; depress; discourage
ab-di-var *v.* to abdicate
ab-do-men *m.* abdomen
ab-do-min-al *adj.* abdominal
a-be-dul *m.* birch
a-be-ja *f.* bee
a-be-jo-rro *m.* bumblebee
a-be-jón *m.* hornet
a-be-rra-cion *f.* aberration
a-ber-tu-ra *f.* aperture; gap
a-be-to *m.* fir
a-bier-ta-mem-te *adv.* outright
a-bier-to, -ta *adj.* open; clear
a-bi-ga-rra-do, -da *adj.* many-colored variegated; motley
a-bis-mal *adj.* abysmal
a-bis-mo *m.* abyss
ab-ju-rar *v.* to abjure
a-blan-dar(se) *v., n.* to soften; mollify

a-bla-tivo *m.* ablative
a-blu-ción *f.* ablution
ab-ne-ga-ción *f.* abnegation
ab-ne-gar *v.* to renounce; abnegate
a-bo-car *v.* to decant
a-bo-car-dar *v.* to ream
a-bo-chor-na-do, -da *adj.* suffocating
a-bo-chor-nar *v.* to blush; suffocate
a-bo-fe-tear *v.* to slap
a-bo-ga-cía *f.* bar; law; advocacy
a-bo-ga-do *m.* attorney; counsel; lawyer
a-bo-gar *v.* to plead; to advocate
a-bo-len-go *m.* ancestry
a-bo-li-ción *f.* abolition
a-bo-li-cio-nis-ta *m., f.* abolitionist
a-bo-lir *v.* to abolish
a-bo-lla-du-ra *f.* dent
a-bo-llar *v.* to emboss; dent
a-bo-mi-na-ble *adj.* abominable
a-bo-mi-na-ción *f.* abomination
a-bo-mi-nar *v.* to abominate; loathe
a-bo-nar *v.* to fertilize; give credit
a-bo-no *m.* manure; fertilizer; subscription; guarantee
a-bo-ri-gen *adj. m., pl.* aboriginal
a-bo-rre-cer *v.* to hate; abhor
a-bo-rre-ci-ble *adj.* detestable; abhorrent; loathsome; hateful
a-bo-ree-ci-mien-to *m.* hate; hatred; abhorrence; loathing
a-bor-tar *v.* to abort
a-bor-tivo, a *adj.* abortive
a-bor-to *m.* abortion
a-bo-to-nar *v.* to button up
a-bo-za-lar *v.* to muzzle
a-bra *f.* cove
a-bra-sion *f.* abrasion
a-bra-si-vo *adj.* abrasive

a-bra-za-de-ra *f.* clamp; brace

a-bra-zar(se) *v.* to hug; cuddle; embrace

a-bra-zo *m.* hug; embrace

a-bre-car-tas *m.* letter opener

a-bre-var *v.* to soak; water

a-bre-via-ción *f.* abbreviation

a-bre-viar *v.* to abridge; abbreviate; curtail; condense

a-bri-gar(se) *v.* to shelter; harbor; protect

a-bri-go *m.* shelter; coat; overcoat

a-bril *m.* April

a-bri-llan-tar *v.* to cut into parts; polish; brighten

a-brir(se) *v.* to open up; to spread out; open

a-bro-char *v.* to button up; fasten; buckle

a-bro-ga-ción *f.* abrogation

a-bro-gar *v.* abrogate; repeal

a-bru-ma-dor, a *adj.* crushing

a-bru-mar *v.* to overwhelm

a-brup-to, -ta *adj.* abrupt; steep; blunt

a-bru-ta-do, -da *adj.* bestial

abs-ce-so *m.* abscess

ab-so-lu-ción *f.* absolution

ab-so-lu-to,-ta *adj.* complete; absolute

ab-sol-ven-te *adj.* absolving

ab-sol-ver *v.* to acquit; clear; absolve

ab-sor-ben-cia *f.* absorbence

ab-sor-ben-te *m.* absorbent

ab-sor-ber *v.* to soak up; engross; absorb

ab-sor-ción *f.* absorption

ab-sor-to, -ta *adj.* abosrbed; intent

abs-ten-cion *f.* abstention

abs-te-ner-se *v.* to abstain; refrain

abs-ti-nen-cia *f.* abstinence

abs-trac-to, -ta *adj.* abstract

abs-tra-er *v.* to abstract

abs-tru-so, -sa *adj.* abstruse

ab-sur-di-dad *f.* absurdity

ab-sur-do, -da *adj.* silly; preposterous; absurd

a-bue-la *f.* grandmother

a-bue-lo *m.* grandfather; grandparent

a-bun-da-mien-to *m.* abundance

a-bun-dan-cia *f.* abundance; amplitude

a-bun-dan-te *adj.* plentiful; aboundant; ample

a-bun-dar *v.* to abound

a-bun-do-so *adj.* abundant

a-bu-rri-do *adj.* boring; bored

a-bu-rri-mien-to *m.* boredom

a-bu-rrir *v.* to bore

a-bu-sar *v.* to misuse; maltreat; abuse; impose

a-bu-si-vo, a *adj.* abusive

a-bu-so *m.* encroachment; abuse

ab-yec-ción *f.* abjectness

ab-yec-to, -ta *adj.* abject

a-cá *adv.* here

a-ca-ba-do, -da *adj.* end; conclusion

a-ca-bar *v.* to accomplish; end; fail

a-ca-de-mia *f.* academy

a-ca-dé-mi-co *adj.* academic

a-ca-li-zar *v.* to alkalize

a-cam-par *v.* to camp

a-ca-ri-ciar *v.* to pet; pat

a-ca-rrear *v.* to cart

a-ca-rreo *m.* cartage

ac-ce-der *v.* to accede

ac-ce-si-ble *adj.* accessible

ac-ce-so *m.* approach; access

ac-ce-so-rio, a *m.* accessory

ac-ci-den-ta-do, a *adj.* uneven; broken; eventful

ac-ci-den-te *m.* casualty; accident

ac-ción *f.* movement; action

a-ce-bo *m.* holly

a-ce-char *v.* to lurk; watch for

a-cei-te *m.* oil

a-cei-tu-na *f.* olive

a-ce-le-rar(se) *v.* to speed; accelerate

a-cen-to *v.* stress; emphasis; accent

a-cen-tuar(se) *v.* to emphasize; accent; stress

a-cep-tar *v.* adopt; accept; agree to something

a-cer-car(se) *v.* to bring near

a-ce-ro *n.m.* steel

a-cer-ti-jo *m.* riddle

a-cé-ti-co *adj.* acetic

a-ce-to-na *f.* acetone

á-ci-do *m.* acid

á-ci-do bo-ri-co *m.* boric acid

á-ci-do ci-tri-co *m.* citric acid

á-ci-do sul-fu-ri-co *m.* sulphuric acid

a-cla-ma-ción *f.* acclaim

a-cla-ra-ción *f.* clarification

a-cla-rar *v.* to clear; to clarify; to rinse

a-cli-ma-tar *v.* acclimate

ac-ne *m.* acne

a-co-bar-dar(se) *v.* to flinch; unnerve; cringe

a-co-gi-da *f.* welcome; shelter

a-col-char *v.* pad

a-có-li-to *m.* altar boy; acolyte

a-co-me-ter *v.* attempt; undertake; overcome; attack

a-co-mo-da-di-zo *adj.* easygoing

a-co-mo-da-dor *m.* usher *f.* usherette

a-co-mo-dar *v.* to suit; to accommodate; put up

a-com-pa-ñan-te *m.* escort *mus.* accompanist

a-com-pa-ñar *v.* to escort; attend; go with; accompany

a-con-di-cio-na-d or de ai-re *m.* air conditioner

a-con-se-jar(se) *v.* to take advice; advise; counsel

a-con-te-cer *v.* to chance; to happen

a-con-te-ci-mien-to *m.* occasion; event; occurrence; happening

a-cor-dar(se) *v.* to agree on; remember; agree

a-cor-de *m.* chord; in tune; harmony; in accord

a-cor-deón *m.* accordion

a-cor-near *v.* to gore

a-co-rra-lar *v.* to round up; corral; intimidate; pen

a-cor-tar(se) *v.* to clip; shorten; lessen; obstruct

a-co-sar *v.* to harass; pursue; beset

a-cos-tar(se) *v.* to lie down; go to bed

a-cos-tum-brar(se) *v.* to be accustomed to; be used to; habituate

a-cre *adj.* acrid; sour

a-cre-cen-tar *v.* to advance; increase

a-cree-dor *m.* creditor

a-cri-mo-nia *f.* bitterness

a-cró-ba-ta *n.m.f.* acrobat

ac-ti-tud *f.* pose; position; attitude

ac-ti-var *v.* to activate

ac-ti-vi-dad *f.* movement; nimbleness; activity

ac-ti-vo, -va *adj.* alive; brisk; active; quick

ac-to *m.* event; act; function

ac-tor *m.* actor

ac-triz *f.* actress

ac-tual *adj.* instant; actual

ac-tual-men-te *adv.* at present; now; actually

ac-tuar *v.* perform; act; set in action

a-cua-rio *m.* aquarium

a-cu-á-til *adj.* aquatic

a-cu-chi-llar *v.* to slash; hack; knife

a-cue-duc-to *m.* aqueduct

a-cueo, a *adj.* watery

a-cuer-do *m.* remembrance; resolution; agreement; accord

a-cu-mu-lar *v.* to amass; stock-pile; accumulate; congest

a-cu-ña-cion *f.* coinage

a-cu-ñar *v.* to coin; mint

a-cu-sar *v.* to impeach; charge; indict; accuse

a-cús-ti-ca *f.* acoustics

a-chi-car *v.* diminish;

humble; bail

a·chis·pa·do, -da *adj.* tipsy

a·da·gio *m.* proverb; adage

a·da·lid *m.* commander

a·dap·ta·ble *adj.* adaptable; versatile

a·dap·ta·ción *f.* adaptation

a·dap·tar *v.* to fit; adapt; adapt oneself to; adjust

a·de·cua·do, -da *adj.* fit; suitable; adequate

a·de·fe·sio *n.* something gaudy; extravagance

a·de·ha·la *f.* tip; bonus

a·de·lan·ta·do, -da *adj.* fast; advanced

a·de·lan·tar(se) *v.* to further; proceed; overtake

a·de·lan·te *adv.* forwards; forward

a·de·lan·to *m.* progress; advance

a·del·ga·zar(se) *v.* to lose weight; taper; make thin; attenuate; slim down

a·de·mán *m.* attitude; gesture

a·de·más *adv.* besides; moreover; in addition

a·den·tro *adv.* inside; within

a·dep·to *m.* adept

a·de·re·zar *v.* adorn; garnish

a·de·re·zo *m.* finery; adornment; dressing

a·des·trar *v.* to train

a·deu·dar *v.* to debit; owe

ad·he·ren·cia *f.* bond; adherence

ad·he·ren·te *adj.* adherent; adhesive

ad·he·rir(se) *v.* to cling; adhere; stick

ad·he·sión *f.* adherence

ad·he·si·vo, -va *adj.* ahesive

a·di·ción *f.* addition

a·di·cio·nal *adj.* more; extra; additional

a·dic·to, -ta *adj.* addicted

a·dies·trar(se) *v.* to exercise; train; practise

a·diós *m.* farewell; goodbye; good day

a·di·po·so, a *m.* fat; adipose

a·di·ta·men·to *m.* attachment; addition

a·di·ti·vo *m.* additive

a·di·vi·nar *v.* to foretell; to guess

ad·je·ti·vo *m.* adjective

ad·ju·di·ca·ción *m.* award; adjudgment

ad·ju·di·car(se) *v.* to allot; to award

ad·jun·tar *v.* to annex

ad·mi·nis·tra·ción *f.* administration; management

ad·mi·nis·tra·dor, -ra *m.* administrator; steward; manager

ad·mi·nis·trar *v.* to manage; dispense; administer

ad·mi·nis·tra·ti·vo, -va *adj.* administrative

ad·mi·ra·ble *adj.* fine; excellent; admirable

ad·mi·ra·ción *f.* admiration

ad·mi·rar(se) *v.* to wonder; admire; amaze

ad·mi·si·ble *adj.* acceptable; admissible

ad·mi·sión *f.* input; admission

ad·mi·tir *v.* to acknowledge; permit; admit

a·do·be *m.* adobe

a·do·les·cen·cia *f.* adolescence

a·dop·tar *v.* to embrace

a·dop·ti·vo, -va *adj.* adoptive

a·do·ra·ble *adj.* adorable

a·do·ra·ción *f.* adoration

a·do·rar *v.* to worship; adore

a·dor·me·cer(se) *v.* to fall asleep; drowse

a·dor·mi·de·ra *f.* poppy

a·dor·na·mien·to *m.* adornment

a·dor·nar *v.* to adorn; deck; ecorate; grace

a·dor·no *m.* adornment; ornament; array

ad·qui·rir *v.* to obtain; secure; acquire

a·dre·na·li·na *f.* adrenaline

ads·cri·bir *v.* assign; ascribe

a·dua·na *f.* customs

a-dua-ne-ro *m.* customs
a-du-cir *v.* to cite; adduce
a-du-ja-da *adj.* coiled
a-du-la-ción *f.* flattery; adulation
a-du-la-dor, a *m.* flatterer
a-du-lar *v.* to flatter; adulate
a-dul-te-ra-ción *f.* adulteration
a-dul-te-ra-dor, a *m.* adulterator
a-dul-te-rar *v.* to adulterate
a-dul-te-rio *m.* adultery
a-dul-to, -ta *m.* adult
a-dul-zar *v.* to make sweet
ad-ver-bi-al *adj.* adverbial
ad-ver-bio *m.* adverb
ad-ver-sa-rio *m.* opponent; adversary
ad-ver-si-dad *f.* adversity
ad-ver-so, -sa *adj.* averse; unfavorable; adverse
ad-ver-ti-do, -da *adj.* skillful; informed; intelligent; capable; sagacious
ad-ver-tir *v.* to notify; advise; caution; take notice of something; observe
ad-ya-cen-te *adj.* adjacent
ae-ra-ción *f.* aeration
aé-reo, -rea *adj.* aerial
ae-ro-di-na-mi-co *adj.* aerodynamic
ae-ro-náu-ti-ca, -co *f.* aeronautics
ae-ro-pla-no *n.* airplane; aeroplane
ae-ro-puer-to *m.* airport
a-fa-bi-li-dad *f.* affability
a-fa-ble *adj.* affable; genial; kind
a-fán *m.* anxiety; travail
a-fa-nar *v.* to urge; toil; strive
a-fa-no-so, -sa *adj.* anxious
a-fec-ción *f.* fondness; affection
a-fec-ta-ción *f.* pretense; affectation
a-fec-ta-do, -da *adj.* affected
a-fec-tar *v.* to affect
a-fec-to *m.* affection
a-fec-tuo-sa-men-te *adv.* fondly; affectionately

a-fec-tuo-so *adj.* affectionate
a-fei-ta-do, -da *m.* shave
a-fei-tar *v.* to shave
a-fei-te *m.* shave; cosmetic
a-fe-rrar(se) *v.* to grasp; furl
a-fian-zar *v.* to bail; clinch; quaranty
a-fi-ción *f.* liking; affection; inclination
a-fi-cio-na-do, -da *m.* fan; amateur; fancier
a-fi-jo, -ja *m.* affix
a-fi-lar(se) *v.* to sharpen
a-fi-liar(se) *v.* to join; affiliate; adopt
a-fin *adj.* related; contiguous; adjacent
a-fi-na-ción *f.* refining; tuning
a-fi-nar *v.* to refine; polish; complete; tune
a-fi-ni-dad *f.* affinity; relationship
a-fir-mar(se) *v.* to secure; assert; contend; affirm; make fast
a-fir-ma-ti-vo *adj.* affirmative
a-flic-ción *f.* anxiety; bereavement; afflication
a-fli-gi-do *adj.* stricken
a-fli-gir(se) *v.* to afflict
a-flo-jar(se) *v.* to loosen; slacken; weaken
a-flo-rar *v.* to emerge; sift
a-fluen-cia *f.* affluence; crowd; jam; fluency; abundance
a-fluen-te *adj.* affluent
a-fo-rar *v.* to appraise; guage; measure
a-fo-ris-mo *m.* aphorism; maxim
a-for-tu-na-do, -da *adj.* prosperous; lucky; fortunate
a-fren-ta *f.* to insult; affront
a-fren-tar(se) *v.* insult; affront; be affronted
a-fro-di-sia-co *adj.* aphrodisiac
a-fue-ra *adv.* outside; outkirts; suburbs
a-ga-char(se) *v.* to crouch; squat; bow down

a-ga-lla *f.* gill
a-ga-rrar(se) *v.* to grasp; seize; clutch; clinch
a-ga-rre *m.* gripping
a-ga-rro *m.* grip; lutch; grab
a-ga-rro-tar *v.* to compress; bind tightly
a-ga-sa-ja-dor *adj.* attentive
a-ga-sa-jar *v.* to entertain; fondle; welcoming
a-gen-cia *f.* bureau; agency
a-gen-ciar *v.* to obtain
a-gen-cio-so *adj.* industrious
a-gen-da *f.* diary; notebook
a-gen-te *m.* officer; agent
a-gil *adj.* nimble; agile; lithe; active; lithesome
a-gi-li-dad *f.* agility
a-gi-a-ción *f.* flurry; flutter; stir; excitement; agitation
a-gi-tar(se) *v.* to stir up; churn; flutter; shake
a-glo-me-ra-ción *f.* agglomeration
a-glo-me-ra-do *adj.* agglomerate
a-glo-me-rar *v.* agglomerate
a-glu-ti-na-ción *f.* agglutination
a-glu-ti-nan-te *m.* cement
a-glu-ti-nar *v.* to agglutinate
a-go-nia *f.* pain; agony
a-go-ni-oso *adj.* persistent
a-go-rar *v.* to foretell
a-gos-tar *v.* to consume
a-gos-to *m.* August; harvest
a-go-ta-mien-to *m.* exhaurstion; depletion
a-go-tar(se) *v.* to drain; give out; tire; exhaust
a-gra-cia-do, a *adj.* attractive
a-gra-ciar *v.* to award; grace
a-gra-da-ble *adj.* gracious; nice; pleasant; agreeable; delightful
a-gra-dar *v.* to please
a-gra-de-cer(se) *v.* to appreciate; acknowledge; thank
a-gra-de-ci-do, -da *adj.* thankful; grateful
a-gra-do *m.* liking; taste
a-gran-dar *v.* to grow bigger
a-gra-va-ción *f.* aggravation

a-gra-van-te *adj.* aggravating
a-gra-viar *v.* to harm; wrong
a-gra-vio *m.* offence; injury; grievance; harm
a-gra-vio-so *adj.* injurious; offensive; insulting
a-gre-dir *v.* to assault
a-gre-sión *f.* aggression
a-gre-si-vo *adj.* aggressive
a-gre-sor, a *m.* aggressor
a-griar *v.* to annoy; sour
a-gri-cul-tu-ra *f.* farming
a-grie-tar *v.* to split
a-gri-men-su-ra *f.* surveying
a-grio, a *adj.* acid; sour
a-gro *m.* farming
a-gro-nó-mi-co, -ca *adj.* agro-nomical
a-gru-pa-ción *f.* group
a-gru-par(se) *v.* to cluster; bunch; group
a-gua *f.* water
a-gua-ca-te *m.* avocado
a-gua-do, -da *adj.* diluted
a-gua-ma-ri-na *f.* aquamarine
a-guan-tar(se) *v.* to support; endure; hold
a-guan-te *m.* endurance
a-guar-dar *v.* to await
a-gu-de-za *f.* acumen; keenness; sharpness; brightness
a-gu-di-zar *v.* to sharpen
a-gu-do, -da *adj.* sharp
a-güe-ro *m.* omen
a-gue-rri-do, a *adj.* seasoned
a-gui-la *f.* eagle
a-gu-ja *f.* needle
a-gu-je-ro *m.* hole
a-guo-so, -sa *adj.* watery
a-gu-zar *v.* to sharpen
a-hi *adv.* there
a-hi-ja-da *f.* goddaughter
a-hi-ja-do *m.* godson
a-hi-jar *v.* to adopt
a-hi-la-do *adj.* faint; soft
a-hi-lar *v.* to faint
a-hi-to, -ta *adj.* stuffed
a-ho-gar *v.* to oppress; drown; choke
a-ho-ra *adv.* now
a-hor-ca-jar(se) *v.* to straddle

a-hor-mar *v.* to fit

a-ho-rrar *v.* to spare

a-ho-rro *m.* savings

a-hue-va-do *adj.* egg-shaped

a-hu-ma-do, -da *adj.* smoky; cured; smoked

a-hu-mar *v.* to cure; smoke

ai-rar *v.* to annoy; anger

ai-re *m.* aspect; air

ai-re-a-do *adj.* aired out

ai-re-ar(se) *v.* to air; cool

ai-re-o *m.* ventilation

ais-la-do, -da *adj.* alone

ais-lar *v.* to seclude; isolate

a-ja-do, -da *adj.* withered

a-jar *v.* to mar; spoil

a-je-dre-cis-ta *f., m.* chess player

a-je-drez *m.* chess

a-jen-jo *m.* bitterness

a-je-no, -na *adj.* alien; strange; foreign

a-je-tre-o *m.* agitation

a-jo *m.* garlic

a-jo-bo *m.* burden

a-jus-tar *v.* to settle; adapt; adjust; fix; tighten

a-jus-te *m.* fitting; accommodation

a-jus-ti-cia-mien-to *m.* execution

a-jus-ti-ciar *v.* to execute

a-la *f.* wing

a-la-ban-za *f.* praise

a-la-bar *v.* to commend

a-la-bas-tro *m.* alabaster

a-la-crán *m.* scorpion

a-la-cri-dad *f.* eagerness

a-la-do, -da *adj.* winged

a-lam-bre *m.* wire

á-la-mo *m.* poplar

a-lar-de-o *m.* bragging

a-lar-gar(se) *v.* to rejoice; cheer; lengthen; extend

a-lar-ma *f.* alarm

a-lar-ma-dor, a *adj.* alarming

a-lar-mar *v.* to alarm

al-ba *f.* daybreak

al-ba-ri-co-que *m.* apricot

al-ber-ca *f.* tank

al-ber-gar *v.* to cherish

al-bi-no, -na *adj.* albino

al-bo-ro-ta-do, -da *adj.* rowdy; excited

al-bo-ro-tar *v.* to excite; incite

al-bo-ro-zo *m.* joy

al-ca-cho-fa *f.* artichoke

al-cal-de *m.* mayor

al-ca-li-no, a *adj.* alkaline

al-ca-loi-de *m.* alkaloid

al-can-for *m.* camphor

al-can-zar *v.* to attain; reach; pass; grasp

al-cau-cil *m.* artichoke

al-cá-zar *m.* castle

al-ce *m.* moose

al-co-ba *f.* bedroom

al-co-hol *m.* alcohol

al-co-hó-li-co *adj.* alcoholic

a-le-a-to-rio *adj.* uncertain

a-le-go-ri-a *f.* allergy

a-le-grar *v.* to happy; cheer; rejoice

a-le-gre *adj.* joyous; gay; glad

a-le-gre-men-te *adv.* gaily

a-le-gria *f.* gladness; gaiety

a-le-grón *m.* joy

a-le-ja-mien-to *m.* distance; withdrawal; estrangement

a-le-la-do *adj.* bewildered

a-len-ta-dor, ra *adj.* encouraging

a-len-tar *v.* to animate

a-ler-gia *f.* allergy

a-ler-gi-co, -ca *adj.* allergic

a-ler-tar *v.* to alert; warn

a-le-te-o *m.* flapping

al-fa-bé-ti-co *adj.* alphabetical

al-fa-be-to *m.* alphabet

al-fa-re-ri-a *f.* pottery

al-fi-le-rar *v.* to pin

al-fom-bra *f.* carpet

al-fom-brar *v.* to carpet

al-for-za *f.* pleat

al-ge-bra *f.* algebra

al-go *pron.* anything; something

al-go-dón *m.* cotton

al-guien *pron.* someone: anyone

al-gún *adj,* some

al-gu-no, a *pron.* anybody

al-ha-ja *f.* gem

al-ho-ce-ma *f.* lavender

a-lia-do, -da *m.* ally
a-lian-za *f.* alliance
a-li-bi *m.* alibi
a-lie-na-ble *adj.* alienable
a-lie-na-ción *f.* alienation
a-lie-nar *v.* to alienate
a-lien-to *m.* courage
a-li-ge-rar(se) *v.* to relieve
a-li-men-tar *v.* to feed
a-li-men-ti-cio *adj.* nutritious
a-li-men-to *m.* food
a-li-ne-a-ción *m.* alignment
a-li-ñar *v.* to tidy
a-li-ño *m.* tidiness
a-li-sar *v.* to smooth
a-lis-tar *v.* to list
a-li-viar *v.* to alleviate; allay
a-li-vio *m.* easing
al-ma *f.* spirit
al-má-ci-ga *f.* nursery
al-me-ja *f.* calm
al-men-dro, a *m.* almond tree
al-mi-don *m.* starch
al-mi-do-nar *v.* to starch
al-miz-cle *m.* musk
al-mo-ha-da *f.* pillow
al-mor-zar *v.* to lunch
al-muer-zo *m.* lunch
a-lo-ca-do, -da *adj.* crazy
a-lo-cu-ción *f.* allocution
a-lo-jar(se) *v.* to house
a-lon-gar *v.* to stretch; to make longer
al-pi-no *adj.* alpine
al-qui-lar *v.* to hire; rent
al-qui-mia *f.* alchemy
al-qui-mis-ta *m.* alchemist
al-re-de-dor, ra *adv.* around
prep. round
al-ta-men-te *adv.* extremely
al-tar *m.* altar
al-te-ra-ción *f.* alteration
al-ter-ca-ción *f.* altercation
al-ter-na-do *adj.* alternate
al-ter-nar *v.* rotate; alternate
al-ter-na-ti-va *f.* alternative
al-ti-me-tri-a *f.* altimetry
al-ti-tud *f.* altitude
al-to, -ta *adj.* upper; high
al-truis-ta *adj.* altruistic
al-tu-ra *f.* elevation; height
a-lu-ci-nar *v.* to hallucinate
a-lu-ci-na-to-rio *adj.* hallu-
cinatory
a-lu-dir *v.* to allude
a-lum-bra-do *m.* lightening
a-lu-mi-nio *m.* aluminum
a-lum-no, -na *m.* student; alumnus
a-lu-sión *f.* allusion
al-za-do *adj.* elevated
al-zar *v.* to hoist; lift up; raise
a-llá *adv.* there
a-lla-nar *v.* overcome; flatten
a-lle-ga-do, -da *adj.* related; close; near
a-llí *adv.* there
a-ma-bi-li-dad *f.* kindness
a-ma-ble *adj.* lovable; amiable; kindly
a-ma-do *adj.* beloved
a-ma-es-trar *v.* to train
a-ma-ne-cer *v.* to nurse
a-ma-ne-ci-da *f.* daybreak
a-man-ser *v.* to soothe; tame
a-ma-na-do *adj.* skillful; fixed
a-ma-ño *m.* skill
a-ma-po-la *f.* poppy
a-mar *v.* to love
a-mar-gar *v.* to make bitter
a-mar-gor *m.* bitterness
a-ma-ri-llo, a *m.* yellow
a-ma-rrar *v.* to fasten; tie
a-ma-teur *adj.* amateur
a-ma-tis-ta *f.* amethyst
ám-bar *m.* amber
am-bi-ción *f.* ambition
am-bi-cio-so *adj.* ambitious
am-bien-ta-ción *f.* atmosphere
am-bi-gue-dad *f.* ambiguity
am-bi-guo *adj.* uncertain; ambiguous
am-bu-lan-cia *f.* ambulance
am-bu-lan-te *adj.* ambulatory
am-bu-lar *v.* amble
a-me-ba *f.* amoeba
a-me-na-za *f.* threat
a-me-na-zar *v.* to menace
a-me-ni-dad *f.* amenity
a-me-ri-ca-no *adj.* American
a-mi-ga *f.* girl friend
a-mi-gar *v.* to reconcile
a-mig-da-la *f.* tonsil
a-mi-go *m.* boy friend

a-mi-la-na-do *adj.* intimidated

a-mi-la-nar *v.* to discourage; intimidate; scare; frighten

a-mis-to-so, a *adj.* friendly

a-mo *m.* master; boss

a-mo-lar *v.* to sharpen

a-mol-dar *v.* to adjust; mold

a-mon-to-nar(se) *v.* to amass; hoard; huddle

amor *m.* lover

a-mo-ra-li-dad *f.* amorality

a-mo-ro-so, -sa *adj.* amorous; loving

am-pa-rar *v.* defend; protect

am-pliar *v.* expand; increase

am-pli-fi-ca-ción *f.* amplification

am-pli-fi-car *v.* to amplify

am-po-lle-ta *f.* hourglass

am-pu-ta-ción *f.* amputation

am-pu-tar *v.* to amputate

a-na-car-do *m.* cashew

a-na-de *m.* duck

a-na-gra-ma *f.* anagram

a-nal-ge-si-co *adj.* analgesic

a-na-li-sis *m.* analysis

a-na-lis-ta *m.* analyst

a-na-li-ti-co *adj.* analytical

a-na-li-zar *v.* to analyze

a-na-lo-gi-a *f.* analogy

a-na-na *m.* pineapple

a-na-quel *m.* shelf

a-na-ran-ja-do, a *adj.* orange

a-nar-quis-ta *m., f.* anarchist

a-na-to-mi-a *f.* anatomy

a-na-to-mi-co *adj.* anatomic

an-cia-no, -na *adj.* aged

an-cla *f.* anchor

an-cho *adj.* broad

an-cho-a *f.* anchovy

an-dar *v.* to go; ambulate

an-dra-jo-so, -sa *adj.* ragged

an-droi-de *m.* android

a-nec-do-ta *f.* anecdote

a-nec-do-tis-ta *m.* anecdotist

a-ne-gar *v.* to flood

a-ne-mi-co, -ca *adj.* anemic

a-nes-te-siar *v.* anesthetize

an-gel *m.* angel

an-ge-li-co, -ca *adj.* angelical

an-go-ra *adj.* angora

an-gui-la *f.* eel

an-gu-lo *m.* angle

an-gu-lo-so *adj.* angular

an-gu-rri *f.* greed

an-gus-tiar *v.* to anguish

an-he-lar *v.* to long for; yearn

a-ni-llo *m.* ring

a-ni-ma-ción *f.* animation

a-ni-ma-do, -da *adj.* lively; animate

a-ni-mal *m.* animal

a-ni-mar *v.* to become animated; enliven

a-ni-qui-lar *v.* to destroy; annihilate

a-ni-ver-sa-rio, -ria *adj.* anniversary

a-no-che *adv.* last night

a-no-ni-mo *adj.* anonymous

a-nor-mal *adj.* subnormal; abnormal

a-no-ta-ción *f.* note

a-no-tar *v.* to note

an-sar *m.* goose

an-sia *f.* yearning

an-siar *v.* to long for

an-sie-dad *f.* anxiety

an-te *prep.* before

an-te-bra-zo *m.* forearm

an-te-ce-der *v.* to anteceed

an-te-de-cir *v.* to predict

an-te-pa-sa-do *m.* ancestor

an-te-rior *adj.* proir; anterior

an-tes de *adv.* before

an-ti-a-ci-do *adj.* antacid

an-ti-bio-ti-co *m.* antibiotic

an-ti-ci-pa-do *adj.* advanced

an-ti-ci-par *v.* advance

an-ti-cuer-po *m.* antibody

an-ti-do-to *m.* antidote

an-ti-guo *adj.* ancient; antique

an-ti-lo-pe *m.* antelope

an-ti-na-tu-ral *adj.* unnatural

an-ti-sep-ti-co *m.* antiseptic

an-ti-so-cial *adj.* antisocial

an-ti-to-xi-co *adj.* antitoxic

an-to-ni-mia *f.* antonymy

an-tro-poi-de *adj.* anthropoid

a-nual *adj.* annual

a-nua-rio *m.* annual

a-nu-blar *v.* to cloud

a-nu-lar *v.* to cancel

a-nun-cia-ción *f.* announce-

ment
a-nun-cian-te *m.* advertiser
a-nun-ciar *v.* to announce
an-zue-lo *m.* fishhook
a-na-di-do *m.* addition
a-na-dir *v.* to add
a-ne-jo, -ja *adj.* old; mature
a-nil *adj., m.* indigo
a-ño *m.* year
a-pa-bu-llar *v.* to squash
a-pa-ci-ble *adj.* gentle
a-pa-ci-guar(se) *v.* appease
a-pa-dri-nar *v.* to support
a-pa-le-o *m.* thrashing
a-pa-nar *v.* to mend; to seize; grasp; repair
a-pa-ra-to *m.* apparatus
a-pa-ra-to-so *adj.* ostentatious
a-par-car *v.* to park
a-pa-ra-cer(se) *v.* to haunt; to come
a-pa-re-jar *v.* to prepare
a-pa-ren-te *adj.* seeming
a-pa-ri-ción *f.* appearance
a-par-ta-do *adj.* isolated
a-par-ta-men-to *m.* apartment
a-par-tar(se) *v.* to divide; to remove
a-par-te *adv.* aside; apart
a-pa-sio-nar *v.* to excite
a-pa-ti-a *f.* apathy
a-pa-ti-co, -ca *adj.* apathetic
a-pe-ar *v.* to chock; fell
a-pe-la-ble *adj.* appealable
a-pe-lar *v.* to appeal
a-pe-lli-dar *v.* to name; called
a-pe-lli-do *m.* name
a-pe-nar *v.* pained; to grieve
a-pen-di-ci-tis *m.* appendictis
a-pe-ro *m.* gear
a-pes-tar *v.* to annoy; infect
a-pe-ten-cia *f.* appetite
ape-ti-to *m.* appetite
a-pe-ti-to-so, a *adj.* delicious
a-pio *m.* celery
a-pla-car *v.* to placate
a-pla-nar *v.* to flatten; stun
a-plas-tar(se) *v.* to flatten
a-plau-dir *v.* to clap; applaud
a-plau-so *m.* clapping
a-pli-ca-ble *adj.* applicable

a-pli-ca-ción *f.* application
a-pli-car *v.* to apply
a-po-ca-do, -da *adj.* timid
a-po-de-rar(se) *v.* empower
a-po-do *m.* nickname
a-po-li-ti-co *adj.* apolitical
a-po-rre-ar(se) *v.* to beat
a-por-tar *v.* to bring; arrive
a-po-sen-to *m.* lodging
a-po-si-ción *f.* apposition
a-pos-tol *m.* apostle
a-pos-tro-fo *m.* apostrophe
a-po-te-ca-rio *m.* apothecary
a-po-te-o-sis *f.* apothesis
a-po-yar(se) *v.* to rest on; to support
a-po-yo *m.* support
a-pre-cia-ción *f.* appreciation
a-pre-ciar *v.* to value; appreciate
a-pre-cio *m.* attention; appraisal
a-pre-hen-der *v.* to seize
a-pre-hen-sión *f.* comprehension; apprehension
a-pren-der *v.* to learn
a-pren-sión *f.* suspicion
a-pre-sar *v.* to seize
a-pre-su-rar *v.* to hurry
a-pre-tar *v.* to crowd; clutch
a-pro-ba-do, a *adj.* approved
a-pro-bar *v.* to pass
a-pro-pia-do *adj.* appropriate
a-pro-piar(se) *v.* appropriate
a-pro-vi-sio-nar *v.* provision
a-pro-xi-mar(se) *v.* to approximate
ap-ti-tud *f.* talent; aptitude
a-pues-to *f.* wager
a-pun-tar(se) *v.* to aim; point
a-pun-te *m.* notation; note
a-pu-rar(se) *v.* to worry
a-que-jar *v.* to distress
a-quel *adj.* that; those
a-quel *pron.* that one
a-qui *adv.* now; here; then
a-quie-tar *v.* to soothe; to calm down
a-ra *f.* altar
a-ra-na *f.* spider
ar-bi-trar *v.* unpire; arbitrate
ar-bi-tra-rio, a *adj.* arbitrary
ar-bi-tro, -tra *m.* arbitrator

ar-bol *m.* tree
ar-bo-re-to *m.* arboretum
ar-bus-to *m.* shrub
ar-ca-da *f.* arcade
ar-ca-is-ta *f.* archaist
ar-can-gel *m.* archangel
ar-ce *m.* maple tree
ar-co *m.* arch
ar-chi-du-que *m.* archduke
ar-chi-du-que-sa *f.* archduchess
ar-chi-var *v.* to file
ar-chi-vo *m.* archives
ar-der(se) *v.* to burn
ar-dien-te *adj.* ardent; burning
ar-di-lla *f.* squirrel
ar-dor *m.* heat
ar-duo *adj.* arduous
a-re-a *f.* area
a-re-no-so *adj.* sandy
a-ren-que *m.* herring
ar-gen-tar *v.* to silver-plate
ar-gen-ta-rio *m.* silversmith
ar-go-lla *f.* ring
ar-guir *v.* to prove; argue
ar-gu-men-tar *v.* to argue
a-ri-do *adj.* dry
a-ris-co, -ca *adj.* wild; unfriendly; surly; churlish
a-ris-to-cra-cia *f.* aristocracy
a-ris-to-cra-ta *f.,m.* aristocrat
a-rit-me-ti-co *adj.* arithmetic
ar-le-quin *m.* harlequin
ar-ma *f.* weapon
ar-ma-do *adj.* armed
ar-mar *v.* to assemble; reinforce; arm; equip
ar-ma-rio, a *m.* buffet; closet
ar-mi-no *m.* ermine
ar-mis-ti-cio *m.* armistice
ar-mo-ni-a *f.* accord
ar-mo-ni-co *m., adj.* harmonicar
ar-mo-ni-zar *v.* to harmonize
a-ro *m.* hoop; ring
a-ro-ma *m.* fragrance
a-ro-mar *v.* to scent; perfume
a-ro-ma-ti-co *adj.* aromatic
a-ro-ma-ti-zar *v.* to perfume; scent
a-ro-mo-so *adj.* aromatic
ar-pis-ta *m., f.* harpist

ar-que-o-lo-gi-a *f.* archaelogy
ar-qui-tec-to *m., f.* architect
ar-qui-tec-tu-ra *f.* architecture
a-rra-ci-ma-do *adj.* bunched
a-rran-car *v.* to seize; pull up; obtain; stem
a-rra-sar *v.* to clear; level
a-rras-trar(se) *v.* to pull; to crawl; to draw
a-rre-ar *v.* to harness; herd
a-rre-ba-ta-dor *adj.* exciting
a-rre-ba-to *m.* rage
a-rre-ci-fe *m.* reef
a-rre-gla-do *adj.* neat
a-rre-glar(se) *v.* order; settle
a-rre-glo *m.* understanding; arrangement
a-rre-me-dar *v.* to copy
a-rre-me-ter *v.* to attack
a-rren-dar *v.* to rent
a-rre-o *m.* drove; herd
a-rre-pen-tir-se *v.* to regret
a-rres-ta-do *adj.* arrested
a-rres-to *m.* arrest
a-rri-ba *adv.* above
a-rri-bar *intr.* to arrive
a-rri-bis-ta, -to *adj.* social-climbing
a-rri-bo *m.* arrival
a-rrien-do *m.* renting
a-rries-ga-do, -da *adj.* hazardous; daring
a-rries-gar(se) *v.* to venture; jeopardize; risk
a-rri-mar *v.* to draw or bring near
a-rri-mo *m.* partition
a-rrin-co-na-do *adj.* distant
a-rrin-co-nar *tr.* to corner; to place in a corner
a-rris-ca-mien-to, -ta *m.* boldness; daring
a-rris-car *v.* to fold up; to turn up
a-rrit-mia *f.* lack of rhythm
a-rro-ba-mien-to *m.* rapture; ecstasy
a-rro-bar *v.* to enrapture
a-rro-di-llar(se) *v.* to kneel
a-rro-gan-te *adj.* proud; arrogant
a-rro-jar(se) *v.* to fling; emit;

throw
a-rro-jo, -ja *m.* boldness
a-rro-lla-dor, ra *adj.* over-
whelming
a-rro-liar *v.* to carry or sweep
away
a-rro-par *v.* to tuck in; to
wrap with clothing
a-rro-rro *m.* lullaby
a-rro-yo *m.* brook; stream
a-rroz *m.* rice pudding
a-rro-zal *m.* rice paddy or
rice field
a-rru-ga *f.* crease; fold;
wrinkle line
a-rru-ga-do *adj.* wrinkled
a-rru-gar(se) *v.* to rumple;
wrinkle
a-mui-nar *v.* to destroy
a-rru-lla-dor *adj.* soothing
a-rru-llar *v.* to lull to sleep;
to coo
a-rru-ma-co *m.* caress
a-rrum-bar *v.* to neglect; to
put or cast aside
ar-se-nal *m.* storehouse;
shipyard
ar-se-ni-co *m.* arsenic
ar-te *f.* craft; art
ar-te-fac-to *m.* appliance
ar-te-ria *f.* artery
ar-te-ro *adj.* sly; cunning
ar-te-sa-ni-a *f.* crafts-
manship
ar-te-sa-no *m,f.* craftswoman
or craftsman
ar-ti-cu-la-ción *f.* joint
ar-ti-cu-lar *v.* to articulate
ar-tis-ta *f., m.* artist
ar-ti-fi-cio, -cia *m.* item;
article; thing
ar-ti-fi-cial *adj.* artificial
ar-tis-ti-co *adj.* artistic
ar-tri-tis *f.* arthritis
ar-zo-bis-po *m.* archbishop
as *m.* ace
a-sa-do *m.* roasted meat;
barbecue
a-sa-dor *m.* grill
a-sa-la-ria-do, -da *adj.*
salaried worker
a-sa-la-riar *v.* to set a salary
for someone

a-sal-ta-dor, a *m.f.* assailant
a-sal-tar *v.* to attack
a-sal-to *m.* attack
a-sam-ble-a *f.* conference;
meeting
a-sam-ble-is-ta *m.f.* assem-
bly member
as-cen-den-cia *f.* ancestry
as-cen-den-te *adj.* ascend-
ing
as-cen-der *v.* to promote;
ascend
as-cen-sión *f.* rise; ascen-
sion
as-cen-so *m.* ascent; promotion
as-cen-sor, a *m.* lift; elevator
as-cen-so-ris-ta *m., f.* one
who operates an elevator
as-co *m.* disgust
a-se-ar *v.* to clean; to wash
a-se-char *v.* to trap
a-se-diar *v.* to bother; to
pester
a-se-dio *m.* siege
a-se-gu-ra-do *adj.* insured
a-se-gu-rar(se) *v.* to fasten;
assure; secure
a-se-me-jar(se) *v.* to
resemble
a-sen-ta-de-ras *f.pl.* buttocks; behind
a-sen-ta-do *adj.* judicious
a-sen-tar *v.* to record
a-sen-ti-mién-to *m.* consent
a-sen-tir *intr.* to agree
a-se-o *m.* tidiness; neatness
a-se-qui-ble *adj.* under-
standable
a-ser-cion *f.* affirmation
a-se-rra-de-ro *m.* sawmill
a-se-rrar *v.* to saw
a-se-rrin *m.* sawdust
a-se-si-nar *v.* to murder
a-se-si-na-to *m.* murder; *pol*
assassination
a-se-si-no *adj.* murderous
pol assassin
a-se-sor, ra *adj.* advisory,
advising
a-se-so-rar *v.* to advise
a-ses-tar *v.* to aim
a-se-ve-rar *v.* to assert

a-se-ve-ra-ti-vo *adj.* affirmative; assertive

a-se-xua-do *adj.* asexual

as-fal-tar *v.* to asphalt

as-fal-to *m.* asphalt

as-fi-xai *f.* suffocation

as-fi-xiar *v.* to asphyxiate

a-si *adv.* so

a-sien-to *m.* seat

a-sig-nar *v.* allot; assign

a-sig-nar *v.* to appoint; to assign

a-sig-na-cion *f.* course or subject in school

a-si-lar *tr.* to give shelter

a-si-lo *m.* asylum

a-si-mi-lar(se) *v.* assimilate

a-si-mis-mo *adj.* in a like manner; likewise

a-sir(se) *v.* grip; hold on to

a-sis-ten-cia *f.* attendance

a-sis-ten-cial *adj.* relier; assisting

a-sis-tir *intr.* to accompnay; to aid; to attend

as-ma *f.* asthma

as-ma-ti-co *adj. & m.f.* asthmatic

as-na-da *f.* stupidity

a-so-cia-cion *f.* association

a-so-cia-do *adj.* associated

a-so-ciar(se) *v.* to associate with

a-so-la-dor *adj.* ravaging

a-so-lar *v.* to scorch

a-so-le-a-mien-to *m.* sunstroke

a-so-le-ar *v.* to place in the sun

a-so-mar *v.* to show; *intr.* to appear

a-som-brar(se) *v.* to amaze; to astonish

as-pi-rar *v.* to breathe; inhale

as-pi-ri-na *f.* aspirin

as-tro-lo-gia *f.* astrology

as-tro-no-mia *f.* astronomy

as-tu-ta *adj.* artful; sly; canny; cunning

a-sun-to *m.* issue; concern

a-ta-car *v.* to assault; charge

a-ta-que *m.* attack

a-tar(se) *v.* to rope; tie; brace

a-ten-ción *f.* attention

a-ten-der *v.* to heed; attend

a-tes-ti-guar *v.* to testify

a-tie-sar(se) *v.* to tighten

at-le-ta *f., m.* athlete

at-le-ti-co, a *adj.* athletic

a-to-mi-co *adj.* atomic

a-to-mo *m.* atom

a-trac-ción *f.* attraction

a-trac-ti-vo *adj.* engaging

a-traer *v.* to engage; lure

a-tras *adv.* aback; back

a-tra-sa-do *adj.* backwards

a-tri-buir *v.* to ascribe

a-tro-ci-dad *f.* atrocity

a-tur-dir(se) *v.* to daze; muddle; bewilder

au-di-ción *f.* audition

au-gus-to *adj.* August

au-men-tar(se) *v.* to augment; enhance

au-men-to *m.* raise; increase

aun *adv.* still

aun-que *conj.* although

au-sen-te *adj.* missing

au-ten-ti-ci-dad *f.* authenticity

au-to-bus *m.* bus

a-to-gra-fo *m.* autograph

au-to-mo-vil *m.* car

au-to-ri-za-ción *f.* authorization

a-van-zar(se) *v.* to advance

a-ve *f.* bird

a-ve-ni-da *f.* avenue

a-ven-tu-ra *f.* adventure

a-ver-sión *f.* aversion

a-via-ción *f.* aviation

a-vión *m.* plane; airplane

a-yú-da *f.* aid; help

a-yu-dar *v.* to assist; help

a-zo-rar *v.* to alarm

a-zo-rra-do *adj.* foxy

a-zo-ta-do *adj.* multicolored

a-so-tar *v.* to beat upon

a-zo-te *m.* spanking; whip

a-zu-car *m.* sugar

a-zu-ca-ra-do *adj.* sweet

a-zu-tre *m.* sulphur

a-zul *m.* blue

a-zu-la-do *adj.* bluish

a-zu-lar *v.* color or dye blue

a-zu-le-jo *m.* glazed tile

ba-ba *f.* spittle
ba-bar-se *tr.* to dribble
ba-ba-za *f.* slime
ba-bear *v.* to drool
ba-bel *m.* confusion
ba-be-ro *m.* bib
ba-bie-ca *adj. m.f.* simple person
ba-bor *m.* port
ba-bo-se-ar *v.* to slobber
ba-ca-la-o *m.* cod
ba-ca-nal *a.* bacchanalian
ba-ci-lo *m.* bacillus
bac-te-ria *f.* bacterium
bac-te-rio-lo-gi-a *f.* bacteriology
bac-te-rio-lo-go, a *m.f.* bacteriologist
ba-che *m.* pothole
ba-da-jo *m.* bell clapper
ba-du-la-que *adj. & m.* follish person
ba-ga-je *m.* luggage
ba-ga-te-la *f.* trinket; trifle
ba-gre *m.* catfish
ba-hi-a *f.* bay
bai-la-dor *m.* dancer
bai-lar *v.* to dance
bai-la-ri-na *f.* ballerina
bai-le *m.* ball; dance
ba-ja *f.* drop
ba-jar(se) *v.* to fall; lower
ba-je-za *f.* lowliness
ba-jo, -ja *adv.* below; *adj.* low; short; small
ba-jon *m.* decline *mus* bassoonist
ba-la *f.* bale
ba-la-da *f.* ballad
ba-la-di *adj.* trivial
ba-la-dro *m.* shout
ba-la-dron *adj.* boasting
ba-la-dro-na-da *f.* boast
ba-la-dro-ne-ar *v.* to brag; to boast
ba-lan-cear(se) *v.* to teeter
ba-lan-ce-o *m.* rocking
ba-lan-za *f.* scale
ba-lar *v.* to bleat
bal-bu-ce-ar *v.* to babble
bal-con *m.* balcony
ba-li-do *m.* bleat
ba-lis-ti-ca *f.* ballistics

ba-lis-ti-co *adj.* ballistic
ba-lon-ces-to *m.* basketball
ba-lon-ma-no *m.* handball
ba-lon-vo-le-a *m.* volleyball
ba-lo-ta *f.* ballot
bal-sa *f.* balsa
bal-sa-mo *m.* balsam
ba-luar-te *m.* bastion
ba-lle-na *f.* whale
ba-lle-na-to *m.* whale calf
ba-lle-ne-ro, -ra *adj.* whaling
ba-lles-ta *f.* crossbow
ba-lles-te-ar *v.* to shoot with a crossbow
ba-lles-te-ria *f.* archery
bam-ba-le-ar *v.* to sway
bam-bo-le-om. wobble
ba-llet *m.* ballet
bam-bu *m.* bamboo
ba-na-na *f.* bananna
ban-ca *f.* banking
ban-ca-rro-ta *f.* bankruptcy
ban-co *m.* bank; band; pew; bench
ban-da-da *f.* flock; group
ban-de-ra *f.* ensign; flag
ban-de-ja *f.* tray
ban-de-ro-la *f.* pennant
ban-di-do *m.* bandit
ban-do-le-ro *m.* bandit
ban-que-ta *f.* stool
ban-que-te *m.* feast
ban-que-tear *v.* to feast
ba-ñar(se) *v.* to bathe
ba-ño *m.* bathtub
ba-ra-jar *v.* to shuffle
ba-ra-to *adv.* cheaply; *adj.* inexpensive; cheap
bar-ba *f.* beard
bar-ba-coa *f.* barbecue
bar-ba-do *adj.* bearded
bar-ba-ri-dad *f.* outrage
bar-ba-ra *f.,* **-ro** *m.* savage
bar-bear *v.* to shave
bar-be-ro *m.* barber
bar-be-lla *f.* chin
bar-bo-tar *v.* to mutter, mumble
bar-bo-te-o *m.* murmuring
bar-bu-do *adj.* heavily bearded
bar-bu-lla *f.* chatter; jabbering

bar-ca *f.* small boat
bar-ca-za *f.* launch
bar-co *m.* ship; boat
ba-ri-to-no *m.* baritone
bar-niz *m.* glaze; varnish; lacquer
bar-ni-zar *v.* varnish; lacquer
ba-ro-me-tro *m.* barometer
ba-ron *m.* baron
ba-ro-ne-sa *f.* baroness
ba-rra *f.* bar
ba-rra-ca *f.* booth
ba-rrer *v.* to sweep
ba-rre-ra *f.* barricade
ba-rri-ga *f.* belly
ba-rril *m.* barrel
ba-rrio *m.* neighborhood
ba-sal-to *m.* basalt
ba-sar *v.* to base
ba-se *f.* foundation
ba-si-co *adj.* basal
ba-si-li-ca *f.* basilica
bas-quet-bol *m.* basketball
bas-tan-te *adj.* sufficient
bas-tar *v.* to suffice
bas-tar-dear *v.* to debase
bas-to *adj.* rough
bas-ton *m.* baton; stick
ba-su-ra *f.* rubbish
ba-ta *f.* negligee
ba-ta-lla *f.* battle
ba-ta-llar *v.* to battle
ba-ta-llon *m.* battalion
ba-te-ria *f.* battery
ba-ti-do *m.* batter
ba-tir(se) *v.* to churn
ba-tu-ta *f.* baton
baul *m.* trunk
bau-tis-mo *m.* christening
bau-ti-zar *v.* to baptize
ba-ya *f.* berry
ba-yo *adj.* bay
ba-zar *m.* bazaar
ba-zu-ca *f.* bazooka
bea-ti-fi-car *v.* to beatify
bea-ti-fi-co *adj.* beatific
bea-ti-tud *f.* beatitude
be-be *m.* baby
be-ber *v.* to drink
be-bi-da *f.* beverage
be-ca *f.* scholarship
be-ce-rro *m.* calf
be-far *v.* to taunt

beige *m.* beige
beis-bol *m.* baseball
be-li-co-so, -sa *adj.* warlike
be-li-ge-ran-te *adj.* belligerent
be-lle-za *f.* beauty
be-llo *adj.* beautiful
be-mol *m.* flat
ben-de-cir *v.* to bless
ben-di-ción *f.* blessing
ben-di-to *adj.* holy
be-ne-fi-ciar(se) *v.* to benefit
be-ne-fi-cio-so *adj.* beneficial
be-ne-fi-co *adj.* charitable
be-ne-vo-lo *adj.* benevolent
ben-ga-la *f.* flare
be-nig-ni-dad *f.* kindness
be-nig-no *adj.* kind; mild
be-rrin-che *m.* tantrum
be-sar(se) *v.* to smooch
be-so, -sa *m.* kiss
bes-tia *f.* animal
bes-tial *adj.* bestial
Bi-blia *f.* Bible
bi-bli-co *adj.* Biblical
bi-blio-gra-fia *f.* bibliography
bi-blio-gra-fo, -fa *m.* bibliographer
bi-blio-te-ca *f.* library
bi-ceps *m.* biceps
bi-ci-cle-ta *f.* bicycle
bi-ci-clis-ta *m., f.* bicyclist
bi-cho *m.* bug
bien *m.* good
bien-ve-ni-da *f.* greeting
bi-fur-car-se *v.* to fork
bi-go-te *m.* mustache
bi-la-te-ral *adj.* bilateral
bi-lio-so *adj.* bilious
bi-lis *f.* bile
bi-llar *m.* billiards
bi-lle-te *m.* bill
bi-llon *m.* trillion
bi-na-rio *adj.* binary
bio-gra-fia *f.* biography
bio-gra-fi-co *adj.* biographic
bio-gra-fo *m.* biographer
bio-lo-gia *f.* biology
bio-lo-gi-co *adj.* biological
bio-lo-go *m.* biologist
biop-sia *f.* biopsy
bi-sa-bue-la *f.* **-lo** *m.* great-grandmother; -father

bi-se-car v. to bisect
bi-sec-cion f. bisection
bi-son-te m. bison
biz-guear v. to squint
blan-co adj. blank; white
blan-dir v. to flourish
blan-do adj. supple; soft
blan-quear v. to whiten
blas-fe-mar v. to swear
blas-fe-mia f. profanity
blin-da-do adj. armored
blo-que m. block
blo-quear v. to block
blu-sa f. blouse
bo-bo m. fool; ninny
bo-ca f. mouth
bo-ca-di-llo m. sandwich
bo-ca-do m. bite
bo-da f. marriage
bo-de-ga f. wine cellar
boi-co-teo m. boycott
bo-la f. fib; ball
bo-le-tin m. bulletin
bo-li-che m. bowling
bo-li-ta f. pellet
bol-sa f. bag; pouch
bol-si-llo m. pocket
bol-sis-ta m. stockbroker
bol-so m. handbag
bo-llo m. bump
bom-ba f. pump
bom-bar-de-ro m. bomber
bom-bear v. to pad; pump
bom-bi-lla f. bulb
bom-bon m. - sweet
bon-dad f. kindness
bon-da-do-so, -sa adj. good
bo-ni-to, -ta adj. pretty
bo-quea-da f. gasp
bo-qui-lla f. nozzle
bor-de m. edge
bor-di-llo m. curb
bo-rra-cho m. drunkard
bo-rra-dor m. eraser
bos-que m. woods
bos-que-jar v. to outline
bo-ta f. wine bag
bo-ta-ni-ca f. botany
bo-te m. jackpot
bo-te-lla f. bottle
bo-ti-ca-rio m. druggist
bo-tin m. loot
bo-ton m. stud

bo-to-nes m. bellhop
bo-ve-da f. vault
bo-vi-no, -na adj. bovine
bo-xea-dor m. boxer
bo-xear v. to box
bo-ya f. buoy
bo-yan-te adj. buoyant
bo-zal m. muzzle
bra-man-te m. twine
bra-mar v. to bluster
bra-mi-do m. bellow
bra-vo, -va adj. brave
bra-za-do m. armful
bra-zo m. arm
bre-ve adj. short
bre-ve-dad f. conciseness
bri-bon adj. lazy
bri-llan-te adj. bright; shiny
bri-llar v. to glow; beam
bri-llo m. glow; shine
brin-car v. to jump; gambol
brio m. jauntiness
bri-sa f. breeze
bro-ca-do m. brocade
bro-che m. brooch
bro-mear(se) v. to joke
bro-mis-ta f. joker
bron-ce m. bronze
bron-cea-do m. suntan; bronze
bron-ce-ar v. to tan; to bronze
bron-co adj. coarse; rough
bron-quial adj. bronchial
bron-quio m. bronchial tube
bron-qui-tis f. bronchitis
bro-quel m. small sheild
bro-ta-du-ra f. budding; sprouting
bro-tar v. to bud
bru-je-ri-a f. witchcraft
bru-jo m. wizard
bru-ju-la f. compass
bru-mo-so adj. foggy; misty
bru-ni-du-ra f. polishing; burnishing
bru-nir v. to burnish; to polish
brus-co, -ca adj. sudden
bru-to m. beast; brute
bu-bon m. swelling or very large tumor
bu-ce-ar v. to swim under water

bu-cle *m.* curl; ringlet
bu-din *m.* pudding
bue-na-ven-tu-ra *f.* good luck; good fortune
bue-no, a *adj.* sound; good
buey *m.* ox
bu-fa-lo *m.* buffalo
bu-fan-da *f.* muffler; scarf
bu-fon *m.* clown; buffoon
bu-ho-ne-ro *m.* hawker; peddler
bui-tre *m.* vulture
bu-jia *f.* candle
bul-bo *m.* bulb
bu-le-var *m.* boulevard
bul-to *m.* mass; heft
bu-lla *f.* uproar; brawl; ctowd; mob
bu-lli-cio *m.* riot; racket; hubbub
bu-llir *v.* to boil
bu-me-ran-ang *m.* boomer-rang
bu-nue-io *m.* fried dough
bu-que *m.* vessel; ship
bu-que *m.* bouquet
bur-bu-ja *f.* bubble
bur-de-os *adj.* deep red in color
bur-do *adj.* rough; coarse
bur-gue-si-a *f.* middle class
bu-ri-lar *v.* to engrave
bur-la *f.* taunt; joke
bur-lar(se) *v.* to gibe; joke
bur-les-co *adj.* burlesque
bu-ro-cra-ta *f.* bureaucrat
bu-rra *f.* stupid woman
bu-rro *m.* donkey; burro
bur-sa *f.* rubbish
bur-sa-til *adj.* stock market
bus-ca *f.* search
bus-ca-pie *m.* feeler
bus-car *v.* to look or search for
bus-ca-vi-das *m.f.* busy-body
bus-que-da *f.* search
bus-to *m.* bust; chest
bu-ta-ca *f.* armchair
bu-ta-no *m.* butane
bu-ti-le-no *m.* butylene
bu-zo *m.* deep-sea diver
bu-zon *m.* mailbox

ca-bal *adj.* fair; precise
ca-ba-la *f. relig.* cabala
ca-bal-gar *v.* to ride on horseback
ca-bal-ga-ta *f.* cavalcade
ca-ba-lle-ria *f. milit.* cavalry
ca-ba-lle-ri-za *f.* stable
ca-ba-lle-ro *m.* gentleman
ca-ba-lle-te *m.* easel; saw-horse
ca-ba-lli-to, -ta *m.* pony, small horse
ca-ba-llo *m.* horse
ca-ba-llón *f.* ridge
ca-ba-na *f.* cabin
ca-ba-ret *m.* cabaret; night club
ca-be-ci-lla *m.* ringleader
ca-be-lle-ra *f.* head of hair
ca-be-llo *m.* hair
ca-ber *v.* to fit
ca-bes-tri-llo *m.* sling
ca-bes-tro *m.* halter
ca-be-za *f.* skull; head
ca-be-zón, o-na *adj.* bigheaded
ca-be-zo-ta *m.f. coll.* mule
ca-bil-dear *v.* to lobby
ca-bil-do *m.* town council
ca-ble *m.* cable
ca-ble-gra-fiar *v.* to cable
ca-ble-gra-ma *m.* cable-gram
ca-ble-vi-sion *f.* cable television
ca-bo *m.* corporal; cape;
ca-bra *f.* goat
ca-brio *m.* rafter
ca-bri-to *m.* young goat, kid
ca-bro-na-da *f. coll.* dirty trick
ca-ca-hue-te *m.* peanut
ca-cao *m.* cocoa
ca-ca-re-ar *v.* to crow; cackle
ca-ca-tua *f.* cockatoo
ca-ce-ro-la *f.* casserole
ca-ci-que *m.* Indian chief
ca-ci-que-ar *intr. coll.* to or-der people around
ca-co *m.* burglar
cac-to *m.* cactus
ca-cha-lo-te *m.* sperm whale

ca-char v. to split; to chip

ca-cha-sa f. sluggish

ca-che-ar v. to frisk, to search

ca-che-mi-ra f. cashmere

ca-che-te-ar v. *Amer.* to slap; hit

ca-che-ti-na f. fist fight

ca-che-tu-do adj. plump or chubby-cheeks

ca-cho-rro m. puppy

ca-da adj. every; each

ca-dal-so m. platform

ca-da-ver m. body; corpse

ca-da-ve-ri-co adj. cadaverous

ca-de-na f. chain

ca-den-cia f. rhythm; cadence

ca-de-ra f. hip, hip joint

ca-de-te m. cadet

ca-du-co, a adj. lapse; to expire

caer(se) v. to fall

ca-fe m. coffee; cafe

ca-fe-i-na f. caffeine

ca-fe-tal m. coffee plantation

ca-fe-te-ri-a f. cafeteria; cafe

cai-da f. downfall; tumble

cai-man m. alligator

ca-ja f. cabinet; chest

ca-je-ro m. cashier; teller

ca-jis-ta m.f. typesetter

cal f. lime

ca-la f. cove

ca-la-ba-za f. pumpkin; gourd; squash

ca-la-bo-zo m. jail; underground prison cell

ca-la-dor m. mech. driller

ca-la-fa-te-ar v. to calk; caulk

ca-la-mar m. squid

ca-lam-bre m. cramp

ca-la-mi-dad f. calamity; misfortune

ca-la-mi-to-so adj. calamitous

ca-la-na f. character; nature

ca-lar(se) v. to swoop; to penetrate

cal-ce-te-ria f. hosiery

cal-ce-tin m. sock

cal-ci-fi-ca-ction f. calcification

cal-ci-fi-car(se) v. to calcify

cal-cio m. calcium

cal-co m. tracing

cal-co-ma-ni-a f. decal

cal-cu-la-dor, ra m.f. calculator

cal-cu-lar v. to estimate; calculate

cal-cu-lis-ta m.f. planner; calculator

cal-cu-lo m. calculation

cal-de-ra f. boiler

cal-do m. soup; broth; stock

ca-le-fac-ción f. heating; heat

ca-le-fac-tor m. heater

ca-len-da-rió m. calendar; schedule

ca-len-ta-dor adj. warming; heating

ca-len-tar(se) v. to heat or to warm

ca-lien-te adj. warm; hot

ca-li-na f. haze

ca-lip-so m. calypso

cal-ma f. calm

cal-man-te adj. sedative m. tranquilizer

cal-mar(se) v. to soothe; to calm; to settle

ca-lo-frí-o m. chill; feaver

ca-lor m. warmth; heat

ca-lo-ria f. calorie

ca-lo-ri-co adj. caloric

ca-lum-nia f. slander; calumny

ca-lum-nia-dor, ra adj. slanderous

ca-lu-ro-so adj. warm; hot

cal-va-rio m. *relig.* Clavary

cal-vi-cie f. baldness

cal-vo adj. bald

cal-za-da f. causeway; drive; highway; road

cal-zo-nes m. shoehorn

cal-zo-nes m., pl. trousers

ca-lia-do adj. silent; quiet

ca-llar(se) v. to keep quiet; hush

ca-lle f. street

ca-lle-jue-la f. alley

ca-llo *m.* callus; corn
ca-ma *f.* bed
ca-ma-da *f.* litter; brood
ca-ma-feo *m.* cameo
ca-ma-ra *f.* room; chamber
ca-ma-ra-da *m.,f.* comrade
ca-ma-re-ra *f.* waitress
ca-ma-re-ro *m.* waiter
ca-ma-ro-te *m.* cabin
cam-biar(se) *v.* to change; to alter
cam-bia-vi-a *m. rail* switch
cam-bio *m.* shift; change
cam-bis-ta *m.f.* broker, moneychanger
ca-me-le-ar *v. coll.* deceive
ca-me-lia *f.* camellia
ca-me-llo *m.* camel
ca-me-ro, a *adj.* double
ca-mi-lla *f.* stretcher
ca-mi-nar *v.* to walk; to travel
ca-mi-na-ta *f.* hike; walk
ca-mi-no *m.* route; road
ca-mion *m.* truck
ca-mio-ne-ro, a *m.f.* truck driver
ca-mio-ne-ta *f.* van
ca-mi-sa *f.* shirt
ca-mi-se-ta *f.* tee-shirt; undershirt
ca-mi-so-la *f.* camisole
ca-mi-son *m.* nightgown
ca-mo-rra *f. coll.* squabble
ca-mo-rre-ar *v. coll* to quarrel; squabble
cam-pa-men-to *m.* camp
cam-pa-na *f.* bell
cam-pa-na *f.* campaign
cam-pe-si-no, -na *adj.* country; peasant
cam-pes-tre *adj.* rural
cam-pis-ta *m.,f* camper
cam-po *m.* country; field
cam-po-san-to *m.* graveyard; cementery
ca-mu-fla-je *m.* camouflage
ca-mu-flar *v.* to camouflage
ca-nal *m.* canal; channel
ca-na-le-te *m.* paddle
ca-nas-ta *f.* hamper; basket
can-ce-la-ción *f.* cancellation
can-ce-lar *v.* to cancel
can-cer *m.* cancer

can-ci-ller *m.* chancellor
can-ci-lle-ri-a *f.* chancellery
can-ción *f.* song
can-cio-ne-ro *m. mus.* songbook
can-cro *m. med.* cancer
can-da-do *m.* padlock
can-del-la *f.* candle
can-de-le-ro *m.* candlestick
can-di-da-to *m.* candidate
can-di-da-tu-ra *f.* candidacy
can-di-do *adj.* unsophisticated
ca-ne-la *f.* cinnamon
ca-ne-ion *m.* roof gutter
ca-ne-lo-nes *m., pl.* canneloni
ca-ne-su *m.* bodice; yoke
can-gre-jo *m.* crab
can-gu-ro *m.* kangaroo
can-ni-bal *m.* cannibal
ca-ni-ca *f.* marble
ca-ni-no *adj.* canine
ca-ni-cu-la *f.* midsummer heat; dog days of summer
ca-ni-lla *f. anat.* shinbone
ca-ni-lli-ta *m.* newspaper boy
ca-ni-no, a *adj.& m.* canine
can-je *m.* trade; exchange
can-je-a-ble *adj.* exchangeable
can-je-ar *v.* to trade; exchange
ca-no, a *adj.* gray-haired
ca-noa *f.* canoe; rowboat
ca-non *m.* canon
can-sa-do *adj.* weary; tired; rundown
can-san-cio *m.* tiredness
can-sar(se) *v.* to weary; tire
can-ta-lu-po *m.* cantaloupe
can-tan-te *m.,f.* singer
can-tar *v.* to sing; chant *m.* song
can-te-ra *f.* pit; quarry
can-ti-dad *f.* quantity; amount
can-tim-plo-ra *f.* canteen
can-to *m.* singing; croak
can-tu-rrear *v.* to croon; hum
ca-na *f.* cane; reed
ca-no *m.* pipe; spout

ca-non *m.* cannon; barrel

ca-os *m.* chaos

ca-pa *f.* cape; coating; layer

ca-pa-ci-dad *f.* capacity; capability

ca-pa-taz *m.* foreman

ca-paz *adj.* roomy; capable

cap-cio-so *adj.* deceitful

ca-pe-llan *m.* chaplain

ca-pe-ru-za *f.* hood

ca-pi-lar *adj. & m.* capillary

ca-pi-la-ri-dad *f.* capillarity

ca-pi-lla *f.* chapel

ca-pi-llo *m.* baby bonnet; cap

ca-pi-ro-ta-zo *m.* flip as with the finger

ca-pi-tal *m.* capital

ca-pi-ta-lis-mo *m.* capitalism

ca-pi-ta-lis-mo *m.* capitalism

ca-pi-tan *m.* captain

ça-pi-to-lio *m.* capitol

ça-pi-tu-lo *m.* chapter

ca-po *m.* bonnet; hood

ca-pon *adj.* casterated

ça-pri-cho *m.* whim; fancy; quick

ca-pri-cho-so *adj.* temperamental; whimsical

cap-su-la *f.* capsule

cap-tu-ra *f.* capture; catch

ca-pu-cha *f.* hood

ca-pu-llo *m.* cocoon

ca-qui *m.* khaki

ca-ra *f.* face

ca-ra-col *m.* snail

ca-rac-ter *m.* nature; character

ca-rac-te-ris-ti-co, -ca *adj.* typical

ca-rac-te-ri-za-do, a *adj.* distinguished

ca-rac-te-ri-za-dor, ra *adj.* distinguishing

ca-rac-te-ri-zar *v.* to characterize

ca-ra-cu *m. Amer.* bone marrow

ca-ram-ba-no *m.* icicle

ca-ra-me-li-zar *v.* to cover with caramel

ca-ra-me-lo *m.* caramel

ca-ra-va-na *f.* caravan

car-bo-hi-dra-to *m.* carbohydrate

car-bɔn *m.* coal

car-bo-na-to *m.* carbonate

car-bo-no *m.* carbon

car-nun-co *m.* carbuncle

car-bu-ra-dor *m.* carburetor

car-bu-ran-te *m.* fuel

car-cel *f.* prison; jail

car-de-nal *m.* cardinal

car-dia-co *adj.* cardiac

ca-re-cer *v.* to lack

ca-ren-cia *f.* need; lack

ca-rey *m.* sea turtle

car-ga *f.* burden; load

car-ga-de-ro *m.* loading platform

car-ga-men-to *m.* cargo

car-gar(se) *v.* to burden; load

car-go *m.* charge; burden; load

ca-riar-se *v.* to decay

ca-ri-dad *f.* charity

ca-ri-no, a *m.* affection; love

ca-ri-ta-ti-vo *adj.* charitable

car-nal *adj.* carnal

car-na-val *m.* carnival

car-ne *f.* pulp; flesh; meat

car-ne-ar *v. Amer.* to slaughter

car-ni-ce-rɪ́a *f.* slaughter; bloodshed

car-ni-ce-ro *m.* butcher

car-pe-ta *f.* folder

car-pin-te-ria *f.* carpentry

car-pin-te-ro *m.* carpenter

ca-rre-ra *f.* career; race

ca-rre-ro *m.* carrier

ca-rre-ta-je *m.* cartage

ca-rre-te *m.* reel; spool; coil; bobbin

ca-rrc-te-ra *f.* road; highway

ca-rro-za *f.* coach; chariot

ca-rrua-je *m.* carriage

ca-rru-sel *m.* merry-go-round

car-ta *f.* card; letter

car-ta-pa-cio *m.* notebook

car-tel *m.* poster

car-te-le-ra *f.* billboard

car-te-ra *f.* billfold; wallet

car-te-ro *m.* postman

car-ti-la-go *m.* gristle; cartilage

car-to-gra-fi-a *f.* mapmaking; cartography

car-to-gra-lo, a *m., f.* mapmaker, catographer

car-ton *m.* cardboard

car-tu-cho *m.* cartridge

ca-sa *f.* home; house

ca-sa-ca *f.* dress coat

ca-sa-do, a *adj.* married

casar(se) *v.* wed; to marry

cas-ca-bel *m.* small bell

cas-ca-be-le-ar *v.* to jingle

cas-ca-do, a *adj.* cracked; decrepit

cas-ca-da *f.* cascade

cas-ca-jo *m.* gravel

cas-ca-ra *f.* hull; shell; skin; rind

ca-se-ta *f.* cottage

ca-se-te *m.f.* tape cartridge; cassette

cas-co-te *m.* rubble

ca-si *adv.* almost

ca-si-mir *m.* cashmere

ca-si-no *m.* casino

ca-so *m.* happening; case

cas-pa *f.* dandruff

cas-ta *f.* breed; caste; cast

cas-ta-ne-te-ar *v.* to chatter

cas-ti-dad *f.* chastity

cas-ti-gar *v.* to punish

cas-ti-llo *m.* castle

cas-tor *m.* beaver

cas-tra-cion *f.* castration

ca-sual *adj.* accidental; coincidental

ca-sua-li-dad *f.* coincidence; chance

ca-ta-le-jo *m.* small telescope; spyglass

ca-ta-lo-gar *v.* to catalog; catalogue

ca-tar *v.* to taste; to sample

ca-ta-ra-ta *f.* waterfall; cataract

ca-tas-tro-fe *f.* catastrophe

ca-te-dral *f.* cathedral

ca-te-go-ria *f.* category

ca-ter-va *f.* gang

ca-te-ter *m.* catheter

ca-tin-ga *f.* body odor

ca-tor-ce *adj.* fourteen

ca-tre *m.* cot made of canvas

cau-ce *m.* channel; riverbed; ditch

cau-cion *f.* bail; caution

cau-cho *m.* rubber; rubber tree or plant

cau-di-lio *m.* leader

cau-sa *f.* cause

cau-te-la *f.* cautiously

cau-te-la *f.* caution

cau-te-lo-so, a *adj.* cautions

cau-te-ri-zar *v.* captivating

cau-ti-ve-rio *m.* captivity

cau-ti-vo, a *adj. & m.f* captive

cau-to, a *adj.* cautions

ca-var *v.* to dig

ca-ver-na *f.* cave, cavern

ca-vial/viar *m.* caviar

ca-vi-dad *f.* cavity

ca-vi-la-cion *f.* rumination, pondering

ca-vi-lar *intr.* to ruminate; ponder

ca-za *f.* hunt game

ca-za-dor, ra *adj.* hunting

ca-zar *v.* to hunt

ca-zo *m.* ladle

ca-zue-la *m.* small shark

ce-bar *v.* to fatten

ce-bo-lla *f.* onion

ce-bra *f.* zebra

ce-ce-o *m.* lisp

ce-dro *m.* cedar

ce-du-la *f.* document

ce-fi-ro *m.* zephyr

ce-gar *v.* to blind

ce-gue-dad-ra *f.* blindness

ce-ja *f.* eyebrow

ce-jar *intr.* to back up

ce-la-da *f.* ambush

ce-la-dor, ra *adj.* vigilant; watchful

ce-lar *v.* to comply with something

cel-da *f.* cell

ce-le-bra-cion *f.* celebration

ce-le-bran-te *adj.* celebrating

ce-le-brar *v.* to celebrate

ce-le-bre *adj.* famous; celebrated

ce-le-bri-dad *f.* celebrity
ce-le-ri-dad *f.* speed
ce-les-te *adj.* sky-blue
ce-les-tial *adj.* heavenly
ce-les-ti-na *f.* madam; procuress
ce-li-ba-to *m.* celibacy
ce-li-be *adj. & m.f.* celibate
ce-lo-tan *m.* cellophane
ce-lo-si-a *f.* latticework
ce-lo-so, a *adj.* zealous
ce-lu-la *f.* cell
ce-lu-loi-de *m.* celluloid
ce-lu-lo-so *adj.* cellulous
ce-llis-ca *f.* sleet
ce-men-te-rio *m.* cemetery
ce-men-to *m.* cement
ce-na *f.* supper; dinner
ce-na-gal *m.* swamp
ce-nar *intr.* to have dinner
cen-ca-rro *m.* cowbell
ce-ni-ce-ro *m.* ashtray
ce-nit *m.* zenith
cen-sor *m.* censor
cen-su-rar *v.* to censor
cen-te-lla *f.* flash
cen-te-lle-an-te *adj.* sparkling
cen-te-na *f.* one hundred
cen-te-nar *m.* one hundred
cen-ta-no *m.* rye
cen-te-si-mo *adj.* hundredth
cen-ti-gra-do *adj.* centrigrade
cen-ti-me-tro *m.* centimeter
cen-ti-me-tro, a *adj.* hundredth
cen-ti-ne-la *m.f.* sentry
cen-to-lla *f.* spider crab
cen-tra-do, a *adj.* centered
cen-tral *adj.* central
cen-tra-li-zar *v.* to centralize
cen-trar *v.* to center
cen-tri-co *adj.* central
cen-tro *m.* core; middle; center
ce-nir *v.* to encircle; to bind; to be tight on
ce-no *m.* frown
ce-pa *f.* stump
ce-pi-llo *m.* brush
ce-ra *f.* wax
ce-ra-mi-ca *f.* ceramics

cer-ca *adv.* near; close
cer-ca *f.* fence
cer-ca-ni-a *f.* nearness *pl.* outskirts
cer-ca-no *adj.* near; close
cer-car *v.* to surround; to fence something in
cer-ce-nar *v.* to cut
cer-cio-rar *v.* to assure
cer-co *m.* circle
cer-da *f.* pig; sow
cer-do *m.* pig
cer-do-so *adj.* bristly
ce-real *m.* cereal
ce-re-bral *adj.* cerebral
ce-re-bro *m.* brain
ce-re-mo-nia *f.* ceremony
ce-re-mo-nial *m.* cermonial
ce-re-za *f.* cherry
ce-ri-lla *f.* match
ce-ro *m.* zero
ce-rra-do *adj.* shut
ce-rra-du-ra *f.* lock
ce-rrar(se) *v.* to close; seal
ce-rro-jo *m.* bolt
cer-ti-fi-ca-do *m.* certificate
cer-ti-fi-car *v.* to certify
cer-va-to *m.* fawn
cer-ve-za *f.* ale; beer
ce-sar *v.* to cease
ce-sion *f.* grant; cession
ces-ped *m.* grass; sod; lawn
ces-ta *f.* basket
ce-tri-no *adj.* sallow
ci-cli-co *adj.* cyclic
ci-clis-ta *m., f.* cyclist
ci-clo *m.* circle
ci-clon *m.* cyclone
ci-cu-ta *f.* hemlock
cie-go *adj.* sightless; blind
cie-lo *m.* heaven; sky
cien *adj.* hundred
cie-na-ga *f.* swamp
cien-cia *f.* science
cien-ti-fi-co *m.* scientist
cien-to *a., m.* hundred
cie-rre *m.* snap
cier-ta-men-te *adv.* certainly
cier-to, -ta *adj.* certain; sure
cier-vo *m.* hart; stag
ci-fra *f.* figure; cipher
ci-frar *v.* to cipher
ci-ga-rri-llo *m.* cigarette

ci-lin-dro *m.* cylinder
ci-ma *f.* crest; summit; top
cin-co *adj.* five
cin-cuen-ta *adj.* fifty
ci-ne *m.* movies
cin-ta *f.* reel; tape; ribbon
cin-to *m.* girdle
cin-tu-ron *m.* belt
ci-pres *m.* cypress
cir-co *m.* circus
cir-cu-la-ción *f.* circulation
cir-cu-lar *adj.* circular
cir-cu-lo *m.* circle
cir-cun-ci-dar *v.* to circumcise
cir-cun-ci-sion *f.* circumcision
ci-rio *m.* candle; taper
ci-rro *m.* cirrus
ci-rue-la *f.* plum
ci-ru-gia *f.* surgery
ci-ru-ja-no *m.* surgeon
cis-ne *m.* swan
ci-ta *f.* meeting; date; appointment
ci-ta-cion *f.* citation; subpena
ci-tar(se) *v.* to quote; summon
clu-dad *f.* town; city
ciu-da-da-no *m.* citizen
ci-vi-co *adj.* civic
ci-vil *adj.* civilian; civil
ci-vi-li-za-cion *f.* civilazation
cal-mor *m.* outcry; noise
cla-mo-ro-so *adj.* clamorous
clan *m.* clan
cla-ra-men-te *adv.* clearly
cla-ri-dad *f.* clearness; clarity
cla-ri-fi-ca-ción *f.* clarification
cla-ri-fi-car *v.* to clarify
cla-rin *m.* bugle
cla-ri-ne-te *m.* clarinet
cla-ro *adj.* clear; light; lucid
cla-se *f.* grade; class; sort
cla-si-co *adj.* classic; classical
cla-si-fi-ca-ción *f.* classification
cla-si-fi-car(se) *v.* to classify; class
cla-var(se) *v.* to nail; to

thrust; stick
cla-ve *adj.* key
cla-vel *m.* carnation
cla-vi-za *f.* peg
cla-vo *m.* spike; nail
cle-men-cia *f.* mercy; clemency
cle-men-te *adj.* clement
cle-ri-cal *adj.* clerical
cle-ri-go *m.* priest; parson
cle-ro *m.* ministry; clergy
clien-te *m., f.* client; customer; patron
cli-ma *m.* climate
cli-max *m.* climax
cli-ni-ca *f.* clinic
clo-quear *v.* to cluck
clo-ro *m.* chlorine
coac-ción *f.* compulsion; constraint
coa-gu-la-ción *f.* coagulation
coa-gu-lar(se) *v.* to coagulate; clot
coa-li-cion *f.* coalition
co-bal-to *m.* cobalt
co-bar-de *adj.* cowardly
co-bra *f.* cobra
co-bra-dor, a *m.* conductor
co-brar(se) *v.* cash; receive
co-bre *m.* copper
co-bro *m.* recovery
co-cai-na *f.* cocaine
co-cer *v.* to bake; cook
co-cien-te *m.* quotient
co-ci-na *f.* kitchen; stove
co-ci-nar *v.* to cook
co-co *m.* coconut
co-co-dri-lo *m.* crocodile
coc-tel *m.* cocktail
co-che *m.* automobile
co-di-cia *f.* greed
codi-ciar *v.* to covet
co-di-cio-so *adj.* greedy
co-di-fi-car *v.* to codify
co-di-go *m.* code
co-do *m.* elbow
co-e-du-ca-ción *f.* coeducation
coe-ta-neo *m.* contemporary
co-fra-dia *f.* gang
co-fre *m.* chest
co-ger *v.* get; choose; take
co-gi-da *f.* toss; catch

co-he-char v. to bribe
co-he-cho m. bribery
co-he-ren-te adj. coherent
co-he-te m. rocket
coin-ci-den-te adj. coincidental
coin-ci-dir v. to coincide
coi-to m. intercourse
co-jear v. to hobble
co-je-ra f. limp
co-jin m. cushion
co-jo adj. lame
col f. cabbage
co-la f. tail
co-la-bo-ra-ción f. collaboration
co-la-no-rar v. to collaborte
co-la-dor m. strainer
co-lap-so m. collapse
col-cha f. quilt; spread
col-chon m. mattress
co-lec-ción f. collection
co-lec-cio-nar v. to collect
co-le-ga m. colleague
co-le-gio m. academy; college; high school
col-ga-du-ra f. drape
co-li-bri m. hummingbird
co-li-co f. colic
co-li-flor f. cauliflower
co-li-na f. hill
col-me-nar f. hive; beehive
col-mi-llo m. fang; tusk
col-mo m. height; climax
co-lo-ca-ción f. location; situation
co-lo-car(se) v. to place; locate; put
co-lon m. colon
co-lo-nia f. colony
co-lo-nial adj. colonial
co-lo-no m. settler
co-lor m. color
co-lo-re-te m. rouge
co-lum-na f. pillar
co-lum-mis-ta m., f. columnist
co-lim-piar(se) v. to swing
co-lu-sion f. colusion
co-ma f. comma
co-ma-dre f. gossip
co-man-dan-te f. commander

co-man-dar v. to command
co-ma-to-so adj. comatose
com-ba f. bend
com-bar(se) v. to bend; sag
com-ba-te m. fight
com-ba-tir(se) v. to combat
com-bi-na-ción f. combination
com-bi-nar(se) v. to blend; combine
com-bus-ti-ble adj. combustible
com-pe-ler v. to compel
com-pen-sa-ción f. compensation
com-pe-ten-cia f. competence
com-pe-tir f. compilation
com-pi-lar v. to compile
com-pin-che m. chum
com-pla-cer(se) v. to please; humor
com-ple-men-to n. complement
com-ple-tar v. to complete
com-ple-to adj. full; absolute; thorough; complete
com-pli-ca-ción f. complication
com-ple-car(se) v. to involve
com-pli-ce m. accessory
com-po-ner(se) v. to make; compose
com-por-ta-mien-to m. behavior
com-por-tar(se) v. to behave
com-po-si-ciona f. composition
com-prar v. purchase; trade
com-pre-hen-sión f. comprehesnion
com-pren-der v. understand
com-pren-si-vo adj. comprehensive
com-pre-sion f. compression
com-pri-mir v. to compress
com-pro-ba-ción f. proof
com-pro-bar v. to verify
com-pues-to m. compound
com-pul-sion f. compulsion
com-pu-ta-dor m. computer
com-pu-tar v. to compute

co-mun *adj.* common

con *prep* towards; with; by

con-ca-vi-dad *f.* hollow

con-ce-bir *v.* to conceive

con-ce-der *v.* allow; accord

con-ce-jo *m.* council

con-cen-tra-ción *f.* concentration

con-cen-trar(se) *v.* to concentrate

con-cep-ción *f.* conception

con-cep-to *m.* concept; notion

con-ce-sion *f.* allowance; concession

con-cien-cia *f.* conscience

con-cier-to *m.* concert

con-cluir(se) *v.* to end; conclude

con-cor-dar *v.* to tally; agree

con-cor-dia *f.* concord

con-cre-to *adj.* concrete

con-cu-bi-na *f.* concurence; turnout

con-cu-rrir *v.* to meet; concur

con-cur-san-te *m., f.* participant

con-cur-so *m.* contest

con-da-do *m.* county

con-de *m.* county

con-de *m.* earl; count

con-de-co-rar *v.* to decorate

con-de-na *f.* sentence

con-de-na-ción *f.* condemnation

con-de-sa *f.* countess

con-di-ción *f.* state; condition

con-di-ció-nal *adj.* conditional

con-di-ció-nar *v.* to condition

con-di-men-to *m.* condiment; seasoning

con-do-len-cia *f.* condolence

con-do-nar *v.* to condone

con-du-cir(se) *v.* to steer; lead; conduct; drive

con-duc-ta *f.* behavior

con-duc-to *m.* duct; conduit

co-nec-tar *v.* to connect

co-ne-ji-to *m.* bunny

co-ne-jo *m.* rabbit

co-ne-xion *f.* connection

con-fec-ción *f.* confection

con-fec-cio-nar *v.* to make up; concoct

con-fe-de-ra-ción *f.* confederation; confederacy

con-fe-ren-cia *f.* lecture; conference

con-fe-rir *v.* to grant; bestow

con-fe-sar(se) *v.* to confess; admit

con-fe-sion *f.* confession; avowal

con-fe-sio-na-rio *m.* confessional

con-fe-so *m.* confessor

con-fe-ti *m.* confetti

con-fia-ble *adj.* reliable

con-fian-za *f.* dependence; confidence

con-fiar *v.* trust; rely; confide

con-fi-den-cial *adj.* confidential

con-fi-gu-ra-ción *f.* configuration

con-fin *m.* confines; bound

con-fir-ma-ción *f.* corroboration

con-fir-mar *v.* ratify; confirm

con-fis-ca-ción *f.* confiscation

con-fis-car *v.* to confiscate

con-fla-gra-ción *f.* conflagration

con-flic-to *m.* clash; conflict

con-for-mar(se) *v.* to adjust; conform

con-for-me *adj.* similar; agreeable

con-for-mi-dad *f.* conformity

con-for-tar *v.* to comfort

con-fron-ta-ción *f.* confrontation

con-fron-tar *v.* to confront

con-fun-dir(se) *v.* to confound; perplex; puzzle; baffle

con-fu-sion *f.* mess; jumble; confusion

con-fu-tar *v.* to disprove; confute

con-ge-la-ción *f.* frostbite

con-ge-lar(se) *v.* to freeze; congeal

con-ge-ni-to *adj.* congenital
con-ges-tion *f.* congestion
con-glo-me-ra-do *m.* conglomerate
con-gre-gar(se) *v.* to flock; assemble
con-gre-so *m.* convention; congress
con-je-tu-ra *f.* surmise; guess; conjecture
con-je-tu-rar *v.* conjecture
con-ju-gar(se) *v.* conjugate
con-jun-ción *f.* conjunction
con-jun-to *m.* whole; ensemble
con-ju-rar *v.* to conjure
con-me-mo-ra-ción *f.* commemoration
con-me-mo-rar *v.* to commemorate
con-me-mo-ra-ti-vo *adj.* memorial
con-mo-cion *f.* stir; concussion; commotion
con-mo-ve-dor *adj.* stirring
con-mo-ver-(se) *v.* to shake; move; thril
co-no *m.* cone
cons-truc-ti-vo *adj.* constructive
cons-truir *v.* to build; structure; construct
con-sue-lo *m.* consolation
con-sul-tar *v.* to consult
con-su-mar *v.* to carry out
con-su-mi-dor *m.* consumer
con-su-mir(se) *v.* to waste away; consume
con-su-mo *m.* consumption
con-sun-cion *f.* consumption
con-tac-to *m.* contact
con-ta-giar(se) *v.* to catch; infect
con-ta-gio *m.* contagion
con-ta-gio-so *adj.* catching
con-ta-mi-na-ción *f.* pollution; contamination
con-ta-mi-nar(se) *v.* to contaminate
con-tar(se) *v.* to number; count; relate; tell
con-tem-pla-ción *f.* contemplation

con-tem-plar *v.* to view; meditate
con-tem-po-ra-neo *adj.* contemporary
con-ten-der *v.* to strive; conten; contest
con-ten-dien-te *v.* contestant
con-te-ner(se) *v.* to hold; include; contain
con-te-ni-do *m.* content
con-ten-to *adj.* happy; contented
con-tes-ta-ción *f.* answer
con-tes-tar *v.* reply; answer
con-tien-da *f.* contest; strife; struggle
con-ti-guo *adj.* adjacent
con-ti-nen-tal *adj.* continental
con-ti-nen-te *m.* mainland; continet; container
con-tin-gen-cia *f.* contingency
con-ti-nua-ción *f.* continuation
con-ti-nuar *v.* to continue
con-ti-nuo *adj.* constant; perpetual; continuous
con-to-near(se) *v.* to strut
con-tor-no *m.* contour; outline
con-tra *prep.* versus; against *adv.* against
con-tra-ba-jo *m.* bass
con-tra-ban-dis-ta *m., f.* smuggler
con-tra-ban-do *m.* smuggling; contraband
con-trac-ción *f.* contraction
con-tra-de-cir *v.* to contradict
con-tra-dic-cion *f.* contradiction
con-traer(se) *v.* to contract
con-tral-to *m., f.* alto; contralto
con-tra-rie-dad *f.* snag; vexation
con-tra-rio *adj.* adverse; contrary
con-tras-tar *v.* contrast
con-tras-te *m.* contrast
con-tra-tiem-po *m.* upset; mishap

con-tra-to *m.* contract; agreement
con-tra-ven-ta-na *f.* shutter
con-tri-bu-ción *f.* task; contribution
con-tri-buir *v.* to contribute
con-trol *m.* control
con-tro-lar *v.* to control
con-tro-ver-sía *f.* controversy
con-tu-sion *f.* bruise; contusion
con-va-le-cen-cía *f.* convalescence
con-va-le-cer *v.* convalesce
con-va-le-cien-te *m., f.* convalescent
con-ven-cer *v.* to satisfy
con-ven-ción *f.* convention
con-ven-ció-nal *adj.* conventional
con-ve-nien-cia *f.* expediency
con-ve-nien-te *adj.* handy; fitting; convenient
con-ve-nir(se) *v.* agree; befit
con-ven-to *m.* abbey
con-ver-gir *v.* to converge
con-ver-sa-ción *f.* conversation
con-ver-sar *v.* to converse
con-ver-tir(se) *v.* to turn into
con-ve-xo *adj.* convex
con-vic-cion *f.* conviction
con-vi-da-do *m.* guest
con-vi-dar(se) *v.* to invite
con-vi-te *m.* invitation
con-vo-ca-ción *f.* convocation
con-vo-car *v.* to summon
con-voy *m.* convoy
con-vul-sion *f.* convulsion
co-nac *m.* brandy
co-o-pe-ra-cion *f.* teamwork
co-o-pe-rar *v.* to cooperate
co-or-di-na-ción *f.* coordination
co-or-di-nar *v.* to coordinate
co-pa *f.* goblet
co-pe-te *m.* tuft
co-pia *f.* imitation; copy
co-piar *v.* to copy
co-pio-so *adj.* copious

co-que-ta *f.* coquette
co-que-tear *v.* to flirt
co-ral *adj.* choral
co-ra-zon *m.* heart
co-ra-zo-na-da *f.* hunch
cor-ba-ta *f.* tie
cor-cel *m.* steed
cor-che-te *m.* clasp
cor-cho *m.* cork
cor-de-ro *m.* lamb
cor-don *m.* cord
co-reo-gra-fo *m.* choreographer
cor-ne-ta *f.* bugler
cor-ni-sa *f.* cornice
co-ro *m.* chorus
co-ro-la *f.* corolla
co-ro-na *f.* crown
co-ro-nar *v.* to crown
co-ro-na-ria *f.* coronary
cor-pi-no *m.* bodice
cor-po-ral *adj.* corporal
cor-po-reo *adj.* bodily
corps *m., pl.* corps
co-rral *m.* corral
co-rrea *f.* strap
co-rrec-ción *f.* propriety
co-rrec-to, -ta *adj.* right
co-rre-dor *m.* broker
co-rre-gir(se) *v.* stream; run
co-rre-ria *f.* foray
co-rres-pon-der(se) *v.* to concern
co-rrien-te *adj.* current
co-rroer(se) *v.* to erode
co-rrom-per(se) *v.* to rot
co-rro-sion *f.* corrosion
co-rro-si-vo *adj.* corrosive
co-rrup-ción *f.* corruption
cor-se *m.* corset
cor-ta-do *adj.* abrupt
cor-ta-du-ra *f.* slit
cor-tan-te *adj.* edged
cor-tar(se) *v.* chop; cut; clip
cor-te *m.* court
cor-tes *adj.* civil; polite
cor-te-sia *f.* civility
cor-ti-jo *m.* grange
cor-to *adj.* brief
co-sa *f.* affair
co-se-cha *f.* crop
co-ser *v.* to sew
cos-me-ti-co *adj.* cosmetic

cos-mos *m.* cosmos
cos-qui-llear *v.* to tickle
cos-ta *f.* cost
cos-tar *v.* to cost
cos-te *m.* price
cos-ti-lla *f.* rib
cos-to-so, -sa *adj.* expensive
cos-tum-bre *f.* custom
cos-tu-ra *f.* joint
co-ti-dia-no *adj.* daily
co-yo-te *m.* coyote
cra-neo *m.* skull
cra-so *adj.* thick
cra-ter *m.* crater
crea-cion *f.* creation
crea-dor *m.* creator
crear *v.* to make; create
cre-cer(se) *v.* to increase
cre-cien-te *m.* crescent
cre-ci-mien-to *m.* growth
cre-di-to *m.* credit
cre-do *m.* credo
cre-du-lo *adj.* credulous
creen-cia *f.* faith
creer(se) *v.* to think
crei-ble *adj.* plausible
cre-ma *f.* cream
cre-sa *f.* maggot
cres-po *adj.* crisp
cre-ta *f.* chalk
cria-da *f.* maid
criar(se) *v.* to raise; nurse
cri-men *m.* felony
crip-ta *f.* crypt
cri-sis *f.* breakdown
cri-sol *m.* crucibile
cris-tal *m.* crystal; glass
cris-tian-nis-mo *m.* Christianity
Christo *m.* Christ
cri-te-rio *m.* criterion
cri-ti-ca *f.* censure; criticism
cri-ti-car *v.* to criticize
cri-ti-co, -ca *adj.* critical
cro-ma-ti-co *adj.* chromatic
cro-mo *m.* chrome
cro-ni-ca *f.* chronicle
cro-ni-co *adj.* chronic
cro-no-me-trar *v.* to tell time
cro-quet *m.* croquet
cro-que-ta *f.* croquette
cru-ce *m.* intersection
cru-ci-fi-car *v.* to crucify

cru-ci-fi-xion *f.* crucifixion
cru-do *adj.* crude; raw
cruel *adj.* heartless; cruel
cru-ji-do *m.* crack
cru-jir *v.* to crunch
cruz *f.* cross
cru-za-da *f.* crusade
cru-za-do, -da *m.* crusader
cru-zar(se) *v.* to cross
cua-dra-do *m.* square
cua-dran-te *m.* quadrant
cua-drar(se) *v.* to tally
cua-dri-lon-go *m.* oblong
cua-dro *m.* square; picture
cua-ja-da *f.* curd
cual *adv.* as; *pron.* which
cua-li-dad *f.* quality
cual-quier *adj.* any; either
cuan *adv.* how
cuan-do *prep.* when; *adv.* when; since
cuan-ti-a *f.* amount
cuan-to *adj.* as much as
cuan-to *adj.* how much?
cua-ren-ta *adj.* forty
cua-ren-ta-vo *adj.* fortieth
cua-res-ma *f.* Lent
cuar-te-ar *v.* to cut up; to quarter
cuar-tel *m. Mil.* barracks
cuar-to *m.* quarter; fourth
cuar-zo *m.* quartz
cua-si *adv.* almost
cua-te *adj.* twin; alike
cua-tre-re-ar *v.* to rustle or steal
cua-tre-ro *adj.* to steal horses
cua-tro *m.* four
cua-tro-cien-tos *adj.* four hundred
cu-be-ta *f.* bucket
cu-bier-to *f.* casing; cover
cu-bil *m.* den
cu-bi-le-te *m.* tumbler
cu-bo *m.* pailful
cu-brir(se) *v.* to conceal; to cover
cu-ca-ra-cha *f.* cockroach
cu-co *adj.* cute
cu-cha-ra *f.* spoon
cu-cha-ra-da *f.* spoonful
cu-che-ta *f.* cabin

cu-chi-che-ar *intr.* to whisper

cu-chi-che-o *m.* whispering

cu-cha-ri-lla *f.* teaspoon

cu-chi-lla *m.* knife

cue-le *m.* collar

cuen-ta *f.* count; bill

cuen-ta-go-tas *m.* eyedropper

cuen-te-ro *adj.* gossipy

cuen-tis-ta *m.* storyteller

cuen-to *m.* tale

cuer-da *f.* cord

cuer-do *adj. & m.f.* sensible; sane person

cuer-no *m.* horn

cue-ro *m.* hide

cuer-pe-ar *intr.* to dodge something

cuer-po *m.* body

cuer-vo *m.* crow

cues-ta *f.* hill; slope

cues-tión *f.* question

cues-tio-na-bel *adj.* debatable; questionable

cues-tio-nar *v.* to debate; discuss

cues-tio-na-rio *m.* questionaire

cue-va *f.* cave

cui-da-do *m.* heed

cui-da-dor *m., f.* caretaker

cui-da-do-so *adj.* careful

cui-dar(se) *v.* to look after

cui-ta *f.* grief

cu-lan-tro *m.* coriander

cu-le-bra *f.* snake

cu-le-bri-lla *f. MED.* ringworm

cu-li-na-rio, a *adj.* culinary

cul-mi-na-ción *f.* culmination

cul-mi-nan-te *adj.* culminating

cul-mi-nar *v.* to culminate

cul-pa *f.* fault

cul-pa-bi-li-dad *f.* guilt

cul-pa-ble *adj.* guilty

cul-par *v.* to criticize; to accuse

cul-ti-va-cion *f.* cultivation

cul-ti-var *v.* farm; to cultivate

cul-ti-vo *m.* cultivation

cul-to *adj.* cultured

cul-tu-ra *f.* culture

cum-bre *f.* peak; top

cum-plea-ños *m.* birthday

cum-pli-do, -da *adj.* perfect; complete

cum-pli-dor *adj.* reliable; trustworthy

cum-pli-men-tar *v.* to compliment

cum-pli-mien-to *m.* fulfillment

cum-plir *v.* to accomplish

cun-dir *intr.* to expand; to spread

cu-ña-da *f.* sister-in-law

cu-ña-do *m.* brother-in-law

cup-le *m.* popular song

cu-po *m.* quota

cu-pon *m.* coupon

cu-ra *f.* cure

cu-ra-ble *adj.* curable

cu-ra-ción *f.* treatment, cure

cu-ran-de-ro, a *m., f.* quack

cu-rar(se) *v.* to heal; recover

cu-ria *f.* court

cu-rio-se-ar *intr.* to pry, snoop

cu-rio-si-dad *adj.* curiosity

cu-rio-so *adj.* curious

cu-rri-cu-lum vi-tae *m.* resume

cur-sar *v.* to study

cur-si *adj.* vulgar

cur-si-vo *adj.* cursive

cur-so *m.* course

cur-ti-do *m.* tanning as in leather

cur-ti-dor *m.* tanner

cur-tiem-bre *m.* tannery

cur-tir(se) *v.* to coarsen

cur-va *f.* bend; curve

cur-va-do, a *adj.* bent; curved

cur-var *v.* to curve

cur-va-tu-ra *f.* curvature

cus-to-dia *f.* keeping

cus-to-diar *v.* to protect; to watch over

cus-to-dio *adj. & m.* guardian

cu-ti-cu-la *f.* curicle

cu-tis *m.* complexion; skin

da-ble *adj.* feasible; possible

dac-ti-lo-gra-ti-a *f.* typewriting; typing

dac-ti-lo-gra-fo *m.f.* typist

da-di-va *f.* gift; present

da-di-vo-si-dad *f.* liberality; generosity

da-di-vo-so, a *adj.* lavish; generous

da-do *m.* die

dal-to-nis-mo *m.* colorblindness

da-ma *f.* lady

da-mi-se-la *f.* damsel

dam-ni-fi-car *v.* to harm; to damage

dam-ni-fi-ca-do, a *adj.* harmed; damaged

dan-za *f.* dance

da-ñar(se) *v.* to hurt; to damage

da-ni-no, -na *adj.* harmful; damaging

da-no *m.* damage

dar(se) *v.* to give; allow

dar-do *m.* arrow; dart

dar-se-na *f.* dock; inner harbor; port

da-ta *f.* items; date

de-tar *v.* to date

da-to *m.* fact

de *prep.* of; frow; with

de-am-bu-lar *intr.* to roam or wander around

de-ba-jo *adv.* underneath; below

de-ba-te *m.* discussion; debate

de-ba-tir *v.* to discuss; to debate

de-be *m.* debit

de-ber *v.* to owe *m.* obligation or duty

de-bi-da-men-te *adv.* duly; properly

de-bi-do *adj.* fitting; due

de-bil *adj.* feeble; weak; faint

de-bi-li-dad *f.* weakness

de-bi-li-tar *tr. & reflex* to weaken

de-but *m.* opening; debut

de-bu-tan-te *f.* debutant *adj.*

beginning

de-ca-den-cia *f.* decline; decadence

de-ca-den-te *adj. & m.f.* decadent

de-ca-er *v.* to decay

de-cal-mien-to *m.* feebleness, weakness; dejection

de-ca-no *m.* dean

de-can-ta-ción *f.* pouring off

de-can-tar *v.* to pour off; to decant

de-ca-pi-tar *v.* to behead

de-cen-cia *f.* decency

de-ce-nio *m.* decade

de-cen-te *adj.* decent

de-cep-cion *f.* deception; disappointment

de-cep-cio-nar *v.* to disappoint

de-ce-so *m.* death; decease

de-ci-di-do, a *adj.* resolute; determined

de-ci-dir *v.* to resolve

de-ci-mal *adj.* decimal

de-cir *v.* to state; say

de-ci-sion *f.* decision; verdict; ruling

de-ci-si-vo *adj.* crucial; conclusive; decisive

de-cla-mar *tr. & intri.* to recite

de-cla-ra-ción *f.* declaration; statement; evidence

de-cla-ra-da-men-te *adv.* openly; manifestly

de-cla-rar(se) *v.* to propose; declare

de-cli-na-cion *f.* decline

de-cli-nar *v.* to decline; to refuse

de-cli-ve *m.* incline; slope

de-co-lo-ra-ción *f.* discoloration

de-co-lo-ran-te *m.* decolorant

de-co-lo-rar *v.* to fade; to discolor

de-co-mi-sar *v.* to seize; confiscation

de-co-ra-do *m.* scenery or set in a theater

de-co-ra-dor, ra *adj.*

ornamental; decorative

de-co-rar v. to decorate

de-co-ra-ti-vo, a adj. ornamental; decorative

de-co-ro m. honor; respect

de-co-ro-so, a adj. decent; honorable

de-cre-cer v. to diminish

de-cre-ci-mien-to m. decrease

de-cre-pi-to, -ta adj. aged; decrepit

de-cre-tar v. to decree; order

de-dal m. thimble

de-di-car(se) v. to devote

de-do m. finger

de-du-cir v. to conclude; deduce; subtract

de-fa-mar v. to defame

de-fec-ción f. defection

de-fec-to m. flaw; defect

de-fec-tuo-so, a adj. faulty; defective

de-fen-der v. to defend

de-fen-sa f. defense

de-fen-sor m. supporter

de-fe-ren-cia f. difference

de-fi-cien-cia f. lacking; deficient

de-fi-ni-ción f. definition; determination

de-fi-nir v. to define

de-for-mar(se) v. to loose shape

de-frau-da-ción f. cheating; fraud

de-frau-dar v. to cheat

de-fun-ción f. death; demise

de-ge-ne-rar v. to decline; to degenerate

de-go-lla-de-ro m. windpipe; throat

de-go-llar v. to cut the throat

de-gra-dar(se) v. to demean

de-gus-ta-cion f. sampling; tasting

dei-dad f. deify

de-ja-do, a adj. negligent; careless

de-jar(se) v. to quit; let

de-jo m. abandonmnet

del contr. of de and el

de-lan-ta adv. ahead; before; in front

de-lan-te-ro adj. forward; front

de-la-tar v. to inform; to denounce, expose

de-le-ga-ción f. delegation

de-le-gar v. to delegate

de-lei-ta-ble adj. enjoyable; delightful

de-lei-tar(se) v. to delight

del-ga-do adj. thin; slim

de-li-be-ra-do, a adj. intentional; deliberate

de-li-ca-do, -da adj. sensitive

de-li-cia f. pleasure; delight

de-lin-cuen-te adj. delinquent

de-li-ne-ar v. to outline; delineate

de-li-ran-te adj. delirious

de-li-rar v. to rave; to be delirious

de-man-da f. challenge; demand

de-man-dar v. to demand; to ask for

de-ma-sí-a f. surplus; more than what is needed

de-ma-sia-do adv. too much

de-me-ri-to m. demerit

de-mo-cra-cia f. democracy

de-mo-le-dor, ra adj. demolishing

de-mo-ler v. to demolish; to destroy

de-mo-li-ción f. destruction

de-mo-nio m. devil; demon

de-mo-ra f. wait; delay

de-mo-rar(se) v. to delay

de-mos-trar v. to display; to demonstrate

de-mos-tra-ti-vo, a adj. & m. demonstrative

de-mu-dar v. to change

de-ne-gar v. to reject; to refuse

de-no-da-do, a adj. bold

de-no-mi-na-ción f. denomination

de-no-mi-na-dor, ra adj. denominating

de-nos-tar v. to insult; to

abuse
de-no-tar v. to denote
den-si-dad f. density
den-so adj. thick; dense
den-ta-du-ra f. denture
den-tal adj. dental
den-te-lle-ar v. to bite; to nibble
den-te-ra f. jealousy; envy
den-ti-fri-co m. toothpaste
den-tis-ta m., f. dentist
den-tro adv. within; inside
de-nue-do m. courage; bravery
de-nues-to m. insult
de-nun-ciar v. to denounce
de-pa-rar v. to supply
de-par-ta-men-to m. office; department; section
de-par-tir v. to converse; to talk
de-pen-den-cia f. dependence; kinship; reliance
de-pen-der v. to depend
de-plo-rar v. deplore
de-po-ner v. depose; to put aside
de-por-ta-ción f. deportation
de-por-tar v. to exile; deport
de-por-te m. sport
de-po-si-tar v. to bank
de-po-si-to m. deposit
de-pra-va-ción f. corruption
de-pra-va-do, a adj. corrupted
de-pra-var v. to deprave
de-pre-car v. to implore
de-pre-ca-to-rio adj. imploring
de-pre-ciar v. to depreciate
de-pre-dar v. to pillage
de-pre-sion f. slump; depression
de-pri-mi-do adj. depressed
de-pri-mir v. to depress
de-re-cho adj. right; upright
de-ri-var(se) v. drift
der-ma-to-lo-gi-a f. dermatology
der-ma-to-lo-go m., f. dermatologist
de-rra-mar(se) v. to overflow; to spill

de-rri-bar v. to overthrow; to knock down
de-rro-char v. to waste
de-rro-che m. squandering
de-rro-tar(se) v. to ruin
des-a-co-plar v. disconnect
des-a-fiar v. to defy
des-a-fio m. challenge
des-a-gra-dar v. to displease
des-a-hu-ciar v. to evict
des-ai-re m. slight
des-a-len-tar v. to dishearten
des-a-ni-mar(se) v. dismay
des-a-ni-mo m. depression
des-a-pro-bar v. disapprove
des-a-rre-glar(se) v. derange
des-a-rre-glo m. disorder
des-a-rro-llar(se) v. to unfold
des-a-rro-llo m. development
des-a-so-sie-go m. unrest
de-sas-tre m. disaster
des-a-tar(se) v. to undo
des-a-ten-to adj. unthinking
de-sa-ti-no m. blunder
des-a-yu-nar(se) v. breakfast
des-a-yu-no m. breakfast
des-ca-li-fi-car v. disqualify
des-can-sar v. to rest
des-can-so m. rest
des-ca-ra-do adj. brazen
des-car-gar(se) v. to unload
des-cen-den-te adj. downward
des-cen-der v. descent
des-ci-frar v. to decipher
des-co-lo-rar(se) v. fade
des-com-po-ner(se) v. to decompose
des-con-cer-tar(se) v. to embarrass
des-con-fiar v. to distrust
des-co-no-cer v. to disavow
des-con-ten-to m. discontent
des-con-ti-nuar v. to discontinue
des-cot-tes adj. impolite
des-co-ser(se) v. to come apart
des-cri-bir v. to describe
des-crip-ción f. description
des-cu-brir v. to find
des-cui-da-do adj. remiss

des-cui-dar v. to neglect
des-de prep. since; from
des-de-nar v. to disdain
des-di-cha f. unhappiness
de-sea-ble adj. elegible
de-sear v. hope; wish; desire
des-e-char v. to reject
des-em-bo-car v. to land
des-em-bol-sar v. disburse
des-en-cov-var v. to unbend
des-en-la-ce m. ending
de-seo m. craving
de-ser-tar v. to defect
de-ser-tor m. deserter
des-es-pe-rar v. to despair
des-fal-car v. to embezzle
des-fi-gu-rar v. to blemish; to disfigure
des-fi-le m. parade
des-ga-rrar(se) v. to tear
des-gas-te m. waste
des-gra-cia f. misfortune
des-gra-cia-do m. unfortunate
des-ha-cer(se) v. to unwrap
des-he-lar(se) v. to thaw
des-hi-dra-ta-cion f. dehydration
des-hon-ra f. disgrace
des-hon-rar v. to disgrace
des-i-gual adj. irregular
des-in-flar v. to deflate
des-in-te-res m. disinterest
de-sis-tir v. to desist
des-leal adj. disloyal
des-li-zar(se) v. to glide
des-lo-car(se) v. dislocate
des-lum-brar v. to blind
des-lus-trar(se) v. to dull
des-lus-tre m. tarnish
des-ma-yo m. swoon
des-mi-ga-jar(se) v. crumble
des-mon-tar(se) v. to dismantle
des-na-tar v. to skim
des-nu-dar(se) v. to undress
des-nu-do, a adj. nude; bare
des-nu-tri-ción f. malnutrition
des-o-be-de-cer v. to disobey
des-o-cu-pa-do adj. free
des-o-do-ri-zar v. deodorize
de-so-la-ción f. desolation

des-or-den m. mess
des-or-ga-ni-zar v. to disrupt
des-pa-cio adv. slowly
des-pa-char v. to speed
des-pe-dir(se) v. to dismiss; to see off
des-pei-na-do adj. unkempt
des-per-di-ciar v. to waste
des-per-tar(se) v. to awaken; to wake up
des-pier-to adj. awake
des-ple-gar(se) v. to unfold
des-po-jar(se) v. to strip
des-po-sar(se) v. to marry
des-pre-cia-ble adj. vile; worthless
des-pre-ciar(se) v. to scorn
des-pues adv. after; later
des-te-rrar v. to banish
des-te-tar(se) v. to wean
des-ti-lar v. to distill
des-tre-za f. dexterity; skill
des-truc-ción f. destruction
des-truir v. to destroy
des-u-nir v. to disunite
des-va-ne-cer(se) v. vanish
des-ver-gon-za-do adj. unabashed
des-viar(se) v. to divert; wander
de-ta-lla-do adj. elaborate
de-ta-llar v. to itemize
de-ta-lle m. detail
de-tec-ti-ve m. sleuth
de-ten-ción f. arrest
de-te-ner(se) v. to arrest
de-te-rio-rar(se) v. to decay
de-ter-mi-nar v. to decide
de-tes-tar v. to hate
de-tras adv. aback; behind
deu-da f. debt
de-va-nar v. to wind
de-vas-tar v. to devastate
de-vo-ción f. devotion
de-vol-ver v. to refund; return
de-vo-rar v. to devour
dia m. day
dia-blo m. devil
dia-co-no m. deacon
dia-frag-ma m. diaphragm
diag-nos-ti-car v. to diagnose
dia-gra-ma m. diagram
dia-lec-to m. dialect

dia-man-te *m.* diamond
dia-rio *m.* daily
di-bu-jan-te *m.* cartoonist
di-bu-jar *v.* to sketch
dic-cio-na-rio *m.* dictionary
di-ciem-bre *m.* December
dic-ta-dor *m.* dictator
dic-tar *v.* to dictate
di-cho *m.* remark; saying
die-ci-nue-ve *adj.* nineteen
die-cio-cho *adj.* eighteen
die-ci-séis *adj.* sixteen
die-ci-sie-te *adj.* seventeen
dien-te *m.* tooth
diez *adj.* ten
di-fe-ren-cía *f.* difference
dife-ren-te *adj.* different
di-fe-rir *v.* to defer
di-fi-cil *adj.* hard; difficult
di-fun-to *adj.* deceased
di-fu-so *adj.* widespread
di-ge-rir *v.* to digest
di-ges-tion *f.* digestion
di-gi-to *m.* digit
dig-ni-dad *f.* dignity
di-la-tar(se) *v.* to dilate
di-li-gen-te *adj.* diligent
di-luir *v.* to dilute
di-lu-viar *v.* to pour
di-men-sion *f.* dimension
di-nas-tia *f.* dynasty
di-ne-ro *m.* money
dios *m.* god
dio-sa *f.* goddess
di-plo-ma-cia *f.* diplomacy
di-rec-ción *f.* direction
di-rec-ta-men-te *adv.* straight
di-rec-to *adj.* straight
di-ri-gir(se) *v.* to lead; control
dis-cer-nir *v.* to discern
dis-ci-pli-na *f.* discipline
dis-ci-pli-nar *v.* discipline
dis-co *m.* record
dis-cre-par *v.* to disagree
dis-cre-to *adj.* discreet
dis-cul-pa *f.* excuse
dis-cul-par *v.* to excuse
dis-cu-sion *f.* discussion
dis-cu-tir *v.* to argue
di-se-mi-nar *v.* to spread
di-se-nar *v.* to design
dis-fraz *m.* costume

dis-fra-zar *v.* to disguise
dis-gus-tar(se) *v.* to annoy
dis-gus-to *m.* displeasure
di-slo-ca-ción *f.* dislocation
di-sol-var(se) *v.* to dissolve
dis-per-sar(se0 *v.* to dispel
dis-po-ner(se) *v.* ready
dis-pues-to *adj.* willing
dis-pu-ta *f.* dispute
dis-pu-tar *v.* fight; quarrel
dis-tan-te *adj.* distant
dis-tin-guir *v.* distinguish
dis-traer(se) *v.* to divert; distract
dis-tri-buir *v.* to distribute
dis-tur-bio *m.* trouble
di-sua-dir *v.* to deter
di-van *m.* couch
di-ver-gir *v.* to diverge
di-ver-sion *f.* amusement
di-ver-so *adj.* varied; different
di-vi-dir(se) *v.* to split; divide
di-vi-no *adj.* divine
di-vor-ciar(se) *v.* to divorce
do-blar(se) *v.* fold; double
do-ce *adj.* twelve
do-ce-na *f.* dozen
do-cil *adj.* meek
do-lar *m.* dollar
do-ler(se) *v.* to pain; hurt
do-lor *m.* ache; pain
do-mes-ti-car(se) *v.* to domesticate
do-min-go *m.* Sunday
do-nan-te *m.* donor
do-ñar *v.* to donate
don-de *adv.* where
dor-mir(se) *v.* to sleep
dos *adj.* two
dra-gon *m.* dragon
dra-ma-ti-co *adj.* dramatic
dro-ga *f.* drug
du-cha *f.* shower
du-char-se *v.* to shower
du-dar *v.* to hesitate; doubt
due-na *f.* owner; master
dul-ce *m.* candy
duo-de-ci-mo *adj.* twelfth
du-pli-car(se) *v.* duplicate
du-que-sa *f.* duchess
du-ra-de-ro *adj.* durable
du-ran-te *prep.* during
du-ro *adj.* stiff; hard

e-ba-no *m.* ebony
e-brie-dad *f.* inebriation
e-brio *m.* drunk
e-clec-ti-co *adj.* eclectic
e-cle-sias-ti-co *adj.* ecclesiastic
e-clip-sar *v.* eclipse
e-clip-se *m.* eclipse
e-co *m.* echo
e-co-lo-gia *f.* ecology
e-co-no-mia *f.* economy
e-co-no-mis-ta *m.* economist
e-co-no-mi-zar *v.* economize
e-cua-ción *f.* equation
e-cua-dor *m.* equator
e-cua-ni-me *adj.* impartial
e-cua-to-rial *adj.* equatorial
ec-ze-ma *m.* eczema
e-cha-da *f.* toss
e-char(se) *v.* throw; cast away
e-dad *f.* age
e-di-cion *f.* edition
e-dic-to *m.* edict
e-di-fi-car *v.* edify
e-di-tar *v.* edict
e-di-tor *m.* editor
e-di-to-rial *m.* editorial
e-du-ca-ción *f.* education
e-du-car *v.* instruct; teach; train; educate
e-fe-bo *m.* adolescent
e-fec-ti-vi-dad *f.* effectiveness
e-fec-to *m.* result; impact; effect
e-fec-tuar *v.* contrive; effect
e-fi-ca-cia *f.* efficacy
e-fi-cien-cia *f.* efficiency
e-fi-cien-te *adj.* efficient
e-fu-sion *f.* effusion
e-fu-si-vo *adj.* effusive
e-go *m.* ego
e-gre-sar *v.* graduate
e-je-cu-ción *f.* execution
e-je-cu-tar *v.* execute
e-je-cu-ti-vo *adj.* executive
e-jem-plar *m.* example
e-jem-pli-fi-car *v.* exemplify
e-jem-plo *m.* example
e-jer-cer *v.* exercise
e-jer-ci-cio *m.* drill; exercise; practice
e-jer-ci-to *m.* army

e-lec-to *adj.* elect
e-lec-to-ra-do *m.* electorate
e-lec-tri-ci-dad *f.* electricity
e-lec-tri-fi-car *v.* to electrify
e-lec-tro-cu-tar *v.* to electrocute
e-lec-trom *m.* electron
e-le-fan-te *m.* elephant
e-le-gan-cia *f.* grace
e-le-gan-te *adj.* elegant
e-le-gi-do *adj.* chosen
e-le-gir *v.* to choose; elect
e-le-men-tal *adj.* elementary; essential; elemental
e-le-va-ción *f.* elevation
e-le-va-do *adj.* high
e-le-var(se) *v.* to elevate; lift
e-li-mi-nar *v.* to eliminate
e-lip-se *f.* ellipse
e-lip-ti-co *adj.* elliptical
e-li-xir *m.* elixir
e-lo-cuen-cia *f.* eloquence
e-lo-cuen-te *adj.* eloquent
e-lo-giar *v.* to eulogize
e-lu-ci-dar *v.* to elucidate
e-lu-dir *v.* to elude
e-lla *pron., f.* she
e-llas *pl. pron., f.* them; they
e-llo *pron.* it
e-llos *pl. pron., m.* them; they
e-ma-nar *v.* to emanate
e-man-ci-par *v.* to emancipate
em-ba-ja-da *f.* embassy
em-ba-ja-dor *m.* ambassador
em-bal-sa-mar *v.* to embalm
em-ba-ra-za-da *adj.* pregnant
em-ba-ra-zo, -za *m.* embarrassment; pregnancy
em-bar-car(se) *v.* to embark
em-bar-que *m.* shipment
em-bas-tar *v.* to tack; quilt
em-be-ber *v.* to wet; absorb
em-be-lle-cer *v.* to embellish
em-bes-tir *v.* to attack
em-blan-que-cer *v.* to bleach
em-ble-ma *m.* emblem
em-bo-lia *f.* embolism
em-bo-rra-char(se) *v.* to get drunk
em-bos-car *v.* to ambush
em-bo-ta-do, -da *adj.* dull
em-bo-tar *v.* to dull

em-bo-te-llar *v.* to bottle

em-bra-ve-cer *v.* to infuriate

em-bria-gar(se) *v.* to intoxicate

em-brion *m.* embryo

em-bro-llar *v.* to embroil

e-mer-gen-cia *f.* emergency

e-mi-gra-do *m.* emigrant

e-mi-grar *v.* to emigrate

e-mi-sa-rio *m.* emissary

e-mi-sion *f.* issue

e-mi-tir *v.* to give off; emit

e-mo-ción *f.* feeling; emotion

e-mo-cio-nar *v.* to affect

e-mo-ti-vo, -a *adj.* emotional

em-pal-mar *v.* to splice; join

em-pa-par(se) *v.* to drench; wet

em-pa-pe-la-do *m.* lining

em-pa-pe-lar *v.* to line with paper

em-pa-re-da-do *m.* recluse; captive; prisoner

em-pa-tar *v.* to tie

em-pa-te *m.* impediment; draw; connection

em-pe-ci-na-do *adj.* obstinate

em-pe-ci-nar *v.* to be obstinate

em-pe-llar *v.* to push

em-pe-no *m.* patron; pledge; insistence

em-peo-rar(se) *v.* to become worse

em-pe-ra-dor *m.* emperor

em-pe-ra-triz *f.* empress

em-pe-ro *conj.* however

em-pe-zar *v.* to start; begin

em-pi-ri-co *adj.* empirical

em-plas-tar *v.* to hamper; plaster

em-plas-to *m.* plaster

em-ple-a-do *m.* employee

em-ple-a-dor *m.* employer

em-ple-ar(se) *v.* to employ

em-pleo *m.* job; work

em-plu-mar *v.* to feater

em-po-bre-ci-do *adj.* impoverished

em-pren-der *v.* to begin

em-pre-sa *f.* company; business

em-pre-sa-rio *m.* director

em-pu-jar *v.* to thrust; push

em-pu-je *m.* push

e-mu-la-ción *f.* emulation

e-mul-sión *f.* emulsion

en *prep.* in

e-na-je-na-ble *adj.* alienable

e-na-je-na-ción *f.* alienation

e-na-je-nar *v.* to alienate

e-na-no *m.* dwarf

e-nar-de-cer *v.* to ignite

en-ca-be-za-mien-to *m.* heading; caption

en-ca-be-zar *v.* to enroll; to head

en-ca-jar *v.* to force; insert

en-ca-je *m.* insertion; lace

en-ca-lle-cer *v.* to develop a callous

en-can-di-lar *v.* to excite; stir

en-can-ta-do *adj.* happy; delighted

en-can-ta-dor *adj.* charming; enchanting

en-can-ta-mién-to *m.* enchantment

en-can-tar *v.* to charm; to enchant

en-can-to *m.* enchantment

en-ca-po-ta-do *adj.* cloudy

en-ca-po-tar *v.* to become overcasted

en-ca-ra-mar *v.* to elevate; to raise; to promote

en-ca-rar *v.* to confront

en-car-gar *v.* to advise; place in charge; request

en-car-go *m.* assignment; task; job

en-car-na-ción *f.* incarnation

en-car-nar *v.* to heal; to mix; to embody

en-car-ni-za-do *adj.* bloody

en-ca-rri-llar *v.* to guide

en-ce-fa-li-tis *f.* encephalitis

en-cen-de-dor *m.* lighter

en-cen-der(se) *v.* to ignite

en-ce-rar *v.* to polish

en-ce-rrar(se) *v.* to confine

en-ci-clo-pe-dia *f.* encyclopedia

en-cie-rro *m.* closing; seclusion; enclosure

en-ci-ma *adv.* above

en-ci-ma de *adv.* upon
en-cin-ta *adj.* pregnant
en-co-co-rar *v.* to annoy
en-co-ger *v.* to shrink; contract; become smaller
en-co-gi-mien-to *m.* shrinkage; contraction
en-co-lar *v.* to glue
en-co-men-dar(se) *v.* to commend
en-co-miar *v.* to extol
en-co-nar *v.* to irritate; anger
en-con-trar(se) *v.* to find; encounter
en-cor-var *v.* to curve
en-cru-ci-ja-da *f.* intersection
en-cua-der-nar *v.* to bind
en-cua-drar *v.* to frame
en-cu-brir *v.* to hide
en-cuen-tro *m.* meeting; collision; encounter
en-cues-ta *f.* inquiry
en-cum-brar *v.* to honor; to lift; to raise
en-cur-tir *v.* to preserve
en-chi-la-da *f.* enchilada
en-chu-far *v.* to couple; to connect; to merge
en-chu-fe *m.* plug; connection; socket
en-de-ble *adj.* weak
en-de-mi-co *adj.* endemic
en-de-re-zar *v.* to direct; to straighten
en-di-bla-do *adj.* diabolical
en-di-bia *f.* endive
en-do-sa-ble *adj.* endorsable
en-do-san-te *m.* endorser
en-do-sar *v.* to endorse
en-do-so *m.* endorsement
en-dul-zar *v.* to make sweet
en-du-re-cer(se) *v.* toughen
e-ne-mi-go *m.* enemy
e-ne-mis-tad *f.* animosity
en-ner-gia *f.* energy
e-ner-gi-co *adj.* energetic
e-ne-ro *m.* January
e-ner-va-ción *f.* enervation
e-ner-var *v.* to weaken
en-fa-dar *v.* to annoy; to make angry
en-fa-sis *m.* stress; emphasis

en-fer-mar *v.* to become ill
en-fer-me-dad *f.* sickness
en-fer-me-ra *f.* nurse
en-fer-mo *adj.* ill
en-fer-vo-ri-zar *v.* to encourage; to enliven
en-fi-lar *v.* to string; to point; direct
en-fo-car(se) *v.* to focus
en-fren-te *adv.* in front of
en-friar(se) *v.* to cool
en-fu-re-cer *v.* to make furious; to infuriate
en-gan-char *v.* to persuade
en-gan-che *m.* hook
en-ga-na-di-zo *adj.* credulous
en-ga-nar(se) *v.* to fool; to deceive
en-ga-no *m.* mistake; trick; error; fraud
en-ga-no-so *adj.* tricking; deceitful; deceiving
en-gar-zar *v.* to curl; to mount; to thread
en-gas-te *m.* mounting
en-gen-drar *v.* to breed
en-gen-dro *m.* fetus
en-go-la-do *adj.* arrogant
en-go-lle-ta-do *adj.* proud
en-go-mar *v.* to glue
en-gor-de *m.* fattening
en-go-rro-so *adj.* troublesome
en-gra-nar *v.* to link; connect
en-gran-de-cer *v.* to praise; increase; heighten; augment; be promoted; exaggerate
en-gra-pa-do-ra *f.* stapler
en-gra-sa-do *m.* lubricant
en-gra-se *m.* lubricant
en-gre-í-do *adj.* arrogant
en-gro-sar *v.* to swell; to enlarge
en-ha-ci-nar *v.* to heap
en-he-brar *v.* to connect; to string; to link
en-hi-lar *v.* to arrange; guide; thread; order
e-nig-ma-ti-co *adj.* enigmatic
en-jam-brar *v.* to swarm
en-jam-bre *m.* swarm
en-ju-gar *v.* to settle; dry

en-jui-ciar v. to examine; to indict; to judge

en-jun-dia f. fat; grease; vitality

en-la-ce m. liaison; link; junction; connection

en-lar-dar v. to baste

en-la-zar v. to connect; to rope; to lace; to lasso

en-lo-que-cer v. to make insane; to drive crazy

en-lo-sa-dor m. tiler

en-lu-cir v. to plaster

en-lu-tar v. to sadden; darken

en-men-da-ble adj. amendable

en-men-da-ción f. amendment

en-ne-gre-cer v. to darken

en-no-ble-cer v. to ennoble

e-no-jar(se) v. to anger one

e-no-jo m. annoyance

e-no-jo-so, -sa adj. annoying

e-no-lo-go m. oenologist

e-nor-me adj. very large; enormous

e-nor-me-men-te adv. enormously

en-ra-ma-da f. arbor

en-ra-sar v. to smooth; level

en-re-da-dor m. gossip

en-re-dar(se) v. to mesh; mix

en-re-do m. muddle; snarl; mess

en-re-ve-sa-do adj. complicated

en-ri-que-cer(se) v. to enrich

en-ris-car v. to lift

en-ro-je-cer v. to turn red; to make red; to redden

en-ro-lar v. to recruit

en-ro-llar v. to involve; entangle

en-ros-car v. to twist

en-sa-la-da f. salad

en-sa-la-de-ra f. bowel for salad

en-sal-zar v. to exalt

en-sam-blar v. to connect

en-san-char v. to extend; to broaden; to expand

en-san-che m. expansion

en-sa-yar v. to practice; train

en-sa-yo m. test

en-sa-na-da f. inlet

en-se-nan-za f. tuition

en-se-nar v. to instruct; to tell; to teach

en-si-mis-ma-do adj. pensive

en-si-mis-ma-mien-to m. vanity; pensiveness

en-som-bre-cer v. to eclipse; to darken

en-sor-de-cer v.to make deaf

en-su-ciar(se) v. to make soiled

en-sue-no m. daydream

en-ta-bla-do m. floor

en-ta-llar v. to engrave; to carve; to groove

en-ten-de-dor, -a adj. sharp; expert

en-ten-der(se) v. to understand

en-ten-di-mien-to m. understanding

en-te-ra-men-te adv. totally; entirely

en-te-rar(se) v. to learn

en-te-re-za f. fortitude; integrity

en-te-ri-zo adj. entire

en-te-ro adj. whole; entire

en-ti-dad f. concern; entity

en-tie-rro m. funeral; burial; grave; internment

en-tin-ta-do m. inking

en-tin-tar v. to ink

en-to-mo-lo-gí-a f. entomolgy

en-to-nar v. to modulate; to intone

en-ton-ces adv. then

en-tor-no m. enviroment

en-tor-pe-cer v. to deaden; to obstruct; to dull

en-tra-da f. entrance

en-tram-par v. to snare; to trick; to entangle

en-tran-te adj. coming; next

en-tra-na-ble adj. beloved; close; dear

en-trar v. to go into; to enter

en-tre prep. among; between

en-tre-ca-no adj. graying

en-tre-cor-tar v. to interrupt

en-tre-ga *f.* delivery
en-tre-gar(se) *v.* to deliver to
en-tre-na-dor *m.* coach
en-tre-na-mien-to *m.* coaching
en-tre-nar *v.* to train
en-tre-ta-llar *v.* to impede; to carve; to engrave
en-tre-te-ner(se) *v.* to entertain
en-tre-te-ni-do *adj.* entertaining
en-tre-ver *v.* to surmise
en-tre-ve-ro *m.* jumble
en-tre-vis-tar *v.* to interview
en-tu-bar *v.* to put a tube into
en-tuer-to *m.* injustice
en-tur-biar *v.* to cloud
en-tu-sias-mar *v.* to enthuse
en-tu-sias-mo *m.* enthusiasm
e-nu-me-ra-ción *f.* enumeration
en-nu-me-rar *v.* to enumerate
e-nun-cia-ción *f.* enunciation
e-nun-ciar *v.* to enunciate
en-va-sar *v.* to package; to bottle
en-va-se *m.* packaging
en-ver-gar *v.* to fasten
en-via-do *m.* envoy
en-viar *v.* to send
en-vi-dia *f.* envy
en-vi-diar *v.* to envy
en-vi-dio-so *adj.* envious
en-vi-o *m.* dispatch; package; sending
en-vol-tu-ra *m.* wrapper
en-vol-ven-te *adj.* enveloping
en-vol-ver(se) *v.* to wrap up
en-ye-sar *v.* to plaster
en-zi-ma *f.* enzyme
e-on *m.* eon
e-pi-cen-tro *m.* epicenter
e-pi-co *f.* epic
e-pi-de-mia *f.* epidemic
e-pi-de-mi-co *adj.* epidemic
e-pi-der-mi-co *adj.* epidermic
e-pi-glo-tis *f.* epiglottis
e-pi-lep-sia *f.* epilepsy
e-pi-lo-go *m.* epilogue
e-pi-so-dio *m.* episode

e-pi-te-lio *m.* epithelium
e-po-ca *f.* age; time period
e-po-pe-ya *f.* epic
e-qui-dad *f.* equity
e-qui-la-te-ro *adj.* equilateral
e-qui-li-bra-do *adj.* well-balanced; reasonable
e-qui-li-brar *v.* to balance
e-qui-li-brio *adj.* equilibrium
e-qui-li-bris-ta *f.* acrobat
e-qui-no *adj.* equine
e-qui-pa-je *m.* baggage
e-qui-par *v.* to equip
e-qui-pa-rar *v.* to compare
e-qui-po *m.* team
e-qui-ta-ti-vo *adj.* fair
e-qui-va-len-te *adj.* equivalent
e-qui-vo-ca-do *adj.* being wrong
e-qui-vo-car(se) *v.* to error
e-qui-vo-co *adj.* equivocal
er-bio *m.* erbium
e-rec-to *adj.* erect
er-guir *v.* to lift up
e-ri-gir *v.* to erect
e-ro-sión *f.* erosion
e-ro-ti-co *adj.* erotic
e-rra-di-car *v.* to uproot; to eradicate
e-rra-do *adj.* mistaken
e-rran-te *adj.* errant
e-rrar(se) *v.* to wander; to miss; to roam; to fail
e-rro-ne-o *adj.* erroneous
e-rror *m.* error
e-ruc-to *m.* burp
e-ru-di-ción *f.* erudition
e-rup-ción *f.* eruption
e-sa *adj.* that
es-bel-to *adj.* slender
es-bo-zo *m.* outline
es-ca-bel *m.* footstool; stool
es-ca-bro-so *adj.* rough; rugged
es-ca-la *f.* range; ladder
es-ca-lar *v.* to climb; to scale
es-ca-le-ra *f.* stairs; staircase
es-cal-far *v.* to poach
es-ca-lo-nar *v.* to stagger
es-ca-par(se) *v.* to escape; to get away
es-car-pa-do, -a *adj.* short;

abrupt
es-ca-so *adj.* scarce
es-ce-na *f.* scene
es-cla-vi-zar *v.* to put into slavery
es-cla-vo, -a *m.* slave
es-co-ba *f.* broom
es-co-ger *v.* decide; choose
es-con-der(se) *v.* to hide
es-cor-pión *m.* scorpion
es-cri-bir *v.* to write
es-cu-char *v.* to listen
es-cue-la *f.* school
es-cul-pir *v.* to carve
es-cul-tu-ra *f.* sculpture
e-se *adj.* that; **e-sos** *pl.* those
e-sen-cial *adj.* essential
es-for-zar(se) *v.* to strive for
es-fuer-zo *m.* exertion; attempt
es-mal-te *m.* enamel
es-me-ral-da *f.* emerald
e-so *pron.* that
e-so-fa-go *m.* esophagus
es-pa-ciar(se) *v.* spread out
es-pa-cio *m.* space
es-pa-da *f.* sword
es-pa-gue-ti *m.* spaghetti
es-pal-da *f.* back
es-pas-mo *m.* spasm
es-pas-ti-co *adj.* spastic
es-pe-cial *adj.* special
es-pe-cia-li-dad *f.* speciality
es-pe-cia-li-zar(se) *v.* to specialize
es-pe-ci-fi-car *v.* to specify
es-pe-ci-men *m.* specimen
es-pec-ta-dor *m.* witness
es-pe-jo *m.* mirror
es-pe-ra *f.* wait
es-pe-rar *v.* to hope; wait
es-piar *v.* to spy
es-pi-na *f.* spine
es-pi-na-zo *m.* backbone
es-pi-ni-lla *f.* shin
es-pi-ral *adj.* spiral
es-pi-rar *v.* to exhale
es-plen-di-do *adj.* splendid
es-plen-dor *m.* splendor
es-pon-ta-neo *adj.* spontaneous
es-po-sa *f.* wife
es-po-so *m.* husband

es-que-le-to *m.* skeleton
es-qui *m.* ski
es-quiar *v.* to ski
es-qui-na *f.* corner
es-ta *adj., f.* this
es-ta *pron., f.* this
es-ta-ble-cer(se) *v.* to settle; to establish
es-ta-ción *f.* station; season
es-ta-dio *m.* stadium
es-ta-do *m.* state
es-ta-llar *v.* to explode
es-tam-par *v.* to stamp
es-tam-pi-da *f.* stampede
es-tan-car(se) *v.* to stagnate
es-tan-dar-te *m.* standard
es-tar *v.* to lie; to be
es-ta-tua *f.* statue
es-ta-tu-ra *f.* stature
es-te *adj.* east
es-te *pron.* this; *pl.* these
es-te-ri-li-dad *f.* sterility
es-ti-bar *v.* to stow
es-ti-lo *m.* style
es-ti-mar(se) *v.* to estimate
es-ti-mu-lar *v.* to stimulate
es-ti-rar *v.* to stretch
es-to-ma-go *m.* stomach
es-tor-bar *v.* block; impede
es-tor-nu-dar *v.* to sneeze
es-tor-nu-do *m.* sneeze
es-tran-gu-lar *v.* to choke
es-tra-te-gia *f.* strategy
es-tra-ti-fi-car(se) *v.* to stratify
es-tre-char(se) *v.* to narrow
es-tré-lla *f.* star
es-tre-llar)se) *v.* smash into
es-tre-me-cer(se) *v.* to shake
es-tric-to *adj.* strict
es-tro-pa-jo *m.* mop
es-tro-pear(se) *v.* to ruin
es-truc-tu-ra *f.* form
es-truen-do *m.* thunder
es-tu-dian-te *m., f.* student
es-tu-diar *v.* to study
es-tu-dio *m.* studio
es-tu-fa *f.* stove
es-tu-pen-do *adj.* stupendous
es-tu-pi-do *adj.* stupid
es-ter-ño *adj.* eternity
e-ti-que-ta *f.* label
eu-fo-ria *f.* euphoria
e-va-cua-ción *f.* evacuation

e-va-cuar v. to evacuate
e-va-dir v. to avoid; dodge
e-va-lua-ción f. evaluation
e-va-po-ra-ción f. evaporation
e-va-po-rar(se) v. evaporate
e-va-sion f. evasion
e-vi-den-cia f. evidence
e-vi-den-te adj. obvious
e-vi-tar v. to shun
e-vo-car v. to evoke
e-o-lu-ción f. evolution
ex-ac-ta-men-te adv. exactly
ex-a-ge-ra-ción f. exaggeration
ex-a-ge-rar v. to exaggerate
ex-a-men m. test; quiz
ex-a-mi-nar(se) v. examine
ex-ca-va-ción f. excavation
ex-ce-der(se) v. to surpass
ex-ce-len-cia f. excellence
ex-ce-len-te adj. excellent
ex-cep-to prep. unless
ex-ci-tar(se) v. to arouse
ex-cla-ma-ción f. exclamation
ex-cla-mar v. to exclaim
ex-cluir v. to exclude
ex-clu-sion f. exclusion
ex-cu-sa f. excuse
ex-cu-sar v. to excuse
ex-ha-lar v. to exhale
ex-i-gir v. to require
ex-is-tir v. to exist
ex-pan-sion f. expansion
ex-pen-der v. to expend
ex-pe-rien-cia f. experience
ex-pe-ri-men-tar v. to experiment
ex-per-to m. expert
ex-pli-ca-cion f. explanation
ex-pli-car(se) v. to explain
ex-plo-ra-ción f. exploration
ex-plo-rar v. to explore
ex-por-ta-ción f. export
ex-por-tar v. to export
ex-pre-sar(se) v. tell; express
ex-pre-sion f. expression
ex-pul-sar v. to put out; expel
ex-ten-der(se) v. expand out
ex-te-rior adj. exterior
ex-tran-je-ro m. alien
ex-tra-ño adj. odd; strange
ex-tre-mo adj. extreme

fa-bri-ca f. mill
fa-bri-ca-ción f. manufacture
fa-bri-car v. to manufacture
fa-bu-la f. fiction; fable
fa-bu-lo-sa-men-te adv. fabulously
fa-bu-lo-so adj. fabulous
fac-ción f. feature; faction
fa-ce-ta f. facet
fa-cil adj. simple
fa-fi-li-dad f. chance; facility
fa-ci-li-tar v. to expedite; to facilitate
fac-ti-ble adj. feasible
fac-tor m. factor
fac-to-ri-a f. foundry; factory
fac-tu-ra-cion f. invoicing
fac-tu-rar v. to invoice
fa-cul-dad f. power
fa-cul-tar v. to empower
fa-cha f. appearance
fai-san m. pheasant
fa-ja f. sash; band
fa-ja-du-ra f. belting
fa-jar v. to belt; wrap
fa-lan-ge f. phalanx
fa-laz adj. deceptive
fal-da f. skirt
fal-don m. tail
fa-li-co adj. phallic
fal-se-dad f. untruth; lie
fal-si-fi-car v. to misrepresent
fal-so adj. dishonest
fal-ta f. fault; shortage; flaw; want; lack
fal-tar v. to fail; to need
fal-to adj. wanting; wretched; short
fa-llar v. to fail
fa-llo adj. judgment; void; decision; ruling
fa-ma f. fame
fa-me-li-co adj. famished
fa-mi-lia f. family
fa-mi-liar adj. familiar; casual; familial
fa-mo-so adj. well-known
fa-na-ti-zar v. to fanaticize
fan-fa-rron adj. showy; bragging
fan-go m. mud
fan-go-si-dad f. muddiness
fan-ta-se-ar v. to dream

fan-ta-sia *f.* fantasy
fan-tas-ti-co *adj.* bizarre; fanciful
fa-ran-du-la *f.* business; theater
fa-ra-on *m.* pharaoh
far-do *m.* bale; pack
fa-rin-ge *f.* pharynx
far-ma-ceu-ti-co *m.* pharmacist
far-ma-cia *f.* pharmacy
fa-ro *m.* beacon; light; lighthouse
fa-rol *m.* light; lantern
far-sa *f.* farce
fas-ci-na-ción *f.* fascination
fas-ci-nan-te *adj.* fascinating
fas-ci-nar *v.* to intrigue; to fascinate
fas-cis-ta *m.* fascist
fas-ti-diar(se) *v.* to hassel; to annoy; to bother
fas-ti-dio *m.* annoyance; repugnance
fas-ti-dio-so *adj.* annoying; tedious; bothersome
fas-to *m.* splendor
fas-tuo-si-dad *f.* splendor
fa-tal *adj.* fatal
fa-ta-li-dad *f.* fatality
fa-tal-men-te *adv.* unhappily; wretchedly
fa-ti-ga *f.* fatigue
fa-ti-gar(se) *v.* to fatigue; tire
fa-ti-go-so *adj.* tiring; fatigued; tired
fa-tuo *m.* fool
fau-na *f.* fauna
fa-vor *m.* favor
fa-vo-ra-ble *adj.* favorable
fa-vo-re-cer *v.* to favor; to help another; to support
fa-vo-ri-to *adj.* favorite
fe *f.* trust; faith
fe-bre-ro *m.* February
fe-bril *adj.* hectic
fe-cu-la *f.* starch
fe-cun-di-dad *f.* fertility
fe-cha *f.* date
fe-char *v.* to date
fe-de-ra-ción *f.* federation
fe-de-ral *adj.* federal
fe-de-ra-lis-ta *adj.* federalist

fe-de-rar *v.* to federate
fe-li-ci-dad *f.* bliss; happiness; felicity
fe-li-ci-ta-ción *f.* congratulation
fe-li-ci-tar *v.* to congratulate
fe-li-no *adj.* feline
fe-liz *adj.* happy
fel-po *m.* rug
fel-po-so *adj.* plush
fel-pu-do *m.* rug
fe-me-ni-no *adj.* feminine
fe-mi-nis-ta *adj.* feminist
fe-mur *m.* femur
fe-ne-cer *v.* to pass away; to settle; to finish
fe-no-bar-bi-tal *m.* phenobarbital
fe-nol *m.* phenol
feo *adj.* ugly
fe-ria *f.* fair; market
fe-ria-do *adj.* holiday
fe-ri-no, -a *adj.* ferocious; fierce
fer-men-ta-cion *f.* fermentation
fer-men-tar *v.* to ferment
fe-ro-ci-dad *f.* ferocity
fe-roz *adj.* fierce
fe-rre-o *adj.* iron
fe-rro-ca-rril *m.* railway
fer-til *adj.* rich
fer-ti-li-zan-te *adj.* fertilizing
fer-ti-li-zar *v.* to fertilize
fer-vi-do *adj.* fervid
fer-vor *m.* fervor
fes-te-jar *v.* to celebrate; to entertain; to court
fes-tin *m.* feast
fes-ti-val *m.* festival
fes-ti-vo, -va *adj.* merry; festive; witty
fe-tal *adj.* fetal
fe-ti-che *m.* fetish
fe-ti-dez *f.* fetidness
fe-to *m.* fetus
feu-dal *adj.* feudal
feu-da-lis-mo *adj.* feudalism
fia-ble *adj.* dependable
fia-dor *m.* bail
fian-za *f.* guarantor; security
fiar *v.* to entrust; to guaranty
fias-co *m.* fiasco

fi-bro-ma *m.* fibroma
fi-bro-so *adj.* stringy; fibrous
fic-ción *f.* fiction
fic-ti-cio *adj.* fictitious
fi-cha *f.* chip; token
fi-de-dig-no *adj.* trustworthy
fi-dei-co-mi-so *m.* trust
fi-de-li-dad *f.* accuracy; fidelity
fie-bre *f.* fever
fiel *adj.* true; loyal; honest; faithful; trustworthy
fiel-tro *m.* felt
fie-re-za *f.* ferocity; deformity; fierceness
fies-ta *f.* feast; party
fi-gu-ra *f.* shape; figure; character
fi-gu-ra-ción *f.* figuration
fi-gu-ra-do *adj.* figurative
fi-gu-rar(se) *v.* to figure
fi-gu-ra-ti-vo *adj.* figurative
fi-ja-dor *adj.* fixative
fi-ja-men-te *adv.* firmly
fi-jar(se) *v.* to determine; set
fi-jo *adj.* permanent; set; steady; fixed
fi-la *f.* row; file; tier
fi-la-men-to *m.* filament
fi-lan-tro-po *m.* philan-thropist
fi-la-te-lis-ta *m.* philatelist
fi-li-gra-na *f.* filigree
fil-mar *v.* to film
fil-mi-co *adj.* movie; film
fi-lo *m.* edge
fi-lo-lo-gi-a *f.* philology
fi-lo-so-fi-a *f.* philosophy
fi-lo-so-fo *m.* philosopher
fil-tra-ción *f.* filtration
fil-trar(se) *v.* to strain; filter
fil-tro *m.* filter
fin *m.* finish
fi-nal *adj.* ending; last; end; final
fi-na-li-dad *f.* finality
fi-na-lis-ta *m.* finalist
fi-na-li-zar *v.* to conclude
fi-nal-men-te *adv.* finally
fin-ca *f.* land; farm
fi-ne-za *f.* politeness; fineness; affection
fin-gir(se) *v.* pretend; sham

fi-ni-to *adj.* finite
fi-no *adj.* acute; fine; elegant; delicate
fir-ma *f.* firm
fir-ma-men-to *m.* firmament
fir-mar *v.* to sign something
fir-me *adj.* hard; strong; firm
fis-ca-li-zar *v.* to investigate; to oversee; to snoop
fi-si-co *adj.* physical
fi-sio-lo-gi-a *f.* physiology
fi-sio-lo-go *m.* physiologist
fi-sion *f.* fission
fis-tu-la *f.* fistula
fi-su-ra *f.* fissure
fla-co *adj.* skinny; gaunt
fla-ge-la-do *adj.* flagellate
fla-gran-te *adj.* flagrant
fla-me-ar *v.* to flame
flan-co *m.* side
fla-que-ar *v.* to weaken
fla-que-za *f.* weakness; leanness
flau-ta *f.* flute
flau-tin *m.* piccolo
flau-tis-ta *f.* flutist
fle-bi-tis *f.* phlebitis
fle-cha *f.* arrow
fle-ma *f.* phlegm
fle-te *m.* cargo; freight
fle-xi-bi-li-dad *f.* flexibility
fle-xi-ble *adj.* flexible
fle-xor *adj.* flexor
flo-je-dad *f.* laziness; debility
flo-je-ra *f.* carelessness
flo-jo *adj.* limp; weak
flor *f.* blossom; flower; bloom
flo-re-cer *v.* bloom; prosper
flo-reo *m.* flourish
flo-ris-ta *m., f.* florist
flo-tar *v.* to float
fluc-tua-ción *f.* vacilation
fluc-tuar *v.* to fluctuate
flui-do *adj.* fluid
fluir *v.* to flow
fo-co *m.* focus
fo-li-cu-lo *m.* follicle
fo-lla-je *m.* foliage
fo-lle-to *m.* brochure
fo-men-tar *v.* to encourage
fon-ta-ne-ro *m.* plumber
for-jar *v.* to forge

for-ma *f.* shape; form
for-ma-cion *f.* formation
for-ma-li-dad *f.* formality
for-mar(se) *v.* make; shape
for-ta-le-cer(se) *v.* to fortify
for-ta-le-za *f.* fortress
for-tui-to *adj.* casual
for-tu-na *f.* fortune
for-zar *v.* to strain; force
fo-sil *m.* fossil
fo-to *f.* picture; photograph
fo-to-gra-fia *f.* photography
fra-ca-sar *v.* to fail
frac-cion *f.* fraction
frac-tu-ra *f.* break; fracture
frac-tu-rar(se) *v.* to fracture
fra-gil *adj.* frail
fran-ca-men-te *adv.* frankly
fran-ces *adj.* French
fran-co *adj.* open; candid
fran-que-za *f.* frankness
fra-se *f.* sentence
fra-ter-ni-dad *f.* fraternity
frau-de *m.* deception
frecuen-cia *f.* frequency
fre-cuen-te *adj.* frequent
fre-gar *v.* to wash; scrub
freirse *v.* to fry
fre-nar *n.* brake
fren-te *f.* front; forehead
fres-co *adj.* fresh
fric-cion *f.* friction
frio *adj.* cold; frigid
fron-tal *adj.* frontal
fron-te-ra *f.* border; limit
fro-tar(se) *v.* to chafe
frun-cir *v.* to gather
frus-tra-cion *f.* frustration
frus-trar(se) *v.* to frustrate
fue-go *m.* fire
fuen-te *f.* spring; fountain
fue-ra *adv.* outside; off
fuer-te *m.* sturdy; strong
fuer-za *f.* power; force
fu-gar-se *v.* to abscond
ful-gu-rar *v.* to gleam
fu-mar *v.* to smoke
fun-da-cion *f.* foundation
fun-dar(se) *v.* to establish
fun-dir(se) *v.* to fuse
fu-ria *f.* fury
fu-rio-so *adj.* furious
fu-tu-ro *m.* future

ga-ban *m.* topcoat
ga-bar-di-na *f.* gabardine
ga-bi-ne-te *m.* boudoir
ga-ce-la *f.* gazelle
ga-ce-ta *f.* gazette
ga-chi *f.* girl
ga-cho *adj.* floppy; bent
ga-fas *f.* glasses
ga-ga *adj.* foolish
gai-te-ro *adj.* gaudy
ga-jo *m.* section; bunch
ga-lac-ti-co *adj.* galactic
ga-la-na-men-te *adv.* elegantly
ga-la-ni-a *f.* elegance
ga-lan-te *adj.* gallant
ga-lan-te-o *m.* flirting; courting another
ga-len-te-ri-a *f.* generosity; grace
ga-lar-do-nar *v.* to reward
ga-la-xia *f.* galaxy
ga-le-on *m.* gallon
ga-le-ra *f.* galley
ga-le-ria *f.* gallery
ga-li-ma-ti-as *m.* nonsense
ga-lon *m.* gallon
ga-lo-pan-te *adj.* galloping
ga-lo-par *v.* to gallop
ga-lo-pe *m.* gallop
gal-va-ni-zar *v.* to galvanize
ga-llar-di-a *f.* gallantry; grace; elegance
ga-llar-do *adj.* graceful; brave
ga-lle-ta *f.* cracker
ga-lli-na *f.* chicken; hen
ga-lli-ne-ro *m.* henhouse; coop
ga-llo *m.* cock; rooster
ga-ma *f.* gamut
gam-ba-do *adj.* bowlegged
gam-be-te-ar *v.* to prance
ga-na *f.* longing; appetite
ga-na-de-ro *m.* cattle
ga-na-do *m.* livestock
ga-nan-cia *f.* profit
ga-nar *v.* to earn; to win
gan-cho *m.* hook
gan-du-le-ri-a *f.* laziness
gan-glio *m.* ganglion
gan-go-so *adj.* nasal
gan-gre-na *f.* gangrene

ga-no-so *adj.* anxious
gan-so *m.* goose
ga-ra-ba-to *m.* grapple
ga-ra-je *m.* garage
ga-ran-tia *f.* warrant; guaranty
ga-ran-tir *v.* to defend; to guarantee
ga-ra-tu-sa *f.* compliment
gar-ban-zo *m.* chickpea
gar-be-ar *v.* to steal; to rob
gar-bi-llo *m.* sieve
gar-bo-so *adj.* graceful; generous
gar-fa *f.* claw
gar-ga-je-ar *v.* to spit
gar-gan-ta *f.* neck
gar-ga-ra *f.* gargling
gar-ga-ri-zar *v.* to gargle
gar-go-la *f.* gargoyle
gar-gue-ro *m.* trachea
ga-rra *f.* talon
ga-rra-fal *adj.* enormous
ga-rra-pa-ta *f.* mite
ga-rra-pi-nar *v.* to grab
ga-rron *m.* claw
ga-ruar *v.* to drizzle
gas *m.* gas
ga-sa *f.* guaze
ga-si-fi-car *v.* to gasify
ga-so-li-na *f.* gas
gas-ta-do, -a *adj.* threadbare; exhausted
gas-tar *v.* to exhaust; to spend; to squander; wear
gas-tri-co *adj.* gastric
gas-tri-tis *f.* gastritis
gas-tro-no-mia *f.* gastronomy
gas-tro-no-mi-co *adj.* gastronomic
ga-te-ar *v.* to climb; to swipe
ga-ti-llo *m.* hammer
ga-to *m.* cat
ga-tu-no *adj.* catlike
gau-cho *adj.* gaucho
ga-ve-ta *f.* drawer
ga-vio-ta *f.* gull
ga-za-pi-na *f.* brawl
gaz-na-te *m.* windpipe; throat
gei-ser *m.* geyser
ge-la-ti-na *f.* gelatin
ge-ma *f.* gem

ge-mi-do *m.* groan
ge-ne-a-lo-gi-a *f.* genealogy
ge-ne-ra-cion *f.* generation
ge-ne-ral *m.* general
ge-ne-ra-li-dad *f.* generality
ge-ne-ra-li-za-cion *f.* generalization
ge-ne-ra-li-zar *v.* generalize
ge-ne-ra-ti-vo *adj.* generative
ge-ne-ri-ca-men-te *adv.* generically
ge-ne-ri-co *adj.* generic
ge-ne-ro-si-dad *f.* generosity
ge-ne-ro-so, -a *adj.* fine; generous
ge-nial *adj.* genial; inspired; pleasant
ge-nio *m.* genius; disposition
ge-no-ci-dio *m.* genocide
ge-no-ti-po *m.* genotype
gen-te *f.* nation; people
gen-til *adj.* genteel; excellent; polite
gen-ti-o *m.* mob
ge-nui-no *adj.* real; true; genuine
ge-o-fi-si-co *adj.* geophysical
ge-o-gra-fia *f.* geography
ge-o-gra-fo *m., f.* geographer
ge-o-lo-gia *f.* geology
ge-o-lo-go *m., f.* geologist
ge-o-me-tria *f.* geometry
ge-ra-nio *m.* geranium
ge-ren-te *m., f.* director
ge-ria-tri-co *adj.* geriatric
ger-ma-nio *m.* germanium
ger-men *m.* germ
ger-mi-na-cion *f.* germination
ger-mi-nar *v.* to germinate
ge-ron-to-lo-gia *f.* gerontology
ges-ta-cion *f.* gestation
ges-ti-cu-la-cion *f.* gesture; grimace
ges-ti-cu-lar *v.* to gesture
gey-ser *m.* geyser
gi-bar *v.* to curve
gi-bon *m.* gibbon
gi-gan-ta *f.* sunflower
gi-gan-te *m.* giant

gi-go-lo *m.* gigolo
gim-na-sia *f.* gymnastics
gim-nas-ta *f., m.* gymnast
gi-mo-te-ar *v.* to whine
gi-ne-co-lo-gia *f.* gynecology
gin-gi-vi-tis *f.* gingivitis
gi-rar *v.* rotate; spin; gyrate
gi-ra-to-rio *adj.* rotating
gi-ro *m.* rotation; turn
gi-ros-co-pio *m.* gyroscope
gi-ta-nes-co *adj.* gypsy-like
gla-cia-cion *f.* glaciation
gla-cial *adj.* glacial; icy
gla-ciar *adj.* glacial
gla-dia-dor *m.* gladiator
glan-du-la *f.* gland
gla-se-ar *v.* to glaze
glau-co-ma *m.* glaucoma
glo-bal *adj.* global
glo-bo *m.* globe
glo-glo *m.* gurgle
glo-ria *f.* glory
glo-ri-fi-ca-cion *f.* glorification
glo-ri-fi-car(se) *v.* to glorify
glo-rio-so *adj.* glorious
glo-sa *f.* gloss
glo-sar *v.* to gloss
glo-sa-rio *m.* glossary
glo-tis *f.* glottis
glu-co-sa *f.* glucose
glu-ti-no-so *adj.* glutinous
go-ber-na-cion *f.* government
go-ber-na-dor *m.* governor
go-ber-nar *v.* to govern
go-bier-no *n.* government
go-la *f.* throat
golf *m.* golf
gol-fo *m.* golf
go-lo-si-na *f.* craving; delicacy; longing
gol-pe *m.* blow; hit
gol-pear *v.* to slug; hit; beat
gol-pe-te-ar *v.* to pummel; hit; to pound; to beat
go-ma *f.* rubber; gum; rubber band
go-mo-so *adj.* gummy
gon-do-la *f.* gondola
gon-do-le-ro *m.* gondolier
go-no-co-co *m.* gonococcus
gor-do *adj.* fat

gor-go-te-o *m.* gurgle
go-ri-la *m.* gorilla
go-te-o *m.* dripping
go-zar *v.* to enjoy; to rejoice
gra-bar *v.* to engrave
gra-cia *f.* kindness; charm; pardon
gra-cio-so *adj.* funny; charming; amusing
gra-do *m.* step; grade; stair
gra-dual *adj.* gradual
gra-fi-to *m.* graphite
gra-ma-ti-co *adj.* grammatical
gra-na-te *m., adj.* garnet
gra-ni-ti-co *adj.* granite
gran-je-ro *m., f.* farmer
gra-pa *f.* staple
gra-ti-fi-car *v.* to gratify
gra-ve *adj.* serious; important; grave
gre-ga-rio *adj.* gregarious
gris *adj.* grey
gri-tar *v.* to yell; to cry
gri-to *m.* yell; scream
gro-se-ria *f.* roughness; stupidity; vulgarity
gro-se-ro *adj.* vulgar; coarse
gro-tes-co *adj.* grotesque
grue-so *adj.* fat; coarse
gru-nir *v.* to grumble; grunt
gru-po *m.* bunch
guan-te *m.* glove •
guan-te-ro *m.* glove maker
gua-pe-ton *adj.* bold; flashy
gua-pe-za *f.* daring
gua-po *adj.* flashy; good-looking
guar-da *f.* custody; guard
guar-dar(se) *v.* keep; guard
guar-dia *f.* guard
guar-dian *m., f.* guardian
guar-ne-cer *v.* border; supply
gu-ber-na-men-tal *adj.* governmental
gue-rra *f.* war
gue-rre-ar *v.* to fight
gui-a *m., f.* leader; guide
guiar *v.* to steer; to guide
gui-ta-rra *f.* guitar
gu-sa-no *m.* worm
gus-tar *v.* to like
gus-to *m.* zest; taste

ha-ber *v.* to have

ha-bil *adj.* skillful

ha-bi-li-dad *f.* ability; skill

ha-bi-ta-cion *f.* habitation; lodging

ha-bi-tar *v.* to dwell

ha-bi-tual *adj.* habitual

ha-bi-tuar *v.* to habituate

ha-bla *f.* speech

ha-bla-do *adj.* spoken

ha-bla-du-ri-a *f.* gossip; chatter

ha-blar *v.* to talk; to speak

ha-ce *adv.* ago

ha-cer(se) *v.* to act; to become; to force; compose

ha-cia *prep.* about; to

ha-cien-da *f.* ranch

ha-ci-na *f.* pile

ha-ci-nar *v.* to pile up

ha-da *f.* fairy

ha-do *m.* fate

ha-la-gue-no *adj.* promising; attractive; pleasing

ha-lar *v.* to tow something

hal-con *m.* falcon

hal-co-ne-ri-a *f.* falconry

hal-co-ne-ro *m.* falconer

ha-llar(se) *v.* to locate

ham-bre *f.* hunger

ham-brien-to *adj.* hungry; starved

ham-bur-gue-sa *f.* hamburger

ha-ra-po-so *adj.* tattered

ha-ren *m.* harem

har-tar *v.* to annoy; to stuff

has-ta *prep.* till

has-tiar *v.* to annoy; to sicken

he-bra *f.* filament; thread

he-chi-ce-ro *m., f.* charmer; sorceress; sorcerer

he-chi-zo *m.* charm; spell

he-der *v.* to stink; smell bad

he-dor *m.* stink

he-la-do *m.* ice cream

he-lar *v.* to freeze

he-li-cop-te-ro *m.* helicopter

he-lio *m.* helium

he-li-puer-to *m.* heliport

hem-bra *f.* female; woman

he-mo-fi-lia *f.* hemophilia

he-mo-glo-bi-na *f.* hemo-globin

he-mo-rra-gia *f.* hemorrhage

hen-der(se) *v.* to crack

he-nil *m.* hayloft

he-no *m.* hay

he-pa-ti-tis *f.* hepatitis

her-ba-rio *adj.* herbal

he-re-di-ta-rio *adj.* hereditary

he-ren-cia *f.* heritage

he-ri-da *f.* wound

he-rir *v.* hurt; injure; wound

her-ma-na *f.* sister

her-man-dad *f.* sisterhood; brotherhood; league

her-ma-no *m.* brother

her-mo-se-ar *v.* to beautify

her-mo-so, -a *adj.* beautiful

her-nia *f.* hernia

he-roi-co *adj.* heroic

he-ro-i-na *f.* heroine

her-pes *m.* herpes

he-rre-ro *m.* blacksmith

he-rrin *m.* rust

he-rrum-brar *v.* to rust

her-vor *m.* boiling

he-si-ta-cion *f.* hesitation

he-si-tar *v.* to hesitate

he-xa-go-no *adj.* hexagonal

hi-ber-na-cion *f.* hibernation

hi-ber-nar *v.* to hibernate

hi-bri-do *m.* hybrid

hi-dra-ta-cion *f.* hydration

hi-dra-tar *v.* to hydrate

hi-dro-car-bu-ro *m.* hydrocarbon

hi-dro-fo-bia *f.* hydrophobia

hi-dro-ge-no *m.* hydrogen

hi-dro-te-ra-pia *f.* hydro-therapy

hi-dro-xi-do *m.* hydroxide

hie-dra *f.* ivy

hie-lo *m.* ice

hier-ba *f.* grass

hi-gie-ne *f.* hygiene

hi-gie-ni-co *adj.* hygienic

hi-ja *f.* daughter

hi-jas-tra *f.* stepdaughter

hi-jas-tro *m.* stepson

hi-jo *m.* son

hi-la-dor *m., f.* spinner

hi-lar *v.* to spin

hi-le-ro *m.* current

hi-lo *m.* filament; thread

hi-men *m.* hymen
him-no *m.* hymn
hin-char *v.* to exaggerate; to swell; to blow up
hi-no-jo *m.* knee
hi-per-bo-la *f.* hyperbola
hi-per-sen-si-ble *adj.* hypersensitive
hi-per-ter-mía *f.* hyperthermia
hip-no-sis *f.* hypnosis
hip-no-tis-mo *m.* hypnotism
hip-no-ti-zar *v.* to hypnotize
hi-po-con-drí-a *f.* hypochondria
hi-po-cre-si-a *f.* hypocrisy
hi-po-cri-ta *f., m.* hypocrite
hi-po-te-ca *f.* mortgage
hi-po-te-car *v.* to mortgage
hi-po-ter-mia *f.* hypothermia
his-te-ria *f.* hysteria
his-to-ria *f.* story; history
his-to-rial *adj.* historical
ho-ci-car *v.* smooch; nuzzle
hoc-key *m.* hockey
ho-gue-ra *f.* bonfire
ho-ja *f.* petal; leaf; sheet
ho-jo-so *adj.* leafy
hol-gan-za *f.* leisure
ho-lo-caus-to *m.* holocuast
hom-bre *m.* man
hom-bre-ra *f.* shoulder pad
hom-bri-llo *m.* yoke
hom-bro *m.* shoulder
ho-mi-ci-da *adj.* homicidal
ho-mi-ci-dio *m.* homocide
ho-mo-ge-nei-zar *v.* to homogenize
ho-mo-ni-mia *f.* homonymy
hon-do *adj.* intense; deep
hon-do-na-da *f.* gorge
ho-nes-ti-dad *f.* honesty
hon-go *m.* mushroom
ho-nor *m.* honor
ho-no-ra-ble *adj.* honorable
hon-ra-dez *f.* honesty
hon-ra-do *adj.* honest
hon-ro-so *adj.* honorable
ho-ra *f.* time; hour
hor-con *m.* pitchfork
ho-ri-zon-tal *adj.* horizontal
ho-ri-zon-te *m.* horizon
hor-mi-go-ne-ra *f.* cement

hor-mo-na *f.* hormone
hor-ne-ar *v.* to bake
hor-ne-ro *f., m.* baker
hor-ni-llo *m.* stove
hor-no *m.* oven
ho-ros-co-po *m.* horoscope
ho-rren-do *adj.* horrendous
ho-rri-ble *adj.* awful; horrible
ho-rri-do *adj.* horrid
ho-rri-fi-car *v.* to horrify
ho-rror *m.* terror; horror
hor-ti-co-la *adj.* horticultural
hor-ti-cul-tu-ra *f.* horticulture
hos-pi-tal *m.* hospital
hos-pi-ta-li-zar *v.* hospitalize
hos-te-rí-a *f.* hostel; inn
hos-ti-gar *v.* to harass; whip
hos-til *adj.* hostile
hos-ti-li-dad *f.* hostility
ho-tel *m.* hotel
hoy *m.* today
ho-ya *f.* hole
hue-co *adj.* deep; hollow
hue-lla *f.* print; footprint
huer-ta *f.* garden
hue-sa *f.* grave
hue-su-do *adj.* bony
hue-vo *m.* egg
huir(se) *v.* to flee; to escape; to avoid; to run from
hu-ma-nar *v.* to humanize
hu-ma-ni-dad *f.* humanity
hu-ma-ni-zar *v.* to humanize
hu-ma-no *m.* human
hu-me-ar *v.* to steam; smoke
hu-me-dad *f.* humidity
hu-me-do *adj.* humid
hu-me-ro *m.* humerus
hu-mil-dad *f.* humility
hu-mi-lla-cion *f.* humiliation
hu-mi-llan-te *adj.* humiliating
hu-mí-llo *m.* pride
hu-mo *m.* smoke
hu-mo-ris-mo *m.* wit
hu-mo-so *adj.* smoky
hun-dir *v.* ruin; sink; plunge
hu-ra-can *m.* hurricane
hur-gon *m.* poker
hu-ron *m.* ferret
hur-tar(se) *v.* to steal; take
hur-to *m.* robbery
hus-me-ar *v.* to pry
hus-me-o *m.* prying

i-bis *f.* ibis
i-ce-berg *m.* iceberg
i-co-no *m.* icon
i-co-no-gra-fía *f.* iconography
ic-te-ri-cía *f.* jaundice
ic-tio-lo-go *m.* ichthyologist
i-dea *f.* notion; thought; image; idea; picture
i-de-al *m.* ideal
i-de-a-lis-ta *adj.* idealist
i-de-a-li-zar *v.* to idealize
i-de-ar *v.* to invent; to plan; to design
i-den-ti-co *adj.* identical
i-den-ti-dad *f.* identity
i-den-ti-fi-ca-ble *adj.* identifiable
i-den-ti-fi-ca-cion *f.* identification
i-den-ti-fi-car *v.* to identify
i-de-o-lo-gí-co *adj.* ideological
i-di-lio *m.* idyll
i-dio-ma-tí-co *adj.* idiomatic
i-dio-sin-cra-sia *f.* idiosyncrasy
i-dio-ta *f., m.* idiot, *adj.* idiotic; foolish
i-do-la-trar *v.* to idolize
i-do-la-tri-a *f.* idolatry
i-do-lo *m.* idol
i-gle-sia *f.* church
ig-ni-cion *f.* ignition
ig-no-mi-nio-so *adj.* ignominious
ig-no-ran-cía *f.* ignorance
ig-no-ran-te *adj.* ignorant; unaware; uneducated
ig-no-to *adj.* undiscovered
i-gual *adj.* level; even; alike; like
i-gua-la-míen-to *m.* equalization
i-gua-lar *v.* to make equal; to equate; to smooth
i-gual-dad *f.* equality
i-gual-men-te *adv.* too; equally
i-gua-na *m.* iguana
i-la-cíon *f.* cohesiveness
i-le-gal *adj.* unlawful; illegal; against the law
i-le-ga-li-dad *f.* illegality
i-le-gi-ble *adj.* illegible
i-le-tra-do *adj.* illiterate
i-lo-gi-co *adj.* illogical
i-lu-mi-na-cion *f.* illumination
i-lu-mi-na-dor *adj.* illuminative
i-lu-mi-nar *v.* light; illuminate
i-lu-sion *f.* illusion
i-lu-so-rio *adj.* illusory
i-lus-tra-cion *f.* illustration
i-lus-tra-dor *adj.* illustrative
i-lus-trar *v.* to illustrate
i-lus-tre *adj.* illustrious
i-ma-gi-na-ble *adj.* imaginable
i-ma-gi-na-cion *f.* imagination
i-ma-gi-nar(se) *v.* to think up; to conceive
i-ma-gi-na-tí-vo *adj.* imaginative
i-ma-nar *v.* to magnetize
im-be-ci-li-dad *f.* imbecility
i-mi-ta-ble *adj.* imitable
i-mi-ta-cion *f.* imitation
i-mi-tar *v.* to imitate
im-pa-cién-cia *f.* impatience
im-pa-cien-te *adj.* impatient
im-par-cial *adj.* impartial
im-par-tir *v.* to concede
im-pa-si-ble *adj.* impassive
im-pe-ca-ble *adj.* impeccable
im-pe-di-men-to *m.* impediment
im-pe-dir *v.* to deter; hinder
im-pen-sa-ble *adj.* inimaginable; unthinkable
im-pe-rar *v.* to reign
im-per-do-na-ble *adj.* inexcusable
im-per-fec-cíon *f.* imperfection
im-pe-rial *adj.* imperial
im-per-me-a-bi-li-dad *f.* impermeability
im-per-me-a-ble *m.* raincoat
im-per-so-nal *adj.* impersonal
im-pe-ti-go *m.* impetigo
im-pe-tu *m.* energy; impetus
im-pe-tuo-so *adj.* impetuous; violent

im-pla-ca-ble *adj.* implacable
im-plan-tar *v.* to implant
im-pli-ca-cion *f.* implication; consequence
im-pli-car *v.* mean; implicate
im-plo-rar *v.* to invoke
im-po-ner *v.* to charge; to inspire; to inform
im-po-pu-lar *adj.* unpopular
im-por-ta-cion *f.* importation
im-por-tan-cia *f.* authority; importance
im-por-tan-te *adj.* important
im-por-tu-nar *v.* to importune
im-por-tu-no *adj.* inopportune
im-po-si-bi-li-dad *f.* impossibility
im-po-si-ble *adj.* impossible; difficult
im-pos-tor *m.* impostor
im-po-ten-cia *f.* impotence
im-prac-ti-ca-ble *adj.* unfeasible; impracticable
im-pre-ci-so *adj.* imprecise
im-preg-nar *v.* to impregnate
im-pre-sion *f.* impression
im-pre-sio-nan-te *adj.* impressive
im-pre-vis-to *adj.* unexpected; sudden
im-pri-mir *v.* to stamp; to print; to imprint
im-pro-ba-ble *adj.* improbable
im-pro-duc-ti-vo *adj.* unproductive
im-pro-vi-sa-cion *f.* improvisation
im-pu-den-cia *f.* impudence
im-pug-nar *v.* to impugn
im-pul-sar *v.* to drive; impel
im-pul-sion *f.* impulse
im-pul-so *m.* impulse
im-pu-ni-dad *f.* impunity
im-pu-re-za *f.* impurity
im-pu-ro *adj.* impure
i-nac-cion *f.* inaction
i-na-cep-ta-ble *adj.* unacceptable
i-nac-ti-vo *adj.* inactive
in-a-de-cua-do *adj.* inadequate

i-nad-ver-ten-cia *f.* carelessness; inadvertence
i-nal-te-ra-ble *adj.* unalterable
i-na-ne *adj.* insane
i-na-ni-dad *f.* inanity
i-na-pli-ca-ble *adj.* inapplicable
i-na-ten-cion *f.* inattention
i-na-ten-to *adj.* unattentive
in-ca-pa-ci-dad *f.* incapacity
in-ca-pa-ci-tar *v.* to incapacitate
in-ca-paz *adj.* unable; incapable
in-cen-dio *m.* fire
in-cen-ti-vo *m.* incentive
in-ces-to *m.* incest
in-cien-so *m.* incense
in-cier-to *adj.* vague; uncertain; doubtful
in-ci-ne-rar *v.* to incinerate
in-ci-sion *f.* incision
in-ci-tar *v.* to urge; to incite
in-cle-men-te *adj.* inclement
in-cli-na-cion *f.* slant; inclination; slope
in-cli-nar(se) *v.* to slant; to sway; to incline; persuade
in-cluir *v.* to contain; include
in-clu-sion *f.* inclusion
in-clu-si-vo *adj.* inclusive
in-co-he-ren-te *adj.* incoherent
in-co-mi-ble *adj.* inedible
in-com-pa-ti-ble *adj.* incompatible
in-com-ple-to *adj.* incomplete
in-con-clu-so *adj.* inconclusive
in-cons-tan-te *adj.* fickle
in-cor-po-ral *adj.* incorporeal
in-cor-po-rar *v.* incorporate
in-co-rrec-to *adj.* incorrect
in-co-rrup-to *adj.* incorrupt
in-cre-du-lo *adj.* incredulous
in-cre-i-ble *adj.* incredible
in-cre-men-tar *v.* to increase
in-cre-men-to *m.* increase
in-cre-par *v.* to reprimand
in-cri-mi-nar *v.* to incriminate
in-crus-tar *v.* to encrust

in-cu-ba-cion *f.* incubation
in-cu-bar *v.* to incubate
in-cul-car *v.* to inculcate
in-cu-ra-ble *adj.* incurable
in-cu-rrir *v.* to incur
in-de-cen-te *adj.* indecent
in-de-ci-sion *f.* indecision
in-de-ci-so *adj.* indecisive
in-de-fen-so *adj.* defenseless
in-de-le-ble *adj.* indelible
in-dem-ne *adj.* unhurt
in-de-pen-di-zar *v.* to liberate
in-de-se-a-ble *adj.* undersirable
in-di-ca-cion *f.* sign; indication; direction
in-di-car *v.* to show; indicate
in-di-fe-ren-te *adj.* indifferent
in-di-gen-cia *f.* indigence
in-di-gen-te *adj.* indigent
in-di-ges-tion *f.* indigestion
in-dig-nar *v.* to infuriate
in-dig-no *adj.* despicable
in-di-go *m.* indigo
in-di-rec-to *adj.* hint; indirect
in-dis-cre-cion *f.* indiscretion
in-dis-cu-ti-ble *adj.* indisputable
in-dis-tin-to *adj.* indistinct
in-di-vi-dual *adj.* individual
in-di-vi-duo *m.* individual
in-di-vi-si-ble *adj.* indivisible
in-do-cil *adj.* indocile
in-do-ci-li-dad *f.* unruliness
in-do-len-cia *f.* indolence
in-do-len-te *adj.* indolent
in-do-ma-ble *adj.* uncontrollable; untamable
in-do-mi-to *adj.* untamable; indomitable
in-duc-cion *f.* induction
in-du-cir *v.* to induce
in-du-da-ble *adj.* certain
in-dul-gen-te *adj.* indulgent
in-dus-tria *f.* industry
in-dus-trial *adj.* industrial
in-dus-tria-li-zar *v.* to become industrialize
in-dus-trio-so *adj.* industrious
i-ne-fa-ble *adj.* ineffable
i-ne-fi-caz *adj.* ineffective
i-nep-ti-tud *f.* ineptitude
i-nep-to *adj.* inept

i-ner-cia *f.* inertia
i-ner-te *adj.* inert
i-nes-pe-ra-do *adj.* unexpected
i-nes-ta-ble *adj.* unstable
i-ne-vi-ta-ble *adj.* inevitable
i-ne-xis-ten-te *adj.* nonexistent; not existing
i-nex-plo-ra-do *adj.* unexplored
in-fa-li-ble *adj.* infallible
in-fa-mar *v.* to slander
in-fa-mia *f.* infamy
in-fan-cia *f.* infancy
in-fan-te *m.* baby; infant
in-fan-til *adj.* childish; baby
in-far-to *m.* infarction
in-fa-tuar *v.* to become conceited
in-fec-cion *f.* infection
in-fec-cio-so *adj.* infectious
in-fec-tar(se) *v.* to infect
in-fe-liz *adj.* wretched
in-fe-ren-cia *f.* inference
in-fe-rior *adj.* under; inferior
in-fe-rio-ri-dad *f.* inferiority
in-fe-rir *v.* to inflict; to infer
in-fes-tar *v.* to infest
in-fiel *adj.* disloyal
in-fier-no *m.* hell
in-fil-trar *v.* to infiltrate
in-fi-mo *adj.* worst; lowest
in-fi-ni-to *m., adj.* infinite
in-fla-cion *f.* inflation
in-fla-ma-ble *adj.* inflammable
in-fla-mar *v.* to inflame
in-flar *v.* to inflate
in-flex-i-ble *adj.* rigid; unyielding
in-fluen-cia *f.* influence
in-flue-ciar *v.* to influence
in-flu-jo *m.* influence
in-for-ma-cion *f.* information
in-for-mal *adj.* informal
in-for-mar(se) *v.* to report; to inform; to find out
in-for-me *adj.* formless
in-for-tu-nio *m.* misfortune
in-fra-rro-jo *adj.* infared
in-fre-cuen-te *adj.* infrequent
in-fruc-tuo-so *adj.* fruitless
in-fun-dir *v.* to arouse

in-fu-sion *f.* infusion
in-ge-nie-ria *f.* engineering
in-ge-nie-ro *m.* engineer
in-ge-nio-so *adj.* witty; clever
in-ge-rir *v.* to ingest
in-ges-tion *f.* ingestion
in-gles *m.* English
in-gra-to *adj.* thankless
in-gre-dien-te *m.* ingredient
in-gre-so *m.* entrance
in-ha-bi-li-dad *f.* incompetence
in-ha-lar *v.* to inhale
in-he-ren-te *adj.* inherent
in-hi-bir *v.* to inhibit
in-hu-ma-no *adj.* inhuman
i-ni-cia-cion *f.* initiation
i-ni-cial *adj.* initial
i-ni-ciar *v.* to initiate
i-ni-cio *m.* beginning
i-ni-gua-la-do *adj.* unequaled
i-ni-mi-ta-ble *adj.* inimitable
in-je-rir *v.* to insert
in-jer-to *m.* transplant
in-ju-ria *f.* injury
in-jus-ti-cia *f.* injustice
in-jus-to *adj.* unjust
in-ma-du-ro *adj.* immature
in-me-mo-rial *adj.* immemorial
in-men-so *adj.* immense
in-mer-sion *f.* immersion
in-mi-grar *v.* to immigrate
in-mi-nen-te *adj.* imminent
in-mo-des-to *adj.* immodest
in-mo-lar *v.* to immolate
in-mo-ral *adj.* immoral
in-mor-tal *adj.* immortal
in-mo-vi-ble *adj.* immovable
in-mo-vil *adj.* immobile
in-mum-do *adj.* filthy
in-mu-ni-dad *f.* immunity
in-mu-ni-zar *v.* to immunize
in-mu-ta-ble *adj.* immutable
in-no-ble *adj.* ignoble
in-no-va-cion *f.* innovation
in-no-var *v.* to innovate
i-no-cen-cia *f.* innocence
i-no-cen-te *adj.* innocent
i-no-cu-lar *v.* to inoculate
i-no-cuo *adj.* innocuous
i-no-pe-ra-ble *adj.* inoperable
i-nor-ga-ni-co *adj.* inorganic

in-quie-tar *v.* to alarm
in-quie-tud *f.* uneasiness
in-qui-li-no *m., f.* tenant
in-qui-rir *v.* to probe
in-sa-no *adj.* insane
ins-cri-bir(se) *v.* to record; to engrave
ins-crip-cion *f.* record; inscription
in-sec-to *m.* insect
in-se-gu-ro *adj.* insecure
in-sen-si-ble *adj.* unfeeling; unconscious; insensible
in-ser-cion *f.* insertion
in-ser-tar *v.* to insert
in-sig-nia *f.* emblem
in-sin-ce-ro *adj.* insincere
in-sis-ten-te *adj.* insistent
in-sis-tir *v.* to insist
in-so-len-cia *f.* insolence
ins-pec-cion *f.* inspection
ins-pi-rar *v.* to inspire
ins-truc-cion *f.* instruction
ins-truir(se) *v.* to teach; to learn; to instruct
in-su-li-na *f.* insulin
in-sul-tar *v.* to insult
in-tac-to *adj.* together; intact
in-te-li-gen-cia *f.* intellect; intelligence
in-te-li-gen-te *adj.* smart; intelligent
in-ten-si-fi-car *v.* to intensify
in-te-re-sar(se) *v.* to concern
in-te-rior *m.* inside
in-ter-no *adj.* inside
in-te-rrup-cion *f.* interruption
in-ter-ve-nir *v.* to mediate; to intervene
in-ti-mo *adj.* intimate
in-tor-duc-cion *f.* introduction
in-va-dir *v.* to invade
in-va-sion *f.* invasion
in-ven-cion *f.* invention
in-ven-tar *v.* to contrive; to think up; to invent
in-ves-tir *v.* to invest
in-vier-no *m.* winter
ir(se) *v.* to depart; to leave
i-rre-gu-lar *adj.* irregular
is-la *f.* island
iz-quier-do, -a *adj.* left

ja-ba-li *m.* boar
ja-ba-lí-na *f.* javelin
ja-bon *m.* soap
ja-bo-na-do *m.* wash
ja-bo-nar *v.* to lather up
ja-bo-ne-ro *m., f.* soapmaker
ja-ca *f.* nag; pony
ja-ca-re-ro *adj.* lively
ja-co *m.* nag
jac-tan-cia *f.* arrogance;
  bragging; boast
jac-tan-cio-so *adj.* arrogant
jac-tar-se *v.* to brag
ja-de *m.* jade
ja-de-ar *v.* to gasp for air
ja-diar *v.* to hoe
ja-guar *m.* jaguar
ja-lar *v.* to pull on
ja-le-a *f.* jelly
ja-le-ar *v.* to urge one
ja-leo *m.* racket; uproar
ja-lo-nar *v.* to mark
ja-más *adv.* never; ever;
  never again
jam-ba *f.* jamb
ja-mel-go *m.* nag
ja-mon *m.* ham
ja-que *m.* check
ja-que-ar *v.* to check
ja-ra-be *m.* syrup
ja-ra-near *v.* to carouse
jar-ca *f.* acacia
jar-din *m.* garden
jar-di-ne-ra *f.* gardener
jar-di-ne-ro *m.* gardener
ja-rra *f.* mug; pitcher
ja-rro *m.* flagon
ja-rrón *m.* vase
jas-pe *m.* jasper
jau-la *f.* cell; cage
az-min *m.* jasmine
je-fa *f.* master; boss
je-fe *m.* head; boss; master
je-mi-que-ar *v.* to whine
jen-gi-bre *m.* ginger
je-rar-qui-a *f.* hierarchy
je-re-mias *m., f.* complainer
jer-ga *f.* jargon; slang
je-ri-gon-za *f.* gibberish
je-rin-gar *v.* to pester
je-rin-ga-zo *m.* injection
je-ro-gli-fi-co *m.* hieroglyph
jer-sey *m.* sweater

ji-fia *f.* swordfish
jin-da *f.* fright
ji-ne-te *m.* equestrian;
  horseman
ji-ne-te-ar *v.* to ride a horse
ji-par *v.* to pant
ji-ra *f.* excursion
ji-ra-fa *f.* giraffe
jo-co-si-dad *f.* joke; wit
jo-co-so *adj.* jocular
jo-cun-di-dad *f.* jocundity
jo-fai-na *f.* washbowel
jor-na-da *f.* trip
jor-nal *m.* wage
jo-ro-ba *f.* hump
jo-ro-bar *v.* to annoy; bother
jo-rrar *v.* to haul
jo-ven *m.* youth
jo-vial *adj.* jovial
jo-ya *f.* gem; jewel
jo-ye-ra *f.* box for jewelry
jo-ye-ria *f.* jewelry store
jo-ye-ro *m.* jeweler
ju-bi-la-do *m., f* retired one
ju-bi-lar(se) *v.* to retire
ju-bi-leo *m.* jubilee
ju-bi-lo *m.* joy
ju-bi-lo-so *adj.* joyful
ju-dia *f.* bean
jue-go *m.* play; game
jue-ves *m.* Tuesday
juez *m.* judge
ju-gar *v.* to game; to play
ju-gue-tear *v.* to play
ju-gue-ton *adj.* playful
jui-cio *m.* verdict; judgment
ju-llo *m.* July
jun-co *m.* junk
ju-nio *m.* June
jun-ta *f.* union
jun-ta-men-te *adv.* together
jun-tar(se) *v.* to connect; join
jun-to *adv.* together
ju-ra-do *m.* jury
ju-rar *v.* to vow; swear; curse
ju-ris-ta *f.* jurist
jus-ta-men-te *adv.* fairly
jus-ti-cia *f.* justice
jus-ti-fi-car *v.* to warrant
jus-to *adj.* fair
ju-ve-nil *adj.* youth
ju-ven-tud *f.* youth
juz-gar *v.* to try; to judge

ki-lo *m.* kilogram
ki-lo-ci-clo *m.* kilocycle
ki-lo-gra-mo *m.* kilogram
ki-lo-me-tri-co *adj.* kilometric
ki-ló-me-tro *m.* kilometer
ki-lo-va-tio *m.* kilowatt
kirsch *m.* cherry-brandy
kum-mel *m.* cumin brandy

la *def. article* the
la-be-rin-to *m.* labyrinth
la-bia *f.* elloquence
la-bio *m.* lip
la-bor *f.* work
la-bo-ra-ble *adj.* working
la-bo-ral *adj.* labor
la-bo-rar *v.* to work
la-bo-ra-to-rio *m.* laboratory
la-bo-re-ar *v.* to work
la-bo-rio-so *adj.* arduous
la-bra-do, -da *adj.* plowed; cultivated; wrought
la-bra-dor, ra *adj.* farming *m.* farmer; peasant
la-bran-za *f.* farmland; farm
la-brar *v.* to carve; work; plow; cultivate; tool
la-ca *f.* shellac; lacquer; hair spray
la-ca-yo *m.* valet; attendant
la-ce-ra-cion *f.* laceration
la-ce-rar *v.* to injure; lacerate
la-ce-ria *f.* want; toil
la-cio *adj.* limp; straight
la-co-ni-co, -ca *adj.* laconic
la-cra *f.* scar
la-cre *m.* a sealing wax
la-cri-mo-ge-no, -na *adj.* tear producing
la-cri-mo-so, -sa *adj.* tearful; sad; sorrowful
lac-ta-cion *f.* nursing
lac-tan-cia *f.* lactation
lac-tar *v.* to suckle
lac-ti-co, -ca *adj.* lactic
lac-to-sa *f.* lactose
la-de-ar *v.* to tilt
la-de-o *m.* inclination
la-de-ra *f.* slope

la-di-no, -na *adj.* astute
la-do *m.* room; side; protection **de** next to; beside; along side
la-drar *v.* to snarl at something; to growl
la-dri-llo *m.* brick
la-dron *m.* robber
la-dro-ne-ri-a *f.* theft
la-gar-ti-ja *f.* a small lizard
la-gar-to *m.* lizard
la-go *m.* lake
lá-gri-ma *f.* tear
la-gri-me-ar *v.* to tear; to weep; to cry
la-gri-mo-so, -sa *adj.* tearful; watery
la-gu-na *f.* lagoon
lai-cal *adj.* laical
la-ja *f.* slab of stone
la-me-du-ra *f.* licking
la-men-ta-ble *adj.* lamentable
la-men-ta-ción *f.* lamentation
la-men-tar *v.* to be sorry for; to regret something
la-men-to *m.* lament
la-men-to-so, -sa *adj.* mournful
la-mer *v.* to lap up
la-me-ta-da *f.* lick
la-mi-do, -da *adj.* polished
la-mi-na-cion *f.* lamination
lá-mi-nar *v.* to laminate
lám-pa-ra *f.* lamp
lam-pa-ri-lla *f.* little or small lamp
lam-pa-ron *m.* stain
lam-pi-ño, -ña *adj.* hairless
la-na *f.* wool
la-na-do, -na *adj.* fleecy
lan-ce *m.* argument; move; occurrence
lan-ce-ar *v.* to lance
lan-ce-ta *f.* lancet
lan-cha *f.* boat
lan-che-ro *m.* boatman
lan-chon *m.* barge
la-ne-ro, -ra *adj.* woolen
lan-gui-de-cer *v.* to languish
lan-gui-dez *f.* feebleness; lethargy

lán-gui-do, -da *adj.* languid
lan-guor *m.* languor
la-no-li-na *f.* lanolin
la-no-so, -sa *adj.* woolly
lan-za *f.* spear
lan-za-da *f.* wound due to a lance
lan-za-mien-to *m.* throwing
lan-zar *v.* to hurl; to fire; to release; to vomit; to throw; to shoot
lá-pi-da *f.* tombstone
la-pi-da-rio, -ria *adj.* concise; lapidary
lá-piz *m.* pencil
lap-so, -sa *m.* interval; lapse
la-que-ar *v.* to varnish
lar-do *m.* fat; lard
lar-gar *v.* to let go; to dismiss; to release; to hurl; to throw
lar-go *adj.* lengthy; long; abundant
lar-gor *m.* length
lar-gue-za *f.* length
lar-gui-ru-cho, -cha *adj.* lanky
la-rin-ge *f.* larynx
la-rin-gi-tis *f.* laryngitis
lar-va *f.* larva
lar-val *adj.* larval
las *pron.* them; *art.* the
la-ser *m.* laser
la-si-tud *f.* lassitude
la-so *adj.* weak; limp
lás-ti-ma *f.* compassion; shame; pity
las-ti-ma-du-ra *f.* wound
las-ti-mar *v.* to hurt; to offend; to injure
las-ti-me-ro, -ra *adj.* pitiful
la-ta *f.* can; tin can; pest
la-te-ar *v.* to bend
la-ten-te *adj.* latent
la-te-ral *adj.* lateral
la-ti-do *m.* beating; throbbing; beat
la-tien-te *adj.* throbbing
la-ti-gue-ar *v.* to whip; to crack the whip
la-tir *v.* to throb
la-ti-tud *f.* breadth; extent; width; scope

la-ti-tu-di-nal *adj.* latitudinal
la-to, -ta *adj.* wide
la-tón *m.* brass
la-to-ne-ro *m.* brassworker
la-to-so, -sa *adj.* bothersome
la-tro-ci-nio *m.* theft
lau-da-ble *adj.* laudable
lau-de *f.* tonbstone
lau-do *m.* verdict
lau-rel *m.* bay; laurel
lau-re-o *adj.* laurel
la-va *f.* lava
la-va-ble *adj.* washable
la-va-da *f.* washing
la-va-de-ro *m.* laundry
la-va-do *m.* wash
la-va-dor *m.* washer
la-van-da *f.* lavender
la-van-de-ra *f.* laundry-woman
la-van-de-ro *m.* laundryman
la-va-pla-tos *m.* dishwasher
la-var *v.* to wash; to clean
la-va-ti-va *f.* enema
la-xar *v.* to slacken
la-xa-ti-vo *adj.* laxative
la-zar *v.* to rope
la-za-ri-no, -na *adj.* leprous
la-zo *m.* lasso; knot; trap; snare
le *pron.* him
le-al *adj.* faithful
le-al-tad *f.* loyalty
lec-ción *f.* lession
lac-tor, a *adj.* reading
lec-tu-ra *f.* reading
le-cha-da *f.* grout; whitewash
le-char *v.* to milk
le-che *f.* milk
le-che-rió, -riá *adj.* dairy; milky
le-cho *m.* layer; bed
le-cho-so *adj.* milky
le-chu-ga *f.* lettuce
le-er *v.* to read
le-ga-ción *f.* legation
le-ga-do *m.* legacy
le-ga-jo *m.* file
le-gal *adj.* legal
le-ga-li-dad *f.* legality
le-ga-lis-ta *f.* legalist
le-ga-li-za-cion *f.* legalization
le-ga-li-zar *v.* to legalize

le-gar *v.* to delegate; to bequeathe

le-gi-ble *adj.* legible

le-gion *f.* legion

le-gis-la-cion *f.* legislation

le-gis-la-dor *m.* legislator

le-gis-la-tu-ra *f.* legislative

le-jos *adv.* far away

len-gua *f.* language

le-on *m.* lion

le-o-na *f.* lioness

le-o-par-do *m.* leopard

les *pron.* for them; for you

le-tal *adj.* lethal

le-tra *f.* letter

le-van-tar *v.* to lift up; erect

ley *f.* rule; law

li-be-ra-ción *f.* liberation

li-be-ral *adj.* liberal

li-ber-tad *f.* freedom

li-bre *adj.* single; open; free

li-bro *m.* book

li-gar *v.* to commit; bind

li-mi-ta-ción *f.* limitation

li-mi-ta-do *adj.* limited

li-mi-tar *v.* to restrict; limit

li-món *m.* lemon

lim-piar *v.* to clear; clean

lim-pie-za *f.* neatness; cleaning

lim-pio *adj.* pure; clean

lí-ne-a *f.* outline; line; boundary

lis-ta *f.* list

lis-to *adj.* ready

li-tro *m.* liter

li-via-no, -na *adj.* faithless; light

li-vi-dez *f.* lividness

li-vi-do *adj.* livid

lo *def. article* the

lo-a *f.* praise

lo-a-ble *adj.* praiseworthy

lo-ar *v.* to praise

lo-ba *f.* the female wolf

lo-bo *m.* the male wolf

lo-bre-go *adj.* somber; dark

ló-bu-lo *m.* lobe

lo-ca-cion *f.* leasing

lo-cal *adj.* local

lo-ca-li-dad *f.* locality

lo-ca-li-zar *v.* to find; to locate

lo-cion *f.* lotion

lo-co *adj.* crazy; extraordinary

lo-grar *v.* to take; obtain

lo-ro *m.* parrot

los *pron.* them; *art.* the

lu-ci-do *adj.* shining

lu-cir *v.* to illuminate; to light

lue-go *adv.* later; then

lu-na *f.* moon

lu-nar *adj.* lunar

lus-trar *v.* to shine

luz *f.* day; light

ma-ca-bro *adj.* funeral

ma-ca-dam *m.* macadam

ma-ca-rrón *m.* macaroon

ma-ce-ra-cion *f.* maceration

ma-ce-rar *v.* to macerate

ma-ce-ta *f.* flowerpot or holder

ma-ci-len-to, -ta *adj.* lean; thin; emaciated

ma-ci-zo, -za *adj.* solid

ma-cro-bio-ti-co *f.* macrobiotics

ma-cu-la *f.* spot

ma-cha-ca *f.* pounder

ma-cha-ca-dor, -ra *adj.* pounding

ma-cha-car *v.* to beat; to pound; to bother

ma-cha-con, -ona *adj.* tiresome *f., m* pest

ma-cha-da *f.* stupidity

ma-cha-do *m.* hatchet

ma-che-te *m.* machete

ma-che-te-ar *v.* to injure or cut with a machete

ma-cho *adj.* manly; male; tough; virile

ma-chu-ca-du-ra *f.* beating; bruising

ma-chu-car *v.* to beat

ma-de-ra *f.* timber; wood; lumber

ma-de-ra-da *f.* raft

ma-de-re-ri-a *f.* lumberyard

ma-de-re-ro, -ra *adj.* timber

ma-de-ro *m.* log
ma-dras-tra *f.* stepmother
ma-dre *f.* mom; mother
ma-dre-sel-va *f.* honeysuckle
ma-dri-gue-ra *f.* hole; burrow; lair
ma-dri-na *f.* bridesmaid; godmother; patroness
ma-dru-ga-dor, -ra *m., f* early riser
ma-dru-gar *v.* to anticipate; to get up early
ma-du-ra-cion *f.* ripening
ma-du-ra-dor, a *adj.* ripening
ma-du-rar *v.* to mature; to ripen; to maturate
ma-du-rez *f.* maturity, ripeness
ma-es-tre *m.* master
ma-es-tro, -tra *adj.* expert; teacher; master
ma-gan-ce-ri-a *f.* trickery
ma-gia *f.* magic
ma-gi-co, -ca *adj.* magic
ma-gis-tra-do *m.* magistrate
ma-gis-tral *adj.* imposing; masterful; magisterial
mag-na-te *m.* magnate
mag-ne-sia *f.* magnesia
mag-ne-sio *m.* magnesium
mag-né-ti-co, -ca *adj.* magnetic
mag-ne-tis-mo *m.* magnetism
mag-ne-to-fo-ni-co, -ca *adj.* magnetic
mag-ni-fi-ca-dor, -ra *adj.* magnifying
mag-ni-fi-car *v.* to exalt; to magnify; to glorify
mag-ni-fi-cen-cia *f.* magnificence
mag-ni-fi-cen-te *adj.* magnificent
mag-ni-fi-co, -ca *adj.* excellent; magnificent
mag-ni-tud *f.* size; importance; magnitude
mag-no-lia *f.* magnolia
ma-go, -ga *adj.* magic
ma-gu-llar *v.* to batter
ma-iz *m.* corn
ma-ja-de-ro, -ra *adj.* foolish

ma-ja-du-ra *f.* pounding
ma-jar *v.* to pound; to bother; to mash
ma-jes-tad *f.* grandeur; majesty
ma-jo, -ja *adj.* showy; attractive; flashy; nice
mal *adj.* bad; evil; disease
mal *adv.* wrongly; badly
ma-la-bar *v.* to juggle
ma-la-ba-ris-ta *m.* juggler
ma-la-cos-tum-bra-do, a *adj.* ill-mannered; have poor or bad habits; spoiled
ma-lan-drin, a *adj.* evil
ma-la-ria *f.* malaria
ma-la-ven-tu-ra *f.* misfortune
ma-la-ven-tu-ran-za *f.* misfortune
mal-ba-ra-tar *v.* to squander
mal-co-mer *v.* to eat badly or poorly
mal-co-mi-do *adj.* underfed
mal-con-ten-to, -ta *adj.* unhappy; rebellious
mal-cria-do, -da *adj.* ill-bred
mal-criar *v.* to spoil
mal-dad *f.* evil
mal-de-cir *v.* to slander; to curse
mal-di-ci-en-te *adj.* defaming; slandering *m., f.* curser; slanderer
mal-di-ción *f.* curse
mal-di-to, -ta *adj.* wicked; bad
ma-le-a-bi-li-dad *f.* malleability
ma-le-a-ble *adj.* malleable
ma-le-an-te *adj.* corrputing; wicked
ma-le-ar *v.* to ruin; to corrupt; to pervert
ma-le-di-cen-cia *f.* slander
ma-le-fi-cen-cia *f.* evil
ma-le-fi-cen-te *adj.* maleficent
ma-les-tar *m.* uneasiness; malaise
ma-le-ta *f.* suitcase; baggage; luggage
ma-le-vo-len-cia *f.* malevolence

mal-for-ma-cion *f.* malformation

mal-gas-tar *v.* to waste

mal-ha-da-do, -da *adj.* unfortunate

mal-he-rir *v.* to injure

mal-hu-mo-ra-do, -da *adj.* bad-tempered

mal-hu-mo-rar *v.* to irritate; to bother; to annoy

ma-li-cia *f.* cunning; wickedness; slyness

ma-li-cio-so, -sa *adj.* malicious; cunning

ma-lig-ni-dad *f.* malignancy

ma-lig-no, -na *adj.* malignant

mal-mi-ra-do, -da *adj.* disfavored

ma-lo *adj.* harmful; nasty; bad

ma-lo-grar *v.* to fail; to lose; to waste

ma-lo-gro *m.* failure

mal-pa-rar *v.* to harm; to damage

mal-quis-tar *v.* to estrange

mal-quis-to, -ta *adj.* unpopular

mal-so-nan-te *adj.* harsh

mal-tra-ta-mien-to *m.* mistreatment

mal-tra-tar *v.* to mistreat

mal-va-do, -da *adj.* wicked

mal-ver-sa-dor, -a *m., f.* embezzler

mal-ver-sar *v.* to embezzle

ma-ma *f.* mommy

ma-mar *v.* to nurse; to suck

ma-ma-rio, -ia *adj.* mammary

ma-me-lon *m.* nipple

ma-na-da *f.* herd; bunch

ma-na-de-ro, -a *m., f.* spring

ma-nan-te *adj.* running

ma-nar *v.* to flow

man-car *v.* to disable

man-ci-lla *f.* blemish

man-ci-llar *v.* to blemish

man-ci-par *v.* to enslave

man-co *adj.* one-armed; disabled

man-co-mu-nar *v.* to join together; to combine

man-co-mu-ni-dad *f.* union; association

man-cha *f.* blot; stain

man-char *v.* to stain; to spot; to soil

man-da *f.* bequest

man-da-do *m.* errand; task; order

man-da-mien-to *m.* command; order

man-dar *v.* to leave; order

man-da-ri-na *f.* mandarin orange

man-da-to *m.* trust; command; order

man-di-bu-ia *f.* mandible

man-do *m.* leadership; power

man-do-lin *f.* mandolin

man-dria *adj.* timid; worthless; useless

man-dril *m.* mandrill

ma-ne-ar *v.* to hobble around

ma-ne-ja-ble *adj.* manageable

ma-ne-jar *v.* to handle; to manage

ma-ne-jo *m.* operation; handling; management

ma-ne-ra *f.* style; way; manner; type

man-ga *f.* strainer; hose

man-ga-ne-so *m.* manganese

man-gar *v.* to swipe; to mooch

man-gos-ta *f.* mongoose

man-gue-ar *v.* to startle

man-gue-ra *f.* garden hose

man-gui-ta *f.* cover

ma-ni *m.* peanut

ma-ni-a *f.* habit; craze

ma-ni-a-co, -ca *adj.* maniac

ma-ni-fes-ta-ción *f.* manifestation

ma-ni-fes-tar *v.* to reveal; to manifest

ma-ni-fies-to, -ta *adj.* manifest

ma-ni-lla *f.* bracelet

ma-ni-pu-la-ción *f.* manipulation

ma-ni-pu-la-dor, a *m.* manipulator

ma-ni-pu-lar v. to manipulate; to manage

ma-ni-qui m. mannequin

ma-no f. hand

ma-no-jo m. handful;bunch

ma-no-se-ar v. to touch

man-so, -sa adj. mild; tame

man-ta f. shawl; blanket

man-te-ca f. fat; lard

man-tel m. tablecloth

man-te-nen-cia f. support; maintenance

man-te-ner v. to support; to keep; to feed; to maintain

man-te-ni-mien-to m. support; sustenance

man-te-que-ri-a f. dairy

man-te-que-ro m. dairyman

man-te-qui-lla f. butter

man-to m. mantle; robe; cloak; cover

ma-nual adj. manual

ma-nu-fac-tu-rar v. to manufacture

ma-nu-ten-ción f. maintenance

man-za-na f. apple

man-za-nar m. apple orchard

man-za-no m. apple tree

ma-ña f. dexterity; skill

ma-ña-na f. morning

ma-ne-ar v. to manage

ma-ñe-ro adj. shrewd

ma-pa f. map

ma-pa-che m. raccoon

ma-que-ar v. to varnish

ma-qui-na f. machine

ma-qui-na-ción f. machination

ma-qui-na-dor m., f. schemer

ma-qui-nar v. to scheme

ma-qui-nis-ta m. machinist

mar m. sea; tide

ma-ra-ton m. marathon

ma-ra-vi-lla f. marvel; astonishment; wonder

ma-ra-vi-llar v. to astonish; to be amazed

ma-ra-vi-llo-so, -sa adj. marvelous

mar-ca f. brand; mark; stamp; trademark

mar-ca-do adj. notable

mar-ca-dor, -ra adj. marking

mar-car v. to stamp; to mark; to note

mar-cia! adj. military; martial

mar-co m. mark; standard

mar-cha f. march; velosity; speed; progress

mar-char v. to run; walk

mar-chi-tar v. to weaken; to wilt; to languish

mar-chi-to, -ta adj. wilted

ma-re-ar v. to sail; to bother

ma-re-ja-da f. turbulence

ma-re-o m. nausea

mar-ga-ri-na f. margarine

mar-ga-ri-ta f. daisy

mar-gen m. fringe; margin

mar-gi-nal adj. marginal

mar-gi-nar v. to marginate

ma-ri-dar v. to wed

ma-ri-do m. spouse

ma-ri-nar v. to marinate

ma-ri-ne-ria f. saloring

ma-ri-ne-ro, -ra adj. marine; seaworthy

ma-ri-no adj. marine

ma-ri-po-sa f. butterfly

ma-ri-qui-ta f. ladybug

ma-ris-cal m. marshal

ma-ris-co m. crustacean

ma-ri-tal adj. marital

ma-ri-ti-mo, -ma adj. maritine

már-mol m. marble

mar-qués m. marquis

ma-rra-no adj. filthy

ma-rrar v. to fail; to miss something

ma-rrón adj. brown

ma-rru-lle-ro, -ra m., f. conniver

mar-so-pa f. porpoise

mar-su-pial adj. marsupial

mar-tes m. Tuesday

mar-ti-llar v. to hammer

mar-ti-llo m. hammer

már-tir m., f. martyr

mar-ti-rio m. martyrdom

mar-zo m. March

mas adv. rather; more

ma-sa-crar v. to massacre

ma-sa-cre *m.* massacre
ma-sa-je *m.* massage
ma-sa-jis-ta *m.* masseur
mas-car *v.* to chew
más-ca-ra *f.* disguise
mas-ca-ra-da *f.* masquerade
mas-co-ta *f.* mascot
mas-cu-li-ni-dad *f.* masculinity
mas-cu-li-no *adj.* manly; male
ma-si-vo, -va *adj.* massive
mas-ti-car *v.* to masticate; to ruminate
más-til *m.* mast
mas-toi-des *adj.* mastoid
ma-ta *f.* shrub
ma-ta-dor, -ra *m., f.* killer
ma-ta-fue-go *m.* fire extinguisher
ma-tan-za *f.* massacre; killing; slaughtering
ma-tar *v.* to extinguish; to kill; to slaughter
ma-ta-ri-fe *m.* slaughterer
ma-ta-se-llar *v.* to cancel
ma-te-ma-ti-co, -ca *adj.* mathematical
ma-te-ria *f.* matter
ma-te-rial *adj.* material
ma-te-ria-li-dad *f.* materiality
ma-te-ria-lis-ta *adj.* materialistic
ma-ter-nal *adj.* maternal
ma-ter-ni-dad *f.* maternity
ma-ter-no *adj.* motherly
ma-ti-nal *adj.* morning
ma-tiz *m.* tint
ma-ti-zar *v.* to tint
ma-tre-ro, -ra *adj.* shrewd
ma-triar-ca-do *m.* matriarchy
ma-triar-cal *adj.* matriarchal
ma-tri-ci-dio *m.* matricide
ma-tri-cu-la *f.* list
ma-tri-cu-la-cion *f.* registration
ma-tri-cu-lar *v.* to natriculate
ma-tri-mo-nial *adj.* matrimonial
ma-tri-mo-nio *m.* matrimony
ma-triz *f.* uterus
ma-tro-na *f.* matron
ma-tro-nal *adj.* matronly

ma-xi-ma-men-te *adv.* chiefly
ma-xi-me *adv.* principally
ma-xi-mo *adj.* maximum
ma-yo *m.* May
ma-yo-ne-sa *f.* mayonnaise
ma-yor *adj.* greatest; larger; older
ma-yo-ria *f.* majority
ma-yo-ri-dad *f.* majority
ma-yus-cu-lo, -la *adj.* important; capital
maz-mo-rra *f.* dungeon
ma-zo *m.* bunch
me *pron.* me
me-ca-ni-co, -ca *adj.* mechanical
me-ca-ni-zar *v.* to mechanize
me-ce-do-ra *f.* rocking chair
me-cer *v.* to sway; to rock
me-cha *f.* match; wick
me-che-ra *f.* shoplifter
me-chón *m.* tuft
me-da-lla *f.* medal
me-da-llon *m.* medallion
me-dia *f.* stocking
me-dia-dor, -ra *m., f.* mediator
me-dia-ne-ro, -ra *adj.* mediating
me-dia-no-che *f.* midnight
me-diar *v.* to intercede
me-di-ca-cion *f.* medication
me-di-car *v.* to medicate
me-di-ci-na *f.* medicine
me-di-ci-nal *adj.* medicinal
me-di-ci-nar *v.* to cure or treat with medicine
me-di-co, -ca *m., f.* doctor
me-di-da *f.* measurement
me-die-val *adj.* medieval
me-dio *adj.* middle; half
me-dio-cre *adj.* mediocre
me-dio-cri-dad *f.* mediocrity
me-dio-di-a *m.* noon
me-dir *v.* to weigh; measure
me-di-ta-ción *f.* meditation
me-di-tar *v.* meditate
me-di-ta-ti-vo, -va *adj.* meditative
me-dium *m.* medium
me-drar *v.* to thrive; prosper

me-dro-so, -sa *adj.* timorous

me-du-la *f.* medulla

me-du-sa *f.* jellyfish

me-gá-fo-no *m.* megaphone

me-ga-tón *m.* megaton

me-ji-lla *f.* cheek

me-jor *adj.* superior; better

me-jo-ra *f.* betterment

me-jo-rar *v.* to make better

me-jo-ría *f.* improvement

me-lan-có-li-a *f.* melancholy

me-la-za *f.* molasses

me-lin-dre-ria *f.* affectation

me-lo-co-tón *m.* peach

me-lo-co-to-ne-ro *m.* peach tree

me-lo-dia *f.* tune

me-lo-di-co *adj.* tuneful

me-lo-dio-so, -sa *adj.* melodious

me-lo-dra-ma *m.* melodrama

me-lo-dra-ma-ti-co, -ca *adj.* melodramatic

me-lón *m.* melon

me-lo-te *m.* molasses

me-llar *v.* to nick; to chip

mem-bra-na *f.* membrane

me-mo-ra-ble *v.* memorable

me-mo-rar *v.* to recall

me-mo-ria *f.* remembrance; memory

me-mo-rial *m.* memorial

me-mo-ri-za-cion *f.* memorization

me-mo-ri-zar *v.* to memorize

men-ción *f.* mention

men-cio-nar *v.* to mention

me-ne-ar *v.* to sway

men-gua *f.* poverty

men-gua-do *adj.* decreased; timid

men-guar *v.* to wane; to diminish

me-nin-gi-tis *f.* meningitis

me-no-pau-sia *f.* menopause

me-nor *adj.* lesser; least; less; younger

me-nos *adv.* least; less

me-nos-ca-bar *v.* to impair

me-nos-ca-bo *m.* damage; diminishing

me-nos-pre-cia-ble *adj.* despicable

me-nos-pre-cio *m.* underestimation; contempt

men-sa-je *m.* message

men-sa-je-ro, -ra *adj.* messenger

men-sual *adj.* monthly

men-su-ra *f.* measurement

men-su-ra-ble *adj.* mensurable

men-su-rar *v.* measure

men-ta *f.* mint

men-ta-do, -da *adj.* reowned

men-tal *adj.* mental

men-ta-li-dad *f.* mentality

men-tar *v.* mention

men-te *f.* intellect; intelligence

men-tir *v.* to lie

men-ti-ra *f.* falsehood

men-ti-ro-so, -sa *adj.* lying

men-tor *m.* mentor

me-nu-do *adj.* little; insignificant

mer-ca-de-o *m.* marketing

mer-ca-do *m.* marketplace

mer-can-te *adj.* merchant

mer-can-til *adj.* mercantile

mer-car *v.* to buy

mer-ced *f.* gift

mer-ce-na-rio, -ria *adj.* mercenary

mer-cu-rial *adj.* mercurial

mer-cu-rio *m.* mercury

me-re-ci-mien-to *m.* worth

me-ri-dia-no, -na *adj.* meridian

me-rien-da *f.* snack

mé-ri-to *m.* value; worth

me-ri-to-rio, -ria *adj.* meritorious

mer-mar *v.* to diminish

me-ro, -ra *adj.* pure

me-ro-de-ar *v.* plunder

mes *m.* month

me-sa *f.* table

me-son *m.* tavern

me-so-ne-ro, -ra *m., f.* innkeeper

me-su-ra *f.* moderation

me-su-ra-do, -da *adj.* moderate

me-ta-bo-li-co, -ca *adj.*

metabolic

me-ta-bo-lis-mo *m.* metabolism

me-ta-fo-ra *f.* metaphor

me-ta-fó-ri-co, -ca *adj.* metaphoric

me-tal *m.* metal

me-tá-li-co *adj.* metallic

me-ta-li-zar *v.* to metalize

me-ta-mor-fi-co, -ca *adj.* metamorphic

me-ta-no *m.* methane

me-te-o-ri-co, -ca *adj.* meteoric

me-te-o-ri-to *m.* meteorite

me-te-o-ro *m.* meteor

me-te-o-ro-lo-gi-a *f.* meteorology

me-te-o-ro-lo-gis-ta *m., f.* meteorologist

me-ter *v.* to insert into; to cause

me-ti-cu-lo-so, -sa *adj.* meticulous

me-ti-lo *m.* methyl

me-tó-di-co, -ca *adj.* methodical

mé-to-do *m.* method

me-to-do-lo-gi-a *f.* methodology

me-tri-co *adj.* metric

me-tro-po-li-ta-no, -na *adj.* metropolitan

mez-cla-dor *adj.* blending

mez-clar *v.* to mingle; blend

mez-quin-dad *f.* miserliness

mez-qui-no, -na *adj.* petty; wretched; miserly

mez-qui-ta *f.* mosque

ni *pron.* me

ni-cro-bio *m.* microbe

ni-cro-bio-lo-gia *f.* microbiology

ni-cro-fil-me *m.* microfilm

ni-cró-fo-no *m.* microphone

ni-cros-co-pi-co, -ca *adj.* microscopic

ni-cros-co-pio *m.* microscope

nie-do *m.* dread

nie-do-so, -sa *adj.* cowardly

niel *f.* honey

niel-ga *f.* alfalfa

miem-bro *m.* member

mien-tras *adv.* meanwhile *conj.* while

miér-co-les *m.* Wednesday

mies *f.* grain

mi-ga *f.* substance; scrap

mi-gra-ción *f.* migration

mi-gra-na *f.* migraine

mil *adj.* thousand

mi-la-gro *m.* miracle

mi-la-gro-so *adj.* miraculous

mi-li-cia *f.* militia

mi-li-cia-no, -na *adj.* military

mi-li-gra-mo *m.* milligram

mi-li-li-tro *m.* milliliter

mi-li-me-tro *m.* millimeter

mi-li-tar *m.* soldier

mi-lla *f.* mile

mi-llón *m.* million

mi-mar *v.* to fondle; pamper

mi-mi-co, -ca *adj.* mimic

mi-mo-so *adj.* spoiled

mi-na *f.* mine

mi-na-dor *adj.* mining

mi-nar *v.* to mine

mi-ne-ral *adj.* mineral

mi-ne-ra-lo-gis-ta *m.* mineralogist

mi-ne-ri-a *f.* mining

mi-nia-tu-ra *f.* miniature

mi-nia-tu-ris-ta *m., f.* miniaturist

mi-ni-fal-da *f.* miniskirt

mi-ni-mi-zar *v.* to minimize

mi-ni-mo, -ma *adj.* least; minimal; minute

mi-nis-te-rial *adj.* ministerial

mi-nis-te-rio *m.* ministry

mi-nis-tro *m.* minister

mi-no-rar *v.* to reduce

mi-no-ria *f.* minority

mi-no-ri-ta-rio *adj.* minority

mi-nu-cio-so, -sa *adj.* minute

mi-nús-cu-lo, -la *adj.* tiny; small

mi-nu-ta *f.* record; note

mi-nu-to *m.* minute

mi-o, -a *adj.* mine

mio-pe *adj.* myopic

mio-pi-a *f.* myopia

mi-ra *f.* sight; intention

mi-ra-do, -da *adj.* regarded; cautious

mi-ra-dor *adj.* watching
mi-rar *v.* to watch; to look at; to observe
mi-ra-sol *m.* sunflower
mi-ri-a-da *f.* myriad
mir-lo *m.* blackbird
mis-ce-lá-ne-o, -a *adj.* miscellaneous
mi-se-ra-ble *adj.* miserable; poor; miserly
mi-se-ria *f.* suffering; miserliness; misery
mi-sil *m.* missile
mi-sión *f.* mission
mi-sio-nal *adj.* missionary
mis-mo *adj.* likewise; same thing
mis-te-rio *m.* mystery
mis-te-rio-so *adj.* mysterious
mis-ti-co, -ca *adj.* mystic
mis-ti-fi-car *v.* to mystify
mis-tu-ra *f.* mixture
mi-tad *f.* half
mi-ti-ga-cion *f.* mitigation
mi-ti-gar *v.* to mitigate
mi-to *m.* myth
mi-ton *m.* mitt
mi-tra *f.* miter
mix-to, -ta *adj.* mixed
mix-tu-ra *f.* mixture
mix-tu-rar *v.* to mix up
mo-bi-lia-rio, -ria *adj.* movable
mo-bla-je *m.* furnishing
mo-blar *v.* to furnish
mo-ce-dad *f.* youth
mo-ción *f.* motion
mo-cho, -cha *adj.* hornless
mo-da *f.* fashion
mo-de-lo *m.* model
mo-de-ra-ción *f.* moderation
mo-de-ra-do *adj.* moderate
mo-de-rar *v.* to regulate; to restrain
mo-der-ni-za-ción *f.* modernization
mo-der-ni-zar *v.* to modernize
mo-der-no *adj.* modern
mo-des-tia *f.* modesty
mó-di-co, -ca *adj.* moderate
mo-di-fi-ca-ción *f.* modification

mo-di-fi-ca-dor *adj.* modifying
mo-di-fi-car *v.* to modify
mo-dis-te-ri-a *f.* shop for dresses
mo-do *m.* way
mo-do-so, -sa *adj.* well-mannered
mo-du-la-cion *f.* modulation
mo-du-la-dor, -ra *m.*, *f.* modulator
mo-jar *v.* to drench; to dip; to wet
mol-de *m.* pattern; mold
mol-de-ar *v.* to shape
mo-lé-cu-lar *adj.* molecular
mo-ler *v.* to grind
mo-les-tar *v.* to annoy; to disrupt
mo-les-tia *f.* annoyance; trouble
mo-les-to *adj.* bothered; annoying
mo-men-to *m.* moment
mo-na *f.* a female monkey
mo-nas-te-rio *m.* monastery
mo-ni-tor *m.* monitor
mo-no *m.* male monkey
mo-no-gra-ma *m.* monogram
mons-truo *m.* monster
mons-truo-so *adj.* monstrous
mon-ta-ña *f.* mountain
mon-tar *v.* to mount
mo-nu-men-to *m.* monument
mo-ral *f.* morale
mo-ra-li-dad *f.* morality
mo-ra-li-zar *v.* to moralize
mo-rar *v.* to dwell; to live
mór-bi-do *adj.* morbid
mo-re-no *adj.* brown
mor-fi-na *f.* morphine
mo-rir *v.* to kill
mor-tal *adj.* fatal; mortal
mor-ta-li-dad *f.* mortality
mor-tuo-rio *m.* mortuary
mos-ca *f.* fly
mos-qui-to *m.* mosquito
mos-ta-za *f.* mustard
mos-trar *v.* to exhibit; to appear; to show
mo-tor *m.* engine

mo-ver v. to move
mo-vi-men-to m. movement
mu-cha-cha f. girl
mu-cha-cho m. boy
mu-cho adj. many; a lot
muer-te f. death
muer-to adj. dead
mu-jer f. female; woman
múl-ti-ple adj. multiple
mul-ti-pli-car v. to multiply
mun-do m. world
mu-ni-ci-pal adj. municipal
mu-ne-ca f. wrist; doll
mus-cu-lo m. muscle
mu-si-ca f. music
mu-si-cal adj. musical
mus-lo m. thigh
muy adv. much; greatly

na-bo m. turnip; mast
na-ca-ri-no adj. narcreous
na-cer v. to rise; to be born;
  to be concieved
na-ci-do, -da adj. born
na-cien-te adj. recent;
  growing; initial; nascent
na-ci-mien-to m. hatching;
  origin; birth; spring
na-ción f. nation
na-cio-nal adj. domestic; na-
  tional
na-cio-na-li-dad f. nationality
na-cio-na-lis-ta m., f. na-
  tionalist
na-cio-na-li-za-cion f. na-
  tionalization
na-cio-na-li-zar v. to na-
  tionalize
na-da pron. no; not
  anything; none; nothing
na-da-dor m., f. swimmer
na-dar v. to swim
na-die pron. no one; nobody
nai-pe m. playing card
nal-ga f. behind; buttocks
na-ran-ja f. orange
na-ran-jal m. orange grove
na-ran-je-ro adj. orange
na-ran-jo m. orange tree

nar-có-ti-co, -ca adj. narcotic
nar-co-ti-zar v. to narcotize
na-riz f. nostril; nose
na-rra-cion f. narration; narrative
na-rra-dor, -ra adj. narrative
na-rrar v. to narrate
na-rra-ti-vo, -va adj. narrative
na-ta-ción f. swimming
na-tal adj. natal
na-ta-li-dad f. natality
Na-ti-vi-dad f. Christmas
na-ti-vo adj. inborn; native
na-to, -ta adj. natural
na-tu-ra f. nature
na-tu-ral adj. native; innate;
  natural
na-tu-ra-le-za f. nature
na-tu-ra-li-dad f. naturalness
na-tu-ra-li-za-ción f. na-
  turalization
nau-fra-gar v. to shipwreck
náu-fra-go, -ga adj. ship-
  wrecked
náu-se-a f. nausea
nau-se-ar v. to feel
  nauseous
náu-ti-co, -ca adj. nautical
na-val adj. naval
na-ve-ga-ble adj. navigable
na-ve-ga-cion f. navigation
na-ve-gar v. to sail
Na-vi-dad f. Christmas
na-ví-o m. vessel; boat
ne-bli-na f. fog
ne-bli-no-so, -sa adj. foggy
ne-bu-lo-si-dad f. haziness
ne-ce-dad f. nonsense
ne-ce-sa-rio adj. necessary
ne-ce-si-dad f. need;
  poverty; necessity
ne-ce-si-ta-do, -da adj. poor;
  needy
ne-ce-si-tar v. to want; to
  require; to need
ne-cio, -cia adj. foolish;
  stubborn
ne-cro-lo-gí-a f. necrology
nec-tar m. nectar
nec-ta-ri-na f. nectarine
ne-fri-tis f. nephritis
ne-ga-ble adj. refutable

ne-ga-ción *f.* denial; refusal; negation

ne-gar *v.* to refuse; to deny; to forbid

ne-ga-ti-vi-dad *f.* negativity

ne-gli-gen-cia *f.* disregard; negligence

ne-go-cia-ble *adj.* negotiable

ne-go-cia-ción *f.* negotiation; transaction

ne-go-ciar *v.* to deal; to negotiate

ne-go-cio *m.* job; work; business; transaction

ne-gro, -a *adj.* black

ne-gru-ra *f.* darkness

ne-gruz-co, -ca *adj.* dark

ne-ne, -na *m., f.* baby

ne-nu-far *m.* water lily

ne-ó-fi-to, -ta *m., f.* neophyte

ne-on *m.* neon

ne-o-na-to *m.* neonate

ner-vo *m.* nerve

ner-vio-si-dad *f.* nervousness

ner-vio-so, -sa *adj.* nervous

ner-vo-si-dad *f.* nervousness

ne-to, -ta *adj.* simple; pure

neu-má-ti-co, -ca *adj.* pneumatic

neu-ro-ci-ru-gi-a *f.* neurosurgery

neu-ro-lo-go *m.* neurologist

neu-ro-ti-co, -ca *adj.* neurotic

neu-to-nio *m.* newton

neu-tral *adj.* neutral

neu-tra-li-dad *f.* neutrality

neu-tra-li-zar *v.* to neutralize

neu-tro, -a *adj.* neutral

neu-trón *m.* neutron

ne-va-do, -da *adj.* snow-covered

ne-var *v.* to snow

ne-ve-ra *f.* refrigerator

ne-xo *m.* link

ni *conj.* neither; nor

ni-co-ti-na *f.* nicotine

ni-cho *m.* vault; recess

ni-dal *m.* nest

ni-do *m.* nest; liar; den

nei-bla *f.* mist

nie-ta *f.* granddaughter

nie-to *m.* grandson

nie-ve *f.* snow

ni-hi-lis-ta *adj.* nihilistic

ni-lon *m.* nylon

nim-bom. halo

ni-mio, -a *adj.* insignificant

nin-fa *f.* nymph

nin-fe-a *f.* water lily

nin-fo *m.* dandy

nin-fo-ma-ni-a *f.* nymphomania

nin-gu-no, -na *adj.* no; none

ni-ne-ri-a *f.* childish

ni-nez *f.* infancy; childhood

ni-no, -na *m. f.* child

ni-quel *m.* nickel

ni-que-lar *v.* to nickel

ni-ti-do, -da *adj.* clear

ni-tra-to *m.* nitrite

ni-tri-to *m.* nitrite

ni-tro-ge-no *m.* nitrogen

ni-tro-gli-ce-ri-na *f.* nitroglycerin

ni-vel *m.* height; standard

ni-ve-lar *v.* to make level

no *adv.* no

no-ble *adj.* honorable; noble

no-ble-za *f.* nobleness; nobility

no-ción *f.* notion

no-ci-vi-dad *f.* noxiousness

no-ci-vo, -va *adj.* noxious

noc-tur-nal *adj.* nocturnal

noc-tur-no, -na *adj.* sad; nocturnal

no-che *f.* night

no-du-lo *m.* nodule

no-gal *m.* walnut

no-ma-da *adj.* nomadic

nom-bra-mein-to *m.* nomination; naming

nom-brar *v.* to name; to nominate

nom-bre *m.* name

no-men-cla-tu-ra *f.* nomenclature

no-mi-na *f.* roll

no-mi-na-ción *f.* nomination

no-mi-nal *adj.* nominal

no-mi-nar *v.* to nominate

non *adj.* uneven

no-na-da *f.* trifle

no-no, -na *adj.* ninth

nor-ma *f.* rule

nor-mal *adj.* normal

nor-ma-li-dad *f.* normality

nor-ma-li-za-cion *f.* normalization

nor-ma-li-zar *v.* to normalize

no-ro-es-te *m.* northwest

nor-te *m.* north

nos *pron.* us

no-ta-ble *adj.* outstanding; notable

no-tar *v.* to observe; note

no-ti-fi-car *v.* to notify

no-ve-no *adj.* ninth

no-ven-ta *adj.* ninety

no-via *f.* girlfriend

no-vio *m.* boyfriend

nu-bo-si-dad *f.* cloudiness

nu-ca *f.* nape

nues-tro *adj.* our

nue-ve *adj.* nine

nue-vo *adj.* new

nú-me-ro *m.* number

nun-ca *adv.* not ever

nu-trir *v.* to feed

ña-me *m.* yam

ña-pa *f.* tip; bonus

ña-que *m.* junk

ñe-que *m.* vigor; *adj.* strength

ño-ñe-ria *f.* timidity

ño-ñez *f.* bashfulness

ño-ño -a *adj., m., f.* timid; bashful

ñu-do *m.* knot

o *conj.* or

o-a-sis *m.* oasis

ob-ce-ca-da-men-to *adv.* blindly

ob-ce-car *v.* to blind

o-be-de-cer *v.* to obey

o-be-dien-cia *f.* obedience

o-be-dien-te *adj.* obedient

o-ber-tu-ra *f.* overture

o-be-si-dad *f.* obesity

o-bi-ce *m.* obstacle

o-bis-po *m.* bishop

ob-je-cion *f.* objection

ob-je-ta-ble *adj.* objectionable

ob-je-tar *v.* to object

ob-je-ti-var *v.* to objectify

ob-je-ti-vi-dad *f.* objectivity

ob-je-ti-vo *adj.* objective

ob-je-to *m.* theme; object

o-bli-cuo, -cua *adj.* oblique

o-bli-ga-ción *f.* responsibility; obligation

o-bli-gar *v.* to force; to oblige; to favor

o-bli-ga-to-rio, -ria *adj.* obligatory

o-blon-go, -ga *adj.* oblong

o-bo-e *m.* oboe

o-bra *f.* work; labor

o-brar *v.* to act; to work

o-bre-ro, -ra *adj.* working

obs-ce-ni-dad *f.* obscenity

obs-ce-no, -na *adj.* obscene

ob-se-quio *m.* present; kindness; gift

ob-se-quio-so, -sa *adj.* obsequious; attentive

ob-ser-va-ción *f.* observation

ob-ser-va-dor, -ra *adj.* observing *m., f.* observer

ob-ser-van-cia *f.* observance

ob-ser-var *v.* to watch; to observe

ob-se-sión *f.* obsession

ob-se-sio-nan-te *adj.* obsessive

ob-se-sio-nar *v.* to obsess about someting

ob-se-so, -sa *adj.* obsessive

obs-ta-cu-li-zar *v.* to hinder

obs-ta-cu-lo *m.* obstacle

obs-tan-te *adj.* obstructing

obs-tar *v.* to hinder; to obstruct something

obs-ti-na-cion *f.* obstinacy

obs-ti-na-do, -da *adj.* obstinate

obs-truc-cion *f.* obstruction

obs-truir *v.* to obstruct

ob-ten-cion *f.* obtaining

ob-te-ner *v.* to get; to have; to obtain

ob-tu-so, -sa *adj.* obtuse
ob-viar *v.* to prevent
ob-vio, -via *adj.* obvious
o-ca-sión *f.* cause; occasion; circumstance
o-ca-sio-nar *v.* to cause; to provoke; to occasion
oc-ci-den-tal *adj.* occidental
oc-ci-pi-tal *adj.* occipital
o-cé-a-no *m.* ocean
o-ce-a-no-gra-fí-a *f.* oceanography
o-ce-a-no-gra-fi-co, -ca *adj.* oceanographic
o-cio *m.* leisure; idleness
oc-ta-vo *adj.* eighth
oc-te-to *m.* octet
oc-to-ge-si-mo *adj.* eightieth
oc-to-go-nal *adj.* octagonal
oc-to-go-no, -na *adj.* octagonal
oc-tu-bre *m.* October
o-cul-tar *v.* to conceal; to silence; to hide
o-cu-lis-ta *m., f.* oculist
o-cul-ta-men-te *adv.* secretly
o-cul-tar *v.* to conceal; to silence; to hide
o-cul-tis-mo *m.* occultism
o-cul-to, -ta *adj.* concealed; occult
o-cu-pa-ción *f.* trade; occupation; job
o-cu-pa-do *adj.* occupied
o-cu-pan-te *adj.* occupying
o-cu-par *v.* to fill; to occupy; to employ; to pay attention to something
o-cu-rren-cia *f.* occurrence
o-cu-rrir *v.* to happen; to take place
o-chen-ta *adj.* eighty
o-chen-ta-vo, -va *adj.* eightieth
o-cho *adj.* eight
o-cho-cien-tos *adj.* eight hundred
o-da *f.* ode
o-da-lis-ca *f.* odalisque
o-diar *v.* to loathe
o-dio *m.* loathing
o-dio-so, -sa *adj.* odious
o-di-se-a *f.* odyssey

o-don-to-lo-go, -ga *m., f.* odontologist
o-es-te *m.* west
o-fen-der *v.* to hurt; offend
o-fen-sa *f.* offense
o-fen-si-vo, -va *adj.* offensive
o-fen-sor *adj.* offending
o-fer-tar *v.* to tender
o-fi-cial *m.* officer
o-fi-cia-li-dad *f.* officers
o-fi-cian-te *m.* officiant
o-fi-ci-na *f.* office
o-fi-ci-nis-ta *m., f.* office clerk
o-fi-cio *m.* work; office
o-fi-cio-so *adj.* obliging; diligent
o-fre-ci-mien-to *m.* offering
o-fren-da *f.* gift
o-fren-dar *v.* to give an offering for
of-tal-mo-lo-gi-a *f.* ophthalmology
of-tal-mo-lo-go *m.* ophthalmologist
o-fus-ca-cion *f.* confusion; dazzling
o-fus-car *v.* to bewilder; to blind
o-í-do *m.* ear
o-ir *v.* to listen; to hear; to attend
o-jal *m.* bottonhole
o-je-a-da *f.* glimpse
o-je-ri-za *f.* grudge
o-jo *m.* eye
o-jo-ta *f.* sandal
o-le-a-da *f.* wave
o-le-a-je *m.* waves
o-ler *v.* to smell
ol-fa-to *m.* instinct
ol-fa-to-rio, -ria *adj.* olfactory
o-li-va *f.* olive
o-li-var *m.* olive grove
o-li-vo *m.* olive tree
ol-mo *m.* elm tree
o-lor *m.* smell
o-lo-ro-so, -sa *adj.* fragrant
ol-vi-da-do, -da *adj.* forgetful; ungrateful
ol-vi-dar *v.* to omit; to forget; to leave out

ol-vi-do *m.* forgetfulness
o-lla *f.* kettle
om-bli-go *m.* navel
o-mi-sión *f.* omission
o-mi-tir *v.* to omit
óm-ni-bus *m.* omnibus
om-ni-po-ten-cia *f.* omnipotence
om-ni-po-ten-te *adj.* omnipotent
o-na-nis-mo *m.* onanism
on-ce *adj.* eleven
on-ce-no *adj.* eleventh
on-co-lo-gi-a *f.* oncology
on-de-ar *v.* to flutter; to ripple
on-du-la-ción *f.* undulation
on-du-lar *v.* to undulate
o-ne-ro-so, -sa *adj.* onerous
o-nix *f.* onyx
o-no-ma-to-pe-ya *f.* onomatopoeia
on-za *f.* ounce
on-za-vo *adj.* eleventh
o-pa *adj.* foolish
o-pa-ci-dad *f.* opacity
o-pa-co, -ca *adj.* opaque
ó-pa-lo *m.* opal
op-cion *f.* option
op-cio-nal *adj.* optional
ó-pe-ra *f.* opera
o-pe-ra-ción *f.* operation
o-pe-ran-te *adj.* operating
o-pe-rar *v.* to operate
o-pe-ra-ti-vo, -va *adj.* operative
o-pi-nion *f.* opinion
o-pio *m.* opium
o-po-ner *v.* to oppose
o-por-tu-na-men-te *adv.* opportunely
o-por-tu-ni-dad *f.* chance
o-por-tu-nis-ta *adj.* opportunist
o-por-tu-no, -na *adj.* opportune; fitting
o-po-si-cion *f.* opposition
o-po-si-tor, -ra *m., f.* opponent
o-pre-sion *f.* opression
o-pre-si-vo, -va *adj.* oppressive
o-pre-so, -sa *adj.* oppressed

o-pri-mi-do, -da *adj.* oppressed
o-pri-mir *v.* to press; to oppress
o-pro-bio *m.* disgrace
o-pro-bio-so, -sa *adj.* disgraceful
op-tar *v.* to select
óp-ti-co, -ca *adj.* optical
op-ti-mis-ta *adj.* optimistic
op-ti-mo, -ma *adj.* optimal
op-to-me-tra *m., f.* optometrist
op-to-me-tri-a *f.* optometry
o-pues-to *adj.* contrary; opposite
o-pu-len-cia *f.* opulence
o-ra *conj.* now
o-ra-ción *f.* oration: speech; sentence
o-rá-cu-lo *m.* oracle
o-ral *adj.* oral
o-ran-gu-tan *m.* orangutan
o-rar *v.* to speak
o-ra-to-rio, -ria *adj.* oratorical
or-be *m.* orb
or-den *m.* order
or-de-na-cion *f.* ordination; ordering
or-de-na-da *f.* ordinate
or-de-nar *v.* to command; to arrange; to put into order
or-de-nar *v.* to milk
or-di-nal *adj.* ordinal
or-di-na-riez *f.* commonness
or-di-na-rio *adj.* ordinary; uncouth; coarse
o-re-ar *v.* to ventilate
or-fa-na-to *m.* orphanage
or-fe-li-na-to *m.* orphanage
or-ga-ni-co *adj.* organic
or-ga-nis-mo *m.* organism
or-ga-nis-ta *m.,f.* organist
or-ga-ni-za-dor, -ra *m., f.* organizer
or-ga-ni-zar *v.* to organize
ór-ga-no *m.* organ
or-gu-llo *m.* conceit
o-rien-ta-cion *f.* orientation
o-rien-tal *adj.* oriental
o-rien-tar *v.* to orient
o-ri-fi-cio *m.* opening

o-ri-gen *m.* source
o-ri-gi-nal *adj.* authentic; original; new
o-ri-gi-na-li-dad *f.* originality
o-ri-gi-nar *v.* to originate
o-ri-gi-na-ria-men-te *adv.* originally
o-ri-lla *f.* edge
o-ri-llar *v.* to edge
o-rin *m.* rust
o-ri-nal *m.* urinal
o-ri-nar *v.* to urinate
or-lar *v.* to edge
or-na-men-tal *adj.* ornamental
or-na-men-tar *v.* to ornament; to decorate
or-na-men-to *m.* ornament
or-nar *v.* to embellish
or-ni-to-lo-gi-a *f.* ornithology
or-ni-to-lo-go *m., f.* ornithologist
o-ro *m.* gold
or-ques-ta *f.* orchestra
or-ques-ta-cion *f.* orchestration
or-ques-tal *adj.* orchestral
or-ques-tar *v.* to orchestrate
or-qui-de-a *f.* orchid
or-ti-ga *f.* nettle
or-to-do-xo, -xa *adj.* orthodox
or-to-gra-fi-a *f.* orthographic
or-to-pe-di-co, -ca *adj.* orthopedic
or-to-pe-dis-ta *m., f.* orthopedist
o-ru-ga *f.* caterpillar
o-ru-jo *m.* residue
os *pron.* you
o-sa-di-a *f.* audacity
o-sa-do, -da *adj.* daring
o-sa-men-ta *f.* bones
o-sar *v.* to dare
os-ci-la-cion *f.* wavering; swinging
os-ci-lar *v.* to oscillate; to swing
os-cu-lo *m.* kiss
os-cu-re-cer *v.* to dim; to obscure; to shade
os-cu-re-ci-mien-to *m.* darkening

os-cu-ri-dad *f.* haziness; obscurity
os-cu-ro, -ra *adj.* unclear; dark; obscure
o-si-fi-car-se *v.* to ossify
os-mo-sis *f.* osmosis
o-so *m.* bear
os-ten-si-ble *adj.* ostensible
os-ten-ta-cion *f.* ostentation
os-ten-tar *v.* to flaunt; to show
os-te-o-lo-go, -ga *m., f.* osteologist
os-tra *f.* oyster
os-tra-cis-mo *m.* ostracism
o-te-ar *v.* to survey
o-to-ñal *adj.* autumnal
o-to-ño *m.* autumn
o-tor-gar *v.* to give
o-tro *adj.* other
o-va-cion *f.* ovation
o-va-cio-nar *v.* to give another an ovation
o-val *adj.* oval
o-va-lo *m.* oval
o-va-rio *m.* ovary
o-ve-ja *f.* the female sheep
o-ver-tu-ra *f.* overture
o-vi-llo *m.* snarl; ball
o-vi-no *m.* ovine
o-vu-la-cion *f.* ovulation
o-vu-lar *adj.* ovular
o-xi-da-cion *f.* oxidation
o-xi-dar *v.* to oxidize
o-xi-do *m.* oxide
o-xi-ge-na-do, -da *adj.* oxygenated
o-xi-ge-nar *v.* to give oxygen to; to oxygenate
o-xi-ge-no *m.* oxygen
o-yen-te *adj.* listening *m., f.* listener
o-zo-no *m.* ozone

pa-be-llon *m.* banner; pavilion
pa-bi-lo *m.* candle wick
pa-bu-lo *m.* pabulum; support

pa-cer v. to graze
pa-cien-cia f. patience
pa-cien-te adj. patient
pa-ci-fi-ca-cion f. pacification
pa-ci-fi-ca-dor, -ra m., f. pacifier
pa-ci-fi-car v. to pacify
pa-ci-fi-co adj. pacific
pa-ci-fis-ta adj. pacifist
pa-cho-rra f. sluggishness
pa-de-cer v. to bear; to suffer; to endure
pa-dras-tro m. stepfather
pa-dre m. dad; father
pa-dri-llo m. stallion
pa-dri-no m. godfather
pa-ga f. payment
pa-ga-de-ro, -ra adj. payable
pa-ga-no, -na adj. pagan
pa-gar v. to repay; pay for
pá-gi-na f. page
pa-gi-nar v. to paginate
pa-go adj. paid
país m. land
pai-sa-je m. landscape
pai-sa-jis-ta adj. landscape
pa-ja f. straw
pa-jar m. barn
pa-ja-re-ra f. cage for birds
pa-ja-re-ri-a f. bird store
pá-ja-ro m. bird
pa-la- f. blade; spade; shovelful
pa-la-bra f. word
pa-la-bre-o m. chatter
pa-la-cie-go, -ga adj. magnificent
pa-la-cio m. palace
pa-la-da f. shovelful
pa-la-de-ar v. to relish
pa-la-dio m. palladium
pa-la-fre-ne-ro m. groom
pa-lan-ca f. shaft; lever
pa-lan-ga-na f. washbasin
pa-le-ar v. to shovel
pa-le-on-to-lo-gi-a f. paleontology
pa-le-ta f. trowel; palette
pa-lia-ti-vo, -va adj. palliative
pá-li-dez f. pallor
pá-li-do, -da adj. pallid
pa-li-to m. small stick

pa-li-za f. thrashing
pal-ma f. palm
pal-ma-do, -da adj. palm-shaped
pal-mar m. palm grove
pal-me-a-do, -da adj. palm-shaped
pal-me-ar v. to applaud
pal-me-ra f. palm tree
pal-mo m. palm
pal-mo-te-ar v. to applaud
pa-lo m. pole; handle
pa-lo-ma f. pigeon
pa-lo-mi-ta f. popcorn
pa-lo-te m. drumstick
pal-pa-ble adj. palpable
pal-par v. to feel
pal-pi-ta-ción f. palpitation
pal-pi-tan-te adj. palpating
pal-pi-tar v. to palpitate; to beat
pal-ta f. avocado
pa-lu-dis-mo m. malaria
pa-lur-do, -da m., f. boor
pam-pa f. pampa
pan m. bread
pa-na f. corduroy
pa-na-de-ri-a f. bakery
pa-na-de-ro, -ra m., f. baker
pa-nal m. honeycomb
pan-cre-as m. pancreas
pan-cre-a-ti-co, -ca adj. pancreatic
pa-cho, -cha adj. unruffled
pan-da f. panda
pan-de-mo-nio m. pandemonium
pan-de-ro m. tambourine
pan-di-lla f. gang
pan-fle-to m. pamphlet
pa-ni-co, -ca m., adj. panic
pa-no-ra-ma f. panorama
pa-no-ra-mi-co, -ca adj. panoramic
pan-ta-ló-nes m. slacks; pants
pan-ta-lla f. movie screen; lamp shade
pan-ta-no m. difficulty
pan-te-on m. pantheon
pan-te-ra f. panther
pan-to-mi-ma f. pantomine
pan-to-rri-lla f. calf

pa-no *m.* cloth
pa-no-le-ta *f.* scarf
pa-no-lon *m.* shawl
pa-nue-lo *m.* kerchief
pa-pa *f.* potato
pa-pa-ga-yo *m.* parrot
pa-pal *adj.* papal
pa-par *v.* to gape
pa-pa-ya *f.* papaya
pa-pel *m.* paper
pa-pe-le-ro, -ra *adj.* paper
pa-pe-le-ta *f.* card
pa-pe-ra *f.* goiter
pa-pi-la *f.* papilla
pa-pi-ro *m.* papyrus
pa-que-te *m.* packet; pack; package
pa-que-te-ri-a *f.* elegance
pa-qui-der-mo *m.* pachyderm
par *adj.* paired; equal
pa-ra *prep.* for; to; towards
pa-ra-bo-la *f.* parable
pa-ra-bri-sas *m.* windshield
pa-ra-ca-i-das *f.* parachute
pa-ra-di-sia-co, -ca *adj.* heavenly
pa-ra-do, -da *adj.* stopped; stationary; idle
pa-ra-do-ja *f.* paradox
pa-ra-do-ji-co, -ca *adj.* paradoxical
pa-ra-fi-na *f.* paraffin
pa-ra-guas *m.* umbrella
pa-ra-i-so *m.* paradise
pa-ra-je *m.* area
pa-ra-le-lo *m.* parallel
pa-ra-le-lo-gra-mo *m.* parallelogram
pa-ra-li-sis *f.* paralysis
pa-ra-li-ti-co, -ca *adj.* paralytic
pa-ra-li-za-cion *f.* paralyzation
pa-ra-li-zar *v.* to paralyze
pa-ra-me-di-co, -ca *adj.* paramedical
pa-ra-me-tro *m.* parameter
pa-ra-no-ia *f.* paranoia
pa-ra-noi-co, -ca *adj.* paranoid
pa-ra-ple-ji-co, -ca *adj.* paraplegic

pa-rar *v.* to halt; to check; to stop
pa-ra-si-ti-co, -ca *adj.* parasitic
pa-ra-si-to, -ta *adj.* parasitic
pa-ra-sol *m.* parasol
par-ce-la *f.* parcel
par-cial *adj.* partial
par-cia-li-dad *f.* partiality
par-do *adj.* brown
pa-re-ar *v.* to pair
pa-re-cer *m.* view; appearance
pa-re-ci-do *adj.* similar
pa-red *f.* wall
pa-re-jo, -ja *adj.* equal; smooth; alike
pa-ren-te-la *f.* relatives
pa-ren-tes-co *m.* kinship
pa-ren-te-sis *m.* parenthesis
pa-ri-dad *f.* parity
pa-ri-ta-rio, -ria *adj.* joint
par-la-men-ta-rio *adj.* parliamentary
par-la-men-to *m.* parliament
par-lar *v.* to chatter
par-lo-te-o *m.* chatter
pa-ro *m.* unemployment
pa-ro-dia *f.* parody
pa-ro-diar *v.* to parody
pa-ro-dis-ta *m., f.* parodist
pa-ro-xis-mo *m.* paroxysm
par-pa-de-ar *v.* to twinkle
par-pa-do *m.* eyelid
par-que *m.* park
par-que-o *m.* parking
par-que-dad *f.* moderation
pa-rra *f.* grapevine
pa-rra-fo *m.* paragraph
pa-rri-ci-dio *m.* parricide
pa-rro-quial *adj.* parochial
par-si-mo-nia *f.* moderation
par-si-mo-nio-so, -sa *adj.* parsimonious
par-te *f.* share; part
par-te-ra *f.* midwife
par-ti-cion *f.* partition
par-ti-ci-pa-cion *f.* participation
par-ti-ci-par *v.* to inform
par-ti-ci-pe *adj.* participating
par-ti-cu-la *f.* particle
par-ti-cu-lar *adj.* particular

par-ti-cu-la-ri-dad *f.* peculiarity

par-ti-cu-lar-men-te *adv.* particularly

par-ti-dis-ta *adj.* party

par-ti-da *f.* group; leaving; departure

par-ti-do *m.* party

par-tir *v.* to depart; to leave

par-ti-ti-vo, -va *adj.* partitive

par-ti-tu-ra *f.* score

pa-sa-di-zo *m.* passage

pa-sa-do *m.* past

pa-sa-dor *adj.* passing

pa-sa-je *m.* passage

pa-sa-por-te *m.* passport

pa-sar *v.* to elapse; to occur; to happen

pa-sa-tiem-po *m.* pastime

pa-se *m.* pass

pa-se-o *m.* stroll; outing

pa-sión *f.* passion

pa-so *m.* footstep; pace

pas-ta *f.* paste

pas-tel *m.* cake

pas-teu-ri-zar *v.* to pasteurize

pas-teu-ri-za-cion *f.* pasteurization

pas-to *m.* pasture; grass

pa-ta *f.* foot; leg; paw; female duck

pa-ta-da *f.* kick

pa-ta-ta *f.* potato

pa-te-ar *v.* to kick

pa-ten-tar *v.* to register

pa-ten-te *adj.* patent; evident; obvious

pa-ter-nal *adj.* paternal

pa-ter-ni-dad *f.* paternity

pa-ti-llas *f.* sideburns

pa-tin *m.* skate

pa-ti-nar *v.* to skate

pa-tion *m.* patio

pa-to *m.* duck

pa-to-lo-gia *f.* pathology

pa-to-lo-go, -ga *m., f.* pathologist

pa-triar-ca *m.* patriarch

pa-trio-ta *m., f.* patriot

pa-trió-ti-co, ca *adj.* patriotic

pa-tro-ci-nar *v.* to patronize

pa-trón *m.* host

pa-tro-nal *adj.* management

pa-tro-na-to *m.* patronage

pa-tru-llar *v.* to patrol

pau-la-ti-no, -na *adj.* gradual

pau-sa *f.* interruption

pau-ta *f.* rule

pa-va-da *f.* foolishness

pa-vi-men-ta-cion *f.* paving

pa-vi-men-to *m.* pavement

pa-vo *m.* turkey

pa-vor *m.* terror

pa-vu-ra *f.* terror

pa-ya-so *m.* clown

paz *f.* peace

paz-gua-to, -ta *adj.* foolish

pe-car *v.* to sin

pe-ce-ra *f.* aquarium

pec-ti-na *f.* pectin

pec-to-ral *adj.* pectoral

pe-cu-liar *adj.* peculiar

pe-cu-lia-ri-dad *f.* peculiarity

pe-cu-lio *m.* peculium

pe-cu-nia *f.* money

pe-char *v.* to pay

pe-cho *m.* breast; chest

pe-dal *m.* pedal

pe-da-le-o *m.* pedaling

pe-dan-te-ri-a *f.* pedantry

pe-da-zo *m.* bit; piece

pe-der-nal *m.* flint

pe-des-tal *m.* pedestal

pe-des-tre *adj.* pedestrian

pe-dia-tri-a *f.* pediatrics

pe-di-cu-lo *m.* peduncle

pe-di-gre-e *m.* pedigree

pe-dir *v.* to order; to beg; to charge

pe-dre-go-so, -sa *adj.* rocky

pe-dris-ca *f.* hail

pe-dun-cu-lo *m.* peduncle

pe-ga-di-zo, -za *adj.* catching

pe-ga-jo-so, -sa *adj.* catching; adhesive

pe-gar *v.* to glue; to attach; to cleave

pei-na-do *m.* hairdresser

pei-ne *m.* comb

pe-la-do, -da *adj.* bare; bald

pe-la-du-ra *f.* peeling

pe-la-gra *f.* pellagra

pe-lar *v.* to peel; to cut

pe-le-a-dor *adj.* fighting

pe-li-ca-no *m.* pelican
pe-li-cu-la *f.* film; movie
pe-li-gro *m.* danger
pe-li-gro-so *adj.* dangerous
pe-lo *m.* fur; hair
pe-lo-ta *f.* ball
pel-tre *m.* pewter
pe-lu-ca *f.* wig
pe-lu-do, -da *adj.* shaggy
pel-vis *f.* pelvis
pe-lliz-car *v.* to nibble
pe-llon *m.* sheepskin
pe-ña *f.* anxiety; penalty; distress
pe-na-cho *m.* crest
pe-na-do, -da *adj.* grieved
pe-na-li-zar *v.* to penalize
pe-nar *v.* to punish
pen-den-ciar *v.* to quarrel; to argue
pen-der *v.* to hover
pen-dien-te *adj.* hanging
pe-ne-tra-ble *adj.* penetrable
pe-ne-tra-ción *f.* penetration
pe-ne-tran-te *adj.* piercing; penetrating
pe-ne-trar *v.* to pierce; to penetrate
pe-ni-ci-li-na *f.* penicillin
pe-nin-su-la *f.* peninsula
pe-ni-que *m.* penny
pe-ni-ten-cia *f.* penitence
pe-ni-ten-te *adj.* penitent
pe-no-so *adj.* grievous; wearing
pen-sa-mien-to *m.* thought
pen-san-te *adj.* thinking
pen-sar *v.* to think about
pen-sa-ti-vo *adj.* thoughtful; pensie
pen-sio-nar *v.* to pension
pen-to-tal *m.* pentothal
pe-na *f.* circle
pe-ñas-co-so, -sa *adj.* rocky
pe-or *adj.* worse
pe-pi-no *m.* cucumber
pep-ti-co, -ca *adj.* peptic
pe-que-ño *adj.* tiny; small
pe-ra *f.* pear
pe-ral *m.* pear tree
per-cep-ción *f.* perception
per-cep-ti-vo, -va *adj.* perceptive

per-ci-bir *v.* to sense; to recieve
per-cu-dir *y.* to dull
per-cu-sión *f.* percussion
per-cu-tir *v.* to percuss
per-cha *f.* hanger; prop
per-der *v.* to waste; to lose
pér-di-da *f.* waste
per-di-do *adj.* missing
per-diz *f.* partridge
per-dón *m.* pardon
per-do-nar *v.* to remit; to excuse; to pardon
per-du-rar *v.* to last
pe-re-cer *v.* to perish
pe-re-gri-na-cion *f.* pilgrimage
pe-re-jil *m.* parsley
pe-ren-ne *adj.* perennial
pe-re-za *f.* laziness
pe-re-zo-so, -sa *adj.* lazy
per-fec-ción *f.* perfection
per-fec-cio-nar *v.* to make something perfect
per-fec-cio-nis-ta *adj.* perfectionist
per-fec-to *adj.* perfect
pér-fi-do, -da *adj.* unfaithful
per-fi-lar *v.* to profile
per-fo-ra-ción *f.* perforation
per-fo-ra-dor *adj.* perforating
per-fo-rar *v.* to perforate
per-fu-mar *v.* to perfume
per-fu-me *m.* perfume
per-fu-me-ri-a *f.* perfumery
pe-ri-car-dio *m.* pericardium
pe-ri-coa *f.* skill
pe-ri-co *m.* parakeet
pe-ri-me-tro *m.* perimeter
pe-rio-di-ca-men-te *adv.* periodically
pe-rio-di-co *m.* periodical
pe-rio-dis-mo *m.* journalism
pe-rio-dis-ta *m., f.* journalist
pe-rio-do *m.* period
pe-ris-to-le *f.* peristalsis
pe-ri-qui-to *m.* parakeet
pe-ris-co-pio *m.* periscope
pe-ri-to-ne-o-m *m.* peritoneum
per-ju-di-car *v.* to harm
per-ju-di-cial *adj.* harmful
per-ju-rio *m.* perjury
per-la *f.* pearl

per-ma-ne-cer *v.* to remain

per-ma-nen-te *adj.* permanent

per-mi-si-ble *adj.* permissible

per-mi-si-vo *adj.* permissive

per-mi-so *m.* consent

per-mi-tir *v.* to allow; to give; to permit

per-mu-tar *v.* to exchange

per-ni-cio-so, -sa *adj.* pernicious

per-no *m.* pin

pe-ro *conj.* but

pe-ro-ne *m.* fibula

pe-ró-xi-do *m.* peroxide

per-pe-tra-cion *f.* perpetuation

per-pe-tuar *v.* to perpetuate

per-ple-ji-dad *f.* perplexity

per-ple-jo, -ja *adj.* perplexed

pe-rro *m.* dog

per-se-cu-ción *f.* persecution

per-se-guir *v.* to follow; to hound; to pursue

per-se-ve-ran-cia *f.* perseverance

per-se-ve-ran-te *adj.* persevering

per-sia-na *f.* blind

per-sig-nar *v.* to cross

per-sis-ten-cia *f.* persistence

per-sis-tir *v.* to persist

per-so-na *f.* person

per-so-na-li-dad *f.* personality

per-so-na-li-zar *v.* to personalize

per-so-ni-fi-ca-cion *f.* personification

pers-pec-ti-va *f.* perspective

per-sua-dir *v.* to persuade

per-sua-sion *f.* persuasion

per-sua-si-vo, -va *adj.* persuasive

per-te-ne-cer *v.* to belong

per-te-ne-cien-te *adj.* pertaining

per-ti-nen-cia *f.* relevancy

per-ti-nen-cia *f.* relevance

per-ti-nen-te *adj.* relevant

per-tre-char *v.* to equip

per-tur-ba-ción *f.* disturbance

per-tur-bar *v.* to upset

per-ver-si-dad *f.* perversity

per-ver-sion *f.* perversion

per-ver-ti-do, -da *adj.* perverted

pe-sa-di-lla *f.* nightmare

pe-sa-do *adj.* dull; heavy; boring

pe-sar *v.* to grieve

pes-ca *f.* fishing

pes-ca-de-ri-a *f.* fish market

pes-ca-di-lla *f.* whiting

pes-ca-do *m.* fish

pes-ca-dor *m.* fisherman

pes-car *v.* to fish

pe-se-bre *f.* manger

pe-si-mis-ta *adj.* pessimistic

pe-so *m.* weight

pes-que-ro, -ra *adj.* fishing

pes-ta-ña *f.* eyelash

pes-ta-ñe-ar *v.* to wink

pes-ta-ne-o *m.* winking

pes-te *f.* plague

pé-ta-lo *m.* petal

pe-ti-ción *f.* petition

pé-tre-o, -a *adj.* rocky

pe-tri-fi-car *v.* to petrify

pe-tró-le-o *m.* petroleum

pe-tu-lan-cia *f.* arrogance

pe-tu-lan-te *adj.* arrogant

pe-tu-nia *f.* petunia

pez *m.* fish

pia-nis-ta *m., f.* pianist

pia-no *m.* piano

piar *v.* to chirp

pi-can-te *adj.* spicy

pi-car *v.* to sting; to chip; to bite

pi-ca-res-co, -ca *adj.* mischievous

pi-ca-ro, -ra *adj.* wicked; sly

pi-ca-zon *f.* itching

pi-co *m.* spout; beak

pi-cor *m.* itching

pi-co-te-ar *v.* to pick; to peck

pic-to-ri-co, -ca *adj.* pictorial

pie *m.* foot

pie-dra *f.* stone

piel *f.* fur; skin

pier-na *f.* leg

pie-za *f.* piece

pi-fiar *v.* to miscue

pig-men-tar *v.* to pigment

pig-me-o *adj.* pygmy
pi-ja-ma *m.* pajamas
pi-lar *m.* pillar
pi-le-ta *f.* sink
pi-lo-tar *v.* to pilot
pi-lo-to *m.* pilot
pi-llar *v.* to plunder
pi-llue-lo, -la *adj.* mischievous
pi-men-ton *m.* paprika
pi-mien-ta *f.* pepper
pim-pan-te *adj.* spruce; graceful
pi-na-cu-lo *m.* pinnacle
pi-nar *m.* pine grove
pin-cel *m.* brush
pin-cha-du-ra *f.* puncture
pin-char *v.* to puncture
pin-cha-zo *m.* puncture
pin-gui-no *m.* penguin
pi-ño *m.* pine
pin-tar *v.* to paint
pin-to, -ta *adj.* speckled
pin-tor, -ra *m., f.* painter
pin-to-res-co, -ca *adj.* picturesque
pin-tu-ra *f.* painting
pi-na *f.* pine cone
pio-jo *m.* louse
pio-la *f.* cord
pi-pa *f.* barrel
pi-per-min *m.* peppermint
pi-pe-ta *f.* pipette
pi-que-ta *f.* pick
pi-que-te *m.* picket
pi-ra-mi-dal *adj.* pyramidal
pi-rá-mi-de *f.* pyramid
pi-ra-ta *m.* pirate
pi-ri-ta *f.* pyrites
pi-rue-ta *f.* pirouette
pi-sa-da *f.* footprint
pi-sar *v.* to walk upon
pis-ci-na *f.* swimming pool
pi-so *m.* story; flat
pi-són *m.* tamper
pi-so-te-ar *v.* to trample
pis-ta *f.* runway; trail
pis-ta-cho *m.* pistachio
pis-to-la *f.* pistol
pis-tón *m.* piston
pi-ti-do *m.* whistling
pi-ti-llo *m.* cigarette
pi-to *m.* whistle

pi-tón *m.* python
pi-to-ni-sa *f.* pythoness
pi-tui-ta-rio, -ria *adj.* pituitary
pi-vo-te *m.* pivot
pla-ca *f.* plaque
pla-ce-bo *m.* placebo
pla-cen-ta *f.* placenta
pla-cen-te-ro, -ra *adj.* placenta
pla-cer *m.* gratification; pleasure
plá-ci-do *adj.* placid
pla-gar *v.* to plague
plan *m.* scheme; plan
plan-cha *f.* sheet
plan-cha-do, -da *adj.* ironing
plan-char *v.* to iron
pla-ne-ar *v.* to plan
pla-ne-ta *f.* planet
pla-ne-ta-rio, -ria *adj.* planetary
pla-ni-cie *f.* plain
pla-ni-fi-ca-cion *f.* planning
pla-ni-fi-car *v.* to plan
pla-no *adj.* level
plan-ta *f.* plant
plan-ta-cion *f.* plantation
plan-tar *v.* to plant
plan-te-ar *v.* to start; to expound
pla-na-do *m.* lament
plas-ma *f.* plasma
plas-mar *v.* to mold
plas-ti-co, -ca *adj.* plastic
plas-ti-fi-car *v.* to shellac something
pla-ta *f.* silver
pla-ta-for-ma *f.* platform
pla-ta-no *m.* banana
pla-te-ar *v.* to silver-plate
pla-te-ro *m.* silversmith
pla-ti-car *v.* to talk
pla-ti-no *m.* platinum
pla-to *m.* dish; plate
pla-to-ni-co, -ca *adj.* platonic
plau-si-ble *adj.* plausible
pla-ya *f.* beach
pla-ye-ro, -ra *adj.* beach
ple-ga-ble *adj.* collapsible
ple-ga-do *m.* folding
ple-gar *v.* to fold; to bend; to pleat

pleu-re-si-a f. pleursiy
pli-sa-do m. pleat
plo-me-ro m. plumber
plo-mo, -ma adj. leaden
plu-ma f. pen; feather
plu-ral adj. plural
plu-ra-li-dad f. plurality
plu-ra-li-zar v. to pluralize
plu-to-nio m. plutonium
po-bla-ción f. population
po-bla-do m. population
po-blar v. to populate
po-bre adj. poor
po-bre-za f. poverty
po-cion f. potion
po-co adv. little
po-dar v. to prune
po-der v. to be able; can
po-de-ri-o m. power
po-di-a-tra m. podiatrist
poe-ma m. poem
po-e-si-a f. poetry
po-e-ta m. poet
poe-ti-co adj. poetical
po-e-ti-sa f. poetess
po-ker m. poker
po-lar adj. polar
po-la-ri-za-cion f. polarization
po-la-ri-zar v. to polarize
po-len m. pollen
po-li-cia f. constable; police
po-li-cial adj. police
po-li-fo-ni-a f. polyphony
po-li-go-no m. polygon
po-li-lla f. moth
po-li-ni-za-cion f. pollination
po-li-no-mio m. polynomial
po-li-po m. polyp
po-li-ti-ca f. policy
po-li-ti-co adj. political
po-li-ti-zar v. to politicize
po-lo m. pole
pol-tron, -na adj. lazy
po-lu-ción f. pollution
pol-vo m. powder; dust
pól-vo-ra f. powder
po-llo m. chicken
po-ma-da f. pomade
pom-pa f. pomp
pom-po-si-dad f. pomposity
pom-po-so, -sa adj. pompous

pon-che m. punch
pon-cho m. poncho
pon-de-ra-ble adj. ponderable
pon-de-rar v. to consider
po-ner v. to place; to don
pon-ti-fi-cal adj. pontifical
pon-ti-fi-car v. to pontificate
pon-zo-no-so, -sa adj. poisonous
po-pu-la-cho m. populace
po-pu-lar adj. popular
po-pu-la-ri-dad f. popularity
po-pu-la-ri-zar v. to popularize
po-pu-rri m. potpourri
po-quer m. poker
por prep. from; via; for
por-cen-ta-je m. percentage
por-cen-tual adj. percentage
por-cion f. part; portion
por-che m. porch
por-fia-do, -da adj. stubborn
po-ro-si-dad f. porosity
po-ro-so, -sa adj. porous
por-qué conj. because
por-qué m. reason
por-tal m. porch
por-ta-til adj. portable
por-ten-to-so, -sa adj. marvelous
por-ve-nir m. future
po-sar v. to rest; to lodge
pos-da-ta f. postscript
po-se-er v. to have
po-se-i-do, -da adj. possessed
po-se-sión f. dependency; possession
po-se-si-vo, -va adj. possessive
po-se-so, -sa adj. possessed
pos-fe-cha f. postdate
po-si-bi-li-dad f. possibility
po-si-bi-li-tar v. to make something possible
po-si-ble adj. possible
po-si-ción f. place; status
po-si-ti-vo, -va adj. positive
pos-po-ner v. to postpone
pos-ta f. slice
pos-tal adj. postal
pos-te m. post

pos-ter-ga-cion *f.* postponement

pos-te-gar *v.* to postpone

pos-te-rior *adj.* posterior

pos-te-rio-ri-dad *f.* posteriority

pos-ti-zo, -za *adj.* artificial

pos-to-pe-ra-to-rio, -ria *adj.* postoperative

pos-tor *m.* bidder

pos-trar *v.* to debilitate; to humiliate

pos-tre *m.* dessert

pos-tre-mo, -ma *adj.* final

pos-tre-ro, -ra *adj.* final

pos-tu-ra *f.* posture

po-ta-ble *adj.* potable

po-ta-sio *m.* potassium

po-te *m.* pot

po-ten-cia *f.* potency

po-ten-cial *adj.* potential

po-ten-ta-do *m.* potentate

po-ten-te *adj.* potent; powerful

po-tre-ar *v.* to frolic

po-tre-ro *m.* pasture

po-tri-llo *m.* colt

po-tro *m.* colt

prác-ti-ca *f.* custom; practice

prac-ti-car *v.* to practice

prác-ti-co *adj.* practical

pra-de-ra *f.* meadow

pra-do *m.* meadow

pre-ám-bu-lo *m.* preamble

pre-ca-rio, -ria *adj.* precarious

pre-cau-ción *f.* precaution

pre-ca-vi-do, -da *adj.* cautious

pre-ce-den-te *adj.* preceeding

pre-ce-der *v.* to forego

pre-cep-to *m.* precept

pre-cep-tor, -ra *m., f.* tutor

pre-cia-do, -da *adj.* precious

pre-cin-ta-do, -da *adj.* sealed

pre-cin-tar *v.* to stamp

pre-cio *m.* fare; cost; price

pre-cio-si-dad *f.* beauty

pre-cio-so *adj.* precious

pre-ci-pi-ta-ción *f.* precipitation

pre-ci-pi-tar *v.* to hasten

pre-ci-sa-men-te *adj.* precisely

pre-ci-sar *v.* to set; to explain

pre-ci-sión *f.* precision

pre-co-ci-dad *f.* precocity

pre-cog-ni-cion *f.* precodnition

pre-con-ce-bir *v.* to preconceive

pre-co-ni-zar *v.* to recommend something

pre-coz *adj.* precocious

pre-de-ce-sor, -ra *m., f.* predecessor

pre-de-cir *v.* to foretell

pre-des-ti-na-cion *f.* predestination

pre-de-ter-mi-nar *v.* to predetermine

pre-di-ca *f.* sermon

pre-di-ca-do *m.* predicate

pre-di-car *v.* to preach

pre-dic-ción *f.* prediction

pre-di-lec-to, -ta *adj.* favorite

pre-dio *m.* property

pre-dis-po-ner *v.* to predispose

pre-dis-po-si-cion *f.* predisposition

pre-do-mi-nan-te *adj.* predominant

pre-do-mi-nar *v.* to prevail

pre-do-mi-nio *m.* predominant

pre-es-co-lar *adj.* preschool

pre-fa-bri-ca-do, -da *adj.* prefabricated

pre-fa-bri-car *v.* to prefabricate

pre-fa-cio *m.* preface

pre-fec-tu-ra *f.* prefecture

pre-fe-ren-te *adj.* preferable

pre-fe-ren-te-men-te *adv.* preferably

pre-fe-ri-do *adj.* preferred

pre-fe-rir *v.* to prefer

pre-go-nar *v.* to divulge; to proclaim

pre-gun-ta *f.* question

pre-gun-tar *v.* to ask; to question

pre-his-to-ria *f.* prehistory
pre-his-to-ri-co, -ca *adj.* prehistoric
pre-juz-gar *v.* to prejudge
pre-lu-dio *m.* prelude
pre-ma-tu-ro-, -ra *adj.* premature
pre-me-di-ta-cion *f.* premeditation
pre-me-di-ta-da-men-te *adv.* deliberately
pre-me-di-tar *v.* to premeditate
pre-miar *v.* to reward
pre-mio *m.* prize
pre-mi-sa *f.* premise
pre-mo-ni-cion *f.* premonition
pre-mu-ra *f.* urgency
pre-na-tal *adj.* prenatal
pren-da *f.* token; guaranty
pren-der *v.* to catch
pren-sa *f.* press
pren-sar *v.* to press
pre-nup-cial *adj.* prenuptial
pre-ñez *f.* pregnancy
pre-o-cu-pa-cion *f.* concern
pre-o-cu-par *v.* to mind; to preoccupy
pre-pa-rar *v.* to ready; fix
pre-pon-de-ran-te *adj.* preponderant
pre-po-si-cion *f.* preposition
pre-po-ten-cia *f.* prepotency
pre-po-ten-te *adj.* prepotent
pre-pu-cio *m.* prepuce
pre-sa *f.* victim; capture
pres-cin-den-cia *f.* omission
pres-cin-di-ble *adj.* nonessential
pres-cin-dir *v.* to ignore
pres-cri-bir *v.* to prescribe
pre-sen-cia *f.* presence
pre-sen-ciar *v.* to witness
pre-sen-ta-cion *f.* presentation
pre-sen-tar *v.* to introduce; to feature
pre-sen-te *adj.* current
pre-ser-va-cion *f.* preservation
pre-ser-var *v.* to preserve
pre-ser-va-ti-vo, -va *adj.* preservative

pre-si-den-cia *f.* presidency
pre-si-den-cial *adj.* presidential
pre-si-den-ta *f.* president
pre-si-den-te *m.* president
pre-si-dia-rio *m.* convict
pre-si-dio *m.* prison
pre-si-dir *v.* to preside
pre-sion *f.* pressure
pre-sio-nar *v.* to press
pres-ta-cion *f.* services
pres-ta-dor, -ra *adj.* lending
pres-ta-men-te *adj.* quickly
prés-ta-mo *m.* lending
pres-tar *v.* to loan
pres-te-za *f.* promptness
pres-ti-gio *m.* prestige
pres-ti-gio-so, -sa *adj.* prestigious
pres-to, -ta *adj.* prompt
pre-su-mi-ble *adj.* presumable
pre-su-mir *v.* to presume
pre-sun-cion *f.* presumption
pre-sun-tuo-so, -sa *adj.* presumptuous
pre-su-po-ner *v.* to presuppose
pre-su-po-si-cion *f.* presupposition
pre-su-pues-ta-rio, -ria *adj.* budgetary
pre-su-ri-zar *v.* to pressurize
pre-ten-cio-so, -sa *adj.* pretentious
pre-ten-der *v.* to attempt; to pretend
pre-ten-dien-te *adj.* pretending to
pre-ten-sion *f.* desire
pre-ten-sio-so, -sa *adj.* pretentious
pre-va-le-cer *v.* to prevail
pre-va-le-cien-te *adj.* prevailing
pre-va-ler *v.* to prevail
pre-ven-cion *f.* prevention
pre-ve-nir *v.* to prepare; to prevent
pre-ven-ti-vo, -va *adj.* preventive
prez *m.* glory

pri-ma, -mo f., m. cousin
pri-ma-rio, -ria adj. primary
pri-ma-te m. primate
pri-ma-ve-ra f. spring
pri-me-ro adj. prime; first
pri-mi-ti-vo adj. primitive
pri-mo-ro-so adj. delicate; exquisite
prin-ce-sa f. princess
prin-ci-pa-do m. principality
prin-ci-pal adj. leading; master; principal
prin-ci-pal-men-te adv. principally
prin-ci-pe m. prince
prin-ci-pes-co, -ca adj. princely
prin-ci-pian-te, -ta adj. beginning
prin-ci-piar v. to begin
prin-ci-pio m. beginning
prin-go-so, -sa adj. greasy
prio-ri-dad f. priority
pri-sa f. haste
pri-sion f. prison
pri-sio-ne-ro, -ra m., f. prisoner
pris-ma m. prism
pris-ti-no, -na adj. pristine
pri-va-do adj. private
pri-va-ti-zar v. to privatize
pri-vi-le-gio m. privilege
pro-ba-bi-li-dad f. probability
pro-ba-ble adj. probable
pro-bar v. to prove; to try
pro-bi-dad f. probity
pro-ble-ma m. problem
pro-ble-má-ti-co, -ca adj. problematic
pro-bo, -ba adj. upright
pro-ce-di-mien-to m. procedure
pro-ce-sar v. to prosecute
pro-ce-sión f. procession
pro-ce-so m. action
pro-cla-ma-cion f. proclamation
pro-cla-mar v. to announce; to proclaim
pro-cre-a-cion f. procreation
pro-cre-ar v. to produce; to procreate
pro-di-gar v. to waste

pró-di-go adj. lavish; spendthrift
pro-di-gio-so, -sa adj. marvelous
pro-duc-cion f. turnout; production
pro-du-cir v. to yield; to produce
pro-duc-ti-vi-dad f. productivity
pro-duc-ti-vo, -va adj. productive
pro-duc-to, -ta m. product
pro-fa-nar v. to disgrace
pro-fe-sar v. to teach; to practice
pro-fe-sion f. vocation; job; profession
pro-fe-sio-nal adj. professional
pro-fe-sor, -ra m., f. professor; teacher
pro-fi-la-xis f. prophylaxis
pro-fun-di-dad f. profundity
pro-fun-do, -da adj. profound; deep
pro-fu-sion f. profusion
pro-du-so, -sa adj. profuse
pro-gra-ma m. program
pro-gra-ma-cion f. programming
pro-gra-mar v. to program
pro-gre-sar v. to progress
pro-gre-sion f. progress
pro-gre-sis-ta adj. progressive
pro-gre-so m. progress
pro-hi-bi-ción f. prohibition
pro-hi-bi-do, -da adj. forbidden
pro-hi-bir v. to prohibit something
pro-hi-bi-ti-vo, -va adj. prohibitive
pro-li-fe-ra-cion f. proliferation
pro-li-fe-rar v. to proliferate
pro-li-fi-co, -ca adj. prolific
pró-lo-go m. prologue
pro-lon-ga-do, -da adj. prolonged
pro-lon-gar v. to lengthen
pro-me-dio m. average

pro-me-sa *f.* vow; promise
pro-me-te-dor, -ra *adj.* promising
pro-me-ter *v.* to promise
pro-mi-nen-te *adj.* prominent
pro-mi-so-rio, -ria *adj.* promising
pro-mo-ción *f.* promotion
pro-mo-cio-nar *v.* to promote
pro-mo-ve-dor, -ra *adj.* promoter; promoting
pro-mo-ver *v.* to promote
pro-no, -na *adj.* prone
pro-nom-bre *m.* pronoun
pro-no-mi-nal *adj.* pronominal
pro-nos-ti-car *v.* to predict
pron-ti-tud *f.* promptness
pron-to *adj.* prompt
pro-nun-cia-ción *f.* pronunciation
pro-nun-ciar *v.* to pronounce
pro-pa-ga-ción *f.* propagation
pro-pa-lar *v.* to divulge
pro-pen-so, -sa *adj.* prone
pro-pie-dad *f.* estate
pro-pi-na *f.* gratuity
pro-pio *adj.* proper
pro-po-ne-dor, -ra *adj.* proposing
pro-po-ner *v.* to intend
pro-por-ción *f.* proportion
pro-por-cio-nal *adj.* proportional
pro-po-si-cion *f.* motion; proposition
pro-pó-si-to *m.* purpose; intention
pro-pues-ta *f.* proposal
pro-pug-nar *v.* to advocate
pro-pul-sar *v.* to push
pro-pul-sión *f.* propulsion
pro-rra-te-ar *v.* to prorate
pró-rro-gar *v.* to extend
pro-sa *f.* prose
pro-sia-co, -ca *adj.* prosaic
pros-cri-bir *v.* to proscribe
pros-crip-ción *f.* proscription
pros-pec-to *m.* prospectus
pros-pe-rar *v.* to thrive; to prosper

pros-pe-ri-dad *f.* prosperity
pros-pe-ro, -ra *adj.* prosperous
prós-ta-ta *f.* prostate
pros-ti-tu-ción *f.* prostitution
pro-tec-ción *f.* protection
pro-tec-tor, -ra *adj.* supporting; protective
pro-te-ger *v.* to defend; to protect
pro-te-í-na *f.* protein
pro-tes-ta *f.* protest
pro-tes-tar *v.* to profess
pro-tes-to *m.* protest
protón *m.* proton
pro-to-ti-po *m.* prototype
pro-to-zo-a-rio *m.* protozoan
pro-ve-cho *m.* profit; benefit
pro-ve-cho-so *adj.* profitable
pro-veer *v.* to cater; to fill; to provide
pro-vi-den-cial *adj.* providential
pro-vi-sión *f.* provision
pro-vo-ca-cion *f.* provocation
pro-vo-car *v.* to antagonize
próx-i-mo *adj.* near
pru-den-cia *f.* prudence
psi-co-lo-gia *f.* psychology
pu-bli-ca-ción *f.* publication
pu-bli-car *v.* to publish
pú-bli-co *m.* public
pue-blo *m.* nation; town
puer-ta *f.* entrance
pues *conj.* then; for
pul-gar *m.* thumb
pu-lir *v.* to shine; to polish
pul-món *m.* lung
pun-ta *f.* point
pun-to *m.* dot; point
pu-ro *adj.* pure
púr-pu-ra *f.* purple

quan-tum *m.* quantum
que *pron.* that; whom
qué *adj.* what; which
que-bra-cho *m.* quebracho
que-bra-da *f.* gap; ravine

que-bra-di-zo, -za adj. fragile

que-bra-do adj. rough; broken; bankrupt

que-bra-du-ra f. rupture; fracture; crack

que-bra-jar v. to crack

que-bran-ta-dor, -ra adj. crushing; breaking

que-bran-ta-mien-to m. cracking; deterioration; breaking

que-bran-tar v. to crush; to break; to weaken

que-bran-to m. sorrow; loss

que-brar v. to break

que-da-men-te adv. calmly

que-dar v. to stay; to be; to remain

que-do, -da adj. calm

que-jar-se v. to complain; to whine

que-ji-do m. groan

que-jo-so adj. complaining

que-ma f. burning

que-ma-de-ro m. incinerator

que-ma-do, -da adj. burnt; burned out

que-ma-dor, -ra adj. burning

que-mar v. to heat up; to burn

que-ma-zón f. burning

que-re-lla f. lament; quarrel

que-re-llan-te adj. complaining

que-rer v. to desire; to want m. love; affection

que-ri-do, -da adj. beloved

que-so m. cheese

quie-bra f. crack

quien pron. who

quie-to, -ta adj. quiet

quí-mi-ca f. chemistry

quí-mi-co adj. chemical

quin-ce adj. fifteen

quin-to adj. fifth

qui-tar v. to forbid; to remove; to take away

rá-ba-no m. radish

ra-bi m. rabbi

ra-bia f. rabies

ra-biar v. to have rabies

ra-bi-no m. rabbi

ra-bio-so adj. furious

ra-bo m. stem; tail

ra-cial adj. racial

ra-ci-mo m. bunch; cluster

ra-ción f. allowance; ration

ra-cio-nal adj. rational

ra-cio-na-li-dad f. rationality

ra-cio-na-lis-mo m. rationalism

ra-cio-na-lis-ta adj. rationalist

ra-cio-na-li-zar v. to rationalize about

ra-cio-nar v. to ration

ra-cha f. gust

ra-da f. bay

ra-dar m. radar

ra-dia-ción f. radiation

ra-diac-ti-vi-dad f. radioactivity

ra-diac-ti-vo, -va adj. radioactive

ra-dia-dor m. radiator

ra-dial adj. radial

ra-dian-te adj. radiant

ra-diar v. to radiate

ra-di-cal adj. radical

ra-dio m. radio; radius

ra-dio-di-fun-dir v. to broadcast

ra-dio-gra-fí-a f. radiography

ra-dio-gra-ma f. radiogram

ra-dio-lo-gi-a f. radiology

ra-dio-lo-go, -ga m., f. radiologist

ra-dios-co-pia f. radioscopy

ra-er v. to scrape

raid m. raid

ra-i-do, -da adj. worn

ra-já f. splinter; crack

ra-ja-do, -da adj. cracked

ra-ja-du-ra f. crack

ra-jar v. to sliver; crack

ra-lo, -la adj. thin

ra-llar v. to grate

ra-ma f. branch

ra-ma-da f. grove

ra-mal m. flight; strand

ram-bla *f.* boulevard
ra-mi-fi-ca-cion *f.* ramification
ra-mi-fi-car-se *v.* to branch
ra-mi-lle-te *m.* cluster
ra-mo *m.* bouquet
ra-mo-ne-ar *v.* to graze
ram-pa *f.* ramp
ra-na *f.* frog
ran-ci-dez *f.* rancidity
ran-cio *adj.* rancid
ran-cho *m.* farm
ra-pa-ci-dad *f.* rapacity
ra-par *v.* to crop; to shave
ra-pi-da-men-te *adv.* rapidly
ra-pi-do *adj.* fast; express; rapid
rap-so-dia *f.* rhapsody
rap-to *m.* rapture
ra-que-ta *f.* racket
ra-qui-tis-mo *m.* rickets
ra-ra-men-te *adv.* rarely
ra-re-za *f.* rarity
ra-ro *adj.* rare; bizarre; odd
ra-sar *v.* to brush
ras-ca-cie-los *m.* skyscraper
ras-ca-du-ra *f.* scratch
ras-car *v.* to scrape
ras-ca-zon *f.* itch
ras-ga-du-ra *f.* tear
ras-gar *v.* to tear
ras-go *m.* feature; trait
ras-gon *m.* tear
ras-gu-ñar *v.* to scratch
ras-gu-no *m.* scratch
ra-so, -sa *adj.* level; flat
ras-pa-dor *m.* scraper
ras-pa-du-ra *f.* rasping
ras-pan-te *adj.* abrasive
ras-par *v.* to erase; to scrape
ras-tra *f.* trail
ras-tre-ar *v.* to trail
ras-tri-llo *m.* rake
ra-su-ra *f.* shaving
ra-su-rar *v.* to shave
ra-ta *f.* rat
ra-te-ro, -ra *m., f.* thief
ra-ti-fi-ca-cion *f.* ratification
ra-ti-fi-car *v.* ratificar
ra-ti-fi-ca-to-rio, -ria *adj.* ratifying
ra-to *m.* while
ra-ton *m.* mouse

ra-ya *f.* stripe; line
ra-yar *v.* to rule; to streak
ra-yo *m.* beam; ray
ra-yon *m.* rayon
ra-za *f.* race
ra-zon *f.* cause
ra-zo-na-ble *adj.* rational; reasonable
ra-zo-na-do, -da *adj.* reasoned
ra-zo-nar *v.* to reason
re-ac-cion *f.* reaction
re-ac-cio-nar *v.* to react
re-ac-ti-va-cion *f.* reactivation
re-ac-ti-var *v.* to reactivate
re-a-dap-ta-cion *f.* readaptation
re-a-dap-tar *v.* to readapt
re-a-fir-mar *v.* to reaffirm
re-a-jus-tar *v.* to readjust
re-a-jus-te *m.* readjustment
real *adj.* true; real; royal
re-a-le-za *f.* royalty
rea-li-dad *f.* reality
rea-lis-ta *adj.* realistic
re-a-li-za-dor, -ra *adj.* fulfilling
rea-li-zar *v.* to accomplish; to fulfil; realize
re-al-zar *v.* to enhance
re-a-ni-mar *v.* to reanimate
re-a-nu-da-cion *f.* resumption
re-a-nu-dar *v.* to resume
re-a-pa-re-cer *v.* to reappear
rea-ta *f.* rope
re-a-vi-var *v.* to revive
re-ba-ja *f.* reduction
re-ba-jar *v.* to reduce
re-ba-na-da *f.* slice
re-ba-nar *v.* to slice
re-ba-ño *m.* flock
re-be-lar-se *v.* to rebel; to revolt
re-bel-de *adj.* rebel
re-be-lion *f.* revolt
re-bor-de *m.* border
re-bo-tar *v.* to bounce
re-buz-no *m.* braying
re-ca-bar *v.* to request
re-ca-do *m.* message
re-ca-er *v.* to relapse

re-cal-car v. to squeeze

re-ca-len-ta-mien-to m. reheating

re-ca-len-tar v. to reheat

re-ca-pa-ci-tar v. to reconsider

re-ca-pi-tu-la-cion m. recapitulation

re-ca-pi-tu-lar v. to recapitulate

re-car-gar v. to overload; to reload

re-cau-dar v. to collect

re-cau-do m. collection

re-ce-lar v. to suspect

re-ce-lo m. jealousy; mistrust; suspicion

re-ce-lo-so, sa adj. suspicious

re-cep-cion f. reception

re-cep-cio-nis-ta m., f. receptionist

re-cep-ta-cu-lo m. receptacle

re-cep-ti-vi-dad f. receptivity

re-cep-ti-vo adj. receptive

re-ce-sion f. recession

re-ce-tar v. to prescribe

re-ci-bi-dor, -ra adj. receiving

re-ci-bi-mien-to m. reception

re-ci-bir v. to accept; receive

re-ci-bo m. receipt

re-ci-clar v. to recycle

re-cién adv. recently

re-cien-te adj. recent

re-cien-te-men-te adv. recently

re-cio, -cia adj. severe; strong

re-ci-pro-car v. to reciprocate

re-ci-pro-ci-dad f. reciprocity

re-ci-ta-ción f. recitation

re-ci-tar v. to recite

re-cla-ma-cion f. complaint

re-cla-ma-dor adj. claiming

re-cla-mar v. to reclaim

re-cli-nar v. to rest on

re-cluir v. to imprison

re-clu-sion f. imprisonment

re-clu-so m. recluse

re-clu-ta f. recruitment

re-clu-ta-mien-to m. recruitment

re-clu-tar v. to recruit

re-co-brar v. to regain; to recover

re-co-bro m. recovery

re-co-do m. bend

re-co-ge-dor, -ra adj. collecting

re-co-gar v. to collect; to gather; to shorten

re-co-gi-mien-to m. retirement

re-co-lec-ción f. collection

re-co-lec-tar v. to gather

re-co-men-da-ble adj. recommendable

re-co-men-da-cion f. recommendation

re-co-men-dar v. to recommend

re-com-pen-sa f. to reward

re-com-pen-sar v. to compensate

re-con-ci-lia-ble adj. reconcilalbe

re-con-ci-lia-ción f. reconciliation

re-con-ci-liar v. to reconcile

re-con-for-tar v. to comfort

re-co-no-cer v. to acknowledge

re-co-no-ci-do, -da adj. gratitude; recognition

re-con-quis-tar v. to recover

re-con-si-de-rar v. reconsider

re-cons-ti-tuir v. to reconstitute

re-cons-truc-cion f. reconstruction

re-cons-truir v. to reconstruct

re-con-tar v. to recount

re-co-pi-la-cion f. compilation

re-co-pi-la-dor m. compiler

re-co-pi-lar v. to compile

re-cor-da-cion f. memory

re-cor-dar v. to remember

re-co-rrer v. to travel

re-cor-tar v. to reduce

re-cre-a-ción f. recreation

re-cre-ar v. to re-create

re-crea-ti-vo adj. recreational

re-creo *m.* recreation

re-cri-mi-na-sion *f.* recrimination

re-cru-de-ci-mien-ti *m.* worsening

rec-tal *adj.* rectal

rec-ta-men-te *adv.* justly

rec-tan-gu-lar *adj.* rectangle

rec-tán-gu-lo *adj.* rectangular

rec-ti-fi-ca-cion *f.* rectification

rec-ti-fi-car *v.* to recify

rec-ti-tud *f.* honesty

rec-to *adj.* right; upright

re-cu-brir *v.* tocover

re-cuen-to *m.* recount

re-cuer-do *m.* menory; remembrance

re-cu-la-da *f.* backing up

re-cu-pe-ra-ble *adj.* recoverable

re-cu-pe-ra-ción *f.* recovery

re-cu-pe-rar *v.* to recover

re-cu-rren-te *adj.* recurrent

re-cu-rrir *v.* to return

re-cur-so *m.* remedy; resource

re-cu-sa-cion *f.* rejection

re-cu-sar *v.* to refuse

re-cha-za-mien-to *m.* rejection

re-cha-zar *v.* to reject; rebuff

re-cha-zo *m.* rejection

re-chi-fla *f.* hissing

re-chi-flar *v.* to hiss

re-dac-cion *f.* writing

re-dac-tar *v.* to edit

ra-da-da *f.* roundup

re-de-ci-lla *f.* mesh

re-den-ción *f.* redemption

re-dil *m.* fold

re-di-mir *v.* to redeem

ré-di-to *m.* rent

re-di-tuar *v.* to yield

re-do-blar *v.* to fold

re-don-dez *f.* roundness

re-don-do, -da *adj.* round

re-duc-ción *f.* reduction

re-du-ci-do *adj.* reduced

re-du-cir *v.* to shorten; reduce

re-duc-tor, -ra *adj.* reducing

re-dun-dan-cia *f.* redundancy

re-dun-dan-te *adj.* redundant

re-dun-dar *v.* to overflow

re-e-le-gir *v.* to reelect

re-em-bol-sa-ble *adj.* reimbursable

re-em-bol-sar *v.* to reimburse

re-em-bol-so *m.* reimbursement

re-em-pla-zar *v.* to replace

re-em-pla-zo *m.* substitution

re-en-car-na-cion *f.* reincarnation

re-es-truc-tu-ra-cion restructuring

re-es-truc-tu-rar *v.* to restructure

re-fec-to-rio *m.* refectory

re-fe-ren-cia *f.* refernce

re-fe-ren-te *adj.* referring

re-fe-rir *v.* to refer; to tell

re-fi-na-do, -da *adj.* refined

re-fi-na-mien-to *m.* refinement

re-fi-nar *v.* to refine

re-fi-ne-ri-a *f.* refinery

re-fle-jar *v.* to speculate; to reflect

re-fle-xión *f.* reflection

re-fle-xi-vo, -va *adj.* reflective

re-for-ma *f.* reform

re-for-ma-cion *f.* reformation

re-for-mar *v.* to reform

re-for-ma-to-rio, -ria *adj.* reformatory

re-for-mis-ta *adj.* reformist

re-for-za-do, -da *adj.* reinforced

re-for-zar *v.* to reinforce

re-frac-ción *f.* refraction

re-frac-tar *v.* to refract

re-fre-nar *v.* to restrain

re-fres-can-te *adj.* refreshing

re-fres-car *v.* to refresh

re-fres-co *m.* refreshment

re-fri-ge-ra-ción *f.* refrigeration

re-fir-ge-ra-dor *m.* refrigerator

re-fri-ge-rar v. to refrigerate
re-fri-to, -ta adj. refried
re-fuer-zo m. reinforcement
re-fu-gia-do, -da adj. refugee
re-fu-gio m. shelter; refuge
re-ful-gen-te adj. refulgent
re-fun-fu-nar v. to grumble
re-fun-fu-no m. grumble
re-fu-ta-cion f. rebuttal
re-fu-tar v. to rebut
re-ga-la-do, -da adj. easy; dainty
re-ga-lar v. to give away
re-ga-liz m. licorice
re-ga-lo m. present
re-ga-ñar v. to argue
re-gar v. to bathe
re-ga-zo m. lap
re-ge-ne-ra-cion f. regeneration
re-ge-ne-ra-dor, -ra m., f. regenerator
re-ge-ne-rar v. to regenerate
re-gen-tar v. to direct
ré-gi-men m. regimen
re-gi-men-tar v. to regiment
re-gio, -gia adj. regal
re-gión f. area; region
re-gio-nal adj. regional
re-gio-na-lis-mo m. regionalism
re-gir v. to govern
re-gis-tra-dor, -ra m., f. register, adj. registering
re-gis-trar v. to record; to register
re-gis-tro m. search; registration; registry; register
re-gla f. rule
re-gla-men-ta-cion f. regulation
re-gla-men-tar v. to regulate
re-glar v. to regulate
re-go-ci-jo m. joy
re-go-de-o m. pleasure
re-gre-sar v. to return
re-gre-sion f. regression
re-gre-si-vo adj. regressive
re-gre-so m. return
re-gue-ro m. trail; stream
re-gu-la-ción f. regulation

re-gu-la-dor m. regulator
re-gu-lar adj. regular
re-gu-la-ri-dad f. regularity
re-gu-la-ri-zar v. to regularize
re-gu-lar-men-te adv. regularly
re-gur-gi-ta-ción f. regurgitation
re-gur-gi-tar v. to regurgitate
re-ha-bi-li-ta-ción f. rehabilitation
re-ha-bi-li-tar v. to rehabilitate
re-ha-cer v. to remake
re-ho-gar v. to brown
re-huir v. to avoid
re-hu-sar v. to refuse
re-im-pri-mir v. to reprint
rei-na f. queen
rei-na-do m. reign
rei-nan-te adj. ruling
rei-nar v. to reign
re-in-ci-den-te adj. relapsing
re-in-ci-dir v. to relapse
re-in-cor-po-ra-ción f. reincorporation
re-in-cor-po-rar v. to reincorporate
re-in-gre-sar v. to re-enter something
rei-no m. kingdom
re-ins-ta-la-ción f. reinstallation
re-ins-ta-lar v. to reinstall
re-in-te-gra-ción f. reintegration
re-in-te-grar v. to reintegrate
re-in-te-gro m. reintegration
re-ir(se) v. to laugh
rei-te-ra-ción f. reiteration
rei-te-rar v. to reiterate
rei-te-ra-ti-vo, -va adj. reiterative
rei-vin-di-car v. to recover
re-jun-tar v. to gather
re-ju-ve-ne-cer v. to rejuvenate
re-la-cion f. account; relation
re-la-cio-na-do, -da adj. related
re-la-cio-nar v. to relate
re-la-ja-ción f. relaxation

re-la-ja-do, -da *adj.* relaxed

re-la-jar *v.* to relax

re-la-mar *v.* to lick

re-lám-pa-go *m.* lightning

re-lám-pa-gue-o *m.* lightning

re-lap-so, -sa *adj.* relapsed

re-la-tar *v.* to narrate

re-la-ti-vi-dad *f.* relativity

re-la-ti-vo, -va *adj.* relative

re-la-to *m.* story; narration

re-le-gar *v.* to relegate

re-le-var *v.* to relieve; to praise

re-li-ca-rio *m.* reliquary

re-li-ve *m.* relief

re-li-gión *f.* religion

re-li-gio-si-dad *f.* religiosity

re-li-gio-so *adj.* religious

re-loj *m.* watch; clock

re-lo-je-ri-a *f.* clockmaking

re-lo-je-ro, -ra *m., f.* watchmaker

re-lu-cir *v.* to shine

re-lum-bran-te *adj.* dazzling

re-lum-brar *v.* to dazzle

re-lle-nar *v.* to refill

re-ma-llar *v.* to mend

re-mar *v.* to row

re-ma-tar *v.* to use up

re-ma-te *m.* conclusion

re-me-dar *v.* to mimic

re-me-dia-ble *adj.* remediable

re-me-diar *v.* to cure; to remedy

re-mem-bran-za *f.* remembrance

re-me-mo-ra-cion *f.* remembrance

re-me-mo-rar *v.* to remember something

re-men-dar *v.* to mend; to repair

re-mem-don, -na *m., f.*

re-mi-sión *f.* remission

re-mi-so, -sa *adj.* remiss

re-mi-tne-te *adj.* remitting

re-mi-tir *v.* to forgive; to remit; to diminish

re-mo *m.* oar

re-mo-la-cha *f.* beet

re-mol-car *v.* to tow

re-mo-io-ne-ar *v.* to loaf

re-mol-que *m.* tow truck

re-mon-tar *v.* to remount; to surmount

re-mor-di-mien-to *m.* remorse

re-mo-to *adj.* faraway

re-mo-ver *v.* to remove; to move; to dismiss

re-mo-zar *v.* to rejuvenate

re-mu-ne-ra-ción *f.* remuneration

re-mu-ne-rar *v.* to remunerate

re-mu-ne-ra-ti-vo, -va *adj.* remunerative

re-na-ci-mien-to *m.* revival

re-nal *adj.* renal

ren-ci-lla *f.* quarrel

ren-cor *m.* spite; bitterness; rancor

ren-co-ro-so *adj.* bitter; resentful

ren-di-do *adj.* submissive; obsequious

ren-di-mien-to *m.* submissiveness; yield

ren-dir *v.* to yield; to surrender; to defeat

ren-gue-ar *v.* to limp

re-no *m.* reindeer

re-nom-bra-do, -da *adj.* renowned

re-nom-bre *m.* renown

re-no-va-ción *f.* renovation

re-no-va-do *adj.* renewed

re-no-var *v.* to renovate; to reform

ren-ta *f.* interest; rent; income

ren-ta-ble *adj.* profitable

ren-tar *v.* to rent

re-nuen-cia *f.* reluctance

re-nuen-te *adj.* reluctant

re-nun-cia *f.* renunciation

re-nun-cia-cion *f.* renunciation

re-nun-ciar *v.* to reject; to surrender; to waive; to renounce

re-ñi-dor, -ra *adj.* quarrelsome

re-ñir *v.* to fight; to quarrel with another

re-or-ga-ni-za-cion f. reorganization

re-or-ga-ni-zar v. to reorganize

re-pa-ra-ción f. repair

re-pa-ra-dor, -ra m., f. repairer

re-pa-rar v. to mend; repair

re-pa-ro m. protection; objection

re-par-ti-cion f. sharing

re-par-ti-dor, -ra m., f. distributor

re-par-tir v. to share; to apportion; to divide

re-par-to m. delivery

re-pa-sar v. to review; to revise

re-pa-so m. review

re-pa-tria-ción f. repatrination

re-pa-triar v. to repatriate

re-pe-len-te adj. repellent

re-pe-ler v. to repel

re-pen-te m. start

re-pen-ti-no, -na adj. repercussion

re-per-cu-sion f. repercussion

re-per-cu-tir v. to reverberate

re-per-to-rio m. repertoire

re-pe-ti-cion f. repetition

re-pe-tir v. to repeat

re-pe-ti-ti-vo, -va adj. repetitive

re-pi-que-te-ar v. to beat; to ring

re-pi-sa f. shelf

re-plan-tar v. to replant

re-plan-te-ar v. to restate

re-ple-to, -ta adj. full

ré-pli-ca f. answer

re-pli-car v. to reply; to respond

re-po-bla-cion f. repopulation

re-po-blar v. to repopulate

re-po-llo m. cabbage

re-po-ner v. to replace; to revive

re-por-tar v. to bring

re-pór-te-ro, -ra adj. reporting

re-po-sa-do adj. quiet

re-po-sar v. to lie

re-po-si-ción f. reposition

re-po-so m. repose

re-pren-der v. to reprimand

re-pren-sión f. reprimand

re-pre-sa-lia f. reprisal

re-pre-sen-ta-ción f. representation

re-pre-sen-tan-te adj. representing

re-pre-sen-tar v. to represent; to appear to be

re-pre-sen-ta-ti-vo, -va adj. representative

re-pre-sión f. repression

re-pre-si-vo, -va adj. repressive

re-pri-men-da f. reprimand

re-pri-mir v. to repress

re-pro-char v. to reproach

re-pro-che m. rebuke; reproach

re-pro-duc-ción f. reproduction

re-pro-du-cir v. to reproduce

rep-tar v. to crawl

rep-til m. reptile

re-pú-bli-ca f. republic

re-pu-bli-ca-no, na adj. republican

re-pu-dia-cion f. repudiation

re-pu-diar v. to repudiate

re-pug-nan-cia f. repugnance

re-pug-nan-te adj. repugnant

re-pul-gar v. to hem

re-pul-sar v. to reject

re-pul-sion f. repulsion

re-pul-si-vo, -va adj. repulsive

re-pun-tar v. to turn

re-pun-te adj. turning

re-que-brar v. to break something again

re-que-ri-mien-to m. requirement

re-que-rir v. to want; to require

re-quiem m. requiem

re-qui-sar v. to requisition

re-qui-si-cion f. requisition

re-qui-si-to *m.* requirement

re-sa-la-do, -da *adj.* charming

re-sar-cir *v.* to indemnify

res-ba-lar *v.* to glide

res-ca-tar *v.* to rescue; to recover

res-ca-te *m.* rescue

res-cin-dir *v.* to rescind

res-ci-sion *f.* rescission

re-sen-ti-do, -da *adj.* resentful

re-sen-ti-mien-to *m.* resentment

re-sen-tir-se *v.* to feel hurt

re-se-ña *f.* account; inspection

re-se-ñar *v.* to review; to inspect

re-ser-va *f.* reserve

re-ser-va-cion *f.* reservation

re-ser-va-do, -da *adj.* reserved; confidential

re-ser-var *v.* to reserve

res-fria-do *m.* cold

res-friar *v.* to cool

res-guar-dar *v.* to protect

res-guar-do *m.* guard; protection

re-si-den-cia *f.* residence

re-si-den-cial *adj.* residential

re-si-den-te *m., f.* resident

re-si-dir *v.* to live; reside

re-si-duo *m.* residue

re-sig-na-cion *f.* resignation

re-sis-ten-cia *f.* endurance; resistance

re-sis-ten-te *adj.* resistant

re-sis-tir *v.* to oppose; to resist

re-so-lu-cion *f.* resolution

re-so-lu-to, -ta *adj.* resolute

re-sol-ver *v.* to settle; to solve; to resolve

re-so-nan-cia *f.* resonance

re-so-nan-te *adj.* resounding

re-so-nar *v.* to resound

re-so-pli-do *m.* puffing

res-pal-dar *v.* to back something or someone

res-pal-do *m.* back

res-pec-ti-vo *adj.* respective

res-pec-to *m.* respect

res-pe-ta-ble *adj.* respectable

res-pe-tar *v.* to respect

res-pe-to *m.* respect

res-pe-tuo-so, -sa *adj.* respectful

res-pi-ra-cion *f.* respiration

res-pi-ra-dor *m.* respirator

res-pi-rar *v.* to inhale and exhale; to breath

res-pi-ro *m.* respite

res-plan-dor *m.* glow; brightness

res-pon-der *v.* to reply; to respond

res-pon-sa-ble *adj.* responsible

res-pues-ta *f.* answer; response

res-que-brar *v.* to crack

res-que-mor *m.* remorse

res-ta-ble-cer *v.* to reestablish

res-ta-ble-ci-mien-to *m.* reestablishment

res-ta-llar *v.* to crack

res-tau-ra-cion *f.* restoration

res-tau-ra-dor, -ra *m., f.* restorer

res-tau-ran-te *m.* restaurant

res-tau-rar *v.* to restore

res-ti-tu-cion *f.* restitution

res-to *m.* remainder

res-tric-cion *f.* restriction

res-tric-ti-vo, -va *adj.* restrictive

res-trin-gir *v.* to restrict

re-su-ci-tar *v.* to resuscitate

re-sul-ta *f.* result

re-sul-ta-do *m.* issue; result

re-sul-tar *v.* to result

re-su-mir *v.* to summarize

re-sur-gir *v.* to reappear

re-su-rrec-cion *f.* resurrection

re-tar-dar *v.* to delay

re-ten-cion *f.* retention

re-te-ner *v.* to keep; to retain

re-ti-na *f.* retina

re-ti-ni-tis *f.* retinitis

re-ti-ra-da *f.* retreat

re-ti-ra-do, -da *adj.* retired

re-ti-rar *v.* to retire; to

withdraw; to retract

re-ti-ro *m.* retreat; withdrawal

re-to *m.* challenge

re-to-ñar *v.* to sprout

re-tor-cer *v.* to twist

re-tor-ci-do, -da *adj.* twisted

re-tor-ci-mien-to *m.* twisting

re-tó-ri-co, -ca *adj.* rhetorical

re-tor-nar *v.* to return

re-to-zar *v.* to frolic

re-to-zo *m.* frolic

re-to-zon, -ona *adj.* frolicsome

re-trac-ción *f.* retraction

re-trac-tar *v.* to recant; to retract

re-trac-til *adj.* retractable

re-tra-er *v.* to dissuade

re-tra-i-do, -da *adj.* withdrawn

re-trai-mien-to *m.* seclusion

re-trans-mi-tir *v.* to retransmit

re-tra-sar *v.* to delay

re-tra-to *m.* portrait

re-tre-ta *f.* retreat

re-tri-bu-ción *f.* retribution

re-tri-buir *v.* to reward

re-tro-ac-ti-vo, -va *adj.* retroactive

re-tro-gra-do, -da *adj.* retrograde

re-tros-pec-ción *f.* retrospection

re-tum-bar *v.* to resound

reu-ma-ti-co *adj.* rheumatic

reu-ma-tis-mo *m.* rheumatism

reu-nión *f.* meeting; reunion

reu-nir *v.* to gather; to mass; to meet

re-va-li-da-ción *f.* revalidation

re-va-li-dar *v.* to revalidate

re-va-lo-ri-zar *v.* to revalue

re-van-cha *f.* revenge

re-ve-la-cion *f.* revelation

re-ve-la-dor, -ra *adj.* revealing

re-ve-lar *v.* to betray; to reveal

re-ven-der *v.* to resell

re-ven-tar *v.* to blow; to

burst

re-ven-tion *m.* burst

re-ver *v.* to review

re-ver-be-rar *v.* to reverberate

re-ve-ren-cia *f.* reverence

re-ve-ren-ciar *v.* to revere

re-ve-ren-do, -da *adj.* reverend

re-ve-ren-te *adj.* respectful

re-ver-so *m.* reverse

re-ver-tir *v.* to revert

re-ves-tir *v.* to cover

re-vi-sar *v.* to review

re-vi-sión *f.* revision

re-vi-sor, -ra *m., f.* inspector

re-vis-ta *f.* magazine

re-vis-te-ro, -ra *m., f.* reviewer

re-vi-ta-li-zar *v.* to revitalize

re-vi-vi-fi-car *v.* to revive

re-vi-vir *v.* to revive

re-vo-ca-ción *f.* revocation

re-vo-car *v.* to repeal; to revoke

re-vol-con *m.* fall

re-vo-lo-te-ar *v.* to flutter

re-vo-lu-ción *f.* revolution

re-vo-lu-cio-nar *v.* to revolutionize

re-vo-lu-cio-na-rio *adj.* revolutionary

re-vól-ver *v.* to revolve; to mix; to shake

re-vol-ver *m.* revolver

re-vo-que *m.* plaster

re-vue-lo *m.* commotion

rey *m.* king

re-zar *v.* to pray; to say something

re-zon-gar *v.* to grumble

ri-be-ra *f.* shore

ri-be-te-a-do *adj.* trimmed

ri-be-te-ar *v.* to hem

ri-ca-men-te *adv.* richly

ri-co *adj.* wealthy; rich

ri-di-cu-la-men-te *adv.* ridiculously

ri-di-cu-li-zar *v.* to ridicule

ri-di-cu-lo *adj.* ridiculous

riel *m.* rail

rien-da *f.* rein

ries-go *m.* danger; risk

ri-fa *f.* raffle
ri-far *v.* to raffle off
ri-fle *m.* rifle
ri-gi-do *adj.* stiff; rigid
ri-gor *m.* rigor
ri-gu-ro-so *adj.* severe; rigorous
ri-ma *f.* rhyme
ri-mar *v.* to rhyme
rim-bom-ban-te *adj.* echoing
rin-cón *m.* corner
ri-no-ce-ron-te *m.* rhinoceros
ri-ña *f.* quarrel
ri-ñón *m.* kidney
rió *m.* river
ri-que-za *f.* riches
ri-sa *f.* laughter
ri-si-ble *adj.* laughable
ris-tra *f.* string
ri-sue-ño, -na *adj.* smiling
rít-mi-co *adj.* rhythmical
ri-to *m.* ceremony
ri-tual *m.* ritual
ri-val *m.* rival
ri-va-li-dad *f.* rivalry
ri-va-li-zar *v.* to rival
ri-zar *v.* to curl up
ro-bar *v.* to steal
ro-ble *m.* oak
ro-bo *m.* robbery
ro-bus-te-cer *v.* to make strong; to strengthen
ro-bus-to *adj.* hardy; strong
ro-ciar *v.* to sprinkle
ro-cin *m.* donkey
ro-cí-o *m.* sprinkle
ro-dar *v.* to tumble; to roll
ro-de-ar *v.* to circle; to ring
ro-de-o *m.* to go around
ro-de-te *m.* bun
ro-di-lla *f.* knee
ro-e-dor, -ra *adj.* gnawing
ro-er *v.* to gnaw
ro-gar *v.* to request; to pray
ro-jo *adj.* red
ro-llo *m.* roll
ro-ma-no, -na *adj.* Roman
ro-mán-ti-co *adj.* romantic
rom-bo *m.* rhombus
ro-me-ro *m.* rosemary
rom-per *v.* to smash; to break
ron *m.* rum

ron-car *v.* to snore
ron-co, -ca *adj.* hoarse
ron-que-ra *f.* hoarseness
ro-no-so, -sa *adj.* filthy
ro-pa *f.* clothing
ro-pe-ro *m.* closet
ro-sa *f.* rose
ro-sa-do, -da *adj.* pink
ro-sal *m.* rosebush
ro-sa-le-da *f.* rose garden
ros-bif *m.* roast beef
ros-ca *f.* circle
ros-tro *m.* face
ro-ta-ción *f.* rotation
ro-ta-to-rio, -ria *adj.* rotating
ro-ton-da *f.* rotunda
ro-tor *m.* rotor
ro-tu-la-do *m.* label
ro-tu-la-dor, -ra *adj.* labeling
ro-tu-lar *v.* to label
ro-za-mien-to *m.* rubbing
ro-zar *v.* to scrape; to skim
ru-be-o-la *f.* rubella
ru-bí *m.* ruby
ru-bi-cun-do, -da *adj.* ruddy
ru-bio *adj.* blonde
ru-bor *m.* blush
ru-bo-ri-zae-se *v.* to blush
ru-da *f.* rue
ru-de-za *f.* rudeness
ru-di-men-tal *adj.* rudimentary
ru-di-men-ta-rio, -ria *adj.* rudimentary
ru-di-men-to *m.* rudiment
ru-do, -da *adj.* rude
rue-da *f.* wheel
rue-do *m.* hem; edge
rue-go *m.* request
ru-gi-do *m.* roar
ru-gi-dor, -ra *adj.* roaring
ru-go-so, -sa *adj.* winkled
rui-do *m.* sound; rattle; noise
rui-do-so, -sa *adj.* noisy
ruin *adj.* poor; despicable
rui-na *f.* ruin
rui-nar *v.* to ruin
rum-bo *m.* direction
ru-mor *m.* rumor
rup-tu-ra *f.* rupture
ru-ral *adj.* rural
ru-ti-lar *v.* to shine
ru-ti-na *f.* route

sá-ba-do *m.* Saturday
sá-ba-na *f.* sheet for a bed
sa-ber *v.* to inform; to know
sa-bi-do, -da *adj.* known
sa-bi-du-rí-a *f.* knowledge
sa-bio, -bia *adj.* learned
sa-ble *m.* saber
sa-bor *m.* flavor; taste
sa-bo-re-ar *v.* to taste
sa-bo-ta-je *m.* sabotage
sa-bo-te-a-dor, -ra *adj.* sabotaging
sa-bo-te-ar *v.* to sabotage
sa-bro-so *adj.* delightful
sa-ca-cor-chos *m.* corkscrew
sa-ca-pun-tas *m.* pencil sharpener
sa-car *v.* to pull out; to get out
sa-ca-ri-na *f.* saccharin
sa-cer-do-cio *m.* priesthood
sa-cer-do-te *m.* priest
sa-cer-do-ti-sa *f.* priestess
sa-co *m.* bag
sa-cra-men-to *m.* sacrament
sa-cri-fi-car *v.* to sacrifice
sa-cri-fi-cio *m.* sacrifice
sa-cri-le-gio *m.* sacrilege
sa-cro *adj.* sacred
sa-cu-di-da *f.* tremor; shake
sa-cu-dir *v.* to beat; to tug
sá-di-co, -ca *adj.* sadistic
sa-ga *f.* saga
sa-ga-ci-dad *f.* sagacity
sa-gaz *adj.* sagacious
sa-gra-do, -da *adj.* sacred
sa-ke *m.* sake
sal *f.* salt
sa-la *f.* living room of a house
sa-la-do, -da *adj.* salted; salty
sa-la-man-dra *f.* salamander
sa-laz *f.* salacious
sal-chi-chon *m.* sausage
sal-dar *v.* to pay off something
sal-do *m.* payment
sa-le-ro *m.* saltshaker
sa-li-da *f.* ` exit; solution
sa-lien-te *adj.* salient
sa-li-no, -na *adj.* saline

sa-lir *v.* to get out; to leave
sa-li-va *n.* saliva
sa-li-val *adj.* salivary
sa-li-var *v.* to salivate
sal-mo *m.* psalm
sal-món *m.* salmon
sa-lo-bre *adj.* briny
sal-pi-car *v.* to splash
sal-pi-men-tar *v.* to season
sal-sa *f.* sauce
sal-ta-dor *m.* jumper
sal-ta-mon-tes *m.* grasshopper
sal-tar *v.* to jump; to leap; to bounce
sal-te-ar *v.* to skip
sal-to *m.* jump
sa-lu-bre *adj.* healthful
sa-lud *f.* health
sa-lu-da-ble *adj.* healthy
sa-lu-dar *v.* to salute
sa-lu-ta-cion *f.* greeting
sal-va-ción *f.* salvation
sal-va-guar-dar *v.* to safeguard
sal-va-guar-dia *f.* safeguard
sal-va-ja-da *f.* savagery
sal-va-je *adj.* untamed; wild; uncivilized
sal-var *v.* to avoid; to save; to cover
sal-via *f.* sage
sal-vo *adj.* safe
sa-an-men-te *adv.* sincerely
sa-nar *v.* to heal
san-ción *f.* sanction
san-cio-nar *v.* to sanction
san-da-lia *f.* sandal
san-da-lo *m.* sandalwood
san-dez *f.* nonsense
san-dí-a *f.* watermelon
sa-ne-a-mien-to *m.* sanitation
sa-ne-ar *v.* to right
san-grar *v.* to bleed
san-gre *f.* blood
san-gri-a *f.* sangria
san-grien-to *adj.* bloody
san-gui-jue-la *f.* leech
san-gui-na-rio, -ria *adj.* cruel
sa-ni-dad *f.* healthiness
sa-ni-ta-rio, -ria *adj.* sanitary
sa-no *adj.* unharmed;

wholesome
san-ti-dad f. sanctity
san-ti-fi-car v. to sanctify
san-to adj. blessed
san-tua-rio m. sanctuary
sa-pien-cia f. wisdom
sa-pien-te adj. wise
sa-po m. toad
sa-que-ar v. to plunder
sa-que-o m. plundering
sa-ram-pión m. measles
sar-cas-mo m. sarcasm
sar-cás-ti-co adj. sarcastic
sar-di-na f. sardine
sar-do-ni-co, -ca adj. sardonic
sar-gen-to m. sergeant
sar-no-so, -sa adj. scabby
sa-rro m. crust
sar-ta f. string
sa-sa-fras m. sassafras
sa-té-li-te m. satellite
sa-ten m. satin
sa-ti-na-do, -da adj. satiny
sá-ti-ra f. satire
sa-ti-ri-co, -ca adj. satirical
sa-ti-ri-zar v. to satirize
sa-ti-ro m. satyr
sa-tis-fac-ción f. satisfaction
sa-tis-fa-cer v. to satisfy
sa-tis-fac-to-rio, -ria adj. satisfactory
sa-tu-ra-cion f. saturation
sa-tu-ra-do, -da adj. saturated
sa-tu-rar v. to saturate
sa-xó-fo-no m. saxophone
sa-yo m. tunic
sa-zon f. season
sa-zo-na-do adj. flavorful
sa-zo-nar v. to season
se pron. herself; oneself; yourself; himself
se-ba-ce-o, -a adj. sebaceous
se-bo m. fat
se-bo-rre-a f. seborrhea
se-ca-do m. drying
se-ca-do-ra f. clothes dryer
se-can-te adj. drying
se-car v. to dry
sec-ción f. section
sec-cio-nar v. to section

se-ce-sion f. secession
se-ce-sio-nis-ta adj. secessionist
se-co adj. dried
se-cre-ción f. secretion
se-cre-ta-men-te adv. secretly
se-cre-ta-ria f. secretary
se-cre-ta-rio m. secretary
se-cre-te-ar v. to whisper
se-cre-te-o m. whispering
se-cre-to m. secret
sec-ta-rio, -ria adj. sectarian
sec-tor m. sector
sec-to-rial adj. sectorial
se-cue-la f. consequence
se-cuen-cia f. sequence
se-cues-trar v. to kidnap
se-cues-tro m. kidnapping
se-cu-lar adj. secular
se-cu-la-ri-zar v. to secularize
se-cun-dar v. to second
se-cun-da-rio, -ria adj. secondary
sed f. thirst
se-da f. silk
se-dan-te adj. sedative
se-dar v. to soothe
se-dar v. to sedate
se-da-ti-vo adj. sedative
se-den-ta-rio, -ria adj. sedentary
se-di-ción f. sedition
se-dien-to, -ta adj. thirsty
se-di-men-to m. sediment
se-do-so adj. silky
se-duc-ción f. seduction
se-du-cir v. to seduce
se-duc-ti-vo, -ra adj. seductive
se-ga-dor, -ra adj. seductive
se-gar v. to mow; to harvest
se-glar adj. secular
seg-men-ta-cion f. segmentation
seg-men-to m. segment
se-gre-ga-cion f. segregation
se-gre-ga-clo-nis-ta adj. segregationist
se-gre-gar v. to segregate
se-gui-da-men-te adv. con-

tinuously

se-gui-do *adj.* consecutive

se-gui-dor, -ra *m., f.* follower

se-guir *v.* to chase; to follow; to watch

se-gún *prep.* according to

se-gun-do *adj.* second

se-gur *m.* sickle

se-gu-ra-men-te *adv.* probably

se-gu-ri-dad *f.* safety

se-gu-ro *adj.* sure; certain

seis *adj.* six

seis-cien-tos, -tas *adj.* six hundred

se-lec-ción *f.* selection

se-lec-cio-nar *v.* to select

se-lec-ti-vo, -va *adj.* selective

se-lec-to, -ta *adj.* select

sel-va *f.* woods

se-llar *v.* to stamp

se-llo *m.* stamp

se-ma-na *f.* week

se-ma-nal *adj.* weekly

se-ma-nal-men-te *adv.* weekly

se-ma-na-rio, -ria *adj.* weekly

se-man-ti-co, -ca *adj.* semantic

sem-bra-dor, -ra *adj.* sowing

sem-brar *v.* to sow

se-me-jan-te *adj.* similar

se-me-jan-za *f.* similarity

se-men-tar *v.* to seed

se-mes-tral *adj.* semiannual

se-mes-tre *m.* semester

se-miau-to-ma-ti-co, -ca *adj.* semiautomatic

se-mi-cir-cu-lar *adj.* semicircular

se-mi-cir-cu-lo *m.* semicircle

se-mi-fi-na-lis-ta *adj.* semifinalist

se-mi-lla *f.* seed

se-mi-lle-ro *m.* nursery for plants

se-mi-nal *adj.* seminal

se-mi-na-rio *m.* seminary

se-mi-na-ris-ta *m.* seminarian

se-mo-la *f.* semolina

sem-pi-ter-no, -na *adj.* everlasting

se-na-do *m.* senate

se-na-dor *m.* senator

sen-ci-lla-men-te *adv.* simply

sen-ci-llez *f.* simplicity

sen-ci-llo, -lla *adj.* simple; easy

sen-da *f.* path; trail

se-nil *adj.* senile

se-no *m.* cavity; hollow

sen-sa-ción *f.* sensation

sen-se-cio-nal *adj.* sensational

sen-sa-cio-na-lis-ta *adj.* sensational

sen-sa-to *adj.* sensible

sen-si-bi-li-dad *f.* sensibility; sensitiveness

sen-si-bi-li-zar *v.* to sensitize

sen-si-ble *adj.* sentimental; sensitive

sen-si-ble-ri-a *f.* sentimentality

sen-si-ti-vo, -va *adj.* sensitive

sen-so-rio, -ria *adj.* sensorial

sen-sual *adj.* sensual

sen-sua-li-dad *f.* sensuality

sen-ta-do, -da *adj.* settled; seated

sen-tar *v.* to sit

sen-ten-cia *f.* sentence

sen-ten-ciar *v.* to sentence

sen-ten-cio-so, -sa *adj.* sententious

sen-ti-do, -da *adj.* heartfelt

sen-ti-men-tal *adj.* sentimental

sen-ti-mien-to *m.* sentiment

sen-tir *v.* to feel; to sense; to experience

se-ña *f.* signal; sign

se-ñal *f.* sign

se-ña-lar *v.* to point; to determine

se-ña-li-zar *v.* to put up signs

se-ñe-ro *adj.* solitary

se-ñor *adj.* Mr.; Mister

se-ño-ri-o *m.* domain; solemnity

se-ño-ri-ta f. lady; girl

se-ño-ri-to m. boy; young man

se-ñue-lo m. trap; bait

se-pa-ra-ción f. separation

se-pa-ra-da-men-te adv. separately

se-pa-ra-do adj. separated

se-pa-rar v. to divide

se-pa-ra-tis-ta adj. separatist

se-pe-lio m. burial

sep-ti-co, -ca adj. septic

sep-tiem-bre m. September

sep-ti-mo adj. seventh

sep-tua-ge-na-rio, -ria adj. septuagenarian

sep-tua-ge-si-mo, -ma adj. seventieth

se-pul-tar v. to bury

se-pul-to, -ta adj. buried

se-pul-tu-ra f. burial

se-que-dad f. dryness

se-quí-a f. drought

ser v. to be; to come from

se-ra-fin m. angel

se-re-nar v. to calm

se-re-na-ta f. serenade

se-re-ni-dad f. serenity

se-re-no, -na adj. calm

se-rial adj. serial

se-ria-men-te adv. seriously

se-rie f. series

se-rie-dad f. seriousness

se-rio adj. serious

ser-món m. sermon

ser-mo-ne-ar v. to lecture

ser-pien-te f. snake

se-rra-do, -da adj. sawed

se-rra-ní-a f. mountains

se-rrar v. to saw

se-rre-ri-a f. sawmill

se-rru-cho m. saw

ser-vi-cio m. help; service

ser-vi-dor, -ra m., f. servant

ser-vil adj. servile

ser-vi-lle-ta f. napkin

ser-vir v. to serve

se-sa-mo m. sesame

se-sen-ta adj. sexty

se-sen-ta-vo, va adj. sixtieth

ses-go m. slant

se-sión f. session

se-so m. brain

se-su-do, -da adj. wise

se-te-cien-tos, -tas adj. seven hundred

se-ten-ta adj. seventy

se-ten-ta-vo, -va adj. seventieth

se-tiem-bre m. September

seu-dó-ni-mo, -ma m. pseudonym

se-ve-ra-men-te adv. relentlessly; severly

se-ve-ri-dad f. graveness; severity

se-ve-ro, -ra adj. unyielding; severe

se-xa-ge-si-mo, -ma adj. sixtieth

sex-te-to m. sextet

sex-to adj. sixth

se-xual adj. sexual

se-xua-li-dad f. sexuality

si conj. if; adv. yes

si-bi-lan-te adj. sibilant

si-co-mo-ro m. sycamore

sie-ga f. harvesting

siem-bra f. sowing

siem-pre adv. forever; always

sien f. temple

sie-rra f. saw

sier-vo m. servant; serf

sies-ta f. nap in the afternoon

sie-te adj. seven

si-fi-lis f. syphilis

si-fi-li-ti-co, -ca adj. syphilitic

si-gi-lo m. secrecy

si-gla f. acronym

si-glo m. century

sig-ni-fi-ca-ción f. significance

sig-ni-fi-ca-do, -da adj. significant

sig-ni-fi-can-te adj. significant

sig-ni-fi-car v. to signify; to indicate

sig-ni-fi-ca-ti-vo, -va adj. significant

sig-no m. sign

si-guien-te adj. next

sí-la-ba f. syllable

si-la-be-ar v. to syllable

si-la-be-o m. syllabication

sil-ba-to *m.* whistle
sil-bi-do *m.* whistle
si-len-cia-dor *m.* silencer
si-len-ciar *v.* to silence
si-len-cio *m.* silence
si-len-cio-so *adj.* silent
si-li-co-na *f.* silicone
si-lo *m.* silo
si-lo-gis-ti-co, -ca *adj.* syllogistic
si-lue-ta *f.* outline
sil-ves-tre *adj.* wild
sil-vi-cul-tor *m.* forester
si-lla *f.* chair
si-llin *m.* seat
si-llon *m.* armchair
sim-bio-sis *f.* symbiosis
sim-bio-ti-co, -ca *adj.* symbiotic
sim-bo-li-zar *v.* to symbolize
sim-bo-lo *m.* symbol
si-me-tri-a *f.* symmetry
si-me-tri-co, -ca *adj.* symmetric
si-mien-te *f.* seed
si-mil *adj.* similar
si-mi-lar *adj.* similar
si-mi-li-tud *f.* similarity
sim-pa-ti-a *f.* congeniality; affection
sim-pa-ti-co, -ca *adj.* pleasant
sim-pa-ti-zan-te *adj.* sympathizing
sim-ple *adj.* simple
sim-ple-za *f.* simplicity
sim-pli-ci-dad *f.* simplicity
sim-pli-fi-ca-cion *f.* simplification
sim-pli-fi-car *v.* to simplify
sim-po-sio *m.* symposium
si-mu-la-cion *f.* pretense
si-mu-la-dor, -ra *m., f.* simulator
si-mul-ta-ne-o, -a *adj.* simultaneous
sin *prep.* without
si-na-go-ga *f.* synagogue
sin-ce-ri-dad *f.* sincerity
sin-ce-ro, -ra *adj.* sincere
sin-co-pa *f.* syncope
sin-co-pa-do, -da *adj.* syncopated

sin-co-pe *m.* syncope
sin-cro-ni-a *f.* synchrony
sin-cro-ni-za-cion *f.* synchronization
sin-cro-ni-zar *v.* to synchronize
sin-di-ca-li-za-cion *f.* unionization
sin-di-ca-li-zar *v.* to unionize
sin-dro-me *m.* syndrome
si-ner-gia *f.* synergy
sin-fo-ni-a *f.* symphony
sin-fo-ni-co, -ca *adj.* symphonic
sin-gu-lar *adj.* single
sin-gu-la-ri-zar *v.* to distinguish
sin-nu-me-ro *m.* countless
si-no *conj.* but; fate
si-no-ni-mia *f.* synonymy
si-no-ni-mo, -ma *adj.* synonymous
si-nop-sis *f.* synopsis
si-nop-ti-co, -ca *adj.* synoptic
sin-ta-xis *m.* syntax
sin-te-sis *f.* synthesis
sin-te-ti-co, -ca *adj.* synthetic
sin-te-ti-za-dor *m.* synthesizer
sin-te-ti-zar *v.* to synthesize
sin-to-ma *m.* symptom
sin-to-ma-ti-co, -ca *adj.* symptomatic
sin-to-ni-zar *v.* to tune
si-nuo-si-dad *f.* sinuosity
si-nuo-so, -sa *adj.* sinuous
si-qui-a-tra *m., f.* psychiatrist
si-quia-tri-a *f.* psychiatry
si-qui-co *adj.* psychic
si-quie-ra *adv.* at least
sir-vien-ta *f.* maid
sir-vien-te *m.* servant
sis-mi-co, -ca *adj.* seismic
sis-mo *m.* earthquake
sis-mo-gra-fo *m.* seismograph
sis-te-ma *m.* system
sis-te-ma-ti-za-cion *f.* systematization
sis-te-ma-ti-zar *v.* to systematize

sis-to-le *f.* systole

si-tio *m.* place

si-to, -ta *adj.* situated

si-tua-ción *f.* situation

si-tuar *v.* to place

so-ba-co *m.* armpit

so-bar *v.* to thrash; to knead

so-be-o *m.* strap

so-be-ra-ni-a *f.* sovereignty

so-be-ra-no, -na *adj.* sovereign

so-ber-bio, -bia *adj.* superb

so-bor-nar *v.* to bribe another

so-bor-no *m.* bribery

so-bra *f.* excess

so-bra-do, -da *adj.* plenty

so-bran-te *adj.* surplus

so-brar *v.* to surpass

so-bre *prep.* over; on; above

so-bre-a-bun-dan-cia *f.* superabundance

so-bre-a-bun-dan-te *adj.* superabundant

so-bre-car-ga *f.* overload

so-bre-car-gar *v.* to overload

so-bre-ce-jo *m.* frown

so-bre-co-ger *v.* to scare

so-bre-cu-bier-ta *f.* cover

so-bre-en-ten-di-do, -da *adj.* understood

so-bre-ex-ci-tar *v.* to overexcite

so-bre-lle-nar *v.* to overfill

so-bre-lle-var *v.* to bear

so-bre-na-tu-ral *adj.* supernatural

so-bre-nom-bre *m.* nickname

so-bren-ten-der *v.* to understand

so-bre-pa-sar *v.* to surpass

so-bre-pe-so *m.* overlaod

so-bre-pre-cio *m.* surcharge

so-bre-sa-lien-te *adj.* outstanding

so-bre-sa-lir *v.* to project

so-bre-sal-tar *v.* to startle

so-bre-fal-to *m.* fright

so-bres-cri-to *m.* address

so-bres-ti-mar *v.* to overestimate

so-bre-to-do *m.* coat; overcoat

so-bre-vi-vien-te *adj.* surviving

so-bre-vi-vir *v.* to survive

so-bri-na *f.* niece

so-bri-no *m.* nephew

so-ca-rrón, -na *m., f.* one who is sarcastic

so-ca-rro-ne-rí-a *f.* sarcasm

so-ca-var *v.* to excavate

so-cia-bi-li-dad *f.* friendliness

so-cia-ble *adj.* sociable

so-cial *adj.* social

so-cie-dad *f.* society

so-cio, -cia *m., f.* member

so-cio-e-co-no-mi-co, -ca *adj.* socioeconomic

so-cio-lo-gí-a *f.* sociology

so-cio-lo-gi-co, -ca *adj.* sociological

so-cio-lo-go, -ga *m., f.* sociologist

so-co-rrer *v.* to aid

so-co-rro *m.* aid

so-dio *m.* sodium

so-fá *f.* sofa

so-fis-ma *m.* sophism

so-fis-ta *adj.* sophistic

so-fis-ti-ca-cion *f.* sophistication

so-fis-ti-ca-do, -da *adj.* sophisticated

so-fo-ca-cion *f.* suffocation

so-fo-ca-dor, -ra *adj.* suffocating

so-fo-car *v.* to suffocate; to suppress

so-ga *f.* rope

so-ja *f.* soybean

so-juz-gar *v.* to subjugate

sol *m.* sun

so-la-men-te *adv.* only

so-la-no *m.* the east wind

so-lar *adj.* solar

so-la-rium *m.* solarium

so-laz *m.* relaxation

sol-da-do *m.* soldier

sol-da-dor *m.* solderer

sol-da-du-ra *f.* soldering

sol-dar *v.* to join

so-le-a-do *adj.* sunny

so-le-cis-mo *m.* solecism

so-le-dad *f.* loneliness
so-lem-ne *adj.* solemn
so-lem-ni-dad *f.* solemnity
so-le-van-tar *v.* to lift
so-li-ci-ta-cion *f.* request
so-li-ci-tan-te *m., f.* petitioner
so-li-ci-tar *v.* to ask for; to request
so-li-ci-to, -ta *adj.* solicitous
so-li-ci-tud *f.* request; solicitude
so-li-da-ri-dad *f.* solidarity
so-li-dez *f.* solidity
so-li-di-fi-ca-cion *f.* solidification
so-li-di-fi-car *v.* to solidify
só-li-do *adj.* solid
so-li-lo-quio *m.* soliloquy
so-lis-ta *f.* soloist
so-li-vian-tar *v.* to irritate
so-li-viar *v.* to lift something
so-lo *adj.* alone
sols-ti-cio *m.* solstice
sol-tar *v.* to let go; to loosen
sol-te-ro *adj.* single
sol-tu-ra *f.* confidence; looseness
so-lu-ble *adj.* soluable
so-lu-ción *f.* solution
so-lu-cio-nar *v.* to solve
sol-ven-cia *f.* solvency
sol-ven-tar *v.* to resolve
sol-ven-te *adj.* solvent
so-ma-ti-co, -ca *adj.* somatic
so-ma-ti-za-cion *f.* somatization
so-ma-ti-zar *v.* to somatize
som-bra *f.* shade
som-brar *v.* to shade
som-bre-ar *v.* to shade
som-bre-ro *m.* hat
som-brí-o, -a *adj.* sullen
so-me-ter *v.* to subordinate
so-me-ti-mien-to *m.* submission
som-no-len-cia *f.* somnolence
so-ña-do, -da *adj.* crazy
so-ñar *v.* to sound
soñ-da *f.* sounding
son-de-ar *v.* to sound
son-de-o *m.* sounding

so-ne-to *m.* sonnet
so-ni-do *m.* sound
so-no-ri-dad *f.* sonority
so-no-ro, -ra *adj.* sonority
so-no-ro, -ra *adj.* sound
son-re-ír *v.* to smile
son-rien-te *adj.* smiling
son-ri-sa *f.* smile
son-ro-jo *m.* blush
son-ro-sar *v.* to turn pink
son-sa-car *v.* to wheedle
so-ña-do, -da *adj.* dream
so-ña-dor, -ra *m., f.* dreamer
so-ñar *v.* to dream
so-ño-len-cia *f.* somnolence
so-ño-lien-to, -ta *adj.* sleepy
so-pa *f.* soup
so-pa-pe-ar *v.* to slap
so-pa-po *m.* slap
so-pe-sar *v.* to wiegh
so-pla-dor, -ra *adj.* blowing
so-plar *v.* to blow
so-por *m.* sleepiness
so-por-ta-ble *adj.* bearable
so-por-tar *v.* to support
so-por-te *m.* support
so-pra-no *m.* soprano
sor-ber *v.* to absorb
sor-be-te *m.* sherbet
sor-bo *m.* sip
sor-de-ra *f.* deafness
sor-di-dez *f.* squalor
sór-di-do, -da *adj.* squalid
sor-do, -da *adj.* deaf
sor-na *f.* sarcasm
sor-pren-den-te *adj.* surprising
sor-pren-der *v.* to surprise
sor-pre-sa *f.* surprise
sor-pre-si-vo, -va *adj.* unexpected
sor-ti-ja *f.* ring
so-se-ga-do, -da *adj.* peaceful
so-se-gar *v.* to calm one down
so-sie-go *m.* quiet
sos-la-yo, -ya *adj.* slanted
so-so, -sa *adj.* dull
sos-pe-cha *f.* suspicion
sos-pe-char *v.* to suspect
sos-pe-cho-so, -sa *adj.* suspicious

sos-tén *m.* support; sustenance

sos-te-ne-dor *m.* supporter

sos-te-ner *v.* to uphold; to support

sos-te-ni-do, -da *adj.* sustained

sos-te-ni-mien-to *m.* sustenance; support

só-ta-na *f.* soutane

so-ta-no *m.* basement

Sr. *abbr.* Senor, *m.* Mr.

Sra. *abbr.* Senora, *f.* Mrs.

stan-dard *adj.* standard

su, sus *adj.* her; his; its; your

sua-ve *adj.* sweet; soft

sua-vi-dad *f.* smoothness; sweetness

sua-vi-za-dor, -ra *adj.* softening

sua-vi-zar *v.* to smooth; to soften

su-bal-ter-no, -na *adj.* subordinate

su-ba-rren-dar *v.* to sublet

su-ba-rrien-do *m.* sublease

su-bas-ta *f.* auction

su-bas-tar *v.* to auction

sub-co-mi-sion *f.* subcommittee

sub-cons-cien-te *adj.* subconscious

sub-cu-ta-ne-o, -a *adj.* subcutaneous

sub-di-vi-sion *f.* subdivision

su-bes-ti-mar *v.* to underestimate

su-bi-ba-ja *m.* seesaw

su-bi-do, -da *adj.* deep

su-bir *v.* to raise; to go up; to come

su-bi-ta-men-te *adv.* suddenly

su-bi-to *adj.* hasty

sub-je-ti-vi-dad *f.* subjectivity

sub-je-ti-vo, -va *adj.* subjective

su-ble-var *v.* to annoy

su-bli-ma-ción *f.* sublimation

su-bli-mar *v.* to sublimate

su-bli-me *adj.* sublime

sub-ma-ri-no, -na *adj.* submarine

su-bor-di-na-ción *f.* subordination

su-bor-di-na-do, -da *adj.* subordinate

su-bor-di-nar *v.* to subordinate

sub-sa-nar *v.* to correct

subs-cri-bir *v.* to subscribe to; to sign

subs-crip-ción *f.* subscription

subs-crip-tor, -ra *m., f.* subscriber

sub-se-cuen-te *adj.* subsequent

sub-si-diar *v.* to subsidize

sub-si-dio *m.* subsidy

sub-sis-ten-cia *f.* subsistence

sub-sis-tir *v.* to subsist

subs-tan-cia *f.* substance

subs-tan-cial *adj.* substantial

subs-tan-ciar *v.* to substantiate

subs-tan-cio-so, -sa *adj.* substantial

subs-ti-tu-ción *f.* substitution

subs-ti-tuir *v.* to substitute

subs-ti-tu-ti-vo, -va *adj.* substitue

subs-trac-ción *f.* subtraction

subs-tra-er *v.* to subtract; to deduce

sub-sue-lo *m.* basement

sub-ter-fu-gio *m.* subterfuge

sub-te-rrá-ne-o, -a *adj.* underground

sub-ti-tu-lo *m.* subtitle

su-bur-ba-no, -na *adj.* suburban

su-bur-bio *m.* suburb

sub-ven-ción *f.* subsidy

sub-ven-cio-nar *v.* to subsidize

sub-yu-gar *v.* to subjugate

suc-ción *f.* suction

su-ce-da-ne-o, -a *adj.* substitute

su-ce-der *v.* to succeed

su-ce-sión *f.* succession

su-ce-si-va-men-te *adv.* successively

su-ce-si-vo, -va *adj.* consecutive

su-ce-so *m.* event

su-ce-sor, -ra *adj.* succeeding

su-cie-dad *f.* filth

su-cio, -cia *adj.* vile; dirty

su-cu-len-cia *f.* succulence

su-cu-len-to, -ta *adj.* succelent

su-cum-bir *v.* to succumb

sud *m.* south

su-dar *v.* to sweat

su-des-te *m.* southeast

su-do-es-te *m.* southwest

su-dor *m.* sweat

su-do-ri-fe-ro, -ra *adj.* sudoriferous

su-do-ro-so, -sa *adj.* sweaty

sue-gra *f.* mother-in-law

sue-gro *m.* father-in-law

sue-lo *m.* floor; soil; ground

suel-to, -ta *adj.* nimble; loose

sue-ño *m.* dream; sleep

sue-ro *m.* serum

suer-te *f.* luck

su-fi-cien-cia *f.* competence

su-fi-cien-te *adj.* sufficient

su-fi-jo *m.* suffix

su-fra-gio *m.* suffrage

su-fra-gis-ta *f., m.* suffragist

su-fri-do, -da *adj.* patient

su-frir *v.* to suffer; to endure something

su-ge-ren-cia *f.* suggestion

su-ge-rir *v.* to suggest

su-ges-tión *f.* suggestion

su-ges-ti-vo, -va *adj.* suggestive

sui-ci-da *adj.* suicidal

sui-ci-dio *m.* suicide

su-je-ción *f.* subjection

su-je-tar *v.* to subject; to fasten

su-je-to, -ta *adj.* subject

sul-fu-ro *m.* sulfide

su-ma-men-te *adv.* extremely

su-mar *v.* to add up

su-ma-ria-men-te *adv.* summarily

su-ma-rio, -ria *adj.* brief

su-mer-gir *v.* to submerge

su-mi-de-ro *m.* drain

su-mi-nis-trar *v.* to supply

su-mi-nis-tro *m.* supply

su-mir *v.* to submerge into something

su-mi-sión *f.* submission

su-mi-so, -sa *adj.* submissive

sun-tuo-si-dad *f.* sumptuousness

sun-tuo-so, -sa *adj.* sumptuous

su-pe-di-tar *v.* to subordinate

su-pe-ra-bun-dar *v.* to superabound

su-pe-rar *v.* to surpass; to beat

su-pe-res-truc-tu-ra *f.* superstructure

su-per-fi-cial *adj.* superficial

su-per-fi-cie *f.* surface

su-per-fi-no, -na *adj.* very fine

su-per-fluo, -a *adj.* superfluous

su-pe-rin-ten-den-te *m., f.* superintendent

su-pe-rior *adj.* superior; better

su-pe-rio-ri-dad *f.* superiority

su-per-mer-ca-do *m.* supermarket

su-per-po-bla-cion *f.* overpopulation

su-per-po-ten-cia *f.* superpower

su-per-pro-duc-cion *f.* overproduction

su-per-só-ni-co, -ca *adj.* supersonic

su-pers-ti-ción *f.* superstition

su-pers-ti-cio-so, -sa *adj.* superstitious

su-per-vi-sar *v.* to supervise

su-per-vi-sion *f.* supervision

su-per-vi-ven-via *f.* survival

su-pi-no, -na *adj.* supine

su-plan-tar *v.* to supplant

su-ple-men-tal *adj.* supplemental

su-plen-te *adj.* substitute

su-pli-car *v.* to implore

su-po-ner *v.* to imagine

something; to suppose

su-po-si-ción f. supposition

su-po-si-to-rio m. suppository

su-pre-mo, -ma adj. supreme

su-pri-mir v. to eliminate

su-pues-to, -ta adj. supposed; assumed

su-pu-rar v. to suppurate

sur m. south

sur-car v. to plow

sur-gir v. to arise

su-rre-a-lis-to adj. surrealistic

sur-ti-do, -da m. selection adj. assorted

sur-ti-dor, -ra m. supplier

sur-tir v. to supply something

sus-cep-ti-bi-li-dad f. susceptibility

sus-cep-ti-ble adj. susceptible

sus-pen-der v. to interrupt

sus-pen-sión f. suspension

sus-pen-si-vo, -va adj. suspensive

sus-pen-so-rio, -ria adj. suspensory

sus-pi-ca-cia f. distrust

sus-pi-caz adj. being distrustful

sus-pi-rar v. to sigh

sus-pi-ro m. sigh

sus-ten-ta-mien-to m. sustenance

sus-ten-tar v. to uphold; to sustain

sus-tne-to m. support; sustenance

sus-to m. scare

su-su-rran-te adj. rustling

su-su-rrar v. to murmur; to whisper

su-su-rro m. whisper

su-til adj. subtle

su-ti-le-za f. sublety

su-tu-ra f. suture

su-tu-rar v. to suture a wound

su-yo, -ya adj. their; her; his; your

ta-ba f. bone of the ankle

ta-ba-cal m. field for tobacco

ta-ba-ca-le-ro, -ra m., f. tabacco dealer

ta-ba-co m. tobacco

tá-ba-no m. gadfly

ta-ba-que-rí-a f. tobacco shop

ta-ber-na f. tavern

ta-ber-ná-cu-lo m. tabernacle

ta-ber-ne-ro, -ra m., f. bartender

ta-bi-que m. partition

ta-bla f. table

ta-ble-a-do, -da m. pleats

ta-ble-ro m. board

ta-ble-ta f. tablet

ta-bu-la-dor m., f. tabulator

ta-bu-re-te m. stool

ta-co-no, -na adj. stingy

tá-ci-to, -ta adj. tacit

ta-ci-tur-no, -na adj. taciturn

ta-co m. pad; wedge

ta-cón m. heel

tác-ti-co, -ca adj. tactical

tac-til adj. tactile

tac-to m. touch; tact

ta-cha f. flaw

ta-char v. to cross something out

ta-cho m. can

ta-chue-la f. tack

ta-fe-tán m. taffeta

ta-hur m. cardsharp

tai-ma-do, -da adj. crafty

ta-ja-da f. profit

ta-jan-te adj. sharp

ta-jar v. to slice

ta-jo m. cut

tal adj. such

ta-la f. ruin

ta-la-dor, -ra adj. cutting

ta-la-drar v. to drill

ta-la-dro m. drill

ta-lar v. to cut something down

tal-co m. talc

ta-le-ga f. wealth

ta-len-to m. talent

ta-len-to-so, -sa adj. talented

ta-lis-man m. talisman

ta-lon *m.* talon; heel
ta-lo-na-rio *m.* checkbook
ta-lla *f.* size; height
ta-lla-do, -da *adj.* engraved; carved
ta-lla-dor *m.* engraver
ta-llar *v.* to carve
ta-lle *m.* figure; shape
ta-ller *m.* shop
ta-loo *m.* stem
ta-ma-no, -na *adj.* very big
tam-ba-le-an-te *adj.* staggering
tam-ba-le-ar *v.* to stagger
tam-bien *adv.* too; also
tam-bor *m.* drum
tam-bo-ra *f.* drum
tam-bo-ril *m.* little drum
tam-bo-ri-le-ar *v.* to beat
tam-bo-ri-le-o *m.* beating
ta-miz *m.* sieve
ta-mi-zar *v.* to filter
tam-po-co *adv.* nor; niether
tan *adv.* as; so
tan-da *f.* shift; turn
tan-gen-te *adj.* tangent
tan-gi-ble *adj.* tangible
tan-go *m.* tango
tan-gue-ar *v.* to tango
tan-que *m.* tanker
tan-te-ar *v.* to consider; to test
tan-to, -ta *adj.* so many
ta-ner *v.* to play
ta-pa *f.* cover; lid
ta-pa-do *m.* coat
ta-par *v.* to block something
ta-pe-te *m.* carpet
ta-piar *v.* to wall something in
ta-pi-ce-ro, -ra *m., f.* upholsterer
ta-pio-ca *f.* tapioca
ta-piz *m.* tapestry
ta-pi-zar *v.* to upholster; to hang tapestries
ta-pon *m.* cork
ta-qui-gra-fi-a *f.* stenography
ta-qui-gra-fiar *v.* to write using shorthand
ta-qui-gra-fo, -fa *m., f.* stenographer
ta-ra *f.* defect

ta-ran-tu-la *f.* tarantula
ta-ras-car *v.* to bite
tar-dan-za *f.* delay
tar-dar *v.* to delay
tar-de *f.* afternoon
tar-di-o, -a *adj.* late
ta-ra-a *f.* homework
ta-ri-fa *f.* tariff
ta-ri-far *v.* to give or apply a tariff to something
tar-je-ta *f.* card
ta-rro *m.* jar
tar-ta *f.* pie
tar-ta-mu-de-o *m.* stammering
tar-tan *m.* tartan
tar-to-ro, -ra *adj.* tartar
ta-sa *f.* rate
ta-sa-cion *f.* appraisal
ta-sa-dor, -ra *adj.* appraising
ta-sa-je-ar *v.* to jerk something
ta-sa-jo *m.* jerky
tas-ca *f.* joint
ta-ta-ra-bue-la *f.* great-great-grandmother
ta-ta-ra-bue-lo *m.* great-great-grandfather
ta-ta-ra-nie-ta *f.* great-great-granddaughter
ta-ta-ra-nie-to *m.* great-great-grandson
ta-tau-je *m.* tattoo
ta-taur *v.* to tattoo
tau-ro-ma-quia *f.* bullfighting
ta-xi *m.* taxi
ta-xi-der-mia *f.* taxidermy
ta-xis-ta *m., f.* one who drives a taxie
ta-xo-no-mi-a *f.* taxonomy
ta-za *f.* bowl; cup
te *pron.* you
te-a *f.* torch
te-a-tral *adj.* theatrical
te-a-tra-li-dad *f.* theatricality
te-a-tro *m.* theater
te-cia *f.* key
te-cla-do *m.* keyboard
tec-ni-co, -ca *adj.* technical
tec-no-cra-cia *f.* technocracy
tec-no-lo-gi-a *f.* technology
tec-no-lo-gi-co, -ca *adj.* technological

te-char v. to roof a building
te-cho m. ceiling; roof
te-dio m. tedium
te-dio-so, -sa adj. tedious
te-ja f. tile
te-jar v. to tile
te-jer v. to knit
te-ji-do m. weave
te-jón m. badger
te-la f. fabric; film
te-la-ra-ña f. spider's web
te-le-co-mu-ni-ca-ción f. telecommunication
te-le-di-fun-dir v. to telecast
te-le-di-fu-sion f. to telecast
te-le-fo-na-zo m. telephone call
te-le-fo-ne-ar v. to phone someone
te-le-fo-ni-ca-men-te adv. by a phone
te-le-fo-nis-ta m., f. telephone operator
te-lé-fo-no m. telephone
te-le-fo-to m. telephoto
te-le-gra-fi-a f. telegraphy
te-le-gra-fiar v. to telegraph
te-le-grá-fi-co, -ca adj. telegraphic
te-le-gra-fis-ta m., f. telegrapher
te-lé-gra-fo m. telegraph
te-le-gra-ma f. telegram
te-le-man-do m. remote control
te-le-me-trí-a f. telemetry
te-le-pa-tí-a f. telepathy
te-le-pá-ti-co, -ca adj. telepathic
te-les-có-pi-co, -ca adj. telescopic
te-les-co-pio m. telescope
te-le-ti-po m. teletype
te-le-vi-sar v. to televise
te-le-vi-sión f. television
te-le-vi-sor m. television
te-lón m. curtain
te-lu-rio m. tellurium
te-ma f. subject; obsession
te-má-ti-co, -ca adj. thematic
tem-blar v. to tremble
tem-ble-que-ar v. to tremble
tem-blor m. earthquake; tremor

te-mer v. to be afraid of
te-me-ro-so-, sa adj. frightening
te-mor m. fear
tem-pe-ra-men-tal adj. temperamental
tem-pe-ra-men-to m. weather
tem-pe-ran-cia f. temperance
tem-pe-rar v. to calm
tem-pe-ra-tu-ra f. temperature
tem-pes-tad f. storm
tem-pes-tuo-so, -sa adj. stormy
tem-pla-do, -da adj. mild
tem-plan-za f. moderation
tem-plar v. to temper; to tune; to appease
tem-ple m. mood; temper
tem-plo m. temple
tem-po-ra-da f. season
tem-po-ral adj. temporal
tem-po-ra-ne-o, -a adj. temporary
tem-pra-ne-ro, -ra adj. early
tem-pra-no, -na adj. early
te-na-ci-dad f. tenacity
te-naz f. tenacious
ten-den-cia f. tendency
tén-der v. to stretch something out
ten-di-do, -da adj. spead out
ten-don m. tendon
te-ne-bro-so, -sa adj. obscure; dark
te-ne-dor m. one who owns
te-nen-cia f. possession
te-ner v. to contain; to have; to keep
te-nia f. tapeworm
te-nien-te m. lieutenant
te-nis m. tennis
te-nis-ta m., f. one who plays tennis
ten-sar v. to stretch
ten-sión f. tension
ten-so, -sa adj. tense
ten-ta-ción f. temptation
ten-tá-cu-lo m. tentacle
ten-ta-dor, -ra adj. tempting

ten-ta-ti-vo, -va *adj.* tentative

te-ñir *v.* to make dark

te-o-cra-cia *f.* theocracy

te-o-lo-gi-a *f.* theology

te-o-lo-go, -ga *m.*, *f.* theologian

te-o-re-ma *m.* theorem

te-o-re-ti-co, -ca *adj.* theoretical

te-o-ri-a *f.* theory

te-o-re-ti-co, -ca *adj.* theoretical

te-o-ri-zar *v.* to theorize

te-ó-so-fo, -fa *m.*, *f.* theosophist

te-qui-la *f.* tequila

te-ra-peu-ta *m.*, *f.* therapist

te-ra-péu-ti-co, -ca *adj.* therapeutic

te-ra-pia *f.* therapy

ter-ce-ro, -ra *adj.* third

ter-cia-do, -da *adj.* brown

ter-cio, -cia *adj.* third

ter-cio-pe-lo *m.* velvet

ter-co, -ca *adj.* stubborn

ter-gi-ver-sar *v.* to distort

ter-mal *adj.* thermal

ter-mi-na-cion *f.* ending; termination

ter-mi-nal *adj.* terminal

ter-mi-nar *v.* to complete; to end something

tér-mi-no *m.* ending

ter-mi-no-lo-gi-a *f.* terminology

ter-mi-ta *m.* termite

ter-mo-di-ná-mi-ca *f.* thermodynamics

ter-mo-e-lec-tri-co, -ca *adj.* thermoelectric

ter-mó-me-tro *m.* thermometer

ter-mos-ta-to *m.* thermostat

ter-no *m.* a set of three things

ter-nu-ra *f.* tenderness

te-rra-plen *m.* embankment

te-rra-que-o, -a *adj.* terrestrial

te-rra-za *f.* terrace

te-rre-mo-to *m.* earthquake

te-rre-nal *adj.* earthly

te-rre-no, -na *adj.* earthly

te-rres-tre *adj.* terrestrial

te-rri-ble *adj.* terrible

te-rri-to-rial *adj.* territorial

te-rri-to-rio *m.* territory

te-rror *m.* terror

te-rro-ri-fi-co, -ca *adj.* terrifying

te-rro-ris-ta *m.*, *f.* terrorist

ter-so, -sa *adj.* smooth

te-sis *f.* thesis

te-son *m.* tenacity

te-so-ne-ro, -ra *adj.* tenacious

te-so-re-ri-a *f.* treasury

te-so-re-ro, -ra *m.*, *f.* treasurer

te-so-ro *m.* treasure

tes-ti-cu-lo *m.* testicle

tes-ti-fi-car *v.* to testify

tes-ti-go *m.* one who sees something; witness

tes-ti-mo-niar *v.* to testify

tes-ti-mo-nio *m.* testimony

te-ta *f.* udder

té-ta-no *m.* tetanus

te-ti-lla *f.* teat

tex-til *adj.* textile

tex-to *m.* textbook

tex-tu-ra *f.* texture

tez *f.* complexion

ti *pron.* yourself

tí-a *f.* aunt

tia-ra *f.* tiara

ti-bia *f.* tibia

ti-bu-rón *m.* shark

tiem-po *m.* weather; time

tien-da *f.* store; shop

tien-to *m.* caution; touch

tier-no, -na *adj.* tender

tie-rra *f.* land; country

tie-so, -sa *adj.* arrogant

ties-to *m.* flowerpot

ti-foj-de-o, -a *adj.* typhoid

ti-fón *m.* typhoon

ti-fus *m.* typhus

ti-gre *m.* tiger

ti-gre-sa *f.* tigress

ti-je-re-te-ar *v.* to snip

ti-je-re-te-o *m.* snipping

ti-mar-dor, -ra *m.*, *f.* cheat

ti-mar *v.* to cheat

tim-bra-do, -da *adj.* stamped

tim-brar *v.* to stamp

tim-bre *m.* ring
ti-mi-dez *f.* timidity
tí-mi-do, -da *adj.* timid
ti-mo *m.* thymus
ti-mo-ra-to, -ta *adj.* shy
tin-gla-do *m.* platform
ti-no *m.* good judgment
tin-ta *f.* dye
tin-te *m.* dye
tin-te-ro *m.* inkwell
tin-ti-nar *v.* to clink something
tin-tu-ra *f.* tincture
ti-ña *f.* ringworm
tí-o *m.* uncle
tí-pi-co, -ca *adj.* typical
ti-pi-fi-car *v.* to typify
ti-po *m.* type; kind
ti-po-gra-fí-a *f.* typofraphy
ti-ra-da *f.* distance
ti-ra-ní-a *f.* tyranny
ti-ra-ni-zar *v.* to tyrannize
ti-ra-no, -na *adj.* tyrannical
ti-ran-te *adj.* tight
ti-ran-tez *f.* tightness
ti-rar *v.* to throw
ti-ri-tar *v.* to shiver
ti-ro *m.* shot; throw
ti-ro-te-o *m.* shooting
ti-sis *f.* tuberculosis
ti-te-re *m.* puppet
ti-ti-lar *v.* to quiver
ti-ti-le-o *m.* quivering
ti-ti-ri-tar *v.* to tremble
ti-tu-be-o *m.* staggering
ti-tu-la-do, -da *adj.* titled
tí-tu-lo *m.* title
ti-za *f.* chalk
tiz-nar *v.* to smudge
to-a-lla *f.* towel
to-bi-llo *m.* ankle
to-bo-gán *m.* sled
to-ca-dor *m.* dressing room
to-car *v.* to ring; to handle; to touch
to-da-vi-a *adj.* every; all
to-do, -da *adj.* all; every
to-le-ran-cia *f.* tolerance
to-le-ran-te *adj.* tolerant
to-le-rar *v.* to tolerate
to-lon-dron, -ona *m., f.* scatterbrain
to-ma *f.* intake; taking

to-ma-dor, -ra *adj.* drinking
to-mar *v.* to have; to take
to-ma-te *m.* tomato
to-na-da *f.* tune
to-na-li-dad *f.* tonality
to-nel *m.* barrel
to-ne-la-da *f.* ton
to-ne-la-je *m.* tonnage
to-ni-fi-car *v.* to tone
to-ni-na *f.* tuna
to-no *m.* tone
ton-te-rí-a *f.* foolishness
ton-to *m.* fool
tó-pi-co *m.* topic
to-po *m.* mole
to-po-gra-fí-a *f.* topography
to-pó-gra-fo *m.* topographer
to-que *m.* beat; touch
to-que-te-ar *v.* to handle
to-que-te-o *m.* handling
to-ra-ci-co, -ca *adj.* thoracic
tor-ce-du-ra *f.* twist
tor-cer *v.* to sprain; to bend
to-re-a-dor *m.* toreador
to-re-ar *v.* to fight
to-re-o *m.* bullfighting
tor-men-ta *f.* storm
tor-men-to *m.* torment
tor-men-to-so, -sa *adj.* stormy
tor-na-do *m.* tornado
tor-na-sol *m.* sunflower
tor-na-so-la-do, -da *adj.* iridescent
tor-ne-ar *v.* to turn
tor-ne-o *m.* tournament
tor-ni-llo *m.* screw
tor-ni-que-te *m.* tourniquet
to-ro *m.* bull
to-ron-ja *f.* grapefruit
tor-pe-de-ar *v.* to torpedo
tor-pe-za *f.* stupidity
tor-por *m.* torpor
to-rrar *v.* to roast
to-rre *f.* castle
to-rren-cial *adj.* torrential
to-rren-te *m.* torrent
tó-rri-do, -da *adj.* torrid
tor-sión *f.* torsion
tor-so *m.* torso
tor-ta *f.* cake
tor-to-la *f.* turtledove
tor-tu-ga *f.* turtle

tor-tuo-so, -sa *adj.* tortuous
tor-tu-ra *f.* torture
tor-tu-rar *v.* to torture
tos *f.* coughing
tos-co, -ca *adj.* crude
to-ser *v.* to cough
tos-que-dad *f.* coarseness
tos-ta-do, -da *adj.* roasted
tos-ta-dor, -ram., f. toaster
tos-tar *v.* to roast; to toast
to-tal *adj.* total
to-ta-li-dad *f.* totality
to-ta-li-ta-rio, -ria *adj.* totalitarian
to-ta-li-zar *v.* to total
to-xe-mia *f.* toxemia
to-xi-ci-dad *f.* toxicity
tó-xi-co, -ca *adj.* poison
to-xi-co-lo-go, -ga *m., f.* toxicologist
to-xi-na *f.* toxin
to-zu-do, -da *adj.* stubborn
tra-ba *f.* obstacle; bolt
tra-ba-ja-dor *m.* worker
tra-ba-jar *v.* to work
tra-ba-jo *m.* job; work
tra-ba-jo-so, -sa *adj.* demanding
tra-bar *v.* to fasten; to bolt
tra-bu-car *v.* to mix up
trac-ción *f.* traction
trac-tor *m.* tractor
tra-di-ción *f.* tradition
tra-di-cio-nal *f.* traditional
tra-duc-ción *f.* translation
tra-du-cir *v.* to express
tra-duc-tor, -ra *adj.* translating something
tra-er *v.* to wear; to carry; to bring
tra-fi-car *v.* to deal
trá-fi-co *m.* traffic
tra-gl-luz *v.* skylight
tra-gar *v.* to devour; swallow
tra-ge-dia *f.* tragedy
trá-gi-co, -ca *adj.* tragic
tra-gi-co-me-dia *f.* tragicomedy
tra-go *m.* gulp
trai-ción *f.* treason
trai-cio-nar *v.* to betray another
tra-je *m.* dress

tra-je-a-do, -da *adj.* dressed
tra-je-ar *v.* to dress
tra-ji-nar *v.* to carry
tra-ma *f.* plot
tra-ma-dor, -ra *m., f.* weaver
tra-mar *v.* to scheme
tra-mi-ta-ción *f.* transaction
tra-mi-tar *v.* to negotiate
tra-mo *m.* flight
tram-pa *f.* trap
tram-pe-ar *v.* to cheat
tram-po-lin *m.* trampoline
tram-po-so, -sa *adj.* cheating
tran-ce *m.* trance; crisis
tran-qui-li-dad *f.* tranquility
tran-qui-li-zan-te *adj.* tranquilizing
tran-qui-lo, -la *adj.* tranquil
tran-sac-ción *f.* transaction
tran-sat-lan-ti-co, -ca *adj.* transatlantic
trans-bor-dar *v.* to transfer
trans-bor-do *m.* transfer
trans-cen-den-cia *f.* transcendence
trans-cen-den-tal *adj.* transcendental
trans-cen-der *v.* to transcend
trans-con-ti-nen-tal *adj.* transcontinental
trans-cri-bir *v.* to transcribe
trans-crip-cion *f.* transcription
tran-se-un-te *adj.* transient
trans-fe-ren-cia *f.* transference
trans-fe-rir *v.* to transfer
trans-fi-gu-ra-ción *f.* transfiguration
trans-for-ma-ción *f.* transformation
trans-for-ma-dor, -ra *adj.* transforming
trans-for-mar *v.* to convert; to transform
trans-fun-dir *v.* to transfuse
trans-fu-sión *f.* transfusion
trans-gre-dir *v.* to transgress
trans-gre-sión *f.* transgression
tran-si-ción *f.* transition

tran-sis-tor *m.* transistor
tran-si-tar *v.* to travel
tran-si-ti-vo, -va *adj.* transitive
trán-si-to *m.* traffic
tran-si-to-rio, -ria *adj.* temporary
trans-la-ción *f.* translation
trans-lu-ci-do, -da *adj.* translucent
trans-mi-gra-ción *f.* tranmigration
trans-mi-grar *v.* to transmigrate
trans-mi-tir *v.* to transmit
trans-mu-tar *v.* to transmute
trans-pa-ren-te *adj.* transparent
trans-pi-ra-ción *f.* perspiration
trans-pi-rar *v.* to perspire
trans-plan-tar *v.* to transplant
trans-po-ner *v.* to transplant; to move
trans-por-ta-ción *f.* transportation
trans-por-tar *v.* to transport
trans-po-si-cion *f.* transposition
trans-ver-so, -sa *adj.* transverse
tran-vi-a *m.* streetcar
tra-pe-cio *m.* trapezoid
tra-pe-zoi-de *m.* trapezoid
trá-que-a *f.* trachea
tras *prep.* behind; after
tra-sat-lan-ti-co, -ca *adj.* transatlantic
tras-cen-den-te *adj.* transcendent
tras-cen-der *v.* to extend
tra-se-gar *v.* to decant
tras-fon-do *m.* background
tra-sie-go *m.* decanting
tras-la-ción *f.* translation
tras-la-dar *v.* to transcribe; to move
tras-la-do *m.* transfer
tras-no-cha-do, -da *adj.* trite
tras-pa-pe-lar *v.* to misplace something
tras-pa-pe-la-do, -da *adj.* misplaced
tras-pa-sar *v.* to break
tras-pa-so *m.* transfer
trans-plan-tar *v.* to transplant
tras-qui-lar *v.* to shear
tras-to-car *v.* to twist
tras-tor-nar *v.* to disrupt
tras-tro-car *v.* to twist
tra-sun-tar *v.* to summarize
tra-ta-mien-to *m.* treatment; process
tra-tar *v.* to process; to handle
tra-to *m.* treatment
trau-ma *m.* trauma
trau-ma-ti-co, -ca *adj.* traumatic
trau-ma-ti-zar *v.* to traumatize
tra-ve-si-a *f.* crosswind; crossroad
tra-ve-su-ra *f.* mischief
tra-vie-so, -sa *adj.* mischievous
tra-yec-to *m.* way
tra-yec-to-ria *f.* trajectory
tra-za *f.* plan
tra-zar *v.* to outline something
tra-zo *m.* line
tré-bol *m.* clover
tre-ce *adj.* thirteen
tre-cho *m.* in parts; stretch
tre-gua *f.* rest
trein-ta *adj.* thirty
trein-ta-vo *f.* thirtieth
trein-te-na *f.* thirty
tre-men-do, -da *adj.* terrible; horrible
tre-men-ti-na *f.* turpentine
tre-mo-lar *v.* to wave
tre-mo-li-na *f.* rustling
tre-mor *m.* tremor
tren *m.* train
tren-ci-lla *f.* braid
tren-za *f.* braid
tren-zar *v.* to braid
tre-pi-dar *v.* to vibrate
tres *adj.* three
tres-cien-tos *adj.* three hundred
tres-pies *m.* tripod

tre-za-vo, -va *adj.* thirteenth
tri-a-da *f.* triad
trian-gu-lar *adj.* triangular
trián-gu-lo *adj.* triangular
tri-bal *adj.* tribal
tri-bu *f.* tribe
tri-bu-la-ción *f.* tribulation
tri-bu-no *m.* tribune
tri-bu-tar *v.* to pay
tri-bu-ta-rio, -ria *adj.* tributary
tri-bu-to *m.* tribute
tri-cen-te-na-rio *m.* tricentennial
tri-ci-clo *m.* trcycle
tri-co-lor *adj.* tricolor
tri-cus-pi-de *adj.* tricuspid
tri-gal *m.* field of wheat
tri-ge-si-mo, -ma *adj.* thirtieth
tri-go *m.* wheat
tri-go-no-me-tri-a *f.* trigonometry
tri-lin-gue *adj.* trilingual
tri-lo-gi-a *f.* trilogy
tri-lla-dor, -ra *adj.* threshing
tri-lli-zo *m.* triplet
tri-mes-tral *adj.* quarterly
trin-cha-dor, -ra *adj.* carving
trin-char *v.* to carve
tri-no-mio *m.* trinomial
tri-o *m.* trio
tri-ple *adj.* triple
tri-pli-ca-ción *f.* triplication
tri-pli-ca-do *m.* triplicate
tri-pli-car *v.* to triplicate
tri-plo, -pla *adj.* triple
tri-po-de *m., f.* tripod
tri-qui-no-sis *f.* trichinosis
tris-ca *f.* crack
tris-car *v.* to stamp
tris-te *adj.* miserable; sad
tris-te-za *f.* sorrow
tri-tu-rar *v.* to chew; to triturate
triun-fa-dor, -ra *adj.* triumphant
triun-fan-te *adj.* triumphant
triun-fo *m.* triumph
tri-vial *adj.* trivial
tri-via-li-dad *f.* triviality
tri-za *f.* piece
tro-car *v.* to barter

tro-fe-o *m.* trophy
tro-glo-di-ta *adj.* barbarous
tro-le *m.* trolley
trom-bon *m.* trombone
trom-bo-sis *f.* thrombosis
trom-pa *f.* horn
trom-pe-ar *v.* to punch
trom-pe-ta *f.* trumpet
trom-pe-tis-ta *m., f.* trumpeter
trom-pi-car *v.* to trip
trom-po *m.* top
tro-na-da *f.* thunderstorm
tro-na-dor, -ra *adj.* thundering
tro-nan-te *adj.* thundering
tro-nar *v.* to thunder
tron-co *m.* trunk
tron-cha *f.* slice
tro-pel *m.* confusion
tro-pe-li-a *f.* violence
tro-pe-zar *v.* to trip
tro-pi-cal *adj.* tropical
tro-pi-co *m.* tropic
tro-pie-zo *m.* stumble
tro-po *m.* trope
tro-que-lar *v.* to mint
tro-ta-da *f.* trot
tro-ta-dor, -ra *adj.* trotting
tro-va *f.* ballad
tro-zo *m.* chunk; part; piece
tru-co *m.* trick
true-no *m.* thunder
try-far *v.* to lie
tu *pron.* you
tu-ba *f.* tuba
tu-ber-cu-li-na *f.* tuberculin
tu-ber-cu-lo-sis *f.* tuberculosis
tu-be-ro-so, -sa *adj.* tuberous
tu-bo *m.* tube
tu-bu-la-do, -da *adj.* tubular
tu-bu-lar *adj.* tubular
tu-can *m.* toucan
tues-te *m.* toasting
tu-fo *m.* fume
tu-li-pan *m.* tulip
tu-llir *v.* to cripple
tum-ba *f.* tomb
tum-bar *v.* to knock out
tum-bo *m.* jolt
tu-mes-cen-cia *f.* tumes-

cence
tu-mes-cen-te *adj.* tumescent
tu-mor *m.* tumor
tú-mu-lo *m.* tomb
tu-mul-to *m.* tumult
tu-mul-tuo-so, -sa *adj.* tumultuous
tu-nan-ta *adj.* cunning
tun-da *f.* beating
tun-de-ar *v.* to beat
tun-di-dor, -ra *m., f.* one who shears
tun-di-du-ra *f.* shearing
tun-dir *v.* to shear
tun-dra *f.* tundra
tú-nel *m.* tunnel
tungs-te-no *m.* tungsten
tu-ni-ca *f.* tunic
tu-pé *m.* toupee
tu-pi-do, -da *adj.* dense; thick
tu-pir *v.* to weave close together
tur-ba *f.* mob
tur-ba-cion *f.* confusion
tur-ba-dor, -ra *adj.* disturbing
tur-ban-te *m.* turban
tur-bar *v.* to embarrass; to upset another
tur-bie-dad *f.* opaqueness
tur-bi-na *f.* turbine
tur-bio, -bia *adj.* turbulent; muddy
tur-bión *m.* shower
tur-bu-len-cia *f.* turbulence
tur-bu-len-to, -ta *adj.* turbulent
tu-ris-ta *f.* tourist
tu-rís-ti-co, -ca *adj.* tourist
tur-nar *v.* taking turns at something
tur-no *m.* turn
tur-que-sa *f.* turquiose
tu-ru-la-to, -ta *adj.* being stunned
tu-sa *f.* cornhusk
tu-sar *v.* to trim
tu-te-ar *v.* to address another as tu
tu-tor, -ra *m., f.* guardian
tu-yo, -ya *adj.* yours

u-be-rri-mo, -ma *adj.* luxuriant
u-bi-ca-cion *f.* placing
u-bi-car *v.* to locate
u-bre *f.* udder
u-fa-nar-se *v.* to boast about something
u-fa-no, -na *adj.* pleased
ul-ce-ra *f.* ulcer
ul-ce-ra-cion *f.* ulceration
ul-ce-rar *v.* to ulcerate
ul-ce-ro-so, -sa *adj.* ulcerous
ul-te-rior *adj.* subsequent
ul-te-rior-men-te *adv.* subsequently
ul-ti-ma-men-te *adv.* finally
ul-ti-mar *v.* to finish; to conclude
ul-ti-ma-tum *m.* ultimatum
úl-ti-mo, -ma *adj.* final; last
ul-tra *adv.* besides
ul-tra-de-re-cha *f.* the far right
ul-tra-jan-te *adj.* outrageous
ul-tra-jar *v.* to insult
ul-tra-je *m.* insult
ul-tra-ma-ri-no, -na *adj.* overseas
ul-tra-mo-der-no, -na *adj.* ultramodern
ul-tra-so-ni-co, -ca *adj.* ultrasonic
ul-tra-so-ni-do *m.* ultrasound
ul-tra-vio-le-ta *adj.* ultraviolet
um-bi-li-cal *adj.* umbilical
um-bral *m.* threshold
um-bri-o, -a *adj.* shady
um-bro-so, -sa *adj.* shady
un *indef. art.* an; a
u-ña *indef. art.* an; a
u-ná-ni-me *adj.* unanimous
u-na-ni-mi-dad *f.* unanimity
un-cir *v.* to yoke
un-de-ci-mo, -ma *adj.* eleventh
un-du-lan-te *adj.* undulating
un-du-lar *v.* to undulate
un-güen-to *m.* ointment
u-ni-ce-lu-lar *adj.* unicellular
u-ni-ci-dad *f.* uniqueness
ú-ni-co, -ca *adj.* single; sole
u-ni-cor-nio *m.* unicorn
u-ni-dad *f.* unity; each

u-ni-do, -da *adj.* united

u-ni-fi-ca-cion *f.* unification

u-ni-fi-car *v.* to unify

u-ni-for-mar *v.* to make something uniform

u-ni-for-me *adj.* even; uniform

u-ni-for-mi-dad *f.* uniformity

u-ni-la-te-ral *adj.* unilateral

u-nion *f.* joint; unity

u-nir(se) *v.* to unite together

u-ni-se-xo *adj.* unisex

u-ni-so-no, -na *adj.* to be in unison with

u-ni-ta-rio, -ria *adj.* unified

u-ni-ver-sal *adj.* world-wide; universal

u-ni-ver-sa-li-dad *f.* universality

u-ni-ver-sa-li-zar *v.* to universalize

u-ni-ver-si-dad *f.* university

u-ni-ver-si-ta-rio, -ria *adj.* university

u-ni-ver-so *m.* universe

u-no, -na *adj.* one

un-tar *v.* to spread; to grease

un-to *m.* grease

un-tuo-si-dad *f.* greasiness

un-tuo-so, -sa *adj.* greasy

un-tu-ra *f.* greasing

u-na *f.* toenail; fingernail

u-ra-nio *m.* uranium

ur-ba-ni-dad *f.* urbanity

ur-ba-ni-za-cion *f.* urvanization

ur-ba-ni-zar *v.* to develop

ur-ba-no, -na *adj.* urban

u-re-a *f.* urea

u-re-ter *m.* ureter

u-re-tra *f.* urethra

ur-gen-cia *f.* urgency

ur-gen-te *adj.* urgent

u-ri-na-rio, -ria *adj.* urinary

u-san-za *f.* custom

u-sar *v.* to use

u-so *m.* use

us-ted *pron.* you

u-sual *adj.* usual

u-su-ra *f.* usury

u-sur-par *v.* to usurp

u-ten-si-lio *m.* utensil

u-til *adj.* useful

va-ca *f.* cow

va-ca-cion *f.* vacation

va-can-te *adj.* vacant

va-cia-de-ro *m.* dump

va-cia-do *m.* cast

va-ciar *v.* to void; to empty; to drain

va-ci-la-cion *f.* vacillation; hesitation

va-ci-lan-te *adj.* hesitating

va-ci-lar *v.* to falter; to vacillate

va-cio, -cia *adj.* devoid; empty; void; hollow

va-cui-dad *f.* vacuity

va-cu-na-cion *f.* vaccination

va-cu-nar *v.* to vaccinate

va-cu-no, -na *adj.* bovine

va-cuo, -cua *adj.* vacuous

va-de-ar *v.* to overcome

va-ga-bun-do, -da *adj.* vagabond

va-ga-men-te *adv.* vaguely

va-gan-cia *f.* vagrancy

va-gar *v.* to roam; to stray; to wander

va-gi-do *m.* cry

va-go, -ga *adj.* hazy; wandering; vague

va-gon *m.* van

va-gue-ar *v.* to wander

va-gue-dad *f.* vagueness

va-ho *m.* vapor; steam

vai-ni-lla *f.* canilla

vai-ven *m.* fluctuation

va-le *m.* voucher

va-le-de-ro, -ra *adj.* valid

va-len-cia *f.* valence

va-len-tia *f.* courage; valor; bravery

va-len-ton, -ona *adj.* boastful

va-len-to-na *f.* boast

va-ler *v.* to be of value; to have authority over; to be of worth

va-le-ro-so, -sa *adj.* valorous; courageous

va-li-a *f.* worth

va-li-da-cion *f.* validation

va-li-dar *v.* to validate

va-li-dez *f.* validity

va-li-do, -da *adj.* good

va-lien-te *adj.* brave; valiant

va-li-ja f. suitcase

va-lio-so, -sa adj. valuable

va-lor m. valor; worth; importance

va-lo-ra-ción f. appraisal

va-lo-rar v. to appraise something

va-lo-ri-za-ción f. appraisal

va-lo-ri-zar v. to appraise something

vals m. waltz

va-luar v. to value something

vál-vu-la f. valve

va-llar v. to put a fence around; to fence in

va-lle m. valley

vam-pi-ro m. vampire

va-na-glo-ria f. pride

va-na-glo-rio-so, -sa adj. boastful

va-na-men-te adv. foolishly; vainly

van-da-lis-mo m. vandalism

va-ni-dad f. vanity

va-ni-do-so, -sa m., f. one who is vain

va-no, -na adj. vain

va-por m. steam

va-po-ri-za-dor m. vaporizer

va-po-ri-zar v. to vaporize

va-po-ro-so, -sa adj. steamy; vaporous

va-que-ta f. hide of a cow

va-ra f. rod; stalk

va-rar v. to beach

va-re-a-dor, -ra m., f. cowhand

va-re-ar v. to cudgel

va-ria-ble adj. variable

va-ria-ción f. change; variation

va-ria-do, -da adj. varied

va-rien-te adj. varying

va-riar v. to change

va-rie-dad f. variety

va-ri-lla f. rob

va-rio, -ria adj. varied

va-rón m. man

va-ro-nil adj. virile

va-sa-llo, -lla adj. subordinate

vas-cu-lar adj. vascular

va-sec-to-mi-a f. vasectomy

va-si-ja f. container

va-so m. vessel; glass

vas-to, -ta adj. vast

va-ti-ci-nar v. to predict

va-ti-ci-nio m. prediction

va-tio m. watt

ve-ci-nal adj. local

ve-ci-na-men-te adv. next

ve-cin-dad f. vicinity

ve-ci-no, -na adj. near; next

vec-tor m. vector

ve-da f. prohibition

ve-da-do, -da adj. prohibited

ve-dar v. to suspend; to prohibit

ve-ge-ta-ción f. vegetation

ve-ge-tal adj. vegetable

ve-ge-tar v. to vegetate

ve-ge-ta-ria-no, -na adj. vegetarian

ve-ge-ta-ti-vo, -va adj. vegetative

ve-he-men-cia f. vehemence

ve-he-men-te adj. vehement

ve-hí-cu-lo m. vehicle

vein-te adj. twenty

ve-ja-ción f. vexation

ve-ja-men m. vezation

ve-jar v. to persecute; to vex

ve-jez f. old age

ve-li-ga f. bladder

ve-la f. sail

ve-la-da f. evening

ve-la-do, -da adj. veiled

ve-lar v. to guard

ve-lei-do-so, -sa adj. fickle

ve-lo m. viel

ve-lo-ci-dad f. velocity

ve-loz adj. swift

ve-llo m. fuzz

ve-llón m. sheepskin

ve-llu-do, -da adj. hairy

ve-na f. vein

ve-na-blo m. javelin

ve-na-do m. venison

ven-ce-dor, -ra m., f. conqueror

ven-cer v. to conquer; to beat another

ven-ci-do, -da adj. conquered; defeated

ven-ci-mien-to m. defeat; collapse

ven-da-je *m.* bandage
ven-dar *v.* to bandage
ven-de-dor, -ra *m., f.* seller
ven-der *v.* to sell
ven-di-mia-dor, -ar *m., f.* one who picks grapes
ve-ne-no *m.* poison
ve-ne-no-si-dad *f.* poisonousness
ve-ne-no-so, -sa *adj.* poisonous
ve-ne-ra-ble *adj.* venerable
ve-en-ra-ción *f.* veneration
ve-ne-rar *v.* to venerate
ven-gan-za *f.* revenge; vengeance
ven-gar *v.* to avenge
ve-nia *f.* forgiveness
ve-nial *adj.* venial
ve-ni-da *f.* return
ve-ni-de-ro, -ra *adj.* upcoming
ve-nir *v.* to come
ven-ta *f.* sale
ven-ta-ja *f.* benefit
ven-ta-jo-so, -sa *adj.* advantageous
ven-ta-na *f.* window
ven-ti-la-ción *f.* ventilation
ven-ti-la-dor *m.* fan
ven-ti-lar *v.* to air
ven-tis-ca *f.* blizzard
ven-tis-que-ro *m.* blizzard
ven-to-si-dad *f.* gas
ven-to-so, -sa *adj.* windy
ven-tri-cu-lar *adj.* ventricular
ven-trí-cu-lo *m.* ventricle
ven-tri-lo-cuo, -a *m., f.* ventriloquist
ven-tu-ra *f.* happiness
ven-tu-ro-so, -sa *adj.* fortunate
ver *v.* to sight; to see
ve-ra *f.* edge
ve-ra-ci-dad *f.* veracity
ve-ra-ne-o *m.* vacationing
ve-ra-no *m.* summer
ve-ras *f.* earnestness
ve-raz *adj.* truthful
ver-bal *adj.* verbal
ver-bal-men-te *adv.* verbally
ver-bo *m.* verb
ver-bo-rre-a *f.* verbosity

ver-bo-si-dad *f.* verbosity
ver-bo-so, -sa *adj.* verbose
ver-dad *f.* truth
ver-da-de-ro, -ra *adj.* truthful
ver-de *adj.* green
ver-dor *m.* verdancy
ver-do-so, -sa *adj.* greenish
ver-du-ra *f.* greenery
ve-re-dic-to *m.* verdict
ver-gel *m.* orchard
ver-gon-zo-so, -sa *adj.* shameful
ver-güen-za *f.* shyness
ve-rí-di-co, -ca *adj.* true
ve-ri-fi-ca-ción *f.* verification
ve-ri-fi-ca-dor, -ra *m., f.* checker
ve-ri-fi-car *v.* to check on; to verify something
ver-mi-ci-da *adj.* vermicidal
ver-nal *adj.* vernal
ve-ro-si-mi-li-tud *f.* probability
ver-sa-do, -da *adj.* versed
ver-sa-til *adj.* versatile
ver-sa-ti-li-dad *f.* versatility
ver-sí-cu-lo *m.* versicle
ver-si-fi-car *v.* to versify
ver-sión *f.* version
ver-so *m.* verse
ver-te-bra *f.* vertebra
ver-te-bra-do, -da *adj.* vertebrate
ver-te-bral *adj.* vertebral
ver-ter *v.* to shed
ver-ti-cal *adj.* vertical
ver-ti-ca-li-dad *f.* verticality
ver-tien-te *f.* spring
vér-ti-go *m.* vertigo
ve-sí-cu-la *f.* vesicle
ve-si-cu-lar *adj.* vesicular
ves-tí-bu-lo *m.* vestibule
ves-ti-do *m.* clothing; dress
ves-ti-du-ra *f.* garment
ves-ti-gio *m.* vestige
ves-ti-men-ta *f.* clothes
ves-tir *v.* to attire; to wear; to dress
ve-tar *v.* to veto
ve-te-ar *v.* to streak
ve-te-ra-no, -na *m., f., adj.* veteran
ve-te-ri-na-rio, -ria *m., f.* vet-

erinarian
vez *f.* time
vía *f.* means; way
via-ble *adj.* viable
via-jar *v.* to journey; to travel
via-je *m.* journey; trip
vial *adj.* traffic
vian-da *f.* food
vi-bo-ra *f.* viper
vi-bra-ción *f.* vibration
vi-brar *v.* to shake; to vibrate
vi-ce-pre-si-den-cia *f.* vice-presidency
vi-ce-pre-si-den-te *m.* vice-president
vi-ciar *v.* to corrupt; to falsify; to pollute
vi-cio *m.* vice
vi-cio-so, -sa *adj.* depraved
vi-ci-si-tud *f.* vicissitude
víc-ti-ma *f., m.* victim
vic-to-ra-ar *v.* to cheer
vic-to-ria *f.* victory
vic-to-rio-so, -sa *adj.* victorious
vid *f.* grapevine
vi-da *f.* life
vi-de-o *m.* video
vi-de-o-ca-se-te *m.* video-cassette
vi-de-o-cin-ta *f.* videotape
vi-dria-do, -da *adj.* glazed
vi-drie-ro, -ra *m., f.* glazier
vi-drio *m.* glass
vi-drio-so, -sa *adj.* glassy
vie-jo, -ja *adj.* aged; old
vien-to *m.* wind
vier-nes *m.* Friday
vi-gen-cia *f.* force
vi-gi-lan-cia *f.* vigilance
vi-gi-lan-te *adj.* heedful; vigilant
vi-gi-lar *v.* to guard
vi-gi-lia *f.* vigil
vi-gor *m.* strength; vigor
vi-go-ro-so, -sa *adj.* forceful; vigorous
vi-hue-la *f.* guitar
vi-le-za *f.* vileness
vi-lla *f.* village
vi-lla-no, -na *adj.* peasant
vi-na-gre *m.* vinegar
vi-na-gre-ta *f.* vinaigrette

vin-cu-lar *v.* to link
vin-di-ca-ción *f.* cindication
vin-di-car *v.* to vindicate
vi-ni-lo *m.* vinyl
vi-no *m.* wine
vi-ne-do *m.* vineyard
vio-la *f.* viola
vio-la-ce-o, -a *adj.* violet
vio-la-ción *f.* violation
vio-lar *v.* to violate
vio-len-cia *f.* violence; enbarrassment; rape
vio-len-tar *tr.* to force; to distort; to break into
vio-len-to, -ta *adj.* violent
vio-le-ta *f., adf* violet
vio-lín *f.* violin
vio-li-nis-ta *m., f.* violinist
vio-lón *m.* double bass player; double bass
vi-pe-ri-no, *adj.* venomous
vi-ra-je *m.* turning point; veering turn
vi-rar *tr.* to turn; to tone; to swerve
vir-gen *adf., f.* virgin
vir-il *adj.* virile
vir-tual *adj.* virtual
vi-ru-len-to, -ta *adj.* virulent
vi-rus *m., inv.* virus
vi-ru-ta *f.* shavings
vi-sar *tr.* to sight; to endorse
vis-co-si-dad *f.* viscosity
vi-se-ra *f.* visor
vi-si-llo *m.* windo curtain
vi-sión *f.* vision
vi-si-tar *v.* to visit
vis-ta *f.* sight; view
vis-to-so, -a *adj.* colorful
vi-sual *adj.* visual
vi-tal *adj.* vital
vi-ta-mi-na *f.* vitamin
vi-to-re-ar *tr.* to cheer
vi-tral *m.* stained-glass window
viu-da *f.* widow
viu-do *m.* widower
vi-vaz *adj.* lively
vi-ven-cia *f.* experience
vi-ve-res *m., pl.* provisions
vi-ve-ro *m., BOT.* fish hatchery; nursery
vi-ve-za *f.* liveliness;

sharpness; quickness

vi-vi-do, -da *adj.* vivid

vi-vien-da *f.* dwelling; housing

vi-vien-te *adj.* living

vi-vi-fi-ca-dor, -ra *adj.* vivifying

vi-vir *v.* to reside; to live

vi-vo, -va *adj.* vivid; lively

vo-ca-blo *m.* term

vo-ca-bu-la-rio *m.* vocabulary

vo-ca-ción *f.* job; occupation; vocation

vo-cal *adj.* vocal

vo-ca-li-za-ción *f.* vocalization

vo-ce-ar *intr., tr.* to shout

vo-ce-o *m.* shouting

vo-ce-ro, -a *m., f.* spokesman; spokeswoman

vo-la-da *f.* short flight

vo-lan-do *adv.* in a flash

vo-lan-te *adj.* balance wheel; steering wheel

vo-lar *v.* to fly; to blow up; to disappear

vo-la-tin *m.* acrobatic stunt

vo-la-ti-ne-ro, -a *m., f.* tightrope walker

vol-cán *m.* volcano

vo-le-ar *ARG.* to scatter

vo-li-ción *f.* volition

vol-ta-je *m.* voltage

vol-tear *v.* to upset; to turn over

vol-te-re-ta *f.* somersault

vol-tí-me-tro *m.* voltmeter

vol-tio *m.* volt

vo-lu-ble *adj.* fickle; voluble

vo-lu-men *m.* volume

vo-lun-tad *f.* will; wish; intention

vo-lun-ta-rio, -ria *adj.* voluntary

vo-lun-ta-rio-so, -a *adj.* willing; willful

vo-lup-tuo-si-dad *f.* voluptuousness

vol-ver *v.* to turn; to return; to recur; to restore

vo-mi-tar *tr.* to spew; to vomit; to spill

vo-mi-ti-vo, -a *adj., m.* vomi-

tive

vo-ra-ci-dad *f.* voracity

vo-ra-gi-ne *f.* whirlpoool

vo-ra-gi-no-so, -a *adj.* turbulent

vo-raz *adj.* voracious

vór-ti-ce *m.* center of a cyclone; vortex

vos *pron., m., f.* you

vo-se-ar *tr.* to address

vo-se-o *m.* used in addressing someone

vo-so-tras *pron., f.* you

vo-so-tros *pron., m.* you

vo-ta-ción *f.* voting; vote

vo-tan-te *m., f.* voter

vo-tar *v.* to vote

vo-ti-vo *adj.* votive

voz *f.* voice

vo-za-rrón *m.* booming voice

vuel-co *m.* to overturn; overturning

vue-lo *m.* flight

vuel-to, -a *m., f.* revolution

vues-tra *adj.* your

vul-ca-ni-zar *tr.* to vulcanize

vul-gar *adj.* vulgar; common

vul-ga-ri-dad *f.* vulgarity

vul-ga-ris-mo *m.* vulgarism

vul-ga-ri-zar *tr.* to popularize; to vulgarize

vul-go *m.* masses

vul-ne-ra-bi-li-dad *f.* vulnerability

vul-ne-rar *tr.* to violate; to wound

vul-va *f.* vulva

wat *m.* watt

wel-ter *m.* welterweight

whis-ky *m.* whiskey

xe-no-fo-bia *f.* xenophobia

xi-ló-fo-no *m.* xylophone

xi-lo-gra-fí-a *f.* xylography

ya-ca-fe *m.* alligator
ya-cer *intr.* to lie; to be
ya-guar *m.* jaguar
yam-bi-co *adj.* iambic
yan-qui *adj., m., f.* Yankee
yar-da *f.* yard
ya-te *m.* yacht
ye-gua *f.* mare
ye-gua-da *f.* herd of horses
yel-mo *m.* helmet
ye-ma *f.* yolk
yen *m., FIN.* yen
yer-ba *f.* grass
yer-bal *m. F.P.* field of mate
yer-mar *tr.* to strip
yer-mo, -a *adj.* barren
yer-no *m.* son-in-law
ye-rra *f.* cattle branding
ye-rro *m.* fault; sin
yer-to *adj.* frozen stiff
ye-se-ro *adj.* plaster
ye-so *m.* gypsum
yo *pron.* I; me
yo-da-do, -a *adj.* iodized
yo-da-to *m.* iodate
yo-do *m.* iodine
yo-du-ro *m.* iodide
yo-ga *m.* yoga
yo-g(h)i *m.* yogi
yo-gur(t) *m.* yogurt
yo-yo *m.* yo-yo
yu-ca *f.* manioc
yu-cal *m.* yucca field
yu-do *m.* judo
yuu-ga-da *f.* day's plowing;
  yoke
yu-gu-lar *adj., f.* jugular
yun-que *m.* anvil
yun-ta *f.* yoke
yu-te *m.* jute

yux-ta-po-ner *tr* to juxtapose
yux-ta-po-si-cion *f.* jux-
  taposition
yu-yal *m.* weed patch
yu-yo *m.* weed
yu-yu-ba *f.* jujube

za-far(se) *v.* loosen
za-gal *m.* boy; lad
za-ga-la *f.* lass
za-ma-rro *m.* sheepskin
zam-bu-lli-da *f.* dive
zam-bu-llir *v.* plunge into
za-na-ho-ria *f.* carrot
zan-ja *f.* trench; ditch
za-pa-te-ria *f.* shoestore
za-pa-te-ro *m.* shoemaker
za-pa-ti-lla *v.* slipper
za-pa-to *m.* shoe
zar *m.* czar
za-ri-na *f.* czarina
zar-za-mo-ra *f.* blackberry
zo-co *adj.* left-handed
zo-dia-co *m.* zodiac
zo-na *f.* zone
zoo-lo-gia *f.* zoology
zoo-lo-gi-co *adj.* zoological
zoo-lo-go *m.* zoologist
zo-rra *f.* fox
zo-rro *m.* fox
zo-zo-brar *v.* overturn
zum-bar *v.* whirr; buzz
zu-mo *m.* juice
zu-mo-so *adj.* juicy
zur-cir *v.* stitch

a *indef. article* una; un
a-back *adv.* atras
a-ba-cus *n.* ábaco
a-ban-don *v.* abandonar
a-base *v.* humillar; rebajar
a-bate *v.* disminuir; reducir
ab-bey *n.* monasterio
ab-bre-vi-a-tion *n.* abreviación
ab-di-cate *v.* abdicar
ab-do-men *n.* abdomen
ab-duct *v.* secuestrar
ab-er-ra-tion *n.* aberración
a-bet *v.* instigar; ayudar
ab-hor *v.* aborrecer
a-bide *v.* habitar; soportar
a-bil-i-ty *n.* habilidad
ab-ject *adj.* abyecto
ab-jure *v.* abjurar
a-ble *adj.* capaz; competente
ab-ne-gate *v.* renunciar; negar
ab-nor-mal *adj.* anormal
a-board *adv.,prep.* a bordo
a-bode *n.* domicilio
a-bol-ish *v.* abolir
a-bom-i-nate *v.* abominar
ab-o-rig-i-nes *n.* aborigenes
a-bor-tion *n.* aborto
a-bound *v.* abundar
a-bout *prep.* sobre; alrededor de
a-bove *prep.* sobre; encima de
a-bra-sion *n.* abrasión
a-breast *adv.* de frente; al lado
a-bridge *v.* abreviar; resumir
a-broad *adv.* fuera de casa; en el extranjero
ab-ro-gate *v.* abrogar
ab-rupt *adj.* brusco
ab-scess *n.* absceso
ab-scond *v.* fugarse
ab-sent *adj.* ausente
ab-so-lute *adj.* completo; absoluto
ab-solve *v.* absolver
ab-sorb *v.* absorber
ab-stain *v.* abstenerse
ab-ste-mi-ous *adj.* abstemio
ab-stract *v.* abstraer
ab-surd *adj.* absurdo

a-bun-dant *adj.* abundante
a-buse *v.* abstraer
a-but *v.* confinar
a-byss *n.* abismo
ac-a-dem-ic *adj.* academico
a-cad-e-my *n.* academia
ac-cede *v.* acceder; consentir; subir
ac-cel-er-ate *v.* acelerar
ac-cent *n.* acento
ac-cept *v.* recibir
ac-cess *n.* acceso
ac-ces-si-ble *adj.* accesible
ac-ces-so-ry *n.,pl.* accesorios; complice
ac-ci-dent *n.* accidente
ac-claim *v.* aclamar
ac-cli-mate *v.* aclimatar
ac-co-lade *n.* acolada
ac-com-mo-date *v.* acomodar
ac-com-pa-ny *v.* acompanar
ac-com-plice *n.* cómlice
ac-com-plish *v.* cumplir; acabar
ac-cord *n.* acuerdo
ac-cor-di-on *n.* acordéon
ac-count *v.* explicar
ac-count-a-ble *adj.* responsable
ac-cum-u-late *v.* acumular
ac-cu-ra-cy *n.* exactitude
ac-cu-rate *adj.* exacto; fiel
ac-cuse *v.* acusar; culpar
ac-cus-tom *v.* acostumbrar
a-ce-tic *adj.* acetico
ac-c-tone *n.* acetone
ache *n.* dolor
a-chieve *v.* acabar
ac-id *adj.* ácido
ac-knowl-edge *v.* reconocer; confesar; agradecer
ac-me *n.* cima
ac-ne *n.* acne
ac-o-lyte *n.* acolito
a-corn *n.* bellota
a-cous-tics *n.* acustica
ac-quaint *v.* enterar
ac-quaint-ance *n.* conocido
ac-qui-esce *v.* consentir
ac-quire *v.* adquirir
ac-quit *v.* absolver
a-cre *n.* acre

ac-rid *adj.* acre
ac-ri-mo-ny *n.* acrimonia
ac-ro-bat *n.* acrobata
a-cross *prep.* a traves de
act *v.* fingir; hacer
ac-tion *n.* acción
ac-ti-vate *v.* activar
ac-tive *adj.* activo
ac-tor *n.* actor
ac-tress *n.* actriz
ac-tu-al *adj.* actual; real
a-cu-i-ty *n.* agudeza
a-cu-men *n.* agudeza
a-cute *adj.* agudo; fino
ad-age *n.* adagio
ad-a-mant *adj.* firme
a-dapt *v.* adaptar
add *v.* sumar; anadir
ad-di-tion *n.* adición
ad-dress *v.* dirigir (se a)
a-dept *n., adj.* experto
ad-e-quate *adj.* adecuado; suficiente
ad-here *v.* adherirse; pegarse; cumplir
ad-he-sive *adj., n.* adhesivo
ad-ja-cent *adj.* adyacente
ad-jec-tive *n.* adjetivo
ad-join *v.* juntar; estar contiguo
ad-journ *v.* suspender
ad-judge *v.* juzgar; sentenciar
ad-just *v.* ajustar; adaptar
ad-ju-tant *n.* ayudante
ad-lib *v.* improvisar
admin-is-ter *v.* administrar
ad-min-is-tra-tion *n.* administración
ad-mire *v.* admirar
ad-mis-si-ble *adj.* admisible
ad-mis-sion *n.* entrada; confesion
ad-mit *v.* confesar; admitir
ad-mon-ish *v.* amonestar
a-do-be *n.* adobe
ad-o-les-cence *n.* adolescencia
a-dopt *v.* adoptar; aceptar
a-dore *v.* adorar
a-dorn *v.* adornar
a-dren-a-line *n.* adrenalina
a-droit *adj.* habil; diestro

ad-u-la-tion *n.* adulación
a-dult *adj.* mayor
a-dul-ter-y *n.* adulterio
ad-vance *v.* avanzar
ad-van-tage *n.* ventaja
ad-ven-ture *n.* aventura
ad-ven-ture-some *adj.* aventurado
ad-verb *n.* adverbio
ad-ver-sar-y *n.* adversario
ad-verse *adj.* adverso; contrario
ad-ver-si-ty *n.* adversidad
ad-ver-tise *v.* publicar
ad-vice *n.* consejo
ad-vise *v.* avisar
ad-vo-cate *v.* abogar
adz, adze *n.* azuela
ae-gis *n.* egido
aer-ate *v.* airear
aer-i-al *adj.* aereo
aer-o-naut-ics *n. pl.* aeronautica
aes-thete *n.* esteta
aes-thet-ic *adj.* estetico
a-far *adv.* lejos
af-fa-ble *adj.* afable; cortes
af-fair *n.* amorosa
af-fect *v.* afectar
af-fec-ta-tion *n.* afectación
af-fec-tion *n.* afeccion
af-fec-tion-ate *adj.* carinoso
af-fi-ance *v.* desposarse
af-fi-da-vit *n.* declaración jurada
af-fil-i-ate *v.* afiliar
af-fin-i-ty *n.* afinidad
af-firm *v.* afirmar
af-firm-a-tive *n.* aserción
af-fix *v.* anadir; fijar
af-flic-tion *n.* aflicción
af-flu-ence *n.* afluencia
af-flu-ent *adj.* rico; opulento
af-ford *v.* tener medios para; dar
af-front *v.* afrentar
a-fire *adj., adv.* ardiendo
a-flame *adj., adv.* en llamas
a-float *adj., adv.* a flote
a-foul *adj., adv.* enredado
a-fraid *adj.* atemorizado
a-fresh *adv.* de nuevo; otra vez

aft adj., adv. en (a) popa
af-ter prep. detras de
af-ter-birth n. secundinas
af-ter-noon n. tarde
af-ter-ward adv. despues
a-gain adv. otra vez
a-gainst prep. contra
a-gape adj., adv. boqui-abierto
agen. edad
a-ged adj. viejo
a-gen-cy n. agencia; accion; medio
a-gen-da n. pl. orden del dia
a-gent n. agente; repre-sentante
ag-glom-er-ate v. aglomerar
ag-gran-dize v. engrandcer
ag-gra-vate v. agravar
ag-gre-gate v. agregar; jun-ter
ag-gres-sion n. agresión
ag-gres-sive adj. agresivo
a-ghast adj. horrorizado
a-gil adj. agil
a-gil-i-ty n. agilidad
ag-i-tate v. agitar; inquietar
a-glow adj. ardiente
ag-nos-tic n. agnostico
a-go adj. pasado
ag-o-ny n. agonia; angustia
a-grar-i-an adj. agrario
a-gree v. acordar
a-gree-a-ble adj. agradable; conforme
a-gree-ment n. acuerdo
ag-ri-cul-ture n. agricultura
a-gron-o-my n. agronomia
a-ground adv. encallado
a-head adv. al frente
aid n. ayuda
ail-ment n. enfermedad; dolencia
aim v. aspirar
air n. aire
air con-di-tion-er n. acon-dicionador de aire
air-plane n. avion
air-port n. aeropuerto
air-raid n. ataque aereo
air-y adj. ligero; alegre
aisle n. nave lateral; pasillo
a-jar adj., adv. entreabierto

a-kin adj. semejante; con-sanguineo
al-a-bas-ter n. alabastro
a-lac-ri-ty n. alacridad
a-larm n. alarma
a-larm-ist n. alarmista
al-ba-tross n. albatros
al-be-it conj. aunque
al-bi-no n. albino
al-bum n. album
al-bu-men n. albumen
al-bu-min n. albumina
al-che-my n. alquimia
al-co-hol n. alcohol
ale n. cerveza
a-lee adv. a sotavento
a-lert adj. alerte
al-fal-fa n. alfalfa
al-ga n. alga
al-ge-bra n. algebra
a-li-as n. alias
al-i-bi n. coartada; excusa
al-ien n. extranjero
al-ien-ate v. enajenar
a-light v. bajar; posarse
a-lign v. alinera; aliar
a-like adj. semejante
al-i-ment n. alimento
al-i-men-ta-ry adj. alimen-ticio
al-i-mo-ny n. alimentos
a-live adj. activo
al-ka-lize v. alcalizar
all adj. todo
al-lay v. aliviar; aquietar
al-le-ga-tion n. alegación
al-lege v. alegar; declarar
al-leged adj. supuesto; alegado
al-le-giance n. lealtad
al-le-go-ry n. alegoria
al-ler-gy n. alergia
al-le-vi-ate v. calmar
al-le-vi-a-tion n. aligeramiento
al-ley n. callejuela
al-li-ance n. alianza
al-li-ga-tor n. caiman
al-lo-cate v. asignar
al-lo-ca-tion n. reparto; cupo
al-lot v. asignar; distribuir; adjudicar
al-low v. dar; permitir

al-low-ance *n.* ración; permision
al-loy *n.* aleación
al-lude *v.* aludir
al-lure *v.* tentar
al-lu-sion *n.* alusion
al-lu-vi-um *n.* derrubio
al-ly *n.* aliado; confederado
al-ma-nac *n.* almanaque
al-might-y *adj.* omnipotente; todopoderoso
al-mond *n.* almendra; almendro
al-most *adv.* casi
alms *n.* limosna
a-loft *adv.* en alto
a-lone *adj.* solo
a-long *adv., con., prep.* a lo largo
a-loof *adv. lejos* reservado
a-loud *adv.* en voz alta; alto
al-pha-bet *n.* alfabeto
al-read-y *adv.* ya
al-so *adv.* también; ademas
al-tar *n.* altar
al-ter *v.* cambiar; alterar; modificar
al-ter-a-tion *n.* alteración
al-ter-ca-tion *n.* altercación
al-ter e-go *n.* alter ego
al-ter-nate *v.* alternar
al-ter-na-tive *n.* alternativa
al-though *conj.* aunque
al-tim-e-ter *n.* altimetro
al-ti-tude *n.* altura; altitude
al-to *n.* alto; contralto
al-to-geth-er *adv.* en total
a-lu-mi-num *n.* aluminio
a-lum-na *n., f.* graduada
a-lum-nus *n.* graduado
al-ways *adv.* siempre
a.m. antemeridiano
a-mal-gam *n.* amalgama
a-mal-gam-ate *v.* amalgamar
a-mass *v.* acumular; amontonar
am-a-teur *n.* aficionada
am-a-to-ry *adj.* amatorio
a-maze *v.* asombrar
a-maze-ment *n.* sorpresa
am-a-zon *n.* amazona
am-bas-sa-dor *n.* embajador

am-ber *n.* ambar
am-bi-dex-trous *adj.* ambidextro
am-bi-gu-i-ty *n.* ambiguedad; doble sentido
am-big-u-ous *adj.* ambiguo
am-bi-tion *n.* ambición
am-bi-tious *adj.* ambicioso
am-biv-a-lence *n.* ambivalencia
am-ble *v.* amblar; andar lentamente
am-bu-late *v.* andar
am-bu-la-to-ry *a.* ambulante
am-bus-cade *n.* emboscada
am-bush *n.* emboscada; docil; respinsable
a-me-ba *n.* amiba
a-mel-io-rate *v.* mejorar
a-mel-io-ra-tion *n.* mejora; mejoramiento
a-men *int.* amen
a-me-na-ble *adj.* docil
a-mend *v.* enmendar; corregir
a-mends *n., pl.* compensación
a-men-i-ty *n.* amenidad
A-mer-i-can *adj.* americano
am-e-thyst *n.* amatista
a-mi-a-ble *adj.* amable
am-i-ca-ble *adj.* amistoso
a-mid *prep.* en medio de; entre.
a-mid-ships *adv.* en medio del navio
a-miss *adv., adj.* impropiamente; mel
am-mo-nia *n.* municion
am-ne-sia *n.* amnesia
am-nes-ty *n.* amniastia
a-moe-ba *n.* amiba
a-mong *prep.* en medio de
a-mor-al *adj.* amoral
am-o-rous *adj.* amoroso
a-mor-phous *adj.* amoroso
am-or-tize *v.* amortizar
a-mount *n.* cantidad; suma
am-pere *n.* amperio
am-phib-i-an *adj., n.* anfibio
am-phib-i-ous *adj.* anfibio
am-phi-the-a-ter *n.* anfiteatro

am-ple *adj.* abundante
am-pli-fy *v.* amplificar
am-pli-tude *n.* amplitud; abundancia
am-pu-tate *v.* amputar
am-pu-ta-tion *n.* amputación
a-muck *adv.* furiosamente
am-u-let *n.* amuleto
a-muse-ment *n.* pasatiempo
an *indef. article* una; un; uno
a-nach-ro-nism *n.* anacronismo
an-a-con-da *n.* anaconda
a-nae-mi-a *n.* anemia
an-a-gram *n.* anagrama
a-nal *adj.* anal
an-al-ge-sic *adj.* analgesico
a-nal-o-gize *v.* analogizar
a-nal-o-gy *n.* analogia
a-nal-y-sis *n.* analisis
an-a-lyst *n.* analizador
an-a-lyze *v.* analizar
an-ar-chism *n.* anarquismo
an-ar-chist *n.* anarquista
an-ar-chy *n.* anarquia
a-nat-o-my *n.* anatomia
an-ces-tor *n.* antepasado
an-ces-try *n.* linaje; abolengo
an-chor *n.* ancla; ancora
an-cho-vy *n.* anchoa
an-cient *adj.* antiguo
and *conj.* y
an-ec-dote *n.* anecdota
a-ne-mi-a *n.* anemia
an-e-mon-e-ter *n.* anemometro
an-es-the-sia *n.* anestesia
an-es-thet-ic *n., adj.* anestesico
a-new *adv.* de nuevo; otra vez
an-gel *n.* angel
an-gel-ic *adj.* angelico
an-ger *n.* ira; colera
an-gle *n.* angulo
an-gle-worm *n.* lombriz
An-glo-Sax-on *v., adj.* anglosajon
an-gor-a *n.* angora
an-gry *adj.* enfadado
an-quish *n.* angustia; ansioa
an-gu-lar *adj.* angular; an-
guloso
an-hy-drous *adj.* anhidro
an-i-mad-ver-sion *n.* animadversion
an-i-mad-vert *v.* censurar
an-i-mal *n.* animal
an-i-mal-ize *v.* animalizar
an-i-mate *v.* dar vida
an-i-ma-tion *n.* animación
an-i-mos-i-ty *n.* animosidad
an-ise *n.* anis
an-kle *n.* tobillo
an-nals *n., pl.* anales
an-neal *v.* templar
an-nex *v.* anexar; adjuntar
an-nex-a-tion *n.* anexión
an-ni-hi-late *v.* aniquilar
an-ni-hi-la-tion *n.* aniquilación
an-ni-ver-sa-ry *n.* aniversario
an-no-tate *v.* anotar
an-nounce *v.* proclamar
an-nounce-ment *n.* anuncio
an-noy *v.* molestar
an-noy-ance *n.* fastidio
an-nu-al *adj.* anual
an-nu-i-ty *n.* renta vitalicia
an-nul *v.* anular
an-nul-ment *n.* anulación
an-nun-ci-ate *v.* anunciar
an-nun-ci-a-tion *n.* anunciación
an-ode *n.* anodo
a-noint *v.* untar; ungir
a-nom-a-lous *adj.* anomalo
a-nom-a-ly *n.* anomalia
a-non-y-mous *adj.* anonimo
an-oth-er *adj., pron.* otro
an-swer *v.* contestar; responder
ant *n.* hormiga
ant-ac-id *n.* antiacido
an-tag-o-nist *n.* antagonista
an-tag-o-nize *v.* contender
ant-arc-tic *adj.* antartico
ant-eat-er *n.* oso hormiguero
an-te-cede *v.* anteceder
an-te-ced-ent *n.* antecendente
an-te-date *v.* antedatar; preceder
an-te-di-lu-ve-an *adj.* antediluviano

an-te-lope *n.* antilope
an-ten-na *n.* antena
an-te-ri-or *adj.* anterior
an-te-room *n.* antecamara
an-them *n.* antifona. **na-tion-al an-them** himno nacional
an-ther *n.* antera
an-thol-o-gy *n.* antologia
an-thra-cite *n.* antracita
an-thrax *n.* antrax
an-thro-poid *adj.* antropoide
an-thro-pol-o-gist *n.* antropologo
an-thro-pol-o-gy *n.* antropologia
an-ti *prefix* anti; contra
an-ti-bi-ot-ic *n.* antibiotico
an-ti-bod-y *n.* anticuerpo
an-tic *n.* travesura; cabriola
an-tic-i-pate *v.* anticipar; esperar
an-tic-i-pa-tion *n.* anticipacion; expectacion
an-ti-cli-max *n.* anticlimax
an-ti-dote *n.* antidoto
an-tip-a-thy *n.* antipatia
an-tip-odes *n.* antipoda
an-ti-quate *v.* anticuar
an-ti-quat-ed *adj.* viejo; anticuado
an-tique *adj.* antiguo
an-tiq-ui-ty *n.* antiguedad
an-ti-Sem-i-tism *n.* antisemitismo
an-ti-sep-tic *adj., n.* antiseptico
an-ti-so-cial *adj.* antisocial
an-tith-e-sis *n.* antitesis
an-ti-tox-in *n.* antitoxina
ant-ler *n.* cuerna; asta
an-to-nym *n.* antonimo
a-nus *n.* ano
an-vil *n.* yunque
anx-i-e-ty *n.* inquietud; ansia
anx-ious *adj.* impaciente
an-y *adj., pron.* alguno; algun
an-y-bod-y *pron.* alguien
an-y-how *adv.* de cualquier modo; de todas formas
an-y-one *pron.* alguien; alguno
an-y-thing *pron.* algo

an-y-way *adv.* de cualquier modo; de todas formas
an-y-where *adv.* en todas partes; dondequiera
a-or-ta *n.* aorta
a-part *adv.* aparte. **a-part from** aparte de
a-part-ment *n.* apartamento
ap-a-thet-ic *adj.* indiferente
ap-a-thy *n.* apatia
ape *n.* mono
ap-er-ture *n.* abertura
a-pex *n.* apice
aph-o-rism *n.* aforismo
aph-ro-dis-i-ac *n.* afrodisiaco
a-pi-a-rist *n.* colmenero
a-pi-ar-y *n.* colmenar
a-piece *adv.* cada uno; por persona
a-plomb *n.* aplomo
a-poc-a-lypse *n.* apocalipsis
a-pol-o-gize *v.* disculparse
a-pol-o-gy *n.* apologia; disculpa
ap-o-plec-tic *adj.* apopletico
ap-o-plex-y *n.* apoplejia
a-port *adv.* a babor
a-pos-tate *n.* apostata
a-pos-ta-tize *v.* apostatar
a-pos-tle *n.* apostol
ap-os-tol-ic *adj.* apostolico
a-pos-tro-phe *n.* apostrofo
a-poth-e-car-y *n.* boticario
ap-pall, ap-pal *v.* aterrar
ap-pa-rat-us *n.* aparato
ap-pa-rel *n.* ropa
ap-par-ent *a.* claro; aparente
ap-pa-ri-tion *n.* fantasma
ap-peal *n.* apelacion
ap-pear *v.* parecer
ap-pear-ance *n.* apariencia
ap-pease *v.* apaciguar
ap-pel-lant *n.* apelante
ap-pel-la-tion *n.* nombre
ap-pend *v.* anexar
ap-pen-dage *n.* apendice
ap-pen-dec-to-my *n.* apendectomia
ap-pen-di-ci-tis *n.* apendicitis
ap-pen-dix *n.* apendice
ap-per-tain *v.* pertenecer

ap-pe-tite *n.* gana
ap-pe-tiz-ing *adj.* apetitoso; apetitivo
ap-plaud *v.* aplaudir
ap-plause *n.* aplauso
ap-ple *n.* manzana
ap-pli-cant *n.* suplicante
ap-pli-ca-tion *n.* aplicación
ap-ply *v.* aplicar
ap-point *v.* senalar; nombrar
ap-point-ment *n.* cita; nombramiento
ap-por-tion *v.* repartir
ap-po-si-tion *n.* aposición
ap-prais-al *n.* valoración
ap-praise *v.* valorar
ap-pre-ci-ate *v.* apreciar; volorar; agradecer
ap-pre-ci-a-tion *n.* aprecio; aumento en valor
ap-pre-hend *v.* entender
ap-pre-hen-sion *n.* aprenhension
ap-pren-tice *n.* aprendiz, *v.* poner de aprendize
ap-prixe, ap-prize *v.* informar
ap-proach *v.* aproximarse
ap-pro-ba-tion *n.* aporobación
ap-pro-pri-ate *v.* apropiarse; destinar. *adj.* apropiado
ap-prov-al *n.* aprobación
ap-prove *v.* aprobar
ap-prox-i-mate *v.* aproximar
ap-ri-cot *n.* albaricoque
A-pril *n.* abril
a-pron *n.* delantal, *m.*
ap-ro-pos of *prep.* a proposito de
apt *adj.* apto; listo
ap-ti-tude *n.* aptitud
a-quar-i-um *n.* acuario
a-quat-ic *adj.* acuatico
aq-ue-duct *n.* acueducto
a-que-ous *adj.* acueo
aq-ui-line *adj.* aguileño
Ar-ab *n., adj.* arabe, *m., f.*
Ar-a-bic nu-me-rals *n.* numeros arabigos
ar-a-ble *adj.* labrantio; cultivable
ar-bi-ter *n.* arbitro

ar-bi-trar-y *adj.* arbitrario
ar-bi-trate *v.* arbitrar
ar-bi-tra-tion *n.* arbitraje
ar-bo-re-al *adj.* arboreo
ar-bo-re-tum *n.* jardin botanico
arc *n.* arce. *v.* formar un arco voltaico
ar-cade *n.* arcada; galeria
arch *n.* arco. *v.* arquear
arch- *prefix* principal
ar-chae-ol-o-gy, ar-che-ol-o-gy *n.* arqueología
ar-cha-ic *adj.* arcaico
arch-an-gel *n.* arcangel
arch-bish-op *n.* arzobispo
arch-duch-ess *n.* archiduquest
arch-duke *n.* archiduque
arch-er *n.* arquero
ar-cher-y *n.* ballesteria
ar-che-type *n.* arquetipo
ar-chi-pel-a-go *n.* archipielago
ar-chi-tect *n.* arquitecto
ar-chi-tec-tur-al *adj.* arquitectonico
ar-chi-tec-ture *n.* arquitectura
ar-chive *n.* archivo
arch-priest *n.* arcipreste
arc-tic *adj.* artico
ar-dent *adj.* ardiente; fervoroso
ar-dor *n.* ardoι
ar-du-ous *adj.* arduo; dificil
a-re-na *n.* areña
ar-gon *n.* argo
ar-got *n.* jerga
ar-gue *v.* razonar
ar-gu-ment *n.* disputa
ar-gu-men-ta-tive *adj.* argumentador
a-ri-a *n.* aria
ar-id *adj.* arido
a-rid-i-ty *n.* aridez
a-rise *v.* alzarse; surgir
ar-is-toc-ra-cy *n.* aristocracía
a-ris-to-crat *n.* aristocrata
a-ris-to-crat-ic *adj.* aristocratico
a-rith-me-tic *n.* aritmetica
a-rith-me-ti-cian *n.* arit-

metico
ark *n.* arca
arm *n.* brazo
ar-ma-da *n.* armada
ar-ma-dil-lo *n.* armadillo
ar-ma-ment *n.* armamento
arm-ful *n.* brazado
ar-mi-stice *n.* armisticio
ar-moire *n.* armario
ar-mor *n.* armadura
ar-mored *adj.* blindado
ar-mor-y *n.* armeria
arm-pit *n.* sobaco
ar-my *n.* ejercito
a-ro-ma *n.* aroma
ar-o-mat-ic *adj.* aromatico
a-round *adv.* alrededor
a-rouse *v.* despertar; excitar
ar-range *v.* arreglar; prevenir
ar-range-ment *n.* orden
ar-rant *adj.* consumado
ar-ray *n* orden; formación; adorno. *v.* colocar; ataviar
ar-rest *v.* detener
ar-ri-val *n.* llegada
ar-rive *v.* llegar
ar-ro-gance *n.* arrogancia
ar-ro-gant *adj.* arrogante
ar-row *n.* flecha
ar-row-head *n.* punta de lfecha
ar-sen-al *n.* arsenal
ar-sen-ic *n.* arsenico
ar-son *n.* incendio premeditado
art *n.* arte
ar-te-ri-al *adj.* arterial
ar-ter-y *n.* arteria
art-ful *adj.* ingenioso; astuto
ar-thrit-ic *adj.* artrico
ar-thri-tis *n.* artritis, *f.*
ar-ti-cle *n.* articulo; objeto
ar-tic-u-late *v.* articular
ar-tic-u-la-tion *n.* articulación
ar-ti-fi-cial *adj.* artificial
ar-til-ler-y *n.* artilleria
art-ist *n.* artista
ar-tis-tic *adj.* artistic
as *conj., adv.* como
as-bes-tos, as-bes-tus *n.* asbesto
as-cend *v.* subir; ascender

as-cen-sion *n.* ascensión
as-cent *n.* subida; cuesta
as-cer-tain *v.* averiguar
as-ce-tic *adj.* ascetico. *n.* asceta *m., f.*
as-cet-i-cism *n.* ascetismo
as-cribe *v.* atribuir
a-sex-u-al *adj.* asexual
ash *n.* ceniza; fresno
a-shamed *adj.* avergonzado
a-side *adv.* a un lado *n.* aparte
as-i-nine *adj.* asnal
ask *v.* rogar; preguntar
a-skance *adv.* con recelo
a-slant *adv.* al sesgo. *prep.* a traves de
a-sleep *adv., adj.* dormido
asp *n.* aspid
as-par-a-gus *n.* esparrago
as-pect *n.* aspecto; aire
as-per-i-ty *n.* aspereze
as-per-sion *n.* calumnia
as-phalt *n.* asfalto
as-phyx-i-ate *v.* asfixiar
as-phyx-i-a-tion *n.* asfixia
as-pi-ra-tion *n.* aspiración; anhelo
as-pire *v.* aspirar
as-pi-rin *n.* aspirina
ass *n.* burro; tonto
as-sail *v.* acometer
as-sail-ant *n.* asaltador
as-sas-in *n.* asesino
as-sas-si-na-tion *n.* asesinato
as-sault *v.* atacar
as-sem-ble *v.* juntar
as-sem-bly *n.* asamblea
as-sent *n.* asentimiento
as-sert *v.* afirmar
as-sess *v.* fijar; tasar
as-set *n.* haber
as-sev-er-ate *v.* aseverar
as-sid-u-ous *adj.* asiduo
as-sign *v.* asignar
as-sign-ment *n.* asignación
as-sim-i-late *v.* asimilar
as-sist *v.* ayudar
as-sist-ance *n.* ayuda
asth-ma *n.* asma
asth-mat-ic *adj.* asmatico
as-ton-ish *v.* asombrar

as-ton-ish-ment *n.* asombro
as-trol-o-gy *n.* astrología
as-tron-o-my *n.* astronomia
at *prep.* a; en
ath-lete *n.* atleta
ath-let-ic *adj.* atletico
at-om *n.* atomo
a-tom-ic *adj.* atomico
a-top *prep.* sobre
at-tach *v.* pegar; sujetar
at-tack *v.* atacar
at-tempt *v.* intentar
at-tend *v.* asistir
at-ten-tion *n.* atención
at-tract *v.* atraer
at-trac-ion *n.* atracción
a-typ-i-cal *adj.* atipico
au-di-ence *n.* publico
au-di-tion *n.* audición
au-di-to-ry *adj.* auditivo
Au-gust *n.* agosto
aunt *n.* tia
au-then-tic-i-ty *n.* autenticidad
au-thor *n.* autor
au-thor-i-ty *n.* autoridad
au-thor-ize *v.* autorizar
au-to-bi-og-ra-pher *n.* autobiografo
au-to-bi-og-ra-phy *n.* autobiografia
au-to-ma-tic *adj.* automatico
au-to-ma-tion *n.* automatización
au-to-mo-bile *n.* automovil; coche
au-ton-o-mous *a.* autonomo
a-venge *v.* vengar
av-e-nue *n.* avenida
a-ver *v.* afirmar
av-er-age *adj.* medio
a-vert *v.* apartar
a-wait *v.* esperar
a-wake *v.* despertar(se)
a-way *adv.* lejos
aw-ful *adj.* horrible
awk-ward *adj.* embarazoso
ax-i-om *n.* axioma
ax-i-o-mat-ic *adj.* axiomatico
ax-is *n.* axis; eje
ax-le *n.* eje
aye, ay *int., n.* si
az-ure *adj., n.* azul celeste

bab-ble *v.* murmurar; barbotar; susurrar
ba-boon *n.* mandril
ba-bush-ka *n.* pañuelo
ba-by *n.* nino
ba-by-hood *n.* infancia
ba-by-ish *adj.* infantil
bac-cha-nal *n.* bacanal
bach-e-lor *n.* soltero
bach-e-lor-hood *n.* solteria
ba-cil-lus *n.* bacilo
back *n.* espalda
back-ache *n.* dolor de espalda
back-bit-ing *n.* murmuración
back-bone *n.* espinazo
back-break-ing *adj.* agobiador
back-date *v.* antedatar
back-er *n.* promotor
back-gam-mon *n.* chaquete
back-ground *n.* fondo
back-hand-ed *adj.* ambiguo
back-lash *n.* sacudida
back-pack *n.* mochila
back-side *n.* trasero
back-stairs *adj.* furtivo
back-track *v.* desandar
back-up *n.* suplente; reserva
back-ward *adv.* atras
back-ward-ness *n.* retraso
ba-con *n.* tocino
bac-te-rial *adj.* bacteriaño
bac-te-ri-cide *n.* bactericida
bac-ter-i-um *n.* bacteria
bad *adj.* malo
badge *n.* insignia
bad-ger *n.* tejon
bad-ly *adv.* mal
bad-min-ton *n.* volante
baf-fle *v.* desconcertar; confundir
baf-fle-ment *n.* confusion
baf-fling *adj.* desconcertante
bag *n.* bolso; saco
bag-gage *n.* equipaje
bag-pipe *n.* gaita
bail *v.* afianzar
bail-iff *n.* alguacil
bail-or *n.* fiador
bait *n.* carnada
bake *v.* cocer en horno
bak-er *n.* panadero

bak-er-y *n.* panaderia
bak-ing *n.* cocción
bal-ance *n.* equilibrio
bal-anced *adj.* balanceado
bal-co-ny *n.* balcon
bald *adj.* calvo
bald-ness *n.* calcicie
bale *n.* bala
bale-ful *adj.* funesto
balk *v.* oponerse
ball *n.* pelota
bal-lad *n.* balada
bal-le-ri-na *n.* bailarina
bal-let *n.* ballet
bal-lis-tic *adj.* balistico
bal-loon *n.* globo
bal-lot *n.* votación
balm *n.* balsamo
bal-sa *n.* balsa
bam-boo *n.* bambu
ban *v.* prohibir
ba-nal *adj.* banal
ba-nan-a *n.* platano
band *n.* banda
band-age *v.* vendar
ban-dit *n.* bandido
ban-do-leer *n.* bandolera
bane-ful *adj.* nocivo
bang *v.* golpear
bangs *n.* flequillo
ban-gle *n.* esclava
ban-ish *v.* desterrar
ban-ish-ment *n.* proscripción; exilio
ban-is-ter *n.* baranda
ban-jo *n.* banjo
bank *n.* banco
bank-er *n.* banquero
bank-ing *n.* banca
bank-rupt *adj.* arruinado
ban-ner *n.* bandera
ban-quet *n.* banquete
ban-ter *f.* broma
bap-tism *n.* bautismo
bap-tist *n.* bautista
bap-tis-ter-y *n.* baptisterio
bap-tize *v.* bautizar
bar *v.* excluir
bar-br-i-an *adj.* barbaro
bar-bar-ic *adj.* barbaro
bar-bar-i-ty *n.* barbaridad
bar-ba-rous *adj.* barbaro
bar-ber *n.* peluquero

bar-ber-shop *n.* peluqueria
bar-bi-tu-rate *n.* barbiturico
bare *adj.* desnudo; *v.* des nudar
bare-faced *adj.* descarado
bare-ly *adv.* simplemente; apneas
bar-gain *n.* ganga; convenio
bar-gain-ing *n.* negociación
barge *n.* gabarra
bar-i-tone *n.* baritono
bar-i-um *n.* bario
bark *v.* ladrar; *n.* ladrido
bar-ley *n.* cebada
bar-maid *n.* cantinera
barn *n.* granero
bar-na-cle *n.* percebe
ba-rom-et-er *n.* barometro
bar-o-met-ric *adj.* barometrico
bar-on *n.* baron
bar-on-ess *n.* baronesa
ba-roque *adj.* barroco
bar-racks *n.* barraca
bar-rel *n.* barril
bar-ren *adj.* infecundo; infructuoso; yermo
bar-ri-cade *n.* barricada
bar-ri-er *n.* barrear
bar-tend-er *n.* camarero
bar-ter *v.* trocar
bas-al *adj.* basico
ba-salt *n.* basalto
base *n.* base
base-ball *n.* béisbol
base-board *n.* zocalo
base-less *adj.* infundado
base-ment *n.* sotaño
bash *v.* golpear
bash-ful *adj.* timido
ba-sic *adj.* basico
ba-sic-i-ty *n.* basicidad
bas-il *n.* albahaca
ba-sil-i-ca *n.* basilica
ba-sin *n.* jofaina
ba-sis *n.* base
bask *v.* complacerse
bas-ket *n.* cesta
bas-ket-ball *n.* baloncesto
bas-ket-ry *n.* cesteria
baste *v.* hilvanar
bat *v.* golpear; *n.* maza
batch *n.* hornada

bate v. disminuir
bath n. baño
bathe v. bañar(se)
bath-ing suit n. traje de bano
bath-tub n. bañera
ba-ton n. batuta
bat-tal-ion n. batallon
bat-ter v. estropear; golpear
bat-ter-y n. bateria
bat-tle v. luchar, n. lucha
bat-tle-ground n. campo de batalla
bat-tle-ship n. acorazado
bau-ble n. baratija
baud n. baudio
bawl v. llorar
bay n. bahia
bay-o-net n. bayoneta
ba-zaar n. bazar
ba-zoo-ka n. bazuca
be v. estar; ser
beach n. playa
bea-con n. almenara; faro
bead n. abalorio
beak n. pico
beam n. rayo
bean n. frijol; habichuela
bear n. oso; v. llevar
bear-a-ble adj. soportable
beard n. barba
beard-ed adj. barbudo
bear-er n. portador
bear-ing n. porte
beast n. bestia
beast-ly adj. bestial
beat v. vencer; golpear
beat-en adj. derrotado
beat-er n. batidor
be-a-tif-ic adj. beatifico
be-at-i-fy v. beatificar
beat-ing n. latido; paliza
be-at-i-tude n. beatitud
beau-ti-ful adj. hermoso
beau-ti-ful-ly adj. ballamente
beau-ti-fy v. embellecer
beau-ty n. belleza
bea-ver n. castor
be-cause conj. porque
beck-on v. llamar
be-come v. hacer(se)
be-com-ing adj. apropiado
bed n. cama

be-daz-zle v. deslumbrar
bed-cham-ber n. alcoba
bed-lam n. alboroto
bed-room n. alcoba
bed-side adj. (de) cabecera
bee n. abeja
beech n. haya
beef-y adj. musculoso
bee-hive n. colmena
beer n. cerveza
bees-wax n. cera
beet n. remolacha
bee-tle n. escarabajo
be-fit v. convenir
be-fit-ting adj. conveniente
be-fore prep. antes de, adv. delante
be-fore-hand adv. antes
be-fud-dle v. confundir
beg v. pedir
beg-gar n. pobre
beg-gar-ly adj. misero
be-gin v. comenzar
be-gin-ner n. novato
be-gin-ning n. comienzo
be-grudge v. envidiar
be-guile v. seducir
be-have v. funcionar; comportarse
be-hav-ior n. comportamiento
be-head v. descabezar
be-hind adv. atras; detras; prep. detras de
be-hold v. contemplar
be-hold-en adj. obligado
be-hoove v. convenir
beige adj. beige
be-ing n. ser
be-la-bor v. machacar
be-lat-ed adj. tardio
be-lief n. fe
be-liev-a-ble adj. creible
be-lieve v. creer
be-liev-er n. creyente
bell n. cascabel
bellflower n. campanilla
bel-li-cose adj. belicoso
bel-lig-er-ence n. beligerancia
bel-lig-er-ent adj. beligerante
bel-low v. rugir

bel-ly *n.* estomago
be-long *v.* estar
be-long-ings *n.* pertenencias
be-lov-ed *adj.* querido
be-low *adv.* abajo, *prep.* debajo de
belt *n.* cinturon
be-moan *v.* lamentar
bench *n.* banco
bend *v.* doblar; inclinar
bend-er *n.* juerga
be-neath *prep.* debajo de
ben-e-dic-tion *n.* bendición
ben-e-fac-tor *n.* benefactor
ben-e-fice *n.* beneficio
be-nef-i-cent *adj.* benefico
ben-e-fi-cial *adj.* beneficioso
ben-e-fi-ci-ar-y *n.* beneficiario
ben-e-fit *n.* beneficio
be-nev-o-lence *n.* benevolencia
be-nev-o-lent *adj.* benevolo
be-nign *adj.* benigno
bent *adj.* empenado; torcido
be-numb *v.* entorpecer
be-queath *v.* legar
be-quest *n.* legado
be-rate *v.* reprender
be-reave-ment *n.* duelo
be-reft *adj.* privado
ber-ryn. baya
berth *n.* camarote
be-ryl-li-um *n.* berilio
be-seech *v.* implorar
be-set *v.* acosar
be-side *prep.* cerca
be-sides *prep.* ademas de
be-siege *v.* asediar
be-smirch *v.* manchar
best *adj.* mejor
bes-tial *adj.* bestial
bes-ti-al-i-ty *n.* bestialidad
be-stow *v.* conceder
bet *n.* apuesta
be-to-ken *v.* presagiar
be-tray *v.* revelar
be-tray-al *n.* traición
be-trothed *n.* novio
bet-ter *adv., adj.* mejor
bet-ter-ment *n.* mejoramiento
bet-tor *n.* apostador

be-tween *adv.* en medio; *prep.* entre
bev-eled *adj.* biselado
bev-er-age *n.* bebida
bev-y *n.* grupo
be-wail *v.* lamentar
be-wil-der *v.* aturdir
be-wil-der-ment *n.* aturdimiento
be-witch *v.* hechizar
be-witch-ment *n.* hechizo
be-yond *prep.* despues de
bi-an-nu-al *adj.* semestral
bi-as *n.* prejuicio
bib *n.* babero
Bi-ble *n.* Biblia
Bib-li-cal *adj.* biblico
bib-li-og-ra-pher *n.* bibliografo
bib-li-og-ra-phy *n.* bibliografia
bib-li-o-phile *n.* bibliofilo
bi-car-bon-ate *n.* bicarbonato
bi-cen-ten-ni-al *adj.* bicentario
bi-ceps *n.* biceps
bi-cy-cle *n.* bicicleta
bi-cy-clist *n.* biciclista
bid *n.* oferta; *v.* mandar
bid-ding *n.* oferta
bi-en-ni-al *adj.* bienal
bi-fo-cal *adj.* bifocal
bi-fur-cate *v.* bifurcarse
bi-fur-ca-tion *n.* bifurcación
big *adj.* grande
big-a-mist *n.* bigamo
big-a-my *n.* bigamia
big-ness *n.* grandeza
bike *n.* bicicleta
bik-er *n.* motociclista
bi-lat-er-al *adj.* bilateral
bile *n.* bilis
bi-lin-gual *adj.* bilingue
bil-ious *adj.* bilioso
bilk *v.* defraudar
bill *n.* pico; cuenta
bill-board *n.* cartelera
bil-let *v.* alojar
bill-fold *n.* cartera
bil-liards *n.* billar
bil-lion *n.* billon
bil-lion-aire *n.* billonario

bil-low *n.* oleada
bil-low-y *adj.* ondulante
bi-month-ly *adj.* bimestram
bin *n.* cajon
bi-na-ry *adj.* binario
bind *v.* encuadernar; atar
bind-er *n.* atadura; encuadernador
bind-ing *n.* encuadernación
bin-oc-u-lar *n.* gemelos
bi-no-mi-al *adj.* binomio
bi-o-chem-i-cal *adj.* bioquimico
bi-o-chem-ist *n.* bioquimico
bi-o-chem-is-try *n.* bioquimica
bi-og-ra-pher *n.* biografo
bi-o-graph-ic *adj.* biografico
bi-og-ra-phy *n.* biografia
bi-o-log-ic *adj.* biologico
bi-ol-o-gist *n.* biologo
bi-ol-o-gy *n.* biologia
bi-on-ics *n.* bionica
bi-o-phys-ics *n.* biofisica
bi-op-sy *n.* biopsia
bi-par-tite *adj.* bipartito
bi-ped *adj.* bipedo
bi-plane *n.* biplaño
birch *n.* abedul
bird *n.* pajaro
bird-cage *n.* jaula
bird-seed *n.* alpiste
birth *n.* nacimiento
birth-day *n.* cumpleanos
bis-cuit *n.* bizcocho
bi-sect *v.* bisecar
bi-sec-tion *n.* bisección
bish-op *n.* obispo
bis-muth *n.* bismuto
bi-son *n.* bisonte
bit *n.* pedazo
bite *v.* picar
bit-ing *adj.* mordaz; cortante
bit-ter *adj.* cortante; implacable; amargo
bit-ter-ness *n.* rencor; encarnizamiento
bit-ter-sweet *adj.* agridulce
bi-tu-mi-nous *adj.* bituminoso
bi-va-lent *adj.* bivalente
bi-valve *adj.* bivalvo
bi-week-ly *adj.* quincenal

bi-zarre *adj.* raro
blab-ber *v.* cotorrear
black *adj.* negro
black-and-blue *adj.* amoratado
black-ber-ry *n.* zarzamora
black-bird *n.* mirlo
black-board *n.* pizarra
black-en *v.* difamar
black-head *n.* grano
black-mail *v.* chantajear
black-mail-er *n.* chantajista
black-smith *n.* herrero
black-top *n.* asfalto
blad-der *n.* vejiga
blade *n.* pala; hoja
blame *v.* culpar
bland *adj.* insulso
blank *n., adj.* blanco
blan-ket *n.* manta
blare *v.* resonar
blas-pheme *v.* blasfemar
blas-phe-mous *adj.* blasfemo
blas-phe-my *n.* blasfemia
blast *v.* destruir; *n.* explosion
blast-ed *adj.* maldito
bla-tant *adj.* patente
blaze *n.* joguera; llamarada; *v.* arder
bleach *n.* lejia; *v.* blanquear
bleach-ers *n.* gradas
blear *adj.* sombrio; frio
bleat *v.* balar
bleed *v.* sangrar
blem-ish *v.* manchar
blend *n.* mezcla; *v.* mezclar
blend-er *n.* licuadora
bless *v.* bandecir
bless-ed *adj.* santo
bless-ing *n.* bendición
blind *v.* cegar; *adj.* ciego
blind-ers *n.* anteojeras
blind-ing *adj.* cegador
blind-ly *adv.* ciegamente
blind-ness *n.* ceguera
blink *v.* pestanear; ceder
blink-ing *adj.* parpadeante
bliss *n.* felicidad
bliss-ful *adj.* feliz
blis-ter *v.* ampollar(se)
blis-ter-ing *adj.* forzado;

abrasador
bliz-zard *n.* ventisca
block *n.* manzana
block-ade *adj.* bloqueo
block-age *n.* obstrucción
blond *adj.* rubio
blonde *adj.* rubia
blood *n.* sangre
blood-less *adj.* exangue
blood-thrist-y *adj.* sanguinario
blood-y *adj.* sangriento
bloom *v.* florecer
blos-som *n.* flor
blot *n.* mancha
blotch *n.* mancha
blouse *n.* blusa
blow *v.* inflar; soplar
blow-gun *n.* cerbantana
blow-torch *n.* soplete
blow-up *n.* explosión
bludg-eon *v.* aporrear
blue *adj.* azul
blue-bell *n.* campanilla
blue-print *n.* cianotipo
blunt *adj.* abrupto
blur *v.* nublar
blur-ry *adj.* confuso
blush *n.* sonrojo
blus-ter *v.* bramar
boar *n.* verraco
board *n.* consejo
board-er *n.* pensionista
board-ing-house *n.* pensión
boast *v.* alardear
boast-ful *adj.* jactancioso
boast-ing *n.* jactancia
boat *n.* barco
boat-man *n.* lanchero
bob-ber *n.* flotador
bob-bin *n.* bobina
bod-ice *n.* cuerpo
bod-i-ly *adj.* corporal
bod-y *n.* cuerpo
bod-y-guard *n.* guardaespaldas
bog *n.* cienaga
bo-gus *adj.* falso
boil *v.* cocer; hervir
boil-er *n.* caldera
boil-ing *adj.* hirviente
bois-ter-ous *adj.* ruidoso; bullicioso

bold *adj.* descarado; intrepido
bod-ster *v.* apoyar
bolt *n.* perno; pestillo
bomb *n.* bomba
bom-bard *v.* acosar; bombardear
bom-bard-ment *n.* bombardeo
bomb-er *n.* bombardero
bomb-ing *n.* bombardero
bomb-shell *n.* bomba
bo-nan-za *n.* bonanza
bond *n.* atadura; bono
bone *n.* hueso
bon-fire *n.* hoguera
bon-net *n.* cofia
bo-nus *n.* sobresueldo
bon-y *adj.* huesudo
book *n.* libro
book-bind-ing *n.* encuadernación
book-end *n.* sujetalibros
book-ing *n.* reservación
book-sell-er *n.* librero
book-store *n.* libreria
boom *n.* prosperidad
boo-mer-ang *n.* bumerang
boor *n.* patan
boor-ish *adj.* tosco
boost *v.* levantar
boot *n.* bota
booth *n.* puesto; cabina
boot-leg *v.* contrabandear
boo-ty *n.* botin
bor-der *n.* borde; frontera
bor-der-line *n.* frontera
bore *v.* aburrir
bore-dom *n.* aburrimiento
bor-ing *adj.* aburrido
born *adj.* nacido
bor-ough *n.* municipio
bor-row *v.* apropiarse
bor-row-er *n.* prestatario
bos-om *n.* pecho
boss *n.* jefe
bo-tan-ic *adj.* botanico
bot-a-nist *n.* botanico
bot-a-ny *n.* botanica
botch *v.* chapucear
both *adj.* los dos
both-er *v.* molestar(se)
both-er-some *adj.* molesto

bot-tle *n.* botella
bot-tom *n.* base; fondo
bot-tom-less *adj.* sin fondo
bot-u-lism *n.* botulismo
bough *n.* rama
bouil-lon *n.* caldo
boul-e-vard *n.* avenida
bounce *v.* rebotar
bounc-ing *adj.* fuerte
bound *v.* saltar
bound-a-ry *n.* limite
bound-less *adj.* ilimitado
boun-te-ous *adj.* abundante
boun-ti-ful *adj.* generoso
boun-ty *n.* generosidad
bou-quet *n.* ramo
bour-geois *n.* burgues
bour-geoi-sie *n.* burguesia
bout *n.* ataque
bo-vine *n.* bovino
bow *v.* inclinarse; doblegarse
bow-el *n.* intestino
bowl *n.* tazon; fuente
bowl-ing *n.* bolos
box *n.* caja
box-er *n.* boxeador
box-ing *n.* boxeo
boy *n.* chico; niño
boy-cott *v.* boicotear
boy-friend *n.* novio
bra *n.* sosten
brace *n.* puntal
brace-let *n.* brazalete
brac-ing *adj.* fortificante
brack-et *n.* corchete
brack-ish *adj.* salino
brag *v.* jactarse
brain *n.* cerebro
brain-y *adj.* listo
brake *v.* frenar
bran *n.* salvado
branch *n.* rama
brand *n.* modo; marca
brand-ing *n.* hierra
bran-dish *v.* blandir
bran-dy *n.* conac
brash *adj.* insolente; impetuoso
brass *n.* laton
bras-siere *n.* sosten
brass-y *adj.* descarado
brave *adj.* valiente
brav-er-y *n.* valor

brawn-y *adj.* musculoso
bra-zen *adj.* descarado
bra-zier *n.* brasero
breach *n.* rupture; violación
bread *n.* pan
bread-bas-ket *n.* panera
breadth *n.* extension
break *v.* quebrar; romper
break-a-ble *adj.* rompible
break-age *n.* rotura
break-down *n.* depresión; desglose
break-fast *n.* desayuño
break-through *n.* adelanto
break-up *n.* desintegración; separacion
breast *n.* pecho
breast-bone *n.* esternon
breath *n.* respiración
breathe *v.* respirar
breath-ing *n.* respiración
breath-tak-ing *adj.* impresionante
breed *v.* criar; reproducirse
breed-er *n.* criador
breed-ing *v.* crianza
breeze *n.* brisa
breez-y *adj.* ventoso
brev-i-ty *n.* brevedad
brew-er *n.* cervecero
brew-er-y *n.* cerveceria
bribe *v.* cohechar
brick *n.* ladrillo
brick-lay-er *n.* albanil
bri-dal *n.* boda.
bride *n.* novia
bridge *n.* puente
bri-dle *n.* brida
brief *adj.* breve
brief-case *n.* cartera
brief-ing *n.* reunion
bri-gade *n.* brigada
bright *adj.* brillante
bright-en *v.* iluminar(se)
bright-ness *n.* lustre
bril-liance *n.* brillo
bril-liant *adj.* brillante
brim *n.* borde
bring *v.* traer
bri-quet *n.* briqueta
brisk *adj.* vigoroso
bris-tle *n.* cerda
brit-tle *adj.* fragil

broach *n.* broche
broad *adj.* extenso; ancho
broad-cast *v.* transmitir; emitir
broad-cast-ing *n.* transmision
broad-en *v.* ensanchar(se)
broad-mind-ed *adj.* comprensivo
bro-cade *n.* brocado
broc-co-li *n.* brecol
bro-chure *n.* folleto
bro-ken *adj.* roto; quebrado
bro-ken-down *adj.* decrepito
bro-ker-age *n.* corretaje
bro-mide *n.* bromuro
bro-mine *n.* bromo
bron-chi-al *adj.* bronquial
bron-chi-tis *n.* bronquitis
bronze *n.* bronce
brook *n.* arroyo
broom *n.* escoba
broth *n.* caldo
broth-el *n.* burdel
broth-er *n.* hermano
broth-er-hood *n.* fraternidad
broth-er-in-law *n.* cuando
broth-er-ly *adj.* fraterno
brow *n.* ceja
brown *adj.* moreno
brown-out *n.* parcial
browse *v.* pacer; curiosear
bruise *n.* contusión
brunt *n.* impacto
brush *n.* cepillo
bru-tal *adj.* brutal
bru-tal-i-ty *n.* brutalidad
bru-tal-ize *v.* brutalizar
brute *n.* bruto
buc-ca-neer *n.* bucanero
buck-et *n.* balde
buck-le *n.* jebilla
bud *n.* yema
bud-dy *n.* compadre
budge *v.* ceder
budg-et *v.* presupuestar
buf-fa-lo *n.* bufalo
buff-er *n.* intercesor
buf-fet *n.* bofetada
buf-foon *n.* bufon
bug *n.* bicho
bu-gle *n.* clarin
build *v.* construir

build-er *n.* constructor
build-ing *n.* construcción
bulb *n.* bulbo
bulge *n.* bulto
bulk-y *adj.* pesado
bull *n.* toro
bull-dog *n.* buldog
bull-doz-er *n.* excavadora
bul-let *n.* bala
bul-le-tin *n.* boletin
bull-fight-er *n.* torero
bul-rush *n.* espadana
bul-wark *n.* baluarte
bum-ble-bee *n.* abejorro
bump *n.* choque
bump-y *adj.* agitado
bun *n.* bollo
bunch *n.* racimo
bun-dle *n.* fajo; bulto
bun-ny *n.* conejito
buoy *n.* boya
buoy-ant *adj.* boyante
bur *n.* erizo
bur-den *n.* carga
bu-reauc-ra-cy *n.* burocracía
bu-reau-crat *n.* burocrata
burg-er *n.* hamburguesa
bur-glar *n.* ladron
bur-glar-ize *v.* robar
bur-i-al *n.* entierro
bur-lap *n.* arpillera
bur-ly *adj.* robusto
burn *v.* incendiar
burn-er *n.* quemador
burn-ing *adj.* ardiente
burn-out *n.* extinción
burnt *adj.* quernado
burp *n.* eructo
bur-ro *n.* burro
burst *v.* romper
bur-y *v.* enterrar
bus *n.* autobus
bus-boy *n.* ayudante
bush *n.* arbusto
bushed *adj.* agotado
busi-ness *n.* oficio
but *conj.* pero
but-ter *n.* mantequilla
but-ter-fly *n.* mariposa
buy *v.* comprar
buy-er *n.* comprador
by *adv.* cerca, *prep.* cerca de; por

cab *n.* taxi
ca-bal *n.* cabala
cab-a-la *n.* cabala
cab-a-ret *n.* cabaret
cab-bage *n.* col
cab-driv-er *n.* taxista
cab-in *n.* cabana
cab-i-net *n.* gabinete
cab-i-net-mak-er *n.* ebanista
cab-i-net-work *n.* ebanisteria
ca-ble *n.* cable
ca-ble-gram *n.* cablegrama
ca-ca-o *n.* cacao
ca-chet *n.* cacareo
cac-tus *n.* cacto
ca-dav-er *n.* cadaver
ca-dav-er-ous *adj.* cadaverico
cad-die *n.* caddy
ca-dence *n.* cadencia
ca-det *n.* cadete
cad-mi-um *n.* cadmio
ca-du-ce-us *n.* caduceo
ca-fe *n.* cafe
caf-e-te-ri-a *n.* cafeteria
caf-feine *n.* cafeina
caf-tan *n.* tunica
cage *n.* jaula
ca-jole *v.* engatusar
cake *n.* pastel
cal-a-bash *n.* calabaza
cal-a-mine *n.* calamina
ca-lam-i-ty *n.* calamidad
cal-ci-fi-ca-tion *n.* calcificación
cal-ci-fy *v.* calcificar
cal-ci-um *n.* calcio
cal-cu-late *v.* calcular
cal-cu-lat-ed *adj.* intencional
cal-cu-lat-ing *adj.* calculador
cal-cu-la-tion *n.* calculo
cal-cu-la-tor *n.* calculadora
cal-dron *n.* caldera
cal-en-dar *n.* calendario
cal-i-ber *n.* calibre
cal-i-brate *v.* calibrar
cal-i-bra-tion *n.* calibración
cal-i-co *n.* calico
cal-i-per *n.* calibrador
ca-liph *n.* califa
cal-is-then-ics *n.* calistenia
ca-lix *n.* caliz
call *v.* llamar

call-er *n.* cisitante
cal-lig-ra-pher *n.* caligrafo
cal-lig-ra-phy *n.* caligrafia
call-ing *n.* vocación
cal-lous *v.* encallecerse
cal-low *adj.* inmaturo
cal-lus *n.* callo
calm *v.* calmar(se); *n.* calma
calm-ness *n.* tranquilidad
ca-lor-ic *adj.* calorico
ca-lo-rie *n.* caloria
ca-lum-ni-ate *v.* calumniar
cal-va-ry *n.* calvario
ca-lyx *n.* caliz
ca-ma-ra-der-ie *n.* camaraderia
cam-bi-um *n.* cambium
cam-el *n.* camello
ca-mel-lia *n.* camelia
cam-e-o *n.* camafeo
cam-er-a *n.* camara
cam-ou-flage *n.* camuflaje
camp *v.* acampar
cam-paign *n.* campana
camp-er *n.* campista
cam-phor *n.* alcanfor
can *v.* poder
ca-nar-y *n.* canario
can-cel *v.* cancelar; matar; anular
can-cel-la-tion *n.* cancelacion
can-cer *n.* cancer
can-cer-ous *adj.* canceroso
can-des-cent *adj.* candente
can-did *adj.* franco
can-di-da-cy *n.* candidatura
can-di-date *n.* candidato
can-died *adj.* escarchado
can-dle *n.* cirio; vela
can-dle-hold-er *n.* candelero
can-dle-stick *n.* candelero
can-dor *n.* franqueza
can-dy *n.* azucar
cane *n.* cana; baston
ca-nine *adj.* canino
can-is-ter *n.* lata
canned *adj.* enlatado
can-ni-bal *n.* canibal
can-ni-bal-ism *n.* canibalismo
can-ni-bal-is-tic *adj.* canibal
can-non *n.* conon

ca-noe *n.* canoa
ca-non-i-za-tion *n.* canonización
can-on-ize *v.* canonizar
can-ta-loupe *n.* cantalupo
can-teen *n.* cantina
can-vas *n.* lona
can-yon *n.* canon
cap *n.* tapa
ca-pa-bil-i-ty *n.* capacidad
ca-pa-ble *adj.* capaz
ca-pa-cious *adj.* espacioso
ca-pac-i-ty *n.* capacidad
ca-per *n.* cabriola
cap-il-lar-y *n.* capilar
cap-i-tal *n., adj.* capital
cap-i-tal-ism *n.* capitalismo
cap-i-tal-ist *n.* capitalista
cap-i-tal-is-tic *adj.* capitalista
cap-i-tal-i-za-tion *n.* capitalización
cap-i-tal-ize *v.* capitalizar
cap-i-tal-ly *adv.* admirablemente
cap-i-tol *n.* capitolio
ca-pit-u-late *v.* capitular
ca-price *n.* capricho
ca-pri-cious *adj.* caprichoso
cap-sule *n.* capsula
cap-tain *n.* capitan
cap-tion *n.* subtitulo
cap-tious *adj.* capcioso
cap-ti-vate *v.* cautivar
cap-ti-va-tion *n.* encanto
cap-tive *adj.* cautivo
cap-tiv-i-ty *n.* cautividad
cap-tor *n.* capturador
cap-ture *v.* capturar
car *n.* coche
car-a-mel *n.* caramelo
car-at *n.* quilate
car-a-van *n.* caravana
car-bide *n.* carburo
car-bine *n.* carabina
car-bo-hy-drate *n.* carbohifrato
car-bon *n.* carbono
car-bon-ate *v.* carbonatar
car-bun-cle *n.* carbunco
car-bu-re-tor *n.* carburador
car-cin-o-gen-ic *adj.* cancerigeno
card *n.* tarjeta

car-di-ac *adj.* cardiaco
car-di-nal *adj.* cardinal
car-di-o-gram *n.* cardiograma
car-di-ol-o-gy *n.* cardiología
care *v.* cuidar
ca-reer *n.* carrera
care-free *adj.* despreocupado
care-ful *adj.* cuidadoso
care-less *adj.* espontaneo; descuidado
ca-ress *n.* caricia
care-tak-er *n.* portero
car-go *n.* carga
car-i-ca-ture *n.* caricatura
car-nage *n.* carniceria
car-nal *adj.* carnal
car-ni-val *n.* carnaval
car-ni-vore *n.* carnivoro
car-niv-o-rous *adj.* carnivoro
ca-rous-al *n.* jarana
car-ou-sel *n.* carrusel
car-pen-try *n.* carpinteria
car-pet *n.* alfombra
car-riage *n.* carruaje
car-ri-er *n.* carrero
car-rot *n.* zanahoria
car-ry *v.* lograr; llevar
car-sick *adj.* mareado
cart *n.* carro
cart-age *n.* acarreo
car-tel *n.* cartel
car-ti-lage *n.* cartilago
cart-load *n.* carretada
car-toon *n.* tira
car-toon-ist *n.* caricaturista
car-tridge *n.* cartucho
carve *v.* esculpir
carv-ing *n.* escultura
case *n.* caja
cahs *n.* efectivo
cash-ew *n.* anacardo
cash-ier *n.* cajero
cash-mere *n.* cachemira
ca-si-no *n.* casino
cask *n.* barril
cas-se-role *n.* cacerola
cas-sette *n.* casete
cast *v.* dar; fundir; echar
cas-ta-nets *n.* castanuelas
caste *n.* casta
cas-ti-gate *v.* castigar

cas-tle n. castillo
cas-trate v. castrar
cas-tra-tion n. castración
ca-su-al adj. casual
cas-u-al-ly adv. casualmente
ca-su-ist-ry n. casuistica
cat n. gato
ca-tab-o-lism n. catabolismo
cat-a-log n. catalogo
cat-a-lyst n. catalizador
cat-a-lyt-ic adj. catalitico
cat-a-lyze v. catalizar
cat-a-pult n. catapulta
cat-a-ract n. catarata
ca-tas-tro-phe n. catastrofe
cat-a-stroph-ic adj. catastrofico
cat-a-ton-ic adj. catatonico
catch v. prender; coger
catch-er n. receptor
catch-ing adj. contagioso
catch-y adj. capcioso
cat-e-chism n. catecismo
cat-e-gor-ic adj. categorico
cat-e-gor-i-cal-ly adv. categoricamente
cat-e-go-rize v. clasificar
cat-e-go-ry n. categoria
cat-er-pil-lar n. oruga
cat-er-waul v. chillar
ca-thar-sis n. catarsis
ca-the-dral n. catedral
cath-ode n. catodo
cath-o-lic adj. catolico
ca-thol-i-cism n. catolicismo
cat-nip n. nebeda
cat-tail n. espadaña
cat-tle n. ganado
cat-tle-man n. ganadero
cau-li-flow-er n. coliflor
cau-sa-tion n. causalidad
caus-a-tive adj. causativo
cause n. razon; causa
cause-way n. elevada
caus-tic adj. caustico
cau-ter-ize v. cauterizar
cau-tion v. amonestar
cau-tion-ar-y adj. preventivo
cau-tious adj. cauteloso
cav-al-ry n. caballeria
cave n. cueva
cav-ern n. caverna
cav-ern-ous adj. cavernoso

cav-i-ty n. cavidad
ca-vort v. cabriolar
cay n. cayo
cease v. suspender
cease-less adj. continuo
ce-dar n. cedro
cede v. ceder
ceil-ing n. techo
cel-e-brant n. celebrante
cel-e-brate v. celebrar
cel-e-brat-ed adj. celebre
cel-e-bra-tion n. celebración
ce-leb-ri-ty n. celebridad
cel-er-y n. apio
ce-les-tial adj. celestial
cel-i-ba-cy n. celibato
cel-i-bate adj. celibe
cell n. celda
cel-lar n. sotano
cel-lo-phane n. celofan
cel-lu-lar adj. celular
cel-lu-loid n. celuloide
cel-lu-lose n. celulosa
ce-ment n. cemento
cem-e-ter-y n. cementerio
cen-ser n. insensario
cen-sor n. censor
cen-so-ri-ous adj. censurador
cen-sor-ship n. censura
cen-sure v. censurar
cen-sus n. censo
cent n. centavo
cen-taur n. centauro
cen-ten-ni-al adj. centenario
cen-ter n. centro
cen-ti-grade adj. centigrado
cen-ti-gram n. centiframo
cen-ti-li-ter n. centilitro
cen-ti-me-ter n. centimetro
cen-tral adj. central
cen-tral-ize v. centralizar(se)
cen-tric adj. centrico
cen-trif-u-gal adj. centrifugo
cen-tu-ry n. siglo
ce-phal-ic adj. cefalico
ce-ram-ic adj. ceramico
ce-re-al n. cereal
cer-e-bral adj. cerebral
cer-e-brum n. cerebro
cer-e-mo-ni-al adj. ceremonial
cer-e-mo-ni-ous adj. cere-

monioso
cer-e-mo-ny *n.* ceremonia
cer-tain *adj.* seguro; cierto
cer-tain-ly *adv.* ciertamente
cer-tain-ty *n.* certeza
cer-ti-fi-a-ble *adj.* certificable
cer-tif-i-cate *n.* certificado
cer-ti-fi-ca-tion *n.* certificación
cer-ti-fied *adj.* certificado
cer-ti-fy *v.* certificar
cer-ti-tude *n.* certidumbre
cer-vix *n.* cerviz
ces-sa-tion *n.* cesación
ces-sion *n.* cesion
chafe *v.* frotar; rozar
cha-grin *v.* desilusionar
chain *n.* cadeña
chair *n.* silla
chair-man *n.* presidente
chair-man-ship *n.* presidencia
chair-wo-man *n.* presidenta
cha-let *n.* chalet
chal-ice *n.* caliz
chalk *n.* tiza
chalk-board *n.* pizarra
chal-lenge *v.* desafiar
chal-leng-er *n.* desafiador
cham-ber-lain *n.* chambelan
cha-me-leon *n.* camaleon
champ *n.* campeon
cham-pagne *n.* champana
cham-pi-on *n.* campeon
cham-pi-on-ship *n.* campeonato
chance *n.* oportunidad; casualidad
chan-cel-ler-y *n.* cancilleria
chan-cel-lor *n.* canciller
change *v.* transformar; cambiar
change-a-ble *adj.* cambiable
change-o-ver *n.* cambio
chang-er *n.* cambiador
chan-nel *n.* canal
chant *n.* canto
cha-os *n.* caos
cha-ot-ic *adj.* caotico
chap-el *n.* capilla
chap-er-one *n.* carabina
chap-lain *n.* capellan
chap-ter *n.* capitulo

char-ac-ter *n.* caracter
char-ac-ter-is-tic *n.* caracteristica
char-ac-ter-ize *v.* caracterizar
char-coal *n.* carboncillo
charge *v.* pedir; cargar
cha-ris-ma *n.* carisma
char-i-ta-ble *adj.* caritativo
char-i-ty *n.* caridad
charm *n.* encanto
charm-er *n.* encantador
charm-ing *adj.* encantador
chart *v.* trazar
char-ter *n.* carta
chase *v.* perseguir
chaste *adj.* casto
chas-ten *v.* castigar
chas-tise *v.* castigar
chas-ti-ty *n.* castidad
chat *v.* charlar
chat-ter *v.* charlar
chau-vin-ist *n.* chauvinista
chau-vin-is-tic *adj.* chauvinista
cheap *adj.* barato
cheap-en *v.* degradar(se)
cheap-ly *adv.* barato
cheap-ness *n.* tacaneria
cheat *v.* enganar
cheat-er *n.* tramposo
cheat-ing *adj.* tramposo
check *n.* cheque; parada; cuenta
check-book *n.* chequera
check-ered *adj.* a cuadros
cheek *n.* mejilla
cheep *adj.* piada
cheer *v.* alegrar; alentar
cheer-ful *adj.* alegre
cheer-i-ly *adv.* alegremente
cheer-less *adj.* triste
cheese *n.* queso
cheese-cake *n.* quesadilla
chef *n.* cocinero
chem-i-cal *n.* quimico
chem-ist *n.* quimico
chem-is-try *n.* quimica
che-mo-ther-a-py *n.* quimioterapia
cher-ish *v.* abrigar; querer
cher-ry *n.* cerezo
cher-ub *n.* querubin

che-ru-bic *adj.* querubico
chess *n.* ajedrez
chest *n.* pecho
chest-nut *n.* castaña
chew *v.* masticar
chew-ing *n.* masticación
chick-en *n.* pollo
chick-pea *n.* garbanzo
chief *n.* jefe
chif-fon *n.* chifon
child *n.* hijo; niño
child-birth *m.* parto
child-ish *adj.* aninado
child-like *adj.* infantil
chil-i *n.* chile
chill *n.* frio
chill-ing *adj.* frio
chime *n.* carillon
chim-ney *n.* chimenea
chim-pan-zee *n.* chimpance
chin *n.* barba
chi-na *n.* china
chip *n.* astilla; *v.* astillar
chip-per *adj.* jovial
chi-ro-prac-tor *n.* quiroprac-
 tico
chirp *v.* gorjear
chis-el *n.* cincel
chis-el-er *n.* cincelador
chiv-al-rous *adj.* cabal-
 ieresco
chiv-al-ry *n.* caballerosidad
chive *n.* cebollino
chlo-ride *n.* cloruro
chlo-rine *n.* cloro
chlo-ro-phyll *n.* clorofila
choc-o-late *n.* chocolate
choice *adj.* selecto; *n.*
 preferencia
choir *n.* coro
choke *v.* ahogar; atorar;
 estrangular
chol-er-a *n.* colera
chol-er-ic *adj.* colerico
cho-les-ter-ol *n.* colesterol
chomp *v.* ronzar
choose *v.* escoger
choos-ing *n.* selección
chop *v.* cortar
cho-ral *n.* coral
cho-re-og-ra-pher *n.* coreo-
 grafo
cho-re-og-ra-phy *n.* coreo-

grafia
cho-sen *adj.* escogido
chow *n.* comida
Christ *n.* Cristo
chris-ten *v.* bautizar
chris-ten-ing *n.* bautismo
Chris-tian *n.* cristiano
Chris-ti-an-i-ty *n.* cris-
 tianismo
Christ-mas *n.* Navidad
chro-mat-ic *adj.* cromatico
chrome *n.* cromo
chro-mi-um *n.* cromo
chro-mo-some *n.* cro-
 mosoma
chron-ic *adj.* cronico
chron-i-cle *n.* cronica
chron-o-log-ic *adj.* crono-
 logico
chro-nol-o-gy *n.* cronologia
chrys-a-lis *n.* crisalida
chry-san-the-mum *n.* crisan-
 temo
chum *n.* compañero
chunk *n.* trozo
church *n.* iglesia
church-man *n.* clerigo
churn *n.* mantequera
chute *n.* conducto; rampa
ci-ca-da *n.* cigarra
ci-der *n.* sidra
ci-gar *n.* puro
cig-a-rette *n.* cigarrillo
cinch *n.* cincha
cin-der *n.* carbonilla
cin-e-ma *n.* cine
cin-e-mat-ic *adj.* filmico
cin-e-ma-tog-ra-phy *n.* cine-
 matografia
cin-na-mon *n.* canela
ci-pher *v.* cifrar
cir-cle *n.* ciclo
cir-cuit *n.* circuito
cir-cu-lar *adj.* circular
cir-cu-late *v.* circular
cir-cu-lat-ing *adj.* circulante
cir-cu-la-tion *n.* circulación
cir-cum-cise *v.* circuncidar
cir-cum-cised *adj.* circunciso
cir-cum-ci-sion *n.* circunci-
 sion
cir-cum-fer-ence *n.* circun-
 ferencia

cir-cum-nav-i-gate v. circunnavegar

cir-cum-scribe v. circunscribir

cir-cum-spect adj. circunspecto

cir-cum-stance n. circunstancia

cir-cum-stan-tial adj. circunstancial

cir-cus n. circo

cir-rho-sis n. cirrosis

cir-rus n. cirro

cis-tern n. cisterna

cit-a-del n. ciudadela

ci-ta-tion n. citación

cite v. citar

cit-i-zen n. ciudadano

cit-i-zen-ship n. ciudadania

cit-rus adj. citrico

cit-y n. ciudad

civ-et n. civeta

civ-ic adj. civico

civ-il adj. civil

ci-vil-ian n. civil

ci-vil-i-ty n. civilidad

civ-i-li-za-tion n. civilización

civ-i-lize v. civilizar

claim v. merecer; reclamar

clair-voy-ance n. clarividencia

clair-voy-ant adj. clarividente

clam n. almeja

clam-or n. clamor

clam-or-ous adj. clamoroso

clamp n. abrazadera

clan n. clan

clan-gor n. estruendo

clap v. aplaudir

clap-per n. badajo

clap-ping n. aplausos

clar-et n. clarete

clar-i-fi-ca-tion n. clarificación

clar-i-fy v. clarificar

clar-i-net n. clarinete

clar-i-on adj. sonoro

clar-i-ty n. claridad

clash v. entrechocarse

class n. clase

clas-sic adj. clasico

clas-si-cal adj. clasico

clas-si-cism n. clasicismo

clas-si-cist n. clasicista

clas-si-fi-ca-tion n. clasificación

clas-si-fied adj. clasificado

clas-si-fy v. clasificar

class-y adj. elegante

clause n. clausula

claus-tro-pho-bi-a n. claustrofobia

clav-i-chord n. clavicordio

clav-i-cle n. clavicula

claw n. garra

clay n. arcilla

clean v. limpiar

clean-cut adj. definido

clean-er n. limpiador

clean-ing n. limpieza

clean-li-ness n. limpieza

cleanse v. limpiar

cleans-er n. limpiador

clear adj. despejado; transparente

clear-cut adj. claro

clear-ing n. claro

clear-ly adv. claramente

cleav-age n. division

cleave v. adherir; partir

cleav-er n. cuchillo

clem-en-cy n. clemencia

cler-gy n. clero

cler-gy-man n. clerigo

cler-ic adj. clerigo

cler-i-cal adj. clerical

clerk n. oficinista

clev-er adj. listo

clev-er-ness n. inteligencia

cli-ent n. cliente

cli-mac-tic adj. culminante

cli-mate n. clima

cli-mat-ic adj. climatico

cli-max n. climax

climb v. trepar

climb-er n. alpinista

climb-ing adj. trepador

clin-ic n. clinica

clin-i-cal adj. clinico

cli-ni-cian n. clinico

clip v. cortar

cloak n. manto

clock n. reloj

clog n. atasco

clois-ter n. claustro

clone n. clon

close v. cerrar

closed adj. cerrado; vedado

close-down n. cierre

close-ly adv. atentamente; de cerca

close-ness n. proximidad

close-out n. liquidacion

clos-et n. armario

clos-ing n. cierre

clot n. coagulo

cloth n. tela

clothe v. arropar

clothes n. ropa

cloth-ing n. ropa

cloud n. nube

cloud-burst n. aguacero

cloud-y adj. nuboso

clout n. bofetada

clo-ver n. trebol

clown n. payaso

club n. palo; trebol

clue n. pista

clump n. grupo

clum-sy adj. pesado

coach n. vagon; coche

coach-man n. cochero

co-ag-u-late v. coagular(se)

co-ag-u-la-tion n. coagulación

coal n. carbon

co-a-lesce v. unirse

co-a-li-tion n. coalición

coarse adj. tosco

coars-en v. vulgarizar

coarse-ness n. aspereza

coast n. costa

coast-al adj. costero

coast-er n. trineo

coat n. pelo

coat-ed adj. banado

coat-ing n. capa; bano

coat-tail n. faldon

coax v. engatusar

coax-ing n. engatusamiento

cob n. elote

co-balt n. cobalto

cob-bler n. zapatero

co-bra n. cobra

cob-web n. telarana

co-caine n. cocaina

coc-cyx n. coccix

cock n. gallo

cock-ade n. escarapela

cock-a-too n. cacatua

cock-i-ness n. presunción

cock-le n. berberecho

cock-pit n. cancha

cock-roach n. cucaracha

cock-tail n. coctel

co-coa n. cacao

co-coa-nut n. coco

co-coon n. capullo

code n. codigo

co-de-fend-ant n. coacusado

co-deine n. codeina

cod-fish n. bacalao

cod-i-fy v. codificar

co-di-rec-tion n. codireccion

co-ed adj. coeducacional

co-ed-u-ca-tion n. coeducación

co-ed-u-ca-tion-al adj. coeducacional

co-ef-fi-cient n. coeficiente

co-erce v. coercer

co-er-cion n. coercion

co-ex-ist v. coexistir

co-ex-is-tence n. coexistencia

co-ex-ten-sive adj. coextenso

cof-fee n. cafe

cof-fer n. cofre

cof-fin n. ataud

cog n. diente

cog-i-tate v. meditar

cog-nac n. conac

cog-ni-tion n. cognición

cog-ni-zance n. conocimiento

cog-ni-zant adj. enterado

co-hab-it v. cohabitar

co-here v. adherirse

co-her-ence n. coherencia

co-her-ent adj. coherente

co-he-sion n. cohesion

co-he-sive adj. cohesivo

co-hort n. compañero

coil n. rollo

coin v. acunar; n. moneda

co-in-cide v. coincidir

co-in-ci-dence n. coincidencia

co-in-ci-den-tal adj. coincidente

co-la *n.* cola
col-an-der *n.* colador
cold *n., adj.* frio
cold-blood-ed *adj.* impasible
cold-heart-ed *adj.* insensible
cold-ness *n.* frialdad
col-ic *n.* colico
col-i-se-um *n.* coliseo
co-li-tis *n.* colitis
col-lab-o-rate *v.* colaborar
col-lab-o-ra-tion *n.* colaboración
col-lab-o-ra-tion-ist *n.* colaboracionista
col-lab-o-ra-tive *adj.* co-operativo
col-lab-o-ra-tor *n.* colaborador
col-lage *n.* collage
col-lapse *v.* desplomarse; caerse
col-laps-i-ble *adj.* plegable
col-lar *n.* cuello
col-lar-bone *n.* clavicula
col-late *v.* colacionar
col-lat-er-al *adj.* colateral
col-league *n.* colega
col-lect *v.* recoger; reunir; coleccionar
col-lect-ed *adj.* sosegado
col-lec-tion *n.* coleccion
col-lec-tive *adj.* colectivo
col-lec-tiv-ist *n.* colectivista
col-lec-tiv-ize *v.* colectivizar
col-lec-tor *n.* colector
col-lege *n.* colegio
col-le-gian *n.* estudiante
col-le-giate *adj.* universitario
col-lide *v.* chocar
col-li-sion *n.* choque
col-loid *n.* coloide
col-lo-qui-al *adj.* familiar
col-lo-qui-um *n.* cologuio
col-lo-quy *n.* coloquio
col-lude *v.* confabularse
col-lu-sion *n.* confabulación
co-logne *n.* colonia
co-lon *n.* colon
colo-nel *n.* coronel
co-lo-ni-al *adj.* colonial
co-lo-ni-al-ist *n.* colonialista
col-o-nist *n.* colonizador
col-o-ni-za-tion *n.* colon-izació́n

col-o-nize *v.* colonizar
col-o-niz-er *n.* colonizador
col-on-nade *n.* columnata
col-o-ny *n.* colonia
col-or *v.* colorear; *n.* color
col-or-a-tion *n.* coloración
col-ored *adj.* coloreado
col-or-ful *adj.* pintoresco
col-or-ing *n.* coloración
col-or-less *adj.* incoloro
co-los-sal *adj.* colosal
co-los-sus *n.* coloso
co-los-to-my *n.* colostomia
col-umn *n.* columna
col-umn-ist *n.* columnista
co-ma *n.* coma
co-ma-tose *adj.* comatoso
comb *v.* peinar; *n.* peine
com-bat *v.* conbatir
com-bat-ant *n.* combatiente
com-bat-ive *adj.* combativo
com-bi-na-tion *n.* combinación
com-bine *v.* combinar
com-bo *n.* conjunto
com-bus-ti-ble *adj.* conbustible
com-bus-tion *n.* combustion
come *v.* llegar; venir
come-back *n.* replica
co-me-di-an *n.* comediante
co-me-di-enne *n.* comedianta
com-e-dy *n.* comedia
come-on *n.* incentivo
com-et *n.* cometa
com-fort *v.* consolar
com-fort-a-ble *adj.* confortable
com-fort-er *n.* consolador
com-ic *adj.* comico
com-i-cal *adj.* comico
com-ing *adj.* venidero
com-ma *n.* coma
com-mand *n.* mando; *v.* mandar
com-man-dant *n.* comandante
com-mand-er *n.* comandante
com-mand-ing *adj.* imponente

com-man-do *n.* comando

com-mem-o-rate *v.* conmemorar

com-mem-o-ra-tion *n.* conmemoración

com-mence *v.* comenzar

com-mence-ment *n.* comienzo

com-mend *v.* encomendar

com-men-da-tion *n.* recomendación

com-men-su-rate *adj.* proporcionado

com-ment *n.* observación

com-mem-tar-y *n.* comentario

com-men-tate *v.* comentar

com-merce *n.* comercio

com-mer-cial *adj.* comercial

com-mer-cial-ism *n.* comercialismo

com-mer-cial-ize *v.* comercializar

com-mis-er-ate *v.* compadecerse

com-mis-sar *n.* comisario

com-mis-sar-y *n.* economato

com-mis-sion *v.* encargar; *n.* comision

com-mis-sion-er *n.* comisario

com-mit *v.* entregar

com-mit-ment *n.* compromiso

com-mit-tal *n.* obligación

com-mit-ee *n.* comite

com-mode *n.* comoda

com-mo-dore *n.* comodoro

com-mon *adj.* comun

com-mon-place *adj.* ordinario

com-mon-wealth *n.* comunidad

com-mo-tion *n.* tumulto

com-mu-nal *adj.* comunal

com-mune *v.* comulgar

com-mu-ni-ca-ble *adj.* comunicable

com-mu-ni-cate *v.* comunicar(se)

com-mu-ni-ca-tion *n.* comunicación

com-mu-ni-ca-tive *adj.* comunicativo

com-nu-ca-tor *n.* comunicante

com-mun-ion *n.* comunion

com-mu-nism *n.* comunismo

com-mun-ist *n.* comunista

com-mu-nis-tic *adj.* comunista

com-mu-ni-ty *n.* comunidad

com-mu-ta-tion *n.* conmutación

com-mu-ta-tive *adj.* conmutativo

com-mute *v.* conmutar

com-pact *adj.* compacto

com-pan-ion *n.* companero

com-pan-ion-ship *n.* companerismo

com-pa-ny *n.* compañia

com-pa-ra-ble *adj.* comparable

com-par-a-tive *adj.* comparativo

com-pare *v.* comparar

com-par-i-son *n.* comparacion

com-part-ment *n.* compartimiento

com-pass *n.* compas

com-pas-sion *n.* compasión

com-pas-sion-ate *adj.* compasivo

com-pat-i-ble *adj.* compatible

com-pa-tri-ot *n.* compatriota

com-pel *v.* compeler

com-pel-ling *adj.* incontestable

com-pen-sate *v.* compensar

com-pen-sa-tion *n.* conpensación

com-pete *v.* competir

com-pe-tence *n.* competencia

com-pe-tent *adj.* competente

com-pe-ti-tion *n.* competencia

com-pet-i-tive *adj.* competitivo

com-pet-i-tor *n.* competidor

com-pi-la-tion *n.* com-

pilacion
com-plie v. compilar
com-plain v. quejarse
com-plain-ant n. demandante
com-plaint n. queja
com-plai-sant adj. complaciente
com-ple-ment n. complemento
com-ple-men-ta-ry adj. complementario
com-plete adj. completo
com-ple-tion n. terminación
com-plex adj. complejo
com-plex-ion n. caracter
com-plex-i-ty n. complejidad
com-pli-nance n. conformidad
com-pli-ant adj. obediente
com-pli-cate v. complicar
com-pli-cat-ed adj. complicado
com-pli-ca-tion n. complicación
com-plic-i-ty n. complicidad
com-pli-ment n. honor; elogio
com-pli-men-ta-ry adj. elogioso
com-ply v. obedecer
com-po-nent n. componente
com-port-ment n. comportamiento
com-pose v. redactar
com-posed adj. tranquilo
com-pos-er n. compositor
com-pos-ite adj. compuesto
com-po-si-tion n. composicion
com-po-sure n. serenidad
com-pound adj. compuesto
com-pre-hend v. comprender
com-pre-hen-si-ble adj. comprensible
com-pre-hen-sion n. comprensión
com-pre-hen-sive adj. comprensivo; general
com-press n. compresa
com-pressed adj. comprimido

com-pres-sion n. compresión
com-prise v. constar de; comprender
com-pro-mise n. compromiso; v. componer
com-pro-mis-ing adj. comprometedor
com-pul-sion n. compulsión
com-pul-sive adj. obsesivo
com-pul-so-ry adj. compulsorio
com-pu-ta-tion n. calculo
com-pute v. computar
com-put-er n. computador
com-put-er-ize v. computarizae
com-rade n. camarada
con adv. contra
con-cave adj. concavo
con-ceal v. ocultar
con-ceal-ment n. encubrimiento
con-cede v. conceder
con-ceit-ed adj. vanidoso
con-ceiv-a-ble adj. concebible
con-ceive v. concebir
con-cen-trate v. concentrar(se)
con-cen-tra-tion n. concentración
con-cen-tric adj. concentrico
con-cept n. concepto
con-cep-tion n. concepción
con-cep-tu-al adj. conceptual
con-cern v. concernir
con-cerned adj. preocupado
con-cern-ing prep. acerca de
con-cert n. concierto
con-cet-ed adj. conjunto
con-cer-to n. concierto
con-ces-sion n. concesión
con-cil-i-ate v. conciliar
con-cil-i-a-tion n. conciliacion
con-cise adj. conciso
con-clude v. concluir
con-clu-sion n. conclusión
con-clu-sive adj. concluyente

con-coc-tion *n.* confección
con-cord *n.* concordia
con-crete *adj.* concreto
con-cur *v.* concurrir
con-cur-rence *n.* concurrencia
con-cur-rent *adj.* concurrente
con-cus-sion *n.* concusión
con-dem-na-ble *adj.* condenable
con-den-sa-tion *n.* condensación
con-dencse *v.* condensar(se)
con-dens-er *n.* condensador
con-de-scend-ing *adj.* condescendiente
con-di-ment *n.* condimento
con-di-tion *v.* condicionar
con-done *v.* condoñar
con-duc-tor *n.* cobrador
con-fed-er-a-cy *n.* confederación
con-fed-er-a-tion *n.* confederacion
con-fer *v.* oferenciar
con-fess *v.* confesar
con-fide *v.* confiar
con-fi-dence *n.* confianza
con-fi-den-tial *adj.* confidencial
con-firm *v.* confirmar
con-flict *v.* chocar
con-form-i-ty *n.* conformidad
con-fron-ta-tion *n.* confrontación
con-fuse *v.* confundir
con-fu-sion *n.* confusión
con-gest *v.* acumular
con-ges-tion *n.* congestión
con-glom-er-a-tion *n.* conglomeración
con-grat-u-la-tion *n.* felicitación
con-gre-gate *v.* congregar(se)
con-junc-tion *n.* conjunción
con-jure *v.* conjurar
con-nect *v.* conectar
con-no-ta-tion *n.* connotación
con-note *v.* connotar

con-sec-u-tive *adj.* consecutivo
con-serv-a-to-ry *n.* conservatorio
con-serve *v.* conservar
con-sid-er *v.* considerar
con-sid-er-a-tion *n.* consideración
con-sist *v.* consistir
con-sol-i-date *v.* consolidar
con-sol-i-da-tion *n.* consolidación
con-stan-cy *n.* constancia
con-stant *adj.* continuo
con-sti-tu-tion *n.* constitución
con-struc-tion *n.* construcción
con-sult *v.* consultar
con-sume *v.* consumir
con-sump-tion *n.* consuncion
con-tain *v.* contener
con-tam-i-na-tion *n.* contaminación
con-tem-plate *v.* proyectar
con-tem-po-rar-y *n.* contemplación
con-tend *v.* afirmar; contender
con-ti-nen-tal *adj.* continental
con-tin-gen-cy *n.* contingencia
con-tin-ue *v.* seguir; continuar
con-trac-tion *n.* contracción
con-tra-dict *v.* contradecir
con-trast *v.* contrastar
con-tri-bu-tion *n.* contribucion
con-trol *v.* dirigir; controlar
con-va-lesce *v.* convalecer
con-ven-tion *n.* convención
con-verge *v.* convergir
con-ver-sa-tion *n.* conversacion
con-verse *v.* conversar
con-ver-sion *n.* conversión
con-vey *v.* llevar
con-vic-tion *n.* convicción
con-vince *v.* convencer
con-vul-sion *n.* convulsion

cook n. cocinero; v. cocinar
cook-ie n. galleta
cool adj. fresco
co-or-di-nate v. coordinar
co-or-di-na-tion n. coordinación
cop-per n. cobre
cop-y v. copiar
cor-dial-i-ty n. cordialidad
corn n. maiz
cor-po-ral adj. corporal
cor-po-ra-tion n. corporación
cor-pu-lent adj. gordo
cor-pus-cu-lar adj. corpuscular
cor-ral v. acorralar
cor-rect v. corregir
cor-rec-tion n. corrección
cor-re-spond v. escribir
cor-re-spond-ence n. correspondencia
cor-rode v. corroer
cor-ro-sion n. corrosion
cor-rup-tion n. corrupción
cos-met-ic n. cosmetico
cos-mic adj. cosmico
cost v. costar; n. precio
couch n. sofa
count n. cuenta; v. contar
coun-try n. campo; pais
cou-ple n. pareja
cou-ra-geous adj. valiente
course n. plato; dirección
cous-in n. prima; primo
cov-er n. cubierta, v. cubrir
cow n. vaca
cow-boy n. vaquero
coy-o-te n. coyote
crab n. cangrejo
crack-er n. galleta
cra-dle v. mercer
crash n. choque; estallido
crate n. cajon
cra-ter n. crater
crave v. ansiar
crav-ing n. anhelo
crawl v. gatear; arrastrarse
cray-on n. pastel
craze v. enloquecer
crazed adj. loco
cra-zy adj. loco
cream n. crema

cream-y adj. cremoso
crease v. doblar
cre-ate v. producir; crear
cre-a-tion n. creación
cre-a-tive adj. creador
cre-a-tiv-i-ty n. originalidad
cre-a-tor n. creador
crea-ture n. criatura
cre-dence n. credito
cre-den-tial n. credencial
cred-i-ble adj. creible
cred-it n. credito; reconocimiento
cred-it-a-ble adj. loable
cred-u-lous adj. credulo
creed n. credo
creep-y adj. espeluznante
cre-mate v. incinerar
cre-ma-tion n. incineración
crepe n. crespon
cres-cent n. medialuna
crest n. cresta
cre-tin n. cretiño
crew n. equipo
crib n. pesebre
crick-et n. grillo
crime n. crimen
crim-i-nal n., adj. criminal
crin-kle v. arrugar(se)
crip-ple v. mutilar
cri-sis n. crisis
crisp adj. crespo
crisp-y adj. crujiente
crit-ic n. critico
crit-i-cal adj. critico
crit-i-cism n. critica
crit-i-cize v. criticar
cri-tique n. critica
croc-o-dile n. cocodrilo
cro-cus n. azafran
crook n. angulo; baculo
crook-ed adj. corvo
crop n. fusta; cultivo
cross-beam n. traviesa
cross-bow n. ballesta
cross-cur-rent n. contracorriente
cross-ex-am-ine v. interrogar
cross-ing n. cruce
cross-word puz-zle n. crucigrama
crouch v. acuclillarse

cross v. cruzar, n. cruz
crow v. cacarear
crowd n. gentio; multitud
crowd-ed adj. concurrido
crown n. corona
crown-ing n. coronación
cru-ci-ble n. crisol
cru-ci-fix n. crucifijo
cru-ci-fix-ion n. crucifixión
cru-ci-fy v. crucificar
crude adj. tosco; ordinario; crudo
crude-ness n. tosquedad
cru-el adj. cruel
cru-el-ty n. crueldad
cruise v. navegar
crumb n. migaja
crum-ble v. desmigajar(se)
crum-ple v. estrujar(se)
crunch-y adj. crujiente
cru-sade n. cruzada
cru-sad-er n. cruzado
crush v. aplastar
crust n. costra; corteza
crus-ta-cean n. crustaceo
crust-y adj. costroso
cry v. llorar
crypt n. cripta
crys-tal n. cristal
crys-tal-line adj. cristaliño
crys-tal-lize v. cristalizar(se)
crys-tal-log-ra-phy n. cristalografia
cube n. cubo
cu-bic adj. cubico
cu-bi-cle n. compartimiento
cub-ist n. cubista
cu-cum-ber n. pepiño
cud-dle v. abrazar(se)
cue n. taco
cu-li-nar-y adj. culinario
cul-mi-nate v. culminar
cul-pa-ble adj. culpable
cul-prit n. culpable
cult n. culto
cul-ti-vate v. cultivar
cul-ti-va-tion n. cultivo
cul-ti-va-tor n. cultivador
cul-tur-al adj. cultural
cul-ture n. cultura
cul-tured adj. culto
cum-ber v. embarazar
cum-ber-some adj. em-
barazoso
cu-mu-late v. acumular
cu-mu-la-tive adj. acumulativo
cun-ning adj. habil; astuto
cup n. taza
cup-ful n. taza
cur-a-ble adj. curable
curb n. bordillo
curd n. cuajada
cure n. cura
cu-ri-os-i-ty n. curiosidad
cu-ri-ous adj. curioso
curl v. enrollar(se); rizar(se)
cur-ren-cy n. moneda
cur-rent n., adj. corriente
cur-rent-ly adj. actualmente
curse n. desgracia; maldición
curs-ed adj. maldito
cur-sor n. cursor
cur-tain n. telon
cur-va-ture n. curvatura
curve n. curva
curved adj. curvo
cus-to-di-an n. custodio
cus-to-dy n. custodia
cus-tom n. costumbre
cus-tom-ar-i-ly adv. acostumbrado
cut adj. cortado; n. cortadura; v. cortar
cu-ta-ne-ous adj. cutaneo
cute adj. mono
cu-ti-cle n. cuticula
cut-ler-y n. cubiertos
cy-a-nide n. cianuro
cy-cle n. ciclo
cy-clic adj. ciclico
cy-clist n. ciclista
cy-clone n. ciclón
cyl-in-der n. cilindro
cy-lin-dri-cal adj. cilindrico
cym-bal n. cimbalo
cyn-i-cal adj. cinico
cyn-i-cism n. cinismo
cy-press n. cipres
cyst n. quiste
cys-tic adj. enquistado
cys-ti-tis n. cistitis
cy-to-plasm n. citoplasma
czar n. zar
cza-ri-na n. zariña

dab *v.* tocar ligeramente
dab-ble *v.* salpicar
dad *n.* papa
daft *adj.* loco
dag-ger *n.* punal
dai-ly *adj.* diario
dain-ti-ness *n.* delicadeze
dain-ty *adj.* delicado
dair-y *n.* lecheria; queseria
dair-y-man *n.* lechero
da-is *n.* estrado
dale *n.* valle
dal-li-ance *n.* diversión
dal-ly *v.* perder tiempo; entretenerse
dam *v.* represar, *n.* presa
dam-age *v.* danar; perjudicar
damn *v.* condenar
dam-na-ble *adj.* detestable
damned *adj.* condenado
damp *adj.* humedo
damp-en *v.* mojar
dance *n.* baile, *v.* bailar
dan-cer *n.* bailador
dan-druff *n.* caspa
dan-ger *n.* peligro
dan-ger-ous *adj.* peligroso
dan-gle *v.* colgar
dank *adj.* liento
dap-pled *adj.* rodado
dare *v.* arriesgarse
dar-ing *n.* atrevimiento
dark *n.* oscuridad, *adj.* oscuro
dark-en *v.* oscurecer
dark-ness *n.* oscuridad
darl-ing *n.* querido
darn *v.* zurcir
dash *v.* precipitarse; romper
dash-board *n.* tablere de instrumentos
date *n.* cita; fecha
daub *v.* pintarrajar
daugh-ter *n.* hija
daugh-ter-in-law *n.* nuera
daunt-less *adj.* impavido
daw-dle *v.* perder el tiempo
dawn *v.* amanecer
day *n.* dia
day-break *n.* amanecer
day-dream *n.* ensueño
day-light *n.* luz del dia
day-time *n.* dia

daze *v.* aturdir
daz-zle *v.* deslumbrar
dea-con *n.* diacono
dea-con-ry *n.* diaconía
dead *adj.* muerto
dead-en *v.* amortiguar
dead-end *n.* calle sin salida
dead-ly *adj.* mortal
deaf *adj.* sordo
deaf-en *v.* ensordecer
deaf-ness *n.* sordera
deal *n.* cantidad; trato; reparto
deal-er *n.* tratante
dean *n.* decaño; dean
dear *adj.* querido; caro
dear-ness *n.* carestia
death *n.* muerte
death-less *adj.* inmortal
death-ly *adj.* mortal
de-ba-cle *n.* fracaso
de-bar *v.* prohibir
de-bate *v.* debatir
de-bauch *v.* corromper
de-bauch-er-y *n.* libertinaje
de-bil-i-tate *v.* debilitar
de-bil-i-ta-tion *n.* debilitación
de-bil-i-ty *n.* debilidad
deb-it *n.* debe
deb-o-nair *adj.* cortes; elegante
de-bris *n.* escombros
debt *n.* deuda
debt-or *n.* deudor
de-but, de-but *n.* presentación; estreno
deb-u-tant, deb-u-tante *n.* debutante
de-cade *n.* deceñio
dec-a-dence *n.* decadencía
dec-a-dent *adj.* decadente
de-can-ter *n.* garrafa
de-cay *v.* decaer; cariarse; deteriorar
de-cease *v.* morir
de-ceased *adj.* muerto
de-ceit *n.* engano
de-ceit-ful *adj.* enganoso
de-ceive *v.* enganar
De-cem-ber *n.* diciembre
de-cen-cy *n.* decencía
de-cent *adj.* decente

de-cep-tion *n.* fraude
de-cide *v.* decidir
de-cid-ed *adj.* decidido
de-cid-ed-ly *adv.* decididamente
dec-i-mal *n.* decimal
de-ci-pher *v.* descifrar
de-ci-sion *n.* decision; firmeze
de-ci-sive *adj.* decisivo
de-ci-sive-ly *adv.* con resolución
deck *v.* adornar
dec-la-ra-tion *n.* declaración
de-clare *v.* declarar
de-cline *v.* rehusar
de-com-pose *v.* descomponer(se)
de-com-po-si-tion *n.* descomposición
de-cor-ate *v.* adornar; condecorar
dec-o-ra-tion *n.* decoración; ornato
dec-o-ra-tor *n.* decorador
de-coy *n.* senuelo
de-crease *v.* disminuir(se)
de-creas-ing-ly *adv.* en disminucion
de-cree *n.* decreto
de-crep-it *adj.* decrepito
de-cry *v.* rebajar
de-duce *v.* deducir
de-duct *v.* restar
de-duc-tion *n.* descuento
deed *n.* hecho
deem *v.* juzgar
deep *adj.* profundo
deep-en *v.* intensificar
de-face *v.* desfigurar
def-a-ma-tion *n.* difamación
de-fame *v.* difamar
de-fault *n.* a falta de
de-feat *n.* derrota *v.* vencer; frustrar
de-fect *n.* defecto
de-fec-tion *n.* defección
de-fec-tive *adj.* defectuoso
de-fend *v.* defender
de-fend-ant *n.* demandado
de-fense, de-fence *n.* defensa
de-fen-sive *adj.* defensivo

de-fer *v.* diferir; aplazar
def-er-ence *n.* deferencia
de-fer-ment *n.* apazamiento
de-fi-ance *n.* desafio
de-fi-ant *adj.* provocativo
de-fi-cien-cy *n.* deficiencia
de-fi-cient *adj.* insuficiente
def-i-cit *n.* deficit
de-file *v.* manchar
de-fine *v.* definir
def-i-nite *adj.* concreto; definido
de-fi-ni-tion *n.* definición
de-fin-i-tive *adj.* definitivo
de-flate *v.* desinflar
de-fla-tion *n.* desinflación
de-flect *v.* desviar
de-form *v.* desfigurar; deformar
de-form-i-ty *n.* deformidad
de-fraud *v.* defraudar; estafar
de-fray *v.* pagar
deft *adj.* diestro
deft-ness *n.* habilidad
de-funct *adj.* difunto
de-fy *v.* desafiar; contravenir
de-gen-er-ate *v.* degenerar
deg-ra-da-tion *n.* degradación
de-grade *v.* degradar
de-gree *n.* rango
de-hy-drate *v.* deshidratar
de-hy-dra-tion *n.* deshidratación
de-i-fy *v.* deificar
deign *v.* dignarse
de-i-ty *n.* deidad
de-ject-ed *adj.* abatido
de-jec-tion *n.* melancolia; abatimiento
de-lay *v.* aplazar; demorar
de-lec-ta-ble *adj.* deleitable
de-le-gate *v.* delegar
de-le-ga-tion *n.* diputación
de-lete *v.* tachar
de-le-tion *n.* supresión; borradura
de-lib-er-ate *v.* deliberar
del-i-ca-cy *n.* delicadeze
del-i-cate *adj.* delicado; fino
de-li-cious *adj.* delicioso
de-light *v.* deleitar

de-light-ful *adj.* encantador
de-lin-e-ate *v.* delinear
de-lin-e-a-tion *n.* bosquejo
de-lin-quen-cy *n.* delincuencia
de-lin-quent *adj., n.* delincuente
de-lir-i-ous *adj.* delirante
de-lir-i-um *n.* delirio
de-liv-er *v.* entregar
de-liv-er-y *n.* entrega
del-ta *n.* delta
de-lude *v.* inganar
del-uge *n.* diluvio
de-lu-sion *n.* engano; ilusión
de-luxe *adj.* de lujo
delve *v.* cavar
de-mand *v.* demandar; exigir
de-moc-ra-cy *n.* democracia
dem-o-crat *n.* democrata
dem-o-crat-ic *adj.* democratico
dem-on-strate *v.* demostrar
dem-on-stra-tion *n.* demostración
de-mor-al-ize *v.* desmoralizar
dn *n.* estudio
de-nom-i-na-tion *n.* denominación
de-nom-i-na-tor *n.* denominador
de-note *v.* denotar
de-nounce *n.* denunciar
dense *adj.* denso
den-si-ty *n.* densidad
den-tist *n.* dentista
de-nun-ci-ate *v.* denunciar
de-nun-ci-a-tion *n.* denuncia
de-par-ture *n.* salida
de-pend-en-cy *n.* dependencia
de-port *v.* deportar
de-por-ta-tion *n.* deportación
de-prave *v.* depravar
de-praved *adj.* depravado
de-pres-sion *n.* desaliento
depth *n.* fondo
de-ride *v.* mofar
de-ri-sion *n.* irrision
der-i-va-tion *n.* derivación
de-rive *v.* derivar(se)

der-rick *n.* grua
de-scend *v.* bajar; descender
de-scend-ant *n.* descendiente
de-scribe *v.* describir
de-scrip-tion *n.* descripción
de-scrip-tive *adj.* descriptivo
des-ert *n.* desierto
de-sert-er *n.* desertor
de-serve *v.* merecer
de-sign *v.* idear; disenar
des-ig-nate *v.* senalar; nombrar
des-ig-na-tion *n.* nombramiento
de-sing-er *n.* disenador; dibujante
de-sire *v.* desear
de-sist *v.* desistir
desk *n.* pupitre
des-o-la-tion *n.* desolación
de-spair *v.* desesperar
des-per-ate *adj.* desesperado; arriesgado
des-per-a-tion *n.* desesperación
des-pi-ca-ble *adj.* despreciable
de-spise *v.* despreciar
de-spite *prep.* a pesar de
des-sert *n.* postre
de-stroy *v.* destruir
de-struct-i-ble *adj.* destructible
de-struc-tion *n.* destrucción
de-tain *v.* retener
de-ter *v.* disuadir
de-ter-mi-na-tion *n.* determinación
de-ter-mine *v.* resolver; determinar
de-test-a-ble *adj.* detestable
de-val-u-a-tion *n.* devaluación
dev-as-tate *v.* devastar
dev-as-ta-tion *n.* devastación
de-vel-op *v.* desenvolver
de-vice *n.* ingenio; estratagema
dev-il *n.* diablo
de-vi-ous *adj.* tortuoso

de-vise v. inventar
de-void adj. desprovisto
de-vote v. dedicar
dev-o-tee n. devoto
dev-o-tion n. devoción; lealtad
de-vour v. devorar
di-a-be-tes n. diabetes
di-a-bet-ic adj. diabetico
di-ag-nose v. diagnosticar
di-a-bol-ic adj. diabolico
di-a-dem n. diadema
di-ag-nose v. diagnosticar
di-ag-no-sis n. diagnostico
di-ag-o-na. adj., n. diagonal
di-a-gram n. diagrama
di-al v. marcar
di-a-lect n. dialecto
di-a-logue n. dialogo
di-am-e-ter n. diametro
di-a-met-ric adj. diametral
dia-mond n. diamante; oros
dia-per n. panal
di-a-phragm n. diafragma
di-ar-rhe-a n. diarrea
di-a-ry n. diario
dice n. dados
dick-er v. regatear
dic-tate v. mandar; dictar
dic-ta-tion n. dictado
dic-ta-tor n. dictador
dic-tion-ar-y n. diccionaio
die v. morir
dif-fer-ence n. diferencia
dif-fer-ent adj. diferente
dif-fi-cult adj. dificil
dif-fi-cul-ty n. dificultad
dif-fu-sion n. difusion
dig n. excavacion; v. extraer
di-ges-tion n. digestion
dig-it n. dedo
dig-ni-fy v. dignificar
di-lem-ma n. dilema
dil-i-gence n. diligencia
dil-i-gent adj. diligente
di-lute v. diluir
di-lu-tion n. dilución
dim adj. oscuro
di-min-ish v. disminuir(se)
dine v. cenar
din-ner n. cena
di-plo-ma-cy n. diplomacia
dip-lo-mat n. diplomatico

dip-lo-mat-ic adj. diplomatico
di-rect v. dirigir, adj. directo
di-rec-tion n. dirección
di-rec-tor n. director
dis-a-ble v. inutilizar
dis-ap-pear v. desaparecer
dis-ap-pear-ance n. desa-
parición
dis-as-trous adj. desastroso
dis-a-vow v. desconocer
dis-charge v. despedir
dis-ci-pli-nar-y adj. dis-
ciplinario
dis-ci-pline v. disciplinar, n.
castigo
dis-con-nect v. desconectar
dis-con-tin-u-ous adj. dis-
continuo
dis-cov-er v. descubrir
dis-crep-an-cy n. discrepan-
cia
dis-cus-sion n. discusión
dis-ease n. enfermedad
dis-guise n. disfraz, v. dis-
frazar
dish n. plato
dis-hon-or v. deshonrar
dis-hon-or-a-ble adj. des-
honroso
dis-in-fect-ant n. desinfec-
tante
dis-in-ter-est n. desinteres
disk n. disco
dis-lo-cate v. dislocar
dis-lo-ca-tion n. dislocación
dis-o-bey v. desobedecer
dis-or-der n. desorden
dis-pense v. dispensar
dis-play n. demostrar
dis-pute n. disputa, v. dis-
putar
dis-qual-i-fy v. descalificar
dis-solve v. disolver(se)
dis-suade v. disuadir
dis-sua-sion n. disuasion
dis-tance n. distancia
dis-tant adj. distante
dis-till v. destilar
dis-till-er-y n. destileria
dis-tinc-tion n. distinción
dis-tin-guish v. distinguir
dis-tract v. distraer

dis-trac-tion n. distracción
dis-tri-bu-tion n. distribución
dis-turb v. perturbar
dis-turb-ance n. disturbio
di-verge v. divergir
di-ver-gence n. divergencia
di-ver-sion n. diversion
di-ver-si-ty n. diversidad
di-vert v. divertir
di-vide v. dividir(se)
di-vin-i-ty n. divinidad
diz-zy adj. mareado
do v. cumplir; hacer
doc-tor n. medico
doc-u-ment n. documentar
dog n. perro
dog-mat-ic adj. dogmatico
doll n. muneca
dol-lar n. dolar
do-mes-tic adj. domestico
do-mes-ti-cate v. domesticar
dom-i-nant v. dominar
dom-i-na-tion n. dominación
dom-i-neer v. tiranizar
dom-i-neer-ing a. dominante
do-min-ion n. dominio
don v. ponerse
do-nate v. donar
done adj. hecho
do-nor n. donante
doom n. juicio; suerte
door n. puerta
dope n. narcotico
dor-mi-to-ry n. dormitorio
dor-sal adj. dorsal
dos-age n. dosificación
dose n. dosis
dot n. punto
dot-age n. chochez
dou-ble v. doblar(se)
doubt n. duda, v. dudar
dough n. maxa
dough-nut n. buñuelo
dour adj. austero
douse v. mojar; zambullir
dow-a-ger n. vuida de un titulado
dow-dy adj. desalinado; poso elegante
down prep., adv. abajo
down-cast adj. abatido
down-fall n. caida
down-heart-ed adj. desa-

nimadc
down-ward adv. hacia abajo
doze v. dormitar
doz-en n. doceña
drab adj. monotono
draft n. destacamento; giro; borrador
drag v. arrastar
drag-on n. dragon
drain v. agotar; desaguar
drain-age n. desague; drenaje
dra-ma n. drama
dra-mat-ic adj. dramatico
dram-a-tist n. dramaturgo
dram-a-tize v. dramatizar
drape v. poner colgaduras
dra-per-y n. paneria
dras-tic a. drastico; energico
draw v. sacar; dibujar; arrastrar
draw-back n. desventaja
draw-bridge n. puente levadizo
draw-er n. cajon
dread v. temer
dread-ful adj. terrible
dream v. sonar, n. sueño
dream-er n. sonador
dredge v. dragar
dreg n. heces
drench v. empapar
dress n. vestido, v. vestir(se)
dress-er n. aparador
drib-ble v. caer gota a gota
drift n. impulso de la corriente; monton
drift-wood n. madera llevada por el agua
drill v. taladrar
drink n. bebida, v. beber
drip v. gotear
drive v. manejar; empujar; conducir
driz-zle v. lloviznar
droll adj. gracioso
drone n. zangano
drool v. babear
droop v. inclinar
drop n. gota; declive
drop-sy n. hidropesia
dross n. escoria
drought n. sequia

drown v. ahogar; engar
drowse v. adormecer(se)
drow-sy adj. sonoliento
drudg-er-y n. faena penosa
drug n. droga
drug-gist n. farmaceutico; boticario
drum n. tambor
drum-stick n. baqueta
drunk adj. borracho
drunk-ard n. borracho
drunk-en adj. borracho
du-al-i-ty n. dualidad
dub v. armar caballero
du-bi-ous adj. dudoso
duch-ess n. duquesa
duck n. pato
duct n. conducto
dude n. petimetre
due adj. debido; oportuno
duel n. duelo
du-et n. duo
duke n. duque
dull adj. embotado; torpe
dumb adj. mudo
dum-found v. pasmar
dum-my n. maniqui
dump v. descargar
dump-ling n. bola de masa
dunce n. zopenco
dune n. duna
dung n. estiercol
dun-geon n. mazmorra
du-pli-cate adj. duplicado, v. duplicar
du-pli-ca-tion n. duplicación
du-ra-tion n. duración
dur-ing prep. durante
dusk n.. crepusculo
dusk-y adj. oscuro
dust n. polvo
du-ti-ful adj. obediente
du-ty n. derechos
dwell v. habitar
dewll-ing n. morada
dwin-dle v. disminuir
dye n. tinte
dy-nam-ic adj. dinamico
dy-na-mite n. dinamita
dy-na-mo n. dinamo; dinamo
dy-nas-ty n. dinastia
dys-en-ter-y n. disenteria

each adv. para cada uño
ea-ger adj. impaciente
ea-ger-ness n. ansia
ea-gle n. aguila
ea-glet n. aguilucho
ear n. oido; oreja
ear-drum n. timpaño del oido
earl n. conde
ear-li-ness n. precocidad
ear-ly adj. primitivo adv., adj. temprano
earn v. merecer
ear-nest a. fervoroso; serio
ear-nest-ly adv. con seriedad
earn-ings n. sueldo
ear-ring n. pendiente
ear-shot n alcance del oido
earth n. mundo; tierra
earth-en-ware n. loza de barro
earth-ly adj. mundaño
earth-quake n. terremoto
earth-y a. terroso
ease v. facilitar, n. facilidad
ea=sel n. caballete
eas-i-ly adv. facilmente
eas-i-ness n. facilidad
east n. este
east-ern adj. del este
east-ward adv. hacia el este
eas-y adj. facil
eas-y-go-ing a. acomodadizo; de manga ancha
eat v. gastar; comer
eat-a-ble a. comestible
eaves n. alero
eaves-drop v. escuchar a escondidas; espiar
ebb v. menguar.; decaer
eb-on-y n. ebaño
ec-cen-tric adj. excentrico
ec-cen-tric-i-ty n. ex-centricidad
ec-cle-si-as-tic a., n. eclesiastico
ech-o n. eco
e-clipse v. eclipsar
e-clip-tic adj. ecliptico
ec-o-lo-gic a. ecologiso
e-col-o-gist n. ecologo

e-col-o-gy *n.* ecologia
e-co-nom-ic *adj.* economico
e-co-nom-ic-al *a.* economico
e-co-nom-ics *n.* economia
e-con-o-mist *n.* economista
e-con-o-mize *v.* economizar
e-con-o-my *n.* economia
ec-sta-sy *n.* extasis
ec-stat-ic *a.* extatico
ec-u-men-i-cal *n.* ecumenico
ec-ze-ma *n.* eczema; ec-
cema
ed-dy *n.*
remolino
e-den-tate *a.* desdentado
edge *n.* filo; agudeza; borde
ed-i-ble *a.* comestible
e-dict *n.*
edicto
ed-i-fi-ca-tion *n.* edificación
de-i-fice *n.* edificio
ed-i-fy *v.* edificar
ed-it *v.* editar
e-di-tion *n.* edición
ed-i-tor *n.* editor
ed-i-to-ri-al *a.* editorial
ed-i-to-ri-al-ist *n.*
editorialista
ed-u-cate *v.* educar
ed-u-ca-tion *n.* educación
eel *n.* anguila
ee-rie *a.* espantoso; fantastico
ef-face *v.* borrar
ef-fect *v.* efectuar, *n.* resultado
ef-fec-tive *a.* efectivo; eficaz
ef-fec-tu-al *a.* eficaz
ef-fem-i-nate *a.* afeminado
ef-fer-vesce *v.* estar en efer-
vescencia
ef-fer-ves-cence *n.* eferves-
cencia
ef-fer-ves-cent *adj.* eferves-
cente
ef-fe-ca-cious *a.* eficaz
ef-fi-cien-cy *n.* eficiencia
ef-fi-cient *adj.* eficiente
ef-fi-gy *n.* efigie
ef-fort *n.* esfuerzo
ef-fort-less *a.* sin esfuerzo
ef-fuse *v.* derramar
ef-fu-sion *n.* efusion

ef-fu-sive *a.j* exspansivo;
efusivo
egg *n.* huevo
e-go *n.* el yo
e-go-tist *n.* egotista
e-gress *n.* salida
eight *adj.* ocho
eight-een *adj.* dieciocho
eighth *adj.* octavo
eight-y *adj.* ochenta
ei-ther *adv.* tampoco; tam-
bien, *adj.* cualquier
e-ject *v.* echar; expulsar
e-jec-tion *n.* expusion
eke *v.* aumentar
e-lab-o-rate *v.*
elaborar
e-lab-ra-tion *n.* elaboración
e-lapse *v.*
pasar
e-last-ic *a.* elastico
e-las-tic-i-ty *n.* elasticidad
e-late *v.* alegrar
e-la-tion *n.* regocijo
el-bow *n.* codo
eld-er *a.* mayor
el-der-ly *a.* de edad
eld-est *a.* el major
e-lect *v.* elegir
e-lec-tion *n.* elección
e-lec-tive *adj.* electivo
e-lec-tor *n.* elector
e-lec-tor-ate *n.* electorado
e-lec-tric *a.* electrico; vivo
e-lec-tri-cian *n.* electricista
e-lec-tric-i-ty *n.* electricidad
e-lec-tro-cute *v.* electrocutar
e-lec-trode *n.* electrodo
e-lec-tron *n.* electron
e-lec-tron-ic *a.* electronico
el-e-gance *n.* elegancia
el-e-gant *adj.* elegante
el-e-gize *v.* hacer una elegia
el-e-gy *n.* elegia
el-e-ment *n.* elemento
el-e-men-ta-ry *adj.* elemental
el-e-phant *n.* elefante
el-e-vate *v.* elevar
el-e-va-tion *n.* elevación
el-e-va-tor *n.* ascensor
e-lev-en *adj.* once
e-lev-enth *a.,n.* undecimo

elf-in a. e elfo

e-lic-it v. sacar

el-i-gi-bil-i-ty n. elegibilidad

el-i-gi-ble a. elegible; deseable

e-lim-i-nate v. eliminar

e-lim-i-na-tion n. eliminación

e-lite n. lo mejor

e-lix-ir n. elixir

elk n. alce

el-lipse n. elipse

el-lip-ti-cal a. eliptico

elm n. olmo

el-o-cu-tion n. elocución

e-lon-gate v. alargar

e-lope v. fugarse con su amante para casarse

e-lope-ment n. fuga

el-o-quence n. elocuencia

el-o-quent a. elocuente

else a. otro; mas

e-lu-ci-date v. elucidar

e-lude v. eludir; escapar de

e-lu-sive a. esquivo

e-ma-ci-ate v. enflaquecer(se)

e-man-ci-pate v. emancipar

e-man-ci-pa-tion n. emancipación

em-balm v. embalsamar

em-bar-go n. embargo

em-bark v. embarcar(se)

em-bar-rass v. desconcertar

em-bas-sy n. embajada

em-ber n. ascua

em-bez-zle v. desfalcar

em-blem n. emblema

em-boss v. realzar

em-brace v. abrazar; aceptar; abarcar

em-broi-der v. recamar

em-bry-o n. embrion

em-er-ald n. esmeralda

e-merge v. salir

e-mer-gence n. salida

e-mer-gen-cy n. crisis

em-er-y n. esmeril

em-i-grant n. emigrante

em-i-grate v. emigrar

em-i-gra-tion n. emigración

em-i-nence n. eminencia

em-i-nent adj. eminente

em-is-sar-y n. emisario

e-mis-sion n. emision

e-mit v. emitir

e-mo-tion n. emoción

em-per-or n. empreador

em-pha-sis n. enfasis

em-pha-size v. acentuar; recalcar

em-phat-ic a. enfatico

em-pire n. imperio

em-ploy v. emplear

em-ploy-ee n. empleado

em-ploy-er n. amo; patron

em-ploy-ment n. empleo; colocacion

em-pow-er v. autorizar

em-press n. emperatriz

emp-ti-ness n. vacuidad; vacio

emp-ty v. vaciar, adj. desocupado

em-u-late v. emular

e-mul-sion n. emulsion

e-mul-sive a. emulsivo

en-a-ble v. hacer que; permitir

en-act v. decretar; hacer el papel de

e-nam-el n. esmalte

en-am-or v. enamorar

en-case v. encerrar; encajar

en-chant v. encantar

en-chant-ing adj. encantador

en-chant-ment n. encanto

en-cir-cle v. cenir; rodear

en-close v. cercar; encerrar; incluir

en-clo-sure n. cercamiento; carta adjunta

en-com-pass v. cercar; abarcar

en-core n. repeticion

en-coun-ter n. encuentro

en-cour-age v. animar; fomentar

en-croach v. usurpar; pasar los limites

en-cum-ber v. estorbor; gravar

en-cy-clo-pe-dia n. enciclopedia

end n. final; fin

en-dan-ger v. poner en peligro

en-dear v. hacer querer

en-deav-or n. esfuerzo

end-ing n. fin

en-dorse v. endosar

en-dorse-ment n. endoso

en-dow v. dotar

en-dur-ance n. resistencia

en-dure v. durar

en-e-my n. enemigo

en-er-get-ic adj. energico

en-er-gy n. energia

en-force v. hacer cumplir; exigir

en-gage v. engranar; apalabrar

en-gage-ment n. obligación

en-gine n. motor; locomotora

en-gi-neer n. ingeniero

en-gi-neer-ing n. ingenieria

Eng-lish n. ingles

en-grave v. grabar

en-gross v. absorber; monopolizar

en-hance v. aumentar

e-nig-ma n. enigma

en-join v. imponer

en-joy v. disfrutar

en-joy-ment n. disfrute

en-large v. extender(se)

en-large-ment n. aumento; ampliación

en-light-en v. iluminar; instruir

en-list v. alistar(se)

en-liv-en v. avivar

en-mi-ty n. enemistad

e-nor-mous adj. enorme

e-nough adv. bastante

en-slave v. entrar

en-ter-tain-ment n. espectaculo

en-thu-si-asm n. entusiasmo

en-thu-si-ast n. entusiasta

en-tire adj. entero

en-tire-ly adv. totalmente

en-trance n. entrada

en-trust v. entregar

en-try n. partida; entrada

en-vel-op v. envolver

en-zyme n. enzima

ep-i-dem-ic n. epidemia

ep-i-sode n. episodio

ep-och n. epoca

eq-ua-bil-i-ty n. uniformidad

eq-ua-ble a. uniforme

e-qual v. igualar, n. igual

e-qual-i-ty adj. igualdad

e-qual-ly adv. igualmente

e-qual-ize v. igualar

e-qual-ly adv. igualmente

e-qua-nim-i-ty n. ecuanimidad

e-quate v. comparar

e-qua-tion n. ecuación

e-qua-tor n. ecuador

e-ques-tri-enne n. jineta

e-qui-lib-ri-um n. equilibrio

e-quip v. proveer; equipar

e-quip-ment n. equipo

eq-ui-ta-ble a. equitat

eq-ui-ty n. equidad

e-quiv-a-lent adj. equivalente

e-ra n. era

e-rad-i-cate v. desarraigar

e-rase v. borrar

e-ras-er n. borrador

ere conj. antes de que

e-rect v. erigir

e-rec-tion n. erección

er-mine n. armino

e-rode v. corroer

e-ro-sion n. erosion

e-rot-ic a. erotico

err v. vagar; errar

er-rand n. recado

er-rant a. errante

er-ror n. error

er-u-dite a. erudito

er-u-di-tion n. erudicion

e-rupt v. estar en erupción

e-rup-tion n. erupción

es-ca-la-tor n. escalera movil

es-ca-pade n. aventura

es-cape v. escapar; huir

es-chew v. evitar

es-cort v. acompanar, n. acompanante

e-soph-a-gus, oe-soph-a-gus n. esofago

es-o-ter-ic a. esoterico

es-pe-cial adj. especial

es-pe-cial-ly *adv.* especial-
mente
es-pi-o-nage *n.* espionaje
es-pouse *v.* adherirse a;
casarse
es-py *v.* divisar; percebir
es-say *n.* ensayo
es-sence *n.* esencia; perfume
es-sen-tial *adj.* esencial
es-tab-lish *v.* establecer;
probar; fundar
es-tab-lish-ment *n.* es-
tablecimiento
es-tate *n.* finca; propiedad
es-teem *v.* estimar
es-thet-ic *a.* estetico
es--ti-ma-ble *a.* estimable
es-ti-mate *v.* calcular; estimar
es-ti-ma-tion *n.* juicio;
aprecio

es-thet-ic *adj.* estetico
es-ti-mate *v.* estimar
es-ti-ma-tion *n.* juicio;
aprecio
as-trange *v.* apartar
es-tu-ar-y *n.* estuario
et cet-er-a *n.* etcetera
etch *v.* grabar al agua fuerte
etch-ing *n.* aguafuerte
e-ter-nal *adj.* eterno
e-ter-nal-ly *adv.* eternamente
e-ter-ni-ty *n.* eternidad
e-ther *n.* eter
e-the-re-al *a.* etereo
eth-i-cal *adj.* etico
eth-ics *n.* etica
eth-nic *a.* etnico
eth-nol-o-gy *n.* etnologia
et-i-quette *n.* etiqueta
e-tude *n.* estudio
eu-lo-gize *v.* elogiar
eu-lo-gy *n.* elogio
eu-pho-ri-a *n.* euforia
eu-phor-ic *adj.* euforico
e-vac-u-ate *v.* evacuar
e-vac-u-a-tion *n.* evacuación
e-vade *v.* evadir
e-val-u-ate *v.* evaluar
e-val-u-a-tion *n.* evaluación
e-van-gel-i-cal *a.* evangelico

e-van-ge-list *n.* evangelista
e-vap-o-rate *v.* evaporar(se)
e-vap-o-ra-tion *n.*
evaporación
e-va-sion *n.* evasion
e-va-sive *a.* evasivo
eve *n.* vispera
e-ven *adj.* igualar
eve-ning *n.* tarde
e-vent *n.* suceso
e-vent-ful *a.* memorable
e-ven-tu-al-i-ty *n.* even-
tualidad
ev-er *adv.* siempre; junca;
jamas
eve-ry *adj.* todo
e-vict *v.* expulsar
e-vic-tion *n.* desahucio
ev-i-dence *n.* evidencia
ev-i-dent *a.* evidente
e-vil *n.* mal
e-vil-do-er *n.* malhechor
e-voke *v.* evocar
ev-o-lu-tion *n.* desarrollo;
evolución
e-volve *v.* desarrollar
ewe *n.* oveja
ew-er *n.* aguamanil
ex-act *adj.* exacto
ex-act-ing *a.* exigente
ex-ag-ger-ate *v.* exagerar
ex-ag-ger-a-tion *n.* ex-
ageración
ex-alt *v.* exaltar; honrar
ex-al-ta-tion *n.* exaltacion
ex-am-in-a-tion *n.* examen
ex-am-ine *v.* examinar
ex-am-in-er *n.* examinador
ex-am-ple *n.* ejemplo
ex-as-per-ate *v.* exasperar
ex-as-per-a-tion *n.* ex-
asperación
ex-ca-vate *v.* excavar
ex-ca-va-tion *n.* excavación
ex-ceed *v.* superar; exceder
ex-ceed-ing-ly *adv.*
sumamente
ex-cel *v.* sobresalir; aventajar
ex-cel-lence *n.* excelencia
ex-cel-lent *adj.* excelente
ex-cept *v.* exceptuar
ex-cep-tion *n.* excepción
ex-cep-tion-al *a.* excepcional

ex-cerpt *v.* citar un texto
ex-cess *n.* exceso
ex-ces-sive *adj.* excesivo
ex-change *v.* cambiar
ex-cise *n.* impuestos sobre ciertos articulos
ex-cit-a-ble *a.* excitable
ex-cite *v.* excitar
ex-cite-ment *n.* agitacion; emocion
ex-cit-ing *a.* emocionante
ex-claim *v.* exclamar
ex-cla-ma-tion *n.* exclamacion
ex-clude *v.* excluir
ex-clu-sion *n.* exclusion
ex-clu-sive *a.* exclusivo
ex-com-mu-ni-cate *v.* excomulgar
ex-com-mu-ni-ca-tion *n.* excomunion
ex-cre-ment *n.* excremento
ex-cur-sion *n.* viaje; excursion
ex-cuse *v.* excusar; perdonar
ex-e-cute *v.* ejecutar; llevar a cabo
ex-e-cu-tion *n.* ejecución
ex-ec-u-tive *a.* ejecutivo
ex-ec-u-tor *n.* albacea
ex-em-pla-ry *a.* ejemplar
ex-er-cise *n.* ejercicio
ex-hale *v.* exhalar; espirar
ex-haust *v.* agotar
ex-hib-it *v.* mostrar; presentar
ex-hi-bi-tion *n.* exposición
ex-hil-a-rate *v.* vigorizar; alegrar
ex-hort *v.* exhortar
ex-i-gent *a.* exigente
ex-ile *n.* exilado; destierro
ex-ist *v.* existir
ex-ist-ence *n.* existencia
ex-it *n.* salida
ex-o-dus exoo
ex-or-bi-tant *a.* excesivo
ex-o-tic *adj.* exotico
ex-pand *v.* extendeer; ensanchar
ex-panse *n.* extensión
ex-pan-sion *n.* expansion
ex-pan-sive *a.* expansivo

ex-pect *v.* experar; contar con
ex-pect-an-cy *n.* expectacion
ex-pect-ant *a.* expectante
ex-pec-ta-tion *n.* expectacion
ex-pe-di-en-cy *n.* conveniencia
ex-pe-di-ent *a.* conveniente
ex-pe-dite *v.* facilitar; acelerar
ex-pe-di-tion *n.* expedición
ex-pel *v.* expulsar
ex-pend *v.* expender
ex-pend-i-ture *n.* gasto
ex-pe-ri-ence *v.* experimentar
ex-per-i-ment *n.* experimento
ex-pire *v.* terminar
ex-pla-na-tion *n.* explicación
ex-pli-cit *a.* explicito
ex-plode *v.* estallar; volar
ex-ploit *n.* hazaña
ex-plo-ra-tion *n.* exploracion
ex-plor *v.* explorar; examinar
ex-plor-er *n.* explorador
ex-plo-sion *n.* explosion
ex-po-nent *n.* exponente
ex-port *v.* exportar
ex-por-ta-tion *n.* exportacion
ex-pose *v.* exponer; desenmascarar
ex-press *v.* expresar
ex-pres-sion *n.* expresion
ex-pres-sive *adj.* expresion
ex-tend *v.* extender
ex-ten-sion *n.* extension
ex-te-ri-or *adj.* exterior
ex-tinct *adj.* extinto
ex-tinc-tion *n.* extinción
ex-tra *n.* extra
ex-tra-or-di-nar-y *adj.* extraordinario
ex-treme *adj.* extremo
ex-ul-ta-tion *n.* exultación
eye *n.* ojo
eye-let *n.* ojete
eye-sight *n.* vista
eye-tooth *n.* colmillo
eye-wit-ness *n.* testigo ocular

fa-ble *n.* fabula
fab-ric *n.* tela
fab-ri-cate *v.* inventar
fab-u-lous *adj.* fabuloso
fa-cade *n.* fachada
face *n.* cara
fa-cial *adj.* facial
fa-cile *adj.* facil
fa-cil-i-tate *v.* facilitar
fa-cil-i-ty *n.* facilida
fac-sim-i-le *n.* facsimile
fact *n.* hecho
fac-tion *n.* facción
fac-tor *n.* factor
fac-to-ry *n.* fabrica
fac-tu-al *a.* basado en datos
fac-ul-ty *n.* facultad
fad *n.* novedad
fade *v.* descolorar(se)
fag *v.* fatigar
fag-ot *n.* haz de lena
Fahr-en-heit *adj.* de Fahren-
heit
fail *v.* acabar; faltar
fail-ure *n.* fracaso
faint *v.* desmayarse
faint-ness *n.* debilidad
fair *adj.* justo; rubio
fair-ly *adv.* justamente
fair-y *n.* hada
faith *n.* fe
faith-ful *adj.* fiel
faith-less *adj.* desleal
fake *n.* impostura
fal-con *n.* halcon
fall *v.* caer(se)
fal-la-cious *adj.* enganoso
fal-la-cy *n.* error; falacia
fal-li-ble *adj.* falible
fal-low *adj.* en barbecho
false *adj.* falso
false-hood *n.* mentira
false-ly *adv.* falsamente
fal-si-fy *v.* falsificar·
fal-si-ty *n.* falsedad
fal-ter *v.* vacilar; titubear
fame *n.* fama
fa-mil-iar *adj.* familiar
fa-mil-i-ar-i-ty *n.* familiaridad
fam-i-ly *n.* familia
fam-ine *n.* hambre
fam-ish *v.* morirse de
hambre

fa-mous *adj.* famoso
fan *n.* aficionado
fa-nat-ic *n., adj.* fanatico
fa-nat-i-cism *n.* fanatismo
fan-ci-er *n.* aficionado
fan-ci-ful *adj.* fantastico
fan-cy *n.* fantasia
fan-fare *n.* toque de trom-
petas
fang *n.* colmillo
fan-tas-tic *adj.* fan
fan-ta-sy *n.* fantasia
far *adv.* lejos
far-a-way *adj.* remoto
farce *n.* farsa
far-ci-cal *adj.* ridiculo
fare *v.* pasarlo
fare-well *ent.* adios
far-fetched *adj.* improbable
farm *n.* granja
farm-house *n.* alqueria
far-off *adj.* lejano
fas-ci-nate *v.* fascinar
fas-cism *n.* fascismo
fas-cist *n.* facista
fash-ion *n.* estilo; moda; uso
fash-ion-a-ble *adj.* de moda
fast *adj.* rapidamente; rapido
fas-ten *v.* abrochar; asegurar
fas-tid-i-ous *adj.* fino;
esquilimoso
fat *adj.* gordo
fa-tal *adj.* fatal
fa-tal-ism *n.* fatalismo
fa-tal-ist *n.* fatalista
fa-tal-i-ty *n.* fatalidad
fate *n.* suerte
fate-ful *adj.* fatal
fa-ther *n.* padre
fa-ther-hood *n.* paternidad
fa-ther-in-law *n.* suegro
fath-om *n.* braza, *v.*
penetrar
fa-tigue *n.* fatiga
fat-ten *v.* engordar
fau-cet *n.* grifo
fault *n.* culpa; falta
fault-y *adj.* defectuoso
fa-vor *n.* favor
fa-vor-a-ble *adj.* favorable
fa-vored *adj.* favorecido
fa-vor-ite *adj., n.* favorito
fa-vor-it-ism *n.* favoritismo

fawn *n.* cervato
faze *v.* perturbar
fear *n.* miedo
fear-ful *adj.* temeroso
fear-less *adj.* intrepido
fear-some *adj.* temible
fea-si-bil-i-ty *n.* viabilidad
fea-si-ble *adj.* factible
feast *n.* banquete; fiesta
feat *n.* proeze
feath-er *n.* pluma
feath-er-y *adj.* plumoso
fea-ture *n.* facción; rasgo
Feb-ru-ar-y *n.* febrero
fe-ces *n.* excrementos
fe-cund *adj.* fecundo
fed-er-al *adj.* federal
fed-er-a-tion *n.* federación
fee *n.* honorario
fee-ble *adj.* debil
fee-bly *adv.* flojamente
feed *v.* alimentar
feel *v.* sentir(se)
feel-er *n.* antena
feel-ing *n.* emoción
feign *v.* fingir
feint *n.* treta
fe-lic-i-tate *v.* flicitar
fe-lic-i-tous *a.* oportuno; feliz
fe-lic-i-ty *n.* felicidad
fe-line *adj.* felino
fell *v.* talar
fel-low *n.* compañero
fel-low-ship *n.* compañerismo
fel-on *n.* criminal
fel-o-ny *n.* crimen
felt *n.* fieltro
fe-male *n.* hembra
fem-i-nine *adj.* femenino
fe-mur *n.* femur
fence *v.* esgrimir
fenc-ing *n.* esgrima
fend *v.* rechazar
fen-der *n.* guardafango
fer-ment *v.* fermentar
fer-men-ta-tion *n.* fermentacion
fern *n.* helecho
fe-ro-cious *adj.* feroz
fe-ro-ci-ty *n.* ferocidad
fer-ret *n.* huron
fer-ry *n.* transbordador

fer-tile *adj.* fecundo; fertil
fer-til-i-ty *n.* fecundidad
fer-ti-lize *v.* fertilizar
fer-ti-liz-er *n.* abono
fer-vid *adj.* fervido
fer-vor *n.* fervor
fes-ter *v.* enconarse
fes-ti-val *n.* fiesta
fes-tive *adj.* festivo
fes-tiv-i-ty *n.* regocijo; fiesta
fes-toon *n.* feston
fetch *v.* ir por
fetch-ing *adj.* atractivo
fete, fete *n.* fiesta
fet-id *adj.* fetido
fet-ish *n.* fetiche
fet-it *adj.* fetido
fet-ter *n.* grillos
fet-tle *n.* condición
fe-tus *n.* feto
feud *n.* enemistad
feu-dal *adj.* feudal
feu-dal-ism *n.* feudalismo
fe-ver *n.* fiebre
fe-ver-ish *adj.* febril
few *adj.* pocos
fi-an-ce *n.* novio
fi-an-cee *n.* novia
fi-as-co *n.* fiasco
fi-at *n.* fiat
fib *v.* mentir
fi-ber, fi-bre *n.* fibra
fi-brous *adj.* fibroso
fick-le *adj.* inconstante
fic-tion *n.* ficcion
fic-tion-al *adj.* novelesco
fic-ti-tious *adj.* ficticio
fid-dle *n.* violin
fi-del-i-ty *n.* fidelidad
fidg-et *v.* inquietar
fidg-et-y *adj.* inquieto; azogado
field *n.* prado; campo
fiend *n.* demonio
fiend-ish *adj.* diabolico
fierce *adj.* feroz
fier-y *a.* ardiente; apaionado
fif-teen *adj.* quince
fif-teenth *adj.* decimoquinto
fifth *adj.* quinto
fif-ti-eth *adj.* quincuagesimo
fif-ty *adj.* cincuenta
fig *n.* higo

fight v. pelear; luchar, n. pelea; lucha
fight-er n. guerrero
fig-ment n. invención
fig-ur-a-tive adj. figuardo
fig-ure n. tipo; figura
fig-ure-head n. mascaron de proa
fig-ur-ine n. figurin
fil-a-ment n. filamento
filch v. ratear
file n. lima; archivo; fila
fi-let n. filete. Also **fil-let**
fil-i-bus-ter n. obstruccionist
fil-i-gree n. filigraña
fil-ings n. limaduras
fill v. llenar
fill-ing n. empaste; relleno
fil-ly n. potra
film n. película
fil-ter n. filtro
filth n. inmundicia
filth-y adj. sucio
fin n. aleta
fi-nal adj. final
fi-na-le n. final
fi-nal-ist n. finalista
fi-nal-i-ty n. finalidad
fi-nal-ly adv. finalmente; por fin
fi-nance n. finanzas
fi-nan-cial adj. financiero
fin-an-cier n. financiero
finch n. pinzón
find v. hallar; encontrar
fine adj. fino; admirable; multa, v. multar
fin-er-y n. adornos
fi-nesse n. sutileza; diplomacia
fin-ger n. dedo
fin-ger-nail n. uña
fin-ger-print n. huella dactilar
fin-ish v. terminar; acabar
fi-nite adj. finito
fir n. abeto
fire n. fuego
fire-arm n. arma de fuego
fire-crack-er n. petardo
fire en-gine n. bomba de incendios
fire-fly n. luciérnaga

fire-man n. bombero
fire-place n. hogar
firm adj. firme
fir-ma-ment n. firmamento
firm-ly adv. firmemente
firm-ness n. firmeza
first adj. primero
first-class adj. de primera clase
first-hand adj. de primera mano
first-rate a. de primera clase
fis-cal adj. fiscal
fish n. pez
fish-er-man n. pescador
fish-ery n. pesquera
fish-y adj. sospechoso
fis-sion n. fisión
fis-sure n. grieta
fist n. puño
fist-i-cuffs n. punetazor
fit v. probar; acomodar, adj. adecuado
fit-ful adj. espasmodico
fit-ting n. ajuste; adj. propio; conveniente
five adj. cinco
fix v. arreglar
fix-a-tion n. fijación
fix-ed adj. fijo
fix-ture n. cosa o instalación fija
fla-by adj. flojo; debil
flag n. bandera
flag-on n. jarro; frasco
fla-grant adj. notorio
flag-stone n. losa
flail n. mayal
flair n. instinto
flake n. escama, v. formar hojuelas
flak-y adj. escamoso
flam-boy-ant adj. llamativo
flame n. llama; v. flamear
flam-ma-ble adj. inflamable
flank n. ijada; lado, v. lindar; flanquear
flap v. ondear
flare v. brillar; fulgurar, n. bengala
flash n. relampago; rafaga, v. lanzar
flash-light n. linterna

electrica
flash-y *adj.* charro
flask *n.* frasco
flat *adj.* plano; llano
flat-ter-y *n.* adulación
flaunt *v.* lucir
fla-vor *n.* sabor
fla-vor-ing *n.* condimento
flaw *n.* imperfeccion
flax *n.* lino
flay *v.* desollar
flea *n.* pulga
fleck *n.* mancha
flee *v.* fugarse; huir
fleece *n.* vellon
fleec-y *adj.* lanudo
fleet *adj.* veloz
fleet-ing *adj.* fugaz
flesh *n.* carne
flex *v.* doblar
flex-i-ble *adj.* flexible
flick *n.* golpecito
fli-er *n.* aviador
flight *n.* vuelo
flim-sy *adj.* endeble
flinch *v.* acobardarse
fling *v.* arrojar
flint *n.* pedernal
flip *v.* mover de un tiron
flip-pant *adj.* ligero
flirt *v.* flirtear; coquetear
flit *v.* revolotear
float *v.* flotar; hacer flotar
flock *n.* rebano
floe *n.* témpano
flog *v.* azotar
flood *n.* diluvio
floor *n.* suelo; piso
flop *v.* caer pesadamente; fracasar
flo-ra *n.* flora
flo-ral *adj.* floral
flor-id *adj.* florido
flo-rist *n.* florista
floss *n.* seda floja
flo-til-la *n.* flotilla
flounce *v.* moverse airadamente
floun-der *v.* tropezer
flour *n.* harina
flour-ish *v.* florecer; blandir
flout *v.* mofarse
flow *v.* fluir

flow-er *n.* flor
flu *n.* gripe
fluc-tu-ate *v.* fluctuar
flue *n.* canon de chimenea
flu-en-cy *n.* fluidez
flu-ent *adj.* facundo
fluff-y *adj.* plumosa
flu-id *adj.* fluido
flude *n.* chirpia
flunk *v.* no aprobar
flu-o-res-cent *adj.* fluorescente
flur-ry *n.* rafaga; agitación
flush *adj.* nivelado
flus-ter *v.* aturdir
flute *n.* flauta
flut-ter *n.* aleteo, *v.* revolotear
flux *n.* mudanza; flujo
fly *v.* volar, *n.* mosca
fly-er *n.* aviador
fly-wheel *n.* rueda volante
foal *n.* potro
foam *n.* espuma
fo-cus *v.* enfocar
fod-der *n.* forraje
foe *n.* enemigo
fog *n.* niebla
fo-gy *n.* sona de ideas anticuadas
foi-blé *n.* flaco
foil *n.* hoja; florete
foist *v.* encajar
fold *v.* plegar; doblar
fold-er *n.* carpeta
fo-li-age *n.* follaje
folk *n.* gente
folk-lore *n.* folklore
fol-li-cle *n.* foliculo
fol-low *v.* perseguir; seguir
fol-low-er *n.* seguidor
fol-ly *n.* locura; tonteria
fo-ment *v.* fomentar
fond *adj.* carinoso
fon-dle *v.* acariciar
fond-ly *adv.* afectuosamente
food *n.* alimento
fool *n.* tonto
fool-har-dy *adj.* temerario
fool-ish *adj.* necio
fool-proof *adj.* infalible
foot *n.* pata; pie
foot-ball *n.* fútbol

foot-note *n.* nota
foot-print *n.* huella
foot-step *n.* paso
fop *n.* petimetre
for *conj.* pues, *prep.* para; por
for-age *n.* forraje
for-ay *n.* correria
for-bear *v.* contenerse
for-bid *v.* prohibir
for-bid-den *adj.* prohibido
for-ceps *n.* forceps
for-ci-ble *a.* energico; eficaz
ford *n.* vado
fore *adj.* anterior
fore-arm *n.* antebrazo
fore-bode *v.* presagiar
fore-cast *v.* pronosticar
fore-fa-ther *n.* antepasado
fore-fin-ger *n.* dede indice
fore-go *v.* preceder; renunciar
fore-gone *a.* predeterminado
fore-ground *n.* primer plano
fore-head *n.* frente
for-eign *adj.* extranjero
for-eign-er *n.* extranjero
fore-man *n.* capatiz
fore-most *adj.* primero
fore-run-ner *n.* precursor
fore-see *v.* prever
foresight *n.* prevision; perspicacia
fore-skin *n.* prepucio
for-est *n.* bosque
fore-tell *v.* predecir
for-ev-er *adv.* siempre
fore-word *n.* prefacio
for-feit *v.* perder
forge *n.* fragua
for-ger-y *n.* falsificación
for-get *v.* olvidar(se)
for-get-ful *adj.* olvidadizo
for-give *v.* perdonar
fork *n.* tenedor
for-lorn *adj.* abandonado
form *n.* forma
for-mal *adj.* ceremonioso
for-mal-i-ty *n.* formalidad
for-mat *n.* formato
for-ma-tion *n.* formación
for-mer *adj.* anterior
for-mer-ly *adv.* antiguamente

for-mi-da-ble *adj.* formidable
for-mu-la *n.* formula
for-ni-cate *v.* fornicar
for-ni-ca-tion *n.* fornicación
for-sake *v.* abandonar
fort *n.* fuerte
forth *adv.* en adelante
forth-com-ing *adj.* próximo
forth-right *adj.* directo
for-ti-fi-ca-tion *n.* fortificacion
for-tune *n.* fortuna
for-ty *adj.* cuarenta
for-ward *adv.* adelante
fos-sil *n.* fosil
foul *adj.* sucio
foun-da-tion *n.* fundación
foun-tain *n.* fuente
four *adj.* cuarto
four-teen *adj.* catorce
fourth *adj.* cuarto
fox *n.* zorra
fra-cas *n.* rina
frac-tion *n.* fracción
frac-ture *v.* quebrar, *n.* fractura
frag-ile *adj.* frágil
frag-ment *n.* fragmento
fra-grence *n.* fragancia
fra-grant *adj.* oloroso
frail *adj.* debil; fragil
frail-ty *n.* fragilidad
frame *n.* estructura; marco
fframe-work *n.* esqueleto
franc *n.* franco
fran-chise *n.* derecho de sufragio
frank *adj.* franco
frank-in-cense *n.* incienso
frank-ly *adv.* francamente
frank-ness *n.* franqueza
fran-tic *adj.* frenetico
fra-ter-ni-ty *n.* fraternidad
fraud *n.* fraude
fraught *adj.* lleno de
fray *v.* deshilacharse
freak *n.* monstruosidad; finomeno
freck-le *n.* peca
free *v.* libertar, *adj.* libre
free-dom *n.* libertad
free-way *n.* autopista

freeze v. helar(se); congelar
freight n. flete
freight-er n. buque de carga
French n., adj. frances
fre-net-ic adj. frenetico
fren-zy n. frenesi
fre-quen-cy n. frecuencia
fre-quent adj. frecuente
fres-co n. fresco
fresh adj. fresco
fresh-en v. refrescar
fret v. apararse
fret-ful adj. displicente
fri-ar n. fraile
fric-tion n. fricción
Friday n. viernes
friend n. amigo, amiga
friend-ly adj. amistoso
frieze n. friso
fright n. susto
fright-en v. asustar
frig-id adj. frio
frill n. lechuga
fringe n. orla; margen
frisk v. retoar
frit-ter v. desperdiciar
fro adv. atras
frock n. vestido
frog n. rana
from prep. desde; de
front n. frente
fron-tal adj. frontal
frown n. ceno
fru-gal adj. frugal
fruit n. fruta
frus-trate v. frustrar
frus-tra-tion n. frustración
fry v. freir
fu-gi-tive n., adj. fugitivo
full adj. completo; lleno
ful-ly adv. completamente
func-tion v. funcionar
func-tion-al adj. funcional
fun-da-men-tal adj. fundamental
fun-ny adj. comico
fur n. piel
fu-ri-ous adj. furioso
fur-ni-ture n. mueblaje
fur-ther adj., adv. mas lejos
fuse n. fusible; espoleta
fu-tile adj. inutil
fuzz n. pelusa

gab-ar-dine n. gabardina
ga-ble n. aguilon; faldon
gad v. andorrear
gad-fly n. tabaon
gad-get n. aparato
gaff n. arpon
gag v. amordazar
gai-e-ty n. alegria
gai-ly adv. alegremente
gain v. ganar
gain-say v. contradecir
gait n. modo de andar
ga-la n. fiesta
gal-ax-y n. galaxia
gale n. ventarron
gall n. bilis
gal-lant adj. valeroso
gal-lant-ry n. galanteria
gal-ler-y n. galeria
gal-ley n. galera; fogón
gal-lon n. galón
gal-lop n. galope
gal-lows n. horca
gal-va-nize v. galvanizar
gam-bit n. gambito
gam-ble v. jugar
gam-bol v. brincar
game n. partido; juego
gam-ut n. gama
gan-der n. ganso
gang n. pandilla
gan-grene n. gangrena
gang-ster n. gangster; pistolero
gang-way n. pasillo
gap n. hueco
ga-rage n. garaje
garb n. vestido
gar-bage n. basura
gar-ble v. mutilar
gar-den n. jardin
gar-gan-tu-an a. colosal
gar-gle v. gargarizar
gar-ish v. llamativo
gar-land n. guirnalda
gar-ment n. prenda de vestir
gar-ner n. granero
gar-net n. granate
gar-nish v. adornar
gar-ret n. guardilla
gar-ri-son n. guarnición
gar-ru-lous adj. garrulo
gar-ter n. liga

gas *n.* gasolina
gas-e-ous *adj.* gaseous
gash *n.* cuchillada
gas-o-line *n.* gasolina
gasp *v.* boquear
gas-tric *adj.* gastrico
g a s - t r o n - o - m y *n.* gastronomia
gate *n.* puerta
gate-way *n.* paso
gath-er *v.* fruncir; reunir
gauche *adj.* torpe
gaud-y *adj.* chillón
gauge *n.* norma de medida; indicador
gaunt *adj.* flaco
gaunt-let *n.* guantelete
gauze *n.* gasa
gawk-y *adj.* desgarbado
gay *adj.* alegre; vistoso
gaze *v.* mirar
ga-zelle *n.* gacela
ga-zette *n.* gaceta
gaz-et-teer *n.* diccionario geografico
gear *v.* engraner
gel-a-tin *n.* gelatina
ge-lat-i-nous *adj.* gelatinoso
geld *v.* castrar
gem *n.* joya; gema
gen-der *n.* genero
gene *n.* gen
ge-ne-al-o-gy *n.* genealogia
gen-er-al *adj.* general
gen-er-al-i-ty *n.* gèneralidad
gen-er-al-ize *v.* generalizar
gen-er-ate *v.* generar
gen-er-tion *n.* generador
gen-er-a-tor *n.* generador
ge-ner-ic *adj.* generico
g e n - e r - o s - i - t y *n.* generosidad
gen-er-ous *adj.* generosq
gen-e-sis *n.* genesis
ge-net-ic *adj.* genesico
gen-ial *adj.* afable
gen-i-tal *adj.* genital
gen-ius *n.* genio
gen-o-cide *n.* genocidio
gen-teel *adj.* elegante; bien criado
gen-til-i-ty *n.* gentilize
gen-tle *adj.* suave; apacible

gen-tle-man *n.* caballero
gen-tly *adv.* suavemente
gen-u-ine *adj.* genuino; sincero
ge-nus *n.* género
ge-o-gra-pher *n.* geógrafo
ge-o-gra-phic, ge-o-graph-i-cal *adj.* geografico
ge-o-gra-phy *n.* geografia
ge-o-log-ic *adj.* geologico
ge-ol-o-gist *n.* geologo
ge-ol-o-gy *n.* geología
ge-o-met-ric *adj.* geométrico
ge-om-e-try *n.* geometria
ge-o-phys-i-cal *adj.* geofisico
ge-o-phys-ics *n.* geofisica
ger-i-at-rics *n.* geriatria
germ *n.* germen
ger-mane *adj.* relativo
ger-mi-nate *v.* germinar
ger-mi-na-tion *n.* germinación
ger-und *n.* gerundio
ges-tic-u-late *v.* gesticular
ges-ture *n.* gesto
get *v.* lograr; obtener
gey-ser *n.* geiser
ghast-ly *adj.* horrible
gher-king *n.* pepinillo
ghost *n.* fantasma
ghost-ly *adj.* espectral
ghoul *n.* demonio
GI *n.* soldado
giant *adj.* gigantesco
gib-ber-ish *n.* galimatias; jerga
gib-bon *n.* gibón
gibe, jibe *v.* mofarse; burlarse
gib-let *n.* menudillos
gid-di-ness *n.* vertigo
gid-dy *adj.* mareado; ligero
gift *n.* regalo; don
gi-gan-tic *adj.* gigantesco
gig-gle *n.* risa sofocada
gild *v.* dorar
gill *n.* agalla
gilt *adj.* dorado
gim-mick *n.* truco
gin *n.* desmotadera de algodon; ginebra
gin-ger *n.* jengibre
gin-ger ale *n.* cerveza de

jengibre

gin-ger-bread *n.* pan de jengibre

gin-ger-ly *adj.* cauteloso

gis-sy *n.* gitano

gi-raffe *n.* jirafa

gird *v.* cenir

gird-er *n.* viga

gir-dle *n.* cinto; faja

girl *n.* chica; niña

girl-ish *adj.* de niña

girth *n.* cincha

gist *n.* esencial; clave

give *v.* entregar; dar

giv-en *adj.* citado

giz-zard *n.* molleja

gla-cial *adj.* glacial

gla-cier *n.* glaciar

glad *adj.* alegre

glad-den *v.* regocijar

glade *n.* claro

glad-ly *adv.* con mucho gusto

glad-ness *n.* alegria

glad-i-o-lus *n.* gladiolo

glam-our, glam-or *n.* encanto

glam-our-ous *a.* encantador

glance *v.* rebotar; mirar

gland *n.* glandula

glan-du-lar *adj.* glandular

glare *v.* relumbrar

glar-ing *adj.* evidente

glass *n.* vidrio; vaso

glass-y *adj.* vitreo

glau-co-ma *n.* glaucoma

glaze *v.* vidriar

gleam *n.* espigar

glee *n.* jubilo

glen *n.* jubilo

glide *v.* deslizarse

glim-mer *v.* brillar debilmente

glimpse *n.* vislumbre

glint *v.* destellar

glis-ten *v.* relucir

glit-ter *v.* relucir

gloat *v.* manifestar saticfacion maligna

globe *n.* globo; esfera

glob-ule *n.* globulo

gloom *n.* tristeza

gloom-y *adj.* lobrego;

melancolico

glo-ri-fy *v.* glorificar

glo-ri-ous *adj.* glorioso

glo-ry *n.* gloria

gloss *n.* lustre

glos-sa-ry *n.* glosario

gloss-y *adj.* lustroso

glot-tis *n.* glotis

glove *n.* guante

glow *v.* brillar

glow-er *v.* mirar con ceño

glow-worm *n.* luciernaga

glue *v.* encolar

glum *adj.* abatido

glut *v.* hartar

glut-ton *n.* glotón

glut-ton-y *n.* gula

gnarl *v.* torcer

gnash *v.* rechinar

gnat *n.* jejen

gnaw *v.* roer

gnome *n.* gnomo

go *v.* ir

goad *n.* aguijada; incitar

goal *n.* meta; gol

goat *n.* cabra

gob-ble *v.* engullir

gob-let *n.* copa

gob-lin *n.* trasgo

God *n.* Dios

god-child *n.* ahijado

god-daugh-ter *n.* ahijada

god-dess *n.* diosa

god-fa-ther *n.* padrino

god-ly *adj.* piadoso

god-moth-er *n.* madrina

god-par-ent *n.* padrino; madrina

god-send *n.* buena suerte

god-son *n.* ahijado

gog-gles *n.* anteojos

go-ing *n.* ida; estado del camino

gold *n.* oro

golf *n.* golf

gon-do-la *n.* gondola

gon-do-lier *n.* goldolero

gong *n.* gong

gon-or-rhe-a *n.* gonorrea

good *n.* bien

good-by; good-bye *int.* adíos

good-heart-ed *adj.* amable

good-look-ing adj. guapo
good-ly adj. agradable; considerable
good-ness n. bondad
good-y n. golosina
goose n. ganso
goose-ber-ry n. uva espina
gore n. sangre
gorge n. barranco
gor-geous adj. magnifico; vistoso
gos-pel n. evangelio
gos-sa-mer n. gasa sutil
gos-sip n. chisme; comadre
gouge n. gubia
gourd n. calabaza
gour-met n. gastronomo
gout n. gota
gov-ern v. gobernar
gov-ern-ess n. institutriz
gov-ern-ment n. gobierno
gov-er-nor n. gobernador
gown n. vestido
grab v. asir; arrebatar
grace n. gracia
grace-ful adj. gracioso
gra-cious adj. agradable
gra-da-tion n. gradación
grade n. grado; clase
grad-u-al adj. gradual
grad-u-al-ly adv. poco a poco
grad-u-ate v. graduar(se)
grad-u-a-tion n. graduación
graft n. injerto; soborno
grain n. graño; bifra
gram n. graño
gram-mar n. gramatica
gram-mat-i-cal adj. gramatical
gra-na-ry n. granero
grand adj. magnifico; grandioso
grand-child n. nieto
grand-daugh-ter n. nieta
grand-fa-ther n. abuelo
grand-moth-er n. abuela
grand-par-ent n. abuelo
grand-son n. nieto
grange n. cortijo
gran-ite n. granito
grant v. conferir; otorgar
gran-u-late v. granular

gran-ule n. grañulo
grape n. uva
grape-fruit n. toronja
graph n. grafica
graph-ic adj. grafico
graph-ite n. grafito
grap-nel n. arpeo
grap-ple n. arpeo
grasp v. agarrar; comprender
grasp-ing adj. codicioso
grass n. hierba
grass-hop-per n. saltamontes
grass-y adj. herboso
grate n. parrilla de hogar
grate-ful adj. agradecido
grat-i-fi-ca-tion n. gratificación; placer
grat-i-fy v. complacer; satisfacer
grat-ing n. reja
gra-tis adj., adv. gratis
grat-i-tude n. reconocimiento
gra-tu-i-tous adj. gratuito; injustificado
gra-tu-i-ty n. propina
grave n. sepultura
grav-el n. cascajo
grav-en adj. grabado
grave-yard n. cementerio
grav-i-tate v. gravitar
grav-i-ta-tion n. gravitación
grav-i-ty n. seriedad; gravedad
gra-vy n. salsa
gray, grey adj., n. gris
graze v. pacer; rozar
grease n. grasa
greas-y adj. grasiento
great adj. grande; gran
greed n. avaricia; codicia
greed-y adj. avaro; codicioso; goloso
green adj., n. verde
green-er-y n. verdura
greet v. saludar
greet-ing n. saludo
gre-gar-i-ous a. gregario
gre-nade n. granada de mano
grid n. reja; parrilla

grid-dle *n.* tortera
grid-i-ron *n.* campo de fútbol; parrilla
grief *n.* pesar
griev-ance *n.* agravio
grieve *v.* afligirse
griev-ous *adj.* grave; penoso
grif-fin, grif-fon *n.* grifo
grill *v.* asar a la parrilla
grille, grill *n.* verja
grim *adj.* inflexible; severo
grim-ace *n.* visaje
grime *n.* mugre
grim-y *adj.* mugriento
grin *v.* sonreir
grind *v.* moler; pulverizar
grind-stone *n.* muela
grip *n.* agarro; apreton; saco de mano
grippe *n.* gripe
gris-ly *adj.* horroroso
gris-tle *n.* cartilago
grit *n.* arena; firmeza
grit-ty *adj.* arenoso
griz-zled, griz-zly *adj.* gris
groan *v.* gemir
gro-cer *n.* abacero
gro-cer-y *n.* abaceria
groin *n.* ingle
groom *n.* novio; mozo de caballos
groove *n.* estria
grope *v.* buscar a tientas
gross *adj.* bruto; grosero; grueso
gro-tesque *adj.* grotesco
grot-to *n.* gruta
grouch *v.* refunfuñar
ground *n.* tierra; terreno; razon; poso
ground-work *n.* fundamento
group *n.* grupo
grouse *v.* quejarse
grove *n.* abbeleda
grov-el *v.* arrastrarse
gus-to *n.* entusiasmo
gym *n.* gimnasio
gym-nast *n.* gimnasta
gym-nas-tic *adj.* gimnastico
gy-ne-çol-o-gy *n.* gine-cologia
gyp *v.* estafar
gyp-sum *n.* jeso

hab-it *n.* costumbre
hab-it-a-ble *adj.* habitable
hab-i-tat *n.* habitación
hab-i-ta-tion *n.* habitación
ha-bit-u-al *adj.* habitual
ha-bit-u-ate *v.* acos-tumbrarse
hack *v.* acuchillar
hack-neyed *adj.* trillado
had *v. pt. and pp. of* have
hag *n.* bruja
hag-gard *adj.* ojeroso
hag-gle *v.* regatear
hail *n.* granizo, *v.* granizar
hail-stone *n.* piedra de granizo
hair *n.* pelo; cabello
hair-breadth *n.* ancho de un pelo
hair-dress-er *n.* peluquero
hair-pin *n.* horquilla
hale *adj.* robusto
half *n.* mitad
half-way *n.* pasillo
hall *n.* sala
hal-le-lu-jah *int.* aleluya
hal-low *v.* consagrar
hal-lu-çin-a-tion *n.* alucinación
hall-way *n.* pasillo
hal-o *n.* halo; aureola
halt *v.* parar
hal-ter *n.* cabestro
halve *v.* partir por mitad
ham *n.* jamón
ham-burg-er *n.* hambur-guesa
ham-let *n.* aldehuela
ham-mer *v.* martillar, *n.* martillo
ham-mock *n.* hamaca
ham-per *v.* impedir
hand *n.* mano
hand-bag *n.* bolso
hand-book *n.* manual
hand-cuff *n.* esposas
hand-ful *n.* puñado
hand-i-cap *n.* desventaja
hand-ker-chief *n.* panuelo
han-dle *n.* mango; manubrio
hand-some *adj.* hermoso
hand-y *adj.* conveniente; prozimo; habil

hang v. pegar; colgar
hang-er-on n. pegote
hank-er v. anhelar
hap-haz-zard adj. fortuito
hap-pen v. pasar
hap-pen-ing n. acontecimiento
hap-pi-ly adv. alegremente
hap-pi-ness n. alegria
hap-py adj. feliz
har-bor n. puerto
hard adj. firme
har-dy adj. robusto
harm v. dañar
harm-ful adj. dañino
har-mo-ni-ous adj. armonioso
har-mo-ny n. armonia
harsh adj. severo
harsh-ness n. severidad
har-vest v. cosechar
hat n. sombrero
hatch v. empollar, n. portezuela
hatch-et n. machado
hate n. odio, v. odiar
hate-ful adj. odioso
have v. tener
hawk n. halcon
haz-ard v. arriesgar, n. azar
he pron. el
head n. cabeza
head-ache n. dolor de cabeza
head-ing n. tículo
head-land n. promontorio
head-light n. faro
head-quar-ters n. cuartel general
head-way n. progreso
heal v. sanar; curar
health n. salud
health-ful adj. sano
heap n. monton
hear v. oir
hear-ing n. oido
hear-say n. rumor
hearse n. coche funebre
heart n. corazón
heart-ache n. angustia
heart-break n. angustia
hearten v. alentar
heart-felt adj. sincero

hearth n. hogar
heat v. calentar, n. calor
heat-er n. calentador
heath n. brezal
heave v. levantar
heav-en n. cielo
heav-y adj. fuerte
heck-le v. interrumpor
hec-tic adj. febril
hedge n. seto
heed v. escuchar
heel n. talon
heft n. bulto
heif-er n. vaquilla
height n. altura
height-en v. elevar
hei-nous adj. atroz
heir n. heredero
heir-ess n. heredera
heir-loom n. herencia; reliquia de familia
hel-i-cop-ter n. helicoptero
he-li-um n. helio
he-lix n. hélice
hell n. infierno
hell-ish adj. infernal
hel-lo int. hola
helm n. timon
hel-met n. casco
help n. ayuda, v. ayudar
help-ful adj. util
help-ing n. ración
help-less adj. incapaz
hem n. dobladillo
hem-i-sphere n. hemisferio
hem-i-spher-ic adj. hemisferico
hem-or-rhage n. hemorragia
hem-or-rhoid n. hemorroides
hemp n. cañamo
hen n. gallirla
hence adv. de aquí; por lo tanto
her pron. obj. and poss. she
her-ald n. heraldo; precursor
he-ral-dic adj. heraldico
her-ald-ry n. heraldica
herb n. hierba
her-ba-ceous adj. herbáceo
her-cu-le-an adj. hercúleo
herds-man n. pastor

here adv. aquí
here-af-ter adv. en el futuro
he-red-i-tar-y adj. hereditario
he-red-i-ty n. herencia
here-in adv. incluso
her-e-sy n. herejía
her-e-tic n. hereje
here-to-fore adv. hasta ahora
her-it-age n. herencia
her-mit n. ermitaño
her-mit-age n. ermita
her-ni-a n. hernia
he-ro n. heroe
he-ro-ic adj. heroico
her-o-ine n. heroína
her-o-ism n. heroísmo
her-on n. garszo
hers pron. poss of. she
her-self pron. ella misma; si misma
hes-i-tant adj. vacilante
hes-i-tate v. vacilar
het-er-o-ge-ne-ous adj. heterogénio
hew v. tajar
hax-a-gon n. hexágono
hex-ag-o-nal adj. hexagonal
hi-ber-nate v. invernar
hic-cup n. hipo
hide v. ocultar(se)
hid-e-ous adj. horrible; feo
hi-er-ar-chy n. jerarquía
hi-er-oglyphic adj. jeroglícifo
high adj. alto
hike n. caminata
hi-lar-i-ous adj. alegre
hi-lar-i-ty n. alegría
hill n. colina
hilt n. puño
him pron. obj. of he
him-self pron. el mismo
hind adj. trasero
hin-der v. impedir
hind-most adj. postrero
hinge n. gozne
hint n. indirecta
hip n. cadera
hip-po-pot-a-mus n. hipopotamo
hire v. alquilar
hire-ling n. mercenario
his pron. suyo

hiss v. silbar
his-to-ri-an n. historiador
his-tor-ic adj. historico
his-to-ry n. historia
hit n. golpe, v. golpear
hitch v. atar
hitch-hike v. hace autostop
hith-er adv. aca
hive n. colmena
hoard n. provision
hoarse adj. ronco
hoax n. engaño
hob-ble v. cojear
hob-by n. pasatiempo
ho-bo n. vagabundo
hod n. azadon
hog n. puerco
hoist v. alzar
hold v. contener; tener
hold-ing n. tenencia
hole n. hoyo
hol-i-day n. día de fiesta
hol-low adj. vacío
hol-ly n. acebo
hol-o-caust n. holocausto
hol-ster n. pistolera
hom-age n. homenaje
home n. casa
home-ly adj. feo
home-sick adj. nostálgico
home-ward adv. hacia casa
home-y adj. comodo
hom-i-cide adj. homicidio
hom-i-ly n. homilia
ho-mo-gen-e-ous adj. homogéneo
hone n. piedra de afilar
hon-est adj. honrado
hon-es-ty n. honradez
hon-ey n. miel
hon-ey-comb n. panal
hon-ey-moon n. luna de miel
hon-ey-suck-le n. madreselva
hon-or v. honrar, n. honor
hon-or-a-ble adj. honorable
hon-or-ar-y adj. honorario
hood n. capucha
hood-lum n. matón
hood-wink v. enganar
hoof n. casco
hook n. gancho, v.

enganchar; encorvar
hoop *n.* aro
hoot *v.* ulular, *n.* grito
hop *n.* salto, *v.* saltar
hope *v.* desear, *n.* esperanza
hope-less *adj.* desesperado
horde *n.* horda
ho-ri-zon *n.* horizonte
hor-i-zon-tal *adj.* horizontal
hor-mone *n.* hormona
horn *n.* cuerno
hor-o-scope *n.* horoscopo
hor-ri-ble *adj.* horrible
hor-ri-fy *v.* horrorizar
hor-ror *n.* horror
horse *n.* caballo
horse-man *n.* jinete
horse-pow-er *n.* caballo de fuerza
horse-rad-ish *n.* rabaño picante
horse-shoe *n.* herradura
hor-ti-cul-ture *n.* horticultura
hose *n.* medias
hose *n.* manga
ho-sier-y *n.* calceteriá
hos-pi-ta-ble *a.* hospitalario
hos-pi-tal *n.* hospital
hos-pi-tal-i-ty *n.* hospitalidad
host *n.* anfitrion; patron; multitud
hos-tage *n.* rehén
host-ess *n.* huéspeda
hos-tile *adj.* hostil
hos-til-i-ty *n.* hostilidad
hot *adj.* caliente
ho-tel *n.* hotel
hot-house *n.* invernáculo
hound *n.* podenco, *v.* perseguir
hour *n.* hora
house *n.* casa
house-keep-er *n.* ama e llaves
hous-ing *n.* alojamiento
how *adv.* cómo
how-ev-er *adv.* en todo caso, *conj.* sin embargo
howl *v.* aullar
hub *n.* cubo
hud-dle *v.* amontonar(se)
hue *n.* color; matiz

hug *v.* abrazar
huge *adj.* enorme
hulk *n.* casco
hull *n.* cascara; casco
hum *v.* zumbar; canturrear
hu-man *n.* humano
hu-man-i-ty *n.* humanidad
hum-ble *adj.* humilde
hu-mid *adj.* humedo
hu-mid-i-fy *v.* humdedecer
hu-mid-i-ty *n.* humedad
hu-mil-i-ate *v.* humillar
hu-mil-i-a-tion *n.* humillación
hu-mil-i-ty *n.* humildad
hum-ming-bird *n.* colibrí
hu-mor *n.* complacer
hump *n.* giba; joroba
hunch *v.* corazonada
hunch-back *n.* jorobado
hun-dred *adj.* ciento
hun-dredth *adj.* centesimo
hun-ger *n.* hambre
hun-gry *adj.* hambriento
hunt *v.* cazar
hunt-er *n.* cazador
hur-dle *n.* valla; zarzo
hurl *v.* lanzar
hur-ri-cane *n.* huracan
hur-ry *v.* apresurar; darse prisa
hurt *v.* hacer daño; doler; danar
hus-band *n.* esposo
hush *n.* cascara
husk-y *adj.* ronco
hus-sy *n.* picara
hus-tle *v.* empujar
hy-brid *n.* híbrido
hy-drant *n.* boca de reigo
hy-dro-gen *n.* hidrogeno
hy-e-na *n.* hiena
hy-giene *n.* higiene
hymn *n.* himno
hyp-no-sis *n.* hipnosis
hyp-no-tize *v.* hipnotizar
hyp-o-crite *n.* hipocrita
hy-po-der-mic *adj.* hipodérmico
hy-pot-e-nuse *n.* hipotenusa
hy-poth-e-sis *n.* hipotesis
hy-po-thet-i-cal *a.* hipotetico
hys-te-ri-a *n.* histerismo
hys-ter-ic *adj.* histérico

I *pron.* yo
i-bis *n.* ibis
ice *n.* hielo
ice-berg *n.* iceberg
ice cream *n.* helado
i-ci-cle *n.* carambano
ic-ing *n.* garapiña
i-con *n.* icono
i-con-o-clast *n.* iconoclasta
i-cy *adj.* helado
i-de-a *n.* idea
i-de-al *adj.* ideal
i-de-al-ize *v.* idealizaɪ
i-den-ti-cal *adj.* idéntico
i-den-ti-fi-ca-tion *n.* identificación
i-den-ti-fy *v.* identificar
i-den-ti-ty *n.* identidad
i-de-ol-o-gy *n.* ideología
id-i-om *n.* idiotismo
id-i-o-mat-ic *adj.* idiomático
id-i-o-syn-cra-sy *n.* idiosincrasia
id-i-ot *n.* idiota
i-dle *adj.* ocioso
i-dol *n.* idolo
i-dol-a-trous *adj.* idolatra
i-dol-a-try *n.* idolatria
i-dol-ize *v.* idolatrar
if *conj.* si
ig-nite *v.* encender(se)
ig-no-ble *adj.* innoble
ig-no-min-y *n.* ignominia
ig-no-rance *n.* ignorancia
ig-no-rant *adj.* ignorante
ig-nore *v.* no hacer caso de
ill *adj.* enfermo
il-le-gal *adj.* ilegal
il-leg-i-ble *adj.* ilegible
il-le-git-i-ma-cy *n.* ilegitimidad
il-le-git-i-mate *adj.* ilegítimo
il-lic-it *adj.* ilicito
il-lit-er-ate *adj., m.* analfabeto
ill-ness *n.* enfermedad
il-lu-mi-nate *v.* iluminar
il-lu-sion *n.* ilusión
il-lus-trate *v.* ilustrar
il-lus-tra-tion *n.* ilustración; ejemplo
im-age *n.* imagen
im-ag-i-nar-y *adj.* imaginario

im-ag-i-na-tion *n.* imaginación
im-ag-ine *v.* imaginar
im-be-cile *n., adj.* imbécil
im-i-tate *v.* imitar
im-i-ta-tion *n.* imitación; copia
im-ma-ture *adj.* inmaturo
im-meas-ur-a-ble *a.* inmensurable
im-me-di-ate *adj.* inmediato
im-mense *adj.* inmenso
im-mer-sion *n.* inmersion
im-mi-grant *n.* inmigrante
im-mi-grate *v.* inmigrar
im-mi-gra-tion *n.* inmigración
im-mi-nent *adj.* inminente
im-mo-bile *adj.* inmovil
im-mo-dest *adj.* impudico
im-mor-al *adj.* inmoral
im-mor-tal *adj.* inmortal
im-mune *adj.* inmune
im-mu-ni-ty *n.* inmunidad
imp *n.* diablillo
im-pact *n.* impacto
im-pair *v.* deteriorar
im-part *v.* comunicar; relatar; dar
im-par-tial *n.* imparcial
im-pa-tient *a.* impaciente
im-peach *v.* acusar
im-pec-ca-ble *adj.* impecable
im-pede *v.* impedir; estorbr
im-ped-i-ment *n.* impediment; estorbo
im-pel *v.* impulsar
im-pe-ri-al *a.* imperial
im-pe-ri-ous *adj.* imperioso
im-per-son-al *adj.* impersonal
im-per-ti-nent *a.* impertinente
im-per-vi-ous *a.* impenetrable
im-pe-tus *n.* impetu
im-pi-e-ty *n.* impiedad
im-ple-ment *n.* herramienta
im-pli-cate *v.* enredar
im-plore *v.* implorar
im-ply *v.* dar a entender; significar

im-po-lite *adj.* descortes
im-port *v.* importar
im-por-tance *n.* importancia
im-por-tant *adj.* importante
im-pose *v.* imponer
im-pos-si-ble *adj.* imposible
im-pos-ter *n.* impostor
im-pos-tor *n.* impostor
im-po-tence *n.* impotencia
im-pov-er-ish *v.* empobrecer
im-prac-ti-cal *adj.* impracticable
im-press *v.* estampar; imprimir; impresionar
im-pres-sion *n.* impresión
im-print *v.* imprimir
im-prove *v.* mejorar
im-prove-ment *n.* mejora
im-pro-vise *nl* improvisar
im-pulse *n.* impulso
in *adv.* dentro, *prep.* durante, en
in-a-bil-i-ty *n.* inhabilidad
in-ca-pac-i-tate *v.* incapacitar
inch *n.* pulgada
in-ci-den-tal *adj.* incidental
in-cin-er-ate *v.* incinerar
in-ci-sion *n.* incisión
in-cite *v.* incitar
in-cli-na-tion *n.* inclinación
in-clu-sion *n.* inclusión
in-com-pa-ra-ble *adj.* incomparable
in-com-pe-tent *adj.* incompetente
in-com-plete *adj.* incompleto
in-cor-rect *adj.* incorrecto
in-crease *v.* crecer; acrecentar
in-crim-i-nate *v.* incriminar
in-de-cen-cy *n.* indecencia
in-de-cent *adj.* indecente
in-deed *adv.* de veras
in-def-i-nite *adj.* indefinido
in-dem-ni-ty *n.* ondemnización
in-dent *v.* mellar
in-den-ta-tion *n.* mella
in-de-pend-ence *n.* independencia
in-de-pend-ent *adj.* independiente

in-de-struct-i-ble *a.* indestructible
in-dex *n.* indice
in-di-cate *v.* indicar
in-di-ca-tion *n.* indicación
in-dict *v.* acusar
in-dif-fer-ent *adj.* indiferente
in-dig-e-nous *a.* indigena
in-di-gent *a.* indigente
in-di-ges-tion *n.* indigestion
in-dig-nant *a.* indignado
in-dig-ni-ty *n.* indignidad
in-di-go *n.* anil.
in-di-rect *adj.* indirecto
in-dis-creet *a.* indiscreto
in-dis-cre-tion *n.* indiscrecion
in-dis-pen-sa-ble *a.* imprescindible
in-di-vid-u-al *n.* individuo
in-di-vid-u-al-i-ty *n.* individualidad
in-doc-tri-nate *v.* doctrinar
in-do-lent *a.* indolente
in-door *a.* interior; de puertas adentro
in-doors *adv.* dentro
in-duce *v.* inducir
in-duct *v.* iniciar
in-duldge *v.* satisfacer; consentir
in-dus-tri-al *adj.* industrial
in-er-tia *n.* inercia
in-ev-i-ta-ble *adj.* inevitable
in-fa-my *n.* infamia
in-fan-cy *n.* infancia
in-fect *v.* infectar
in-fec-tion *n.* infección
in-fe-ri-or *adj.* inferior
in-fi-del-i-ty *n.* infidelidad
in-fil-trate *v.* infiltrarse
in-fi-nite *adj.* infinito
in-fin-i-tive *n.* infinitivo
in-fin-i-ty *n.* infinidad
in-fir-ma-ry *n.* enfermeria
in-flame *v.* inflamar; provocar
in-flam-ma-ble *adj.* inflamable
in-flate *v.* inflar
in-fla-tion *n.* inflación
in-flec-tion *n.* inflexión
in-flict *v.* infligir; imponer

in-flu-ence *n.* influencia
in-flu-en-za *n.* gripe
in-form *v.* informar
in-for-mal *adj.* sin ceremonia
in-for-ma-tion *n.* informacion
in-for-ma-tive *adj.* informativo
in-fre-quent *adj.* infrecuente
in-fu-ri-ate *v.* enfurecer
in-fuse *v.* infundir
in-fu-sion *n.* infusion
in-gen-ious *adj.* ingenioso
in-ge-nu-i-ty *n.* ingeniosidad
in-got *n.* lingote
in-gre-di-ent *n.* ingrediente
in-hab-it *v.* habitar
in-hab-i-tant *n.* habitante
in-hale *v.* inhalar; aspirar
in-her-ent *a.* inmanente; inherente
in-her-it *v.* heredar
in-her-it-ance *n.* herencia
in-hib-it *v.* inhibir
in-hi-bi-tion *n.* inhibición
in-hu-man *a.* inhumano; cruel
in-iq-ui-ty *n.* iniquidad
in-i-tial *adj.* inicial
in-i-ti-ate *v.* iniciar
in-i-ti-a-tion *n.* iniciación
in-i-ti-a-tive *n.* iniciative
in-ject *v.* inyectar
in-jec-tion *n.* inyección
in-jure *v.* hacer daño a; ofender
in-ju-ry *n.* daño; injuria
in-jus-tice *n.* injusticia
ink *n.* tinta
ink-ling *n.* sospecha
in-let *n.* entrada; ensenada
in-mate *n.* inquilino
inn *n.* posada
in-nate *adj.* innato
in-ner *adj.* interior
in-no-cence *n.* inocencia
in-no-cent *adj.* inocente
in-no-va-tion *n.* innovación
in-nu-en-do *n.* indirecta
in-nu-mer-a-ble *a.* innumerable
in-oc-u-late *v.* inocular
in-oc-u-la-tion *n.* inoculación
in-quest *n.* pesquisa judicial

in-quire *v.* preguntar
in-quir-y *n.* indagación; pregunta
in-qui-si-tion *n.* inquisición
in-sane *adj.* insensato; loco
in-san-i-ty *n.* locura
in-scribe *v.* inscribir
in-scrip-tion *n.* inscripción
in-sect *n.* insecto
in-se-cure *a.* inseguro; precario
in-sert *v.* insertar; meter
in-ser-tion *n.* inserción
in-side *n.* interior
in-sight *n.* perspicacia
in-sig-ni-a- *n.* insignias
in-sig-nif-i-cance *n.* insignificancia
in-sin-u-ate *v.* insinuar
in-sin-u-a-tion *n.* insinuación; indirecta
in-sip-id *adj.* insipido
in-sist *v.* insistir
in-sist-ent *a.* insistente; porfiado
in-so-lence *n.* insolencia
in-so-lent *adj.* insolente
in-som-ni-a *n.* insomnio
in-spect *v.* examinar; inspeccionar
in-spec-tion *n.* inspección
in-spi-ra-tion *n.* inspiración
in-spire *v.* inspirar; estimular
in-stall *v.* instalar
in-stall-ment *n.* plazo; entrega
in-stance *n.* ejemplo
in-stant *n.* instante
in-stan-ta-ne-ous *a.* instantaneo
in-stead *adv.* en lugar; en vez de
in-step *n.* empeine
in-sti-gate *v.* instigar
in-stinct *n.* instinto
in-stinc-tive *adj.* instintivo
in-sti-tute *v.* instituir; empezar
in-sti-tu-tion *n.* institución
in-struct *v.* instruir; ensenar
in-struc-tion *n.* instrucción
in-stru-ment *n.* instrumento
in-suf-fi-cient *adj.* in-

suficiente
in-su-late *v.* sislar
in-su-la-tion *n.* aislamiento
in-su-lin *n.* insulina
in-sult *n.* insulto; ultraje
in-sur-ance *n.* seguro
in-sure *v.* asegurar
in-sur-rec-tion *n.* insurección
in-tact *adj.* intacto
in-te-ger *n.* numero entero
in-te-grate *v.* integrar
in-te-gra-tion *n.* integración
in-teg-ri-ty *n.* integridad
in-tel-lect *n.* intelecto
in-tel-li-gence *n.* inteligencia
in-tel-li-gent *adj.* inteligente
in-tend *v.* proponerse; querer decir
in-tense *adj.* intenso
in-ten-si-ty *n.* intensidad
in-tent *adj.* atento; absorto
in-ter *v.* enterrar
in-ter-cede *v.* interceder
in-ter-cept *v.* interceptar
in-ter-ces-sion *n.* intercesión
in-ter-change *v.* intercambiar
in-ter-course *n.* comercio; trato; coito
in-ter-est *n.* interes
in-trer-fere *v.* intervenir; meterse
in-ter-im *n.* interin
in-te-ri-or *adj.* interior
in-ter-jec-tion *n.* interjección
in-ter-lude *n.* intemedio
in-ter-me-di-ate *adj.* intermedio
in-ter-mis-sion *n.* intermisión
in-tern *n.* interno
in-ter-nal *adj.* interior
in-ter-na-tion-al *adj.* internacional
in-ter-play *n.* interacción
in-ter-[pose *v.* interponer
in-ter-pret *v.* explicar; interpretar; entender
in-ter-pre-ta-tion *n.* interpretación
in-ter-ro-gate *v.* interrogar
in-ter-ro-ga-tion *n.* interrogación

rogación
in-ter-rupt *v.* interrumpir
in-ter-rup-tion *n.* interrupcion
in-ter-sec-tion *n.* intersección
in-ter-twine *n.* entretejer(se)
in-ter-val *n.* intervalo
in-ter-vene *v.* intervenir
in-ter-view *n.* entrevista
in-tes-tine *n.* intestino
in-ti-mate *v.* intimar
in-tim-i-date *v.* intimidar
in-to *prep.* en
in-tol-er-ant *adj.* intolerante
in-to-na-tion *n.* entonación
in-tox-i-cate *v.* emriagar; encitar
in-tran-si-tive *adj.* intransitivo
in-tra-ve-nous *adj.* intravenoso
in-trep-id *adj.* intrepido
in-tri-ca-cy *n.* complejidad; enredo
in-tri-cate *adj.* intrincado
in-trigue *v.* intrigar; fascinar
in-trin-sic *adj.* intrinseco
in-tro-duce *v.* introducir
in-tro-duc-tion *n.* introducción
in-trude *v.* entrəmeterse
in-tu-i-tion *n.* intuición
in-ure *v.* habituar
in-vade *v.* invadir
in-va-lid *adj.* invalido
in-var-i-a-ble *adj.* invariable
in-va-sion *n.* invasion
in-vent *v.* inventar
in-ven-tion *n.* invención
in-ven-to-ry *n.* inventario
in-ver-sion *n.* inversión
in-vert *v.* invertir
in-ver-te-brate *a., n.* invertebrado
in-vest *v.* investir
in-ves-ti-gate *v.* investigar
in-ves-ti-ga-tion *n.* investigacion
in-vig-or-ate *v.* vigorizar
in-vin-ci-ble *adj.* invencible
in-vis-i-ble *adj.* invisible
in-vi-ta-tion *n.* invitación

in-vite v. invitar
in-vo-ca-tion n. invocación
in-voice n. factura
in-voke v. invocar; implorar
in-vol-un-tar-y adj. involuntario
in-volve v. complicar; comprometer; enredar
in-ward adv. hacia dentro
i-o-dine n. yodo
i-on n. ion
i-ron v. planchar, n. plancha
i-ron-ic adj. ironica
i-ro-ny n. ironia
ir-ra-di-ate v. irradiar
ir-ra-tion-al adj. irracionál
ir-rec-on-cil-a-ble adj. irreconciliable
ir-ref-u-ta-ble adj. irrefutable
ir-reg-u-lar adj. irregular
ir-rel-e-vant adj. inaplicable
ir-re-sist-i-ble adj. irresistible
ir-re-spon-si-ble adj. irresponsable
ir-ri-gate v. regar
ir-ri-tate v. irritar; provocar; molestar
is v. third person pres. sing of be
is-land n. isla
isle n. isla
i-so-late v. aislar
i-sos-ce-les adj. isosceles
is-sue v. publicar; salir, n. resultado; emision
isth-mus n. pl. istmo
it pron. le; la; lo; ello; ella; el
i-tal-ic n. usu. pl. letra bastardilla
i-tal-i-cize tr. imprimir en cursiva
itch v. picar
itch-y adj. que da picazon; impaciente
i-tem n. articulo; partida
i-tem-ize v. detallar
it-er-ate tr. iterar; repetir
i-tin-er-ar-y n. itinerario
its pron., adj. poss. case of it
it-self pron. el, ella, ello, o, so, mismo
i-vo-ry n. pl. marfil
i-vy n. hiedra

jab v. golpear
jab-ber v. farfullar
jack n. mozo; marinero; gato; sota
jack-al n. chacal
jack-ass n. burro
jack-et n. chaqueta
jack-nife n. navaja
jack-pot n. bote
jade n. jade
jag-uar n. jaguar
jail v. encarcelar, n. carcel
jam v. apinar; atascar
jamb n. jamba
jam-bo-ree n. francachela
jangle n. sonido discordante
jan-i-tor n. portero
Jan-u-ar-y n. enero
jar n. jarra
jar-gon n. jerga
jas-mine n. jazmin
jaun-dice n. ictericia
jaunt n. excursión
jave-lin n. jabalina
jaw n. quijada
jay n. arrendajo
jazz n. jazz
jeal-ous adj. celoso
Jeep n. trademark. jeep
jeer v. mofarse; befar
jell v. cuajar(se)
jel-ly n. jalea
jel-ly-fish n. medusa
jeop-ar-dize v. arriesgar
jeop-ar-dy n. pelogro
jerk v. arrojar; sacudir
jer-kin n. justillo
jer-sey n. jersey
jest n. chanza
jet n. chorro; surtidor; avion; a reaccion; azabache
jet-same n. echazón
jet-ti-son n. echazón
jet-ty n. malecon; muelle
jew-el n. joya
jew-el-er n. joyero
jew-el-ry n. joyas
jif-fy n. instante
jib n. jiga
jig-saw n. sierra de vaiven
jig-saw puzzle n. rompecabezaw
jilt v. dar calcbazar

jim-my *n.* palanqueta
jin-gle *v.* retinir; tintinear
jinx *n.* gafe
jit-ters *n.* inquietud
job *n.* trabajo
jock-ey *n.* jockey
jo-cose *a.* jocoso
joc-u-lar *a.* jocoso
joc-und *a.* alegre
jog *v.* empujar; correr despacio
join *v.* unir(se)
joint *n.* juntura; union
joist *n.* viga
joke *n.* chiste; broma
jok-er *n.* bromista
jol-ly *adj.* alegre
jolt *v.* sacudir
jon-quil *n.* junquillo
jour-nal *n.* periodico
jour-nal-ism *n.* periodismo
jour-nal-ist *n.* periodista
jour-ney *v.* viajar, *n.* viaje
joy-ous *adj.* alegre
judge *n.* juez; *v.* juzgar
ju-di-cial *adj.* judicial
jug-gle *v.* hacer juegos malabares
jug-u-lar *adj.* yugular
juice *n.* jugo
July *n.* julio
jum-ble *v.* mezclar
jump *n.* salto, *v.* saltar
jump-er *n.* saltador
junc-tion *n.* juntura; empalme
junc-ture *n.* juntura; coyuntura
June *n.* junio
jun-gle *n.* selva
jun-ior *adj.* mas joven; menor
ju-ni-per *n.* enebro
junk *n.* trastos viejos; junco
ju-ris-dic-tion *n.* jurisdicción
ju-ris-pur-dene *n.* jurisprudencia
ju-rist *n.* jurista
ju-ror *n.* jurado
ju-ry *n.* jurado
just *adj.* justo; imparcial
jus-ti-fy *v.* justificar
ju-ve-nile *adj.* joven

kale *n.* col rizada
ka-lei-do-scope *n.* calidoscopio
kan-ga-roo *n.* canguro
kar-at *n.* uilate
keel *n.* quilla
keen *adj.* agudo; perspicaz; entusiasta; afilado
keep *v.* detener; tener; cumplir
keep-ing *n.* custodia
keg *n.* cuñete
ken *v.* saver
ken-nel *n.* perrera
ker-chief *n.* pañuelo
ker-nel *n.* almendra; mucleo
ker-o-sene *n.* ueroseno
ketch *n.* queche
ketch-up *n.* salsa picante de tomate
ket-tle *n.* tetera
key *n.* llave
key-board *n.* teclado
key-stone *n.* piedra clave
khak-i *n.* caqui
kick *v.* dar patadas; dar un puntapié
kid *n.* cabrito
kid-nap *v.* secuestrar
kid-ney *n.* riñón
kill *v.* matar
kiln *n.* horno
kil-o-c-cle *n.* kilociclo
kil-o-gram *n.* kilogramo
kil-o-me-ter *n.* kilómetro
kil-o-watt *n.* kilovation
kin *n.* parientes
kind *adj.* bueno; *n.* genero
kin-der-gar-ten *n.* jardin de la infancia
kind-heart-ed *a.* bondadoso
kin-dle *v.* encender
kind-ly *adj.* bondadoso
kind-ness *n.* benevolencia
kin-dred *n.* parientes
king *n.* rey
king-dom *n.* reino
kink *n.* coca; peculiaridad
kin-ship *n.* parentesco
kins-man *n.* pariente
kiss *n.* beso; *v.* besar
kit *n.* equipo; avios
kitch-en *n.* cocina

kite *n.* equipo; avios
kith *n.* amigos
kit-ten *n.* gatito
knack *n.* mana
knap-sack *n.* mochila
knave *n.* bribón
knav-er-y *n.* bellaquería
knav-ish *adj.* bellaco
knead *v.* amasar
knee *n.* rodilla
knee-cap *n.* rotula
kneel *n.* arrodillarse
knee-pad *n.* rodillera
knell *n.* doble
knick-ers *n.* bombachos
knick-knack *n.* chuchería
knife *v.* acuchillar, *n.* cuchillo
knight *n.* caballero
knight-hood *n.* caballerosidad
knit *v.* hacer punto; juntar
knit-ting *n.* tejido
knob *n.* tirador; buto
knock *v.* golpear
knock-down *adj.* que derriba
knock-er *adj.* picaporte
knock-ing *n.* llamada
knoll *n.* otero
knot *v.* anudar
knot-hole *n.* agujero
knot-ted *adj.* anudado; nudoso
knot-ty *adj.* enredado; nudoso
know *v.* saber; conocer
know-a-ble *adj.* conocible
know-how *n.* pericia
know-ing *a.* astuto; habil
know-ing-ly *adv.* a sabiendas
knowl-edge *n.* saber
knowl-edge-a-ble *adj.* erudito
known *adj.* concido
know-noth-ing *n.* ignorante
knuck-le *n.* nudillo
ko-a-la *n.* koala
kook *n.* excentrico
Ko-ran *n.* Alcorán; Coran
ko-sher *adj.* legitimo; conforme a las reglas
kow-tow *v.* postarse

lab *n.* laboratorio
la-bel *v.* marcar; *n.* etiqueta; rotulo
la-bi-al *adj.* labial
la-bor *v.* trabajar, *n.* trabajo
lab-o-ra-to-ry *n.* laboratorio
la-bored *adj.* peon; trabajador; jornalero
la-bo-ri-ous *adj.* laborioso
lab-y-rinth *n.* laberinto
lac *n.* laca
lace *v.* encordonar; *n.* encaje
lac-er-ate *v.* lacerar
lac-er-ation *n.* laceración
lach-ry-mal *adj.* lagrimal
lack *v.* faltar; hacer falta; *n.* falta
lack-ey *n.* lacayo
lack-ing *adj.* deficiente; *prep.* sin
lack-lus-ter *adj.* deslucido
la-con-ic *adj.* laconico
lac-quer *n.* laca
lac-tase *n.* lactasa
lac-tate *v.* lactar
lac-ta-tion *n.* lactancía
lac-tic *adj.* lactico
lac-tose *n.* lactoxa
la-cu-na *n.* laguna
lac-y *adj.* de encaje
lad *n.* chico
lad-der *n.* escalera
lad-die *n.* chico
lade *v.* agobiar
lad-en *adj.* agobiado; cargado
la-dle *n.* cucharón
la-dy *n.* dama
la-dy-bug *n.* mariquita
lag *v.* trasarse; rezagarse
lag-gard *adj.* rezagado
la-goon *n.* laguna
la-ic *adj.* laico
lair *n.* madriguera
la-i-ty *n.* laicos
lake *n.* lago
lamb *n.* cordero
lame *v.* baldar; *adj.* renco; cojo
la-me *n.* lame
la-ment *v.* deplorar; lamentar
la-men-ta-ble *adj.* lamentable

lam-en-ta-tion *n.* lamen-
tacion
la-ment-ed *adj.* lamentado
lam-i-na *n.* lamina
lam-i-nate *v.* laminar
lam-i-nat-ed *adj.* laminado
lam-i-na-tion *n.* laminación
lamp *n.* lampara
lam-poon *v.* satirizar; *n.*
satira
lam-prey *n.* lamprea
lance *n.* lanza
lan-cet *n.* lanceta
land *v.* pais; tierra
land-ed *adj.* hacendado
land-fall *n.* recalada
land-hold-er *n.* terrateniente
land-ing *n.* amaraje; desem-
barco
land-lord *n.* arrendador
land-mark *n.* mojón
land-own-er *n.* terrateniente
land-scape *n.* panorama
lane *n.* ruta; vereda; camino
lan-guage *n.* lenguaje
lan-guid *adj.* languido
lan-guish *v.* decaer; lan-
guidecer
lan-guish-ing *adj.* languido
lan-guor *n.* languidez
lan-guor-ous *adj.* languido
lan-o-lin *n.* lanolina
lan-tern *n.* linterna
lap *n.* falda; *v.* plegar;
doblar
la-pel *n.* solapa
lap-i-dar-y *n.* lapidario
lapse *v.* faltar; caer; decaer;
deslizarse
lapsed *adj.* caduco
lar-ce-ny *adj.* robo
lard *n.* lardo
large *adj.* grande
lar-gess *n.* donativo;
generosidad
lar-va *n.* larva
lar-val *adj.* larval
lar-yn-gi-tis *n.* laringitis
lar-y-nx *n.* laringe
la-ser *n.* laser
lash *n.* latigo; azote; latigazo
lash-ing *n.* fustigación;
azotaina

lass *n.* muchacha
las-si-tude *n.* lasitude
las-so *n.* lazo
last *adv.* finalmente; *adj.*
final
last-ing *adj.* duradero
last-ly *adv.* finalmente
latch *n.* aldabilla
late *adv.* tarde
late-ly *adv.* ultimamente
la-ten-cy *n.* latencia
late-enss *n.* tardanza
la-tent *adj.* latente
la-ter *adj.* posterior
lat-er-al *adj.* lateral
lat-est *adj.* último
la-tex *n.* latex
lath-er *n.* espuma
lat-i-tude *n.* latitud
la-trine *n.* letrina
lat-ter *adj.* ultimo
lat-ter-day *adj.* reciente
lat-tice *n.* celosia; *v.* enrejar
lat-tice-work *n.* enrejado
laud *v.* alabar; elogiar
laud-a-ble *adj.* laudable
laud-a-to-ry *adj.* laudatorio
laugh *n.* risa, *v.* reir(se)
laugh-a-ble *adj.* absurdo;
comico
laugh-ing *adj.* risueño
laugh-ter *n.* risa
launch *v.* lanzar; iniciar;
botar
launch-er *n.* lanzador
launch-ing *n.* lanzamiento
laun-der *v.* lavar(se)
laun-dered *adj.* lavado
laun-der-er *n.* lavandero
laun-dry *n.* lavanderia
lau-rel *n.* laurel
la-va *n.* lava
lav-en-der *n.* lavanda
lav-ish *adj.* espendido;
generoso
law *n.* derecho; ley
law-ful *adj.* legitimo
law-less *adj.* sin leyes
law-mak-er *n.* legislador
lawn *n.* césped
law-yer *n.* abogado
lax *adj.* laxo
lax-a-tive *adj.* laxante

lax-i-ty n. laxitud
lay v. acostar; poner
lay-er n. estrato
lay-out n. distribución
la-zi-ness n. pereza
la-zy adj. perezoso
lead v. mandar; conducir
lead-en adj. plumbeo
lead-er n. lider
lead-er-ship n. mando
lead-ing n. emplomado
leaf n. hoja
leaf-let n. panfleto
leaf-y adj. hojoso
league n. liga
leak v. gotear; salirse; n. gotera; agujero
lean adj. magro
lean-ing n. inclinación
leap v. saltar
learn v. aprender
learn-ed adj. erudito
learn-er n. principiante
learn-ing n. aprendizaje
lease-hold n. arrendamiento
lease-hold-er n. arrendatario
leash n. trailla
leas-ing n. arrendamiento
least adv. menos, adj. menor
leath-er n. cuero
leath-er-y adj. curtido
leave v. salir; dejar; irse
leav-en v. leudar
leav-ing n. salida
lech-er-ous adj. lujurioso
lech-er-y n. lujuria
lec-tor n. lector
lec-ture v. sermonear; reprender; n. reprimenda; conferencia
lec-tur-er n. conferenciante
leech n. sanguijuela
leek n. puerro
left adj. izquierdo
left-o-ver adj. sobrante
left-y n. zirdo
leg n. pierna
leg-a-cy n. herencia
le-gal adj. legal
le-gal-ist n. legalista
le-gal-is-tic adj. legalista
le-gal-i-ty n. legalidad

le-gal-ize v. legalizar
leg-ate n. legado
le-ga-tion n. legación
leg-end n. leyenda
leg-end-ar-y adj. legendario
leg-gings n. polainas
leg-i-bil-i-ty n. legibilidad
leg-i-ble adj. legible
le-gion n. legion
le-gion-ar-y n. legionario
le-gion-naire n. legionario
leg-is-late v. legislar
leg-is-la-tion n. legislaci-ón
leg-is-la-tor n. legislador
le-git-i-ma-cy n. legitimidad
le-git-i-mate adj. legitimo
le-git-i-mize v. legitimar
lei-sure n. ocio
lem-on n. limon
lem-on-ade n. limonada
lend v. impartir; prestar
lend-er n. prestador
length n. extensión; longitud; tramo; largo
length-en v. prolongar(se); alargar(se)
length-y adj. prolongado
le-nient adj. indulgente
lens n. lente
len-til n. lenteja
le-o-nine adj. leonino
leop-ard n. leopardo
lep-er n. leproso
lep-ro-sy n. lepra
lep-rous adj. leproso
le-sion n. lesión
less adv., adj. menos
less-en v. disminuir
less-er adj. menor
les-son n. lección
let v. dejar; permitir
let-down n. desilusión
le-thal adj. letal
le-thar-gic adj. letargico
leth-ar-gy n. letargo
let-ter n. carta
let-tered adj. letrado
let-ter-ing n. rotulo
let-tuce n. lechuga
leu-ke-mi-a n. leucemia
lev-el n. llano; nivel
lev-i-ta-tion n. levitación
lev-y v. recaudar; exigir

lewd *adj.* lujurioso
lewd-ness *n.* lujuria
lex-i-cog-ra-phy *n.* lexicografia
lex-i-con *n.* lexicon
li-a-bil-i-ty *n.* obligación
li-a-ble *adj.* sujeto; responsable
li-ar *n.* mentiroso
li-ba-tion *n.* libación
lib-er-al *adj.* liberal
lib-er-ate *v.* libertar
lib-er-ty *n.* libertad
li-brar-y *n.* biblioteca
lie *v.* mentir; acostarse
life *n.* vida
lift *v.* levantar(se); elevar
light *n.* lampara; luz
light-ly *adv.* ligeramente
like *n.* gusto, *v.* gustar
like-ness *n.* semejanza
li-lac *n.* lila
lil-y *n.* lirio
lim-bo *n.* limbo
lime *n.* lima
lim-it *v.* limitar
lim-ou-sine *n.* limusina
line *v.* alinear; rayar, *n.* raya; linea
li-on *n.* léon
lip *n.* labio
liq-uid *n.* liquido
liq-ui-date *v.* liquidar
liq-uor *n.* licor
list *n.* lista
lit-er-al *adj.* literal
lit-er-ar-y *adj.* literario
lit-er-a-ture *n.* literatura
lit-tle *n., adj., adv.* poco, *adj.* pequeno
live *v.* vivir
liz-ard *n.* lagarto
lob-ster *n.* langosta
lo-cal *adj.* local
lo-cal-i-ty *n.* localidad
lo-cate *v.* encontrar
lone *adj.* solitario
lone-ly *adj.* solo
lone-ly *adj.* solo
long *adj.* largo
look *n.* mirada, *v.* buscar; mirar
loose *v.* soltar, *adj.* disoluto; suelto
lost *adj.* perdido
lo-tion *n.* loción
lot-ter-y *n.* loteria
loud *adj.* alto
love *v.* amar; querer, *n.* amor
love-ly *adj.* hermoso
low *adv., adj.* bajo, *adv.* abajo
low-er *v.* bajar
loy-al *adj.* fiel
loy-al-ty *n.* fidelidad
lu-bri-cant *n.* lubricante
lu-bri-cate *v.* lubricar
lu-bri-cious *adj.* lúbrico
lu-cent *adj.* luminoso
lu-cid *adj.* cuerdo; lucido
lu-cid-i-ty *n.* lucidez
luck *n.* suerte
luck-less *adj.* desafortunado
luck-y *adj.* fortuito
lu-cra-tive *adj.* lucrativo
lu-di-crous *adj.* ridiculo
lug *v.* halar
lug-gage *n.* equipaje
luke-warm *adj.* tibio
lull *v.* sosegar; embaucar
lum-bar *adj.* lumbar
lum-ber *n.* leno
lum-ber-ing *adj.* torpe; pesado
lu-mi-nance *n.* luminancia
lu-mi-nar-y *n.* luminar
lu-mi-nes-cence *n.* luminiscente
lu-mi-nous *adj.* luminoso
lump *n.* masa; terron
lu-na-cy *n.* locura
lu-nar *adj.* lunar
lunch *v.* almorzar, *n.* almuerz
lus-ter *n.* lustre
lus-ty *a.* robusto
lute *n.* laud
lux-u-ri-ant *a.* lozano
lux-u-ry *n.* lujo
lye *n.* lejia
lymph *n.* linfa
lynch *n.* linchar
lynx *n.* lince
lyre *n.* lira
lyr-ic *adj.* lírico

ma-ca-bre *adj.* macabro

mac-a-ro-ni *n.* macarrones

mac-a-roon *n.* mostachon

ma-chaw *n.* guacamayo

mac-er-ate *v.* macerar(se)

ma-chet-e *n.* machete

mach-i-nate *v.* maquinar

m a c h - i - n a - t i o n *n.* maquinacion

ma-chine *n.* maquina

ma-chine-gun *n.* ametrallar

ma-chin-er-y *n.* maquinaria

ma-chin-ist *n.* maquinista

mack-er-el *n.* caballa

mac-ra-me *n.* macrame

mac-ro-bi-ot-ics *n.* macrobiotica

mac-ro-cosm *n.* macrocosmo

mac-ro-scop-ic *adj.* macroscopico

mad *adj.* furioso

mad-cap *adj.* alocado

mad-den *v.* enloquecer

mad-den-ing *adj.* enloquecedor

made-up *adj.* incentado

mad-ness *n.* locura

mag-a-zine *n.* revista

mag-got *n.* gusano

mag-ic *n.* magia

mag-i-cal *adj.* magico

ma-gi-cian *n.* mago

mag-is-te-ri-al *adj.* magistral

mag-is-trate *n.* magistrado

mag-nate *n.* magnate

mag-ne-si-um *n.* magnesio

mag-net-ic *adj.* magnetico

mag-net-ism *n.* magnetismo

mag-net-ize *v.* magnetizar

m a g - n i - f i - c a - t i o n *n.* ampliación

mag-nif-i-cence *n.* magnificencia

mag-nif-i-cent *adj.* magnifico

mag-ni-fi-er *n.* amplificador

mag-ni-fy *v.* aumentar

mag-ni-tude *n.* magnitud

mag-num *n.* magnum

ma-hog-a-ny *n.* caoba

maid *n.* soltera

mail *n.* correo

mail-box *n.* buzón

mail-man *n.* cartero

main-tain *v.* mantener

main-te-nance *n.* mantenimiento

ma-jes-tic *adj.* majestuoso

maj-es-ty *n.* majestad

ma-jor *adj.* mayor

ma-jor-i-ty *n.* mayoria

make *v.* ganar; crear; hacer

mak-er *n.* fabricante

mak-ing *n.* fabricación

mal-a-dy *n.* dolencia

ma-lar-i-a *n.* malaria

mal-con-tent *adj.* malcontento

male *adj.* masculino; macho

mal-e-dic-tion *n.* maldición

m a - l e v - o - l e n c e *n.* malevolencia

ma-lev-o-lent *adj.* malévolo

mal-func-tion *v.* funcionar mal

mal-ice *n.* malicia

ma-li-cious *adj.* malicioso

ma-lig-nan-cy *n.* malignidad

ma-lig-nant *adj.* maligno

mall *n.* alameda

mal-le-a-ble *adj.* maleable

mal-nour-ished *adj.* desnutrido

mal-nu-tri-tion *n.* desnutrición

malt *n.* malta

mal-treat *v.* maltratar

mal-treat-ment *n.* maltratamiento

mam-mal *n.* mamifero

mam-ma-li-an *adj.* mamifero

mam-ma-ry *adj.* mamario

man *n.* hombre

man-age *v.* manejar

m a n - a g e - a - b l e *adj.* manejable

man-age-ment *n.* gerencia

man-da-rin *n.* mandarin

man-date *n.* mandato

man-da-to-ry *adj.* mandante

man-do-lin *n.* mandolina

ma-neu-ver *v.* maniobrar

m a - n e u - n e r - a - b l e *adj.* maniobrable

man-ga-nese *n.* manganeso

man-gle v. mutilar
man-go n. mango
man-hood n. madurez
ma-ni-a n. mania
ma-ni-ac adj. maniaco
ma-ni-a-cal adj. maniaco
man-ic adj. maniaco
man-i-cure n. manicura
man-i-cur-ist n. manicuro
man-i-fest adj. manifiesto
man-i-fes-ta-tion n. manifestación
man-i-fes-to n. manifiesto
ma-ni-kin n. maniqui
ma-nip-u-late v. manipular
ma-nip-u-la-tion n. manipulación
ma-nip-u-la-tive adj. de manipuleo
ma-nip-u-la-tor n. manipulador
man-li-ness n. hombria
man-ly adj. masculino
man-ne-quin n. maniqui
man-ner n. manera
man-nered adj. amanerado
man-ner-ism n. amaneramiento
man-nish adj. hombruno
man-tel n. manto
man-tle n. manto
man-u-al adj. manual
man-u-fac-ture n. manufactura
man-u-fac-tured adj. manufacturado
man-u-fac-tur-ing adj. manufacturero
man-u-script n. manuscrito
man-y adj. muchos
map n. mapa
ma-ple n. arce
map-mak-er n. cartografia
mar v. desfigurar
mar-a-thon n. maraton
ma-raud-er n. merodeador
mar-ble n. marmol
mar-bled adj. jaspeado
mar-bling n. marmoración
march v. marchar
March n. marzo
mar-ga-rine n. margarina
mar-gin s. margen

mar-gin-al adj. marginal
mar-i-gold n. maravilla
ma-ri-na n. marina
mar-i-nate v. marinar
ma-rine n. marino
mar-i-ner n. marinero
mar-i-tal adj. marital
mar-i-time adj. maritimo
mark n. marca
marked adj. marcado
mark-er n. marcador
mar-ket v. vender; n. mercado
mar-ket-a-ble adj. vendible
mar-ket-er n. vendedor
mark-ing n. marca
mar-ma-lade n. mermelada
ma-roon v. abandonar
mar-quis n. marques
mar-riage n. matrimonio
mar-ried adj. casado
mar-row n. medula
mar-ry v. casar(se)
marsh n. pantano
mar-shal n. mariscal
marsh-y adj. pantanoso
mar-su-pi-al adj. marsupial
mart n. mercado
mar-tial adj. marcial
mar-tyr n. martir
mar-tyr-dom n. martirio
mar-vel s. maravilla
mar-vel-lous adj. maravilloso
mas-cot n. mascota
mas-cu-line adj. masculion
mas-cu-lin-i-ty n. masculinidad
mash v. majar
mash-er n. majador
mask n. mascara
mas-och-ism n. masoquismo
mas-o-chist n. masoquista
mas-o-chis-tic adj. masoquista
ma-son-ary n. albanileria
mas-quer-ade n. mascarada
mass n. masa
mas-sa-cre n. masacre
mas-sage v. masajear
mas-sive adj. masivo
mast n. mastil
mas-tec-to-my n. mastec-

tomia
mas-ter *n.* maestro
mas-ter-ful *adj.* habil
mas-ter-ly *adj.* magistral
mas-ter-y *n.* maestria
mas-tic *adj.* mastique
mas-ti-cate *v.* masticar
mas-toid *n.* mastoides
mat *n.* estera
mate *n.* hembra; compañero
ma-te-ri-al *adj., n.* material
ma-te-ri-al-ist *n.* materialista
ma-te-ri-al-is-tic *adj.* materialista
ma-te-ri-al-i-ty *n.* materialidad
math *n.* matematicas
math-e-mat-i-cal *adj.* matematico
math-e-ma-ti-cian *n.* matematico
math-e-mat-ics *n.* matematicas
mat-i-nee *n.* matinee
ma-tri-arch *n.* matriarca
ma-tri-ar-chal *adj.* matriarcal
ma-tri-ar-chy *n.* matriarcado
ma-tric-u-late *v.* matricular(se)
ma-tric-u-la-tion *n.* matriculación
mat-ri-mo-ni-al *adj.* matrimonial
mat-ri-mo-ny *n.* matrimonio
ma-trix *n.* matriz
ma-tron *n.* matrona
ma-tron-ly *adj.* matronal
mat-ted *adj.* esterado
mat-ter *n.* materia
mat-ting *n.* estera
mat-tress *n.* colchon
mat-u-ra-tion *n.* maduración
ma-ture *v.* madurar, *adj.* maduro
ma-tur-i-ty *n.* madurez
maul *v.* maltratar
mauve *n.* malva
max-im *n.* máxima
max-i-mal *adj.* máximo
max-i-mum *adj.* máximo
May *n.* mayo
may *v.* poder
may-be *adj.* tal vez

may-on-naise *n.* mayonesa
may-or *n.* alcalde
may-or-al-ty *n.* alcadia
me *pron.* mi; me
mead-ow *n.* pradera
mea-ger *adj.* pobre; magro
meal *n.* comida
mean *v.* intentar
me-an-der *v.* vagar
mean-ing *n.* significado
mean-ing-ful *adj.* significativo
mean-ing-less *adj.* insignificante
mea-sles *n.* rubeola
meas-ure *v.* medir
meas-ured *adj.* mesurado
meas-ure-ment *n.* medición
meat *n.* carne
meat-y *adj.* carnoso
me-chan-ic *n.* mecánico
me-chan-i-cal *adj.* mecánico
mech-a-nism *n.* mecánismo
mech-a-nize *v.* mecanizar
med-al *n.* medalla
me-dal-lion *n.* medallon
med-dle *v.* entremeterse
med-dler *n.* entremetido
me-di-an *adj.* mediano
me-di-ate *v.* mediar
me-di-a-tion *n.* mediación
me-di-a-tor *n.* mediador
med-ic *n.* medico
med-i-cal *adj.* medico
med-i-cate *v.* medicinar
med-i-ca-tion *n.* medicación
med-i-cine *n.* medicina
me-di-e-val *adj.* midieval
me-di-o-cre *adj.* mediocre
me-di-oc-ri-ty *n.* mediocridad
med-i-tate *v.* meditar
med-i-ta-tion *n.* meditación
meet *v.* reunirse; encontras(se)
mel-o-dy *n.* melodia
mel-on *n.* melon
mem-ber *n.* miembro
mem-o-ra-ble *adj.* memorable
men-tal *adj.* mental
men-tion *v.* mencionar; *n.* mencion

mer-cu-ry *n.* mercurio
mer-it *v.* merecer
mer-ry *adj.* festivo
mes-sage *n.* comunicación
mes-sen-ger *n.* mensajero
met-al *n.* metal
me-te-or-ol-o-gy *n.* meteorologia
meth-od *n.* metodo
mi-crobe *n.* microbio
mi-cro-phone *n.* microfono
mi-cro-scope *n.* microscopio
mid-dle *n., adj.* medio
mid-night *n.* medianoche
mi-grate *v.* emigrar
mil-i-tar-y *adj.* militar
mi-li-tia *n.* milicia
milk *n.* leche
mil-lion *n.* millón
mil-lion-aire *n.* millonario
mind *v.* obedecer, *n.* mente
min-er-al *n.* mineral
min-is-ter *n.* ministro
mi-nor *adj.* menor
mi-nor-i-ty *n.* minoria
mi-nus *prep.* menos
mir-a-cle *n.* milagro
mir-ror *n.* espejo
mis-chie-vous *adj.* malicioso
miss *v.* perder
mis-sion *n.* misión
mis-sion-ar-y *n.* misionero
mis-take *v.* equivocar(se)
mis-ter *n.* senor
mis-treat *v.* maltratar
mit-i-gate *v.* mitigar
mit-ten *n.* mitón
mix *n.* mezcla, *v.* mezclar(se)
mix-ture *n.* mezcla
mod-el *v.* modelar, *n.* modelo
mod-er-ate *v.* moderar, *adj.* moderno
mod-ern *n.* moderno
mod-est *adj.* modesto
mod-i-fi-ca-tion *n.* modificación
mod-i-fy *v.* modificar
mod-u-late *v.* modular
moist *adj.* humedo
mois-ten *v.* humedecer(se)
moist-ness *n.* humedad

mois-ture *n.* humedad
mois-tur-iz-er *v.* humedecer
mo-lar *n.* molar
mo-las-ses *n.* melaza
mold *v.* moldear, *n.* molde
mold-er *v.* desmoronar(se)
mold-ing *n.* mohoso
mo-lec-u-lar *adj.* molecular
mol-e-cule *n.* molecula
mole-hill *n.* topera
mol-li-fy *v.* molificar
mol-lusk *n.* molusco
mol-ten *adj.* fundido
mom *n.* mama
mo-ment *n.* momento
mo-men-tar-i-ly *adv.* momentáneamente
mo-men-tar-y *adj.* momentaneo
mo-men-tum *n.* momento
mon-arch *n.* monarca
mo-nar-chic *adj.* monarquico
mon-ar-chist *n.* monarquico
mon-ar-chy *n.* monarquia
mon-as-ter-y *n.* monasterio
mo-nas-tic *adj.* monastico
Mon-day *n.* lunes
mon-e-tar-y *adj.* monetario
mon-ey *n.* dinero
mon-eyed *adj.* adinerado
mon-goose *n.* mangosta
mo-ni-tion *n.* admonición
mon-i-tor *n.* monitor
mon-i-to-ry *adj.* admonitorio
monk *n.* monje
mon-key *n.* mono
monk-hood *n.* monacato
monk-ish *adj.* monacal
mon-o-chro-mat-ic *adj.* monocromatico
mo-noc-u-lar *adj.* monocular
mo-nog-a-my *n.* monogamia
mon-o-gram *n.* monograma
mon-o-graph *n.* monografia
mon-o-lith *n.* monolito
mon-o-lith-ic *adj.* monolitico
mon-o-plane *n.* monoplano
mo-nop-o-lize *v.* monopolizar
mo-nop-o-ly *n.* monopolio
mon-o-rail *n.* monocarril
mo-no-tone *n.* monotonia

mo-not-o-nous *adj.* monotono

mo-not-o-ny *n.* monotonía

mon-ox-ide *n.* monoxido

mon-soon *n.* monzon

mon-ster *n.* monstruo

mon-stros-i-ty *n.* monstruosidad

mon-strous *adj.* monstruoso

mon-tage *n.* montaje

month *n.* mes

month-ly *adj.* mensual

mon-u-ment *n.* monumento

mon-u-men-tal *adj.* monumental

moo *v.* mugir

mood *n.* humor

moon *n.* luna

moor *v.* amarrar

moor-age *n.* amarradero

moor-ing *n.n* amarradero

moose *n.* anta

mop *n.* estropajo

mo-ped *n.* ciclomotor

mor-al *adj.* moral

mo-rale *n.* moral

mor-al-ist *n.* moralista

mor-al-is-tic *adj.* moralizador

mo-ral-i-ty *n.* moralidad

mor-al-ize *v.* moralizar

mor-bid *adj.* morboso

mor-bid-i-ty *n.* morbosidad

more *n., adv., adj.* mas

more-o-ver *adv.* ademas

morn-ing *n.* manana

mor-phine *n.* morfina

mor-phol-o-gy *n.* morfología

mor-tal *n., adj.* mortal

mor-tal-i-ty *n.* mortalidad

mor-tu-ar-y *n.* mortuorio

mos-qui-to *n.* mosquito

most *adj.* muy; mas

moth *n.* polilla

moth-er *n.* madre

moth-er-hood *n.* maternidad

moth-er-in-law *n.* suegra

mo-tor-cy-cle *n.* motocicleta

montain *n.* montaña

mouse *n.* ratón

mouth *n.* boca

move *v.* mundar; mover

mov-ie *n.* película

Mr. *n.* señor

Mrs. *n.* señora

Ms. *n.* señora

much *adj.* muy, *n., adv., adj.* mucho

mul-ti-ple *adj.* multiple

mul-ti-pli-ca-tion *n.* multiplicación

mul-ti-ply *v.* multiplicar

mul-ti-pur-pose *adj.* multiuso

mul-ti-tude *n.* multitud

mum-ble *v.* mascullar

mum-my *n.* momia

munch *v.* ronzar

mun-dane *adj.* mundaño

mu-nic-i-pal *adj.* municipal

mu-nic-i-pal-i-ty *n.* municipalidad

mu-ni-fi-cence *n.* munificencia

mu-nif-i-cent *adj.* munifico

mur-der *v.* matanza

mur-der-er *n.* asesiño

mur-der-ous *adj* asesiño

mur-mur *v.* murmurar

mus-cle *n.* musculo

mus-cu-lar *adj.* musculoso

muse *v.* meditar

mu-se-um *n.* museo

mu-sic *n.* musica

mu-si-cal *adj.* musical

mu-si-cal-i-ty *n.* musicalidad

mu-si-cian *n.* musico

mus-ing *n.* contemplación

mus-ket *n.* mosquete

mus-ket-eer *n.* mosquetero

mus-lin *n.* muselina

mus-sel *n.* mejillon

must *v.* deber

mus-tache *n.* bigote

mu-ti-late *v.* mutilar

muz-zle *n.* hocico; boca

my *adj.* mi

myr-i-ad *n.* miriada

my-self *pron.* yo mismo

mys-te-ri-ous *a.* misterioso

mys-ter-y *n.* misterio

mys-tic *a.* mistico

mys-ti-cism *n.* misticismo; mistica

myth *n.* mito

myth-ic *a.* mitico

my-thol-o-gy *n.* mitología

nab v. prender
na-dir n. nadir
nag n. jaca
nail v. clavar, n. clavo
na-ive adj. ingenuo
na-ive-te n. ingenuidad
naked adj. desnudo
name v. apellido; nombre
name-less adj. anonimo
name-ly adv. a saber
name-sake n. tocayo
nap n. siesta
nape n. nuca
nap-kin n. servilleta
nar-cis-sism n. narcisismo
nar-cis-sus n. narciso
nar-cot-ic n. narcotico
nar-rate v. narrar
nar-ra-tion n. narración
nar-ra-tive adj. narrativo
nar-ra-tor n. narrador
nar-row adj. estrecho; limitado; angosto
nar-row-ing n. limitación
na-sal adj. nasal
na-sal-i-ty n. nasalidad
nas-ty adj. antipatico; sucio; obsceno
na-tal adj. natal
na-tal-i-ty n. natalidad
na-tion n. nation
na-tion-al n., adj. nacional
na-tion-al-ist n. nacionalista
na-tion-al-is-tic adj. nacionalista
na-tion-al-i-ty n. nacionalidad
na-tion-al-ize v. nacionalizar
na-tive adj. natal; innato; nativo
na-tiv-i-ty n. natividad
nat-u-ral adj. natural
nat-u-ral-ist n. naturalista
nat-u-ral-is-tic adj. naturalista
nat-u-ral-ize v. naturalizar(se)
nat-u-ral-ly adv. naturalmente
na-ture n. genero; naturaleza
naught n. nada
naugh-ty adj. verde; travieso

nau-se-a n. nausea
nau-se-ate v. dar nauseas a
nau-se-at-ing adj. nauseabundo
nau-seous adj. nauseabundo
nau-ti-cal adj. nautico
na-val adj. naval
nav-i-ga-ble adj. navegable
nav-i-gate v. navegar
nav-i-ga-tion n. navegación
nav-i-ga-tor n. navegante
nay adv. no
near prep. cerca de, adv. cerca, adj. próximo
near-by adj. próximo
near-ly adj. caso
neat adj. claro; limpio; fantastico
neb-u-la n. nebulosa
neb-u-lar adj. nebuloso
nec-es-sar-y adj. necesario
ne-ces-si-tate v. necesitar
ne-ces-si-ty n. necesidad
neck n. cuello
neck-lace n. collar
neck-line n. escote
ne-crol-o-gy n. necrologia
ne-cro-sis n. necrosis
nec-tar n. nactar
nec-tar-ine n. pelon
need v. necesitar
need-ful adj. necessario
nee-dle n. aguja
need-less adj. superfluo
need-y adj. necesitado
ne-far-i-ous adj. nefario
ne-gate v. negar
ne-ga-tion n. negación
neg-a-tive n. negativa
ne-glect v. descuidar
ne-glect-ful adj. negligente
neg-li-gence n. negligencia
neg-li-gent adj. negligente
neg-li-gi-ble adj. insignificante
ne-go-tia-ble adj. negociable
ne-go-ti-ate v. negociar
ne-go-ti-a-tion n. negociación
ne-go-ti-a-tor n. negociador
neigh-bor n. projimo; vecino
neigh-bor-hood n. barrio

neigh-bor-ing adj. vecino
neigh-bor-ly adj. amable
nei-ther pron. ninguno, conj. tampoco; ni
ne-ol-o-gism n. neologismo
ne-ol-o-gist n. neologo
ne-on n. neon
ne-o-phyte n. neofito
neph-ew n. sobrino
nep-o-tism n. nepotismo
nerve n. nervio
nerve-less adj. sin nervios
nerv-ous adj. nervioso
nerv-ous-ness n. nerviosidad
nest n. nido
net n. red
net-ting n. red
net-tle n. ortiga
net-work n red
neu-ral-gia n. neuralgia
neu-ral-gic adj. neuralgico
neu-ri-tis n. neuritis
neu-ro-sis n. nervioso
neu-rol-o-gist n. neurólogo
neu-rol-o-gy n. neurólogia
neu-rot-ic adj. neurótico
neu-tral n., adj. neutral
neu-tral-i-ty n. neutralidad
neu-tral-ize v. neutralizar
neu-tral-iz-er n. neutralizador
neu-tron n. neutron
nev-er adv. jamás; nunca
nev-er-more adv. nunca mas
nev-er-the-less adv. sin embargo
new adj. nuevo
new-found adj. nuevo
new-ly adv. nuevamente
news n. nuevas
news-cast n. noticiario
news-cast-er n. locutor
news-pa-per n. diario
news-y adj. informativo
newt n. tritón
new-ton n. neutonio
next adj. próximo
nib-ble v. mordiscar
nice adj. agradable; amable
ni-ce-ty n. delicadeza; precisión
niche n. nicho

nick n. neusca; mella
nick-el n. niquel
nick-name n. apodo
nic-o-tine n. nicotina
niece n. sobrina
nigh adv. cerca
night n. noche
night-fall n. anochecer
night-gown n. camison
night-in-gale n. ruiseñor
night-light n. lamparilla
night-ly adj. nocturno
night-mare n. pesadilla
night-time n. noche
nine adj. nueve
nine-teen adj. diecinueve
nine-ty adj. noventa
ninth adj. noveno
no n., adv. no
no-bod-y n., pron. nadie
noise n. ruido
nois-y adj. ruidoso
none pron. nadie; nada
noon n. mediodia
nor conj. ni
nor-mal adj. normal
nor-mal-ly adv. normalmente
north n. norte
north-east n. nordeste
north-west n. noroeste
nose n. nariz
not adv. no
no-ta-ble adj. notable
no-ta-tion n. notación
note v. notar, n. nota
no-ti-fy v. notificar
no-tion n. nocion
no-to-ri-ous adj. notorio
No-vem-ber n. noviembre
now adv. ahora
nu-cle-ar adj. nuclear
nude n., adj. desnudo
num-ber v. numerar, n. numero
nu-mer-i-cal adj. numerico
nu-mer-ous adj. numeroso
nut n. nuez
nu-tri-tion n. nutrición
nu-tri-tion-al adj. nutritivo
nu-tri-tious adj. nutritivo
nu-tri-tive adj. nutritivo
nuz-zle v. hocicar
ny-lon n nailon

oak *n.* roble
oak-en *adj.* de roble
oar *n.* remo
o-a-sis *n.* oasis
oat *n.* avena
oath *n.* juramento
oat-meal *n.* gachas de avena
ob-du-ra-cy *n.* obstinación
ob-du-rate *adj.* obstinado; insensible
o-be-di-ence *n.* obediencia
o-be-di-ent *adj.* obediente
ob-e-lisk *n.* obelisco
o-bese *adj.* obeso
o-be-si-ty *n.* obesidad
o-bey *v.* obedecer
ob-fus-cate *v.* ofuscar
ob-fus-ca-tion *n.* ofuscación
o-bit-u-ar-y *n.* obituario
ob-ject *v.* desaprobar; *n.* objeto
ob-jec-tion *n.* objeción
ob-jec-tion-a-ble *adj.* ofensivo
ob-jec-tive *n.*, *adj.* objetivo
ob-li-gate *v.* obligar
ob-li-ga-tion *n.* obligación
o-blig-a-to-ry *adj.* obligatorio
o-blige *v.* obligar
o-blig-ing *adj.* complaciente
o-blique *adj.* oblicuo
o-blit-er-ate *v.* aniquilar; arrasar
o-bliv-i-on *n.* olvido
o-bliv-i-ous *adj.* olvidadizo
ob-long *adj.* oblongo
o b - n o x - i o u s *a d j.* insoportable; desagradable
o-boe *n.* oboe
ob-scene *adj.* obsceno
ob-scen-i-ty *n.* obscenidad
ob-scure *adj.* imperceptible; oscuro
ob-scu-ri-ty *n.* oscuridad
ob-e-qui-ous *adj.* servil
o b - s e r - v a n c e *n.* observacion; cumplimiento
ob-ser-vant *adj.* observador
ob-ser-va-tion *n.* observación
ob-ser-va-to-ry *n.* observatorio
ob-serve *v.* cumplir; observar

ob-serv-er *n.* observador
ob-sess *v.* obsesionar
ob-ses-sion *n.* obsesión
ob-ses-sive *adj.* obsesivo
ob-so-les-cence *n.* obsolencia
ob-so-lete *adj.* obsoleto
ob-sta-cle *n.* obstaculo
ob-stet-ric *adj.* obstetrico
ob-sti-na-cy *n.* obstinación
ob-sti-nate *adj.* obstinado
ob-struct *v.* obstruir
ob-struc-tion *n.* obstrucción
ob-struc-tion-ist *n.* obstruccionista
ob-tain *v.* obtener
ob-trude *v.* introducir
ob-tru-sion *n.* intrusión
ob-tuse *adj.* obtuso
ob-vi-ate *v.* obviar
ob-vi-ous *adj.* obvio
ob-vi-ous-ly *adj.* claro
oc-ca-sion *n.* ocasión
oc-ca-sion-al *adj.* ocasional
oc-clude *v.* ocluir
oc-cu-pan-cy *n.* ocupación
oc-cu-pant *n.* pasajero; inquilino
oc-cu-pa-tion *n.* ocupación
o c - c u - p a - t i o n - a l *adj.* ocupacional
oc-cu-pied *adj.* ocupado
oc-cu-py *v.* ocupar
oc-cur *v.* ocurrir
oc-cur-rence *n.* presencia; suceso
o-cean *v.* oceáno
o-ce-an-ic *adj.* oceánico
oc-ta-gon *n.* octagono
oc-tag-o-nal *adj.* octogonal
oc-tane *n.* octaño
oc-tave *n.* octavo
Oc-to-ber *n.* octubre
oc-to-ge-nar-i-an *adj.* octogenario
oc-to-pus *n.* pulpo
oc-u-lar *adj.* ocular
oc-u-lis *n.* oculista
odd *adj.* raro
odd-i-ty *n.* rareza
odds *n.* probabilidades
o-di-ous *adj.* odioso

o-di-um *n.* odio
o-dom-e-ter *n.* odometro
o-dor *n.* olor
o-dor-less *adj.* inoforo
o-dor-ous *adj.* fragante
od-ys-sey *n.* odisea
of *prep.* de
off *adv.* fuera
of-fend *v.* ofender
of-fend-er *n.* infractor
of-fense *n.* ofense
of-fen-sive *adj.* ofensivo
of-fer *n.* ofrecimiento, *v.* ofrecer
of-fer-ing *n.* ofrecimiento
of-fice *n.* oficina
of-fi-cer *n.* oficial
of-fi-cial *n., adj.* oficial
of-fi-ci-ate *v.* oficiar
of-fi-cious *adj.* oficioso
off-set *v.* compensar
of-ten *adv.* a menudo
oil *n.* aceite
oil-can *n.* alcuzq
oiled *adj.* aceitado
oil-y *adj.* aceitoso
oint-ment *n.* pomada
o-kra *n.* quingombo
old *adj.* anciano; viejo
old-en *adj.* pasado
old-fash-ioned *adj.* anticuado
ol-fac-to-ry *adj.* olfativo
ol-ive *n.* oliva
om-i-nous *adj.* ominoso
o-mis-sion *n.* omisión
o-mit *v.* omitir
om-ni-bus *n.* omnibus
om-nip-o-tence *n.* omnipotencia
om-nip-o-ten *adj.* omnipotente
on *prep.* sobre
once *n., adv.* una vez
on-col-o-gy *n.* oncologia
on-com-ing *adj.* que viene
one *adj.* uno; un
one-di-men-sion-al *adj.* unidimensional
on-er-ous *adj.* oneroso
one-self *pron.* uno
one-sid-ed *adj.* desigual
on-ion *n.* cebolla

on-look-er *n.* espectador
on-ly *adj., adv.* solo
on-rush *n.* embestida
on-to *prep.* sobre; en
on-ward *adj.* hacia adelante
on-yx *n.* onix
o-pac-i-ty *n.* opacidad
o-pal *n.* opalo
o-pal-es-cence *n.* opalescencia
o-paque *adj.* opaco
o-pen *v.* abrir, *adj.* abierto
o-pen-er *n.* abridor
o-pen-ing *n.* abertura
o-pen-mind-ed *adj.* receptivo
o-per-a *n.* opera
op-er-a-ble *adj.* operable
op-er-ate *v.* operar; actuar; manejar
op-er-at-ing *adj.* de mantenimiento
op-er-a-tion *n.* operación
o-per-a-tion-al *adj.* deoperacion
op-er-a-tive *adj.* operante
oph-thal-mol-o-gist *n.* oftalmolgo
oph-thal-mol-ogy *n.* oftalmologia
o-pi-ate *n.* opiato
o-pine *v.* opinar
o-pin-ion *n.* opinion
o-pi-um *n.* opio
op-po-nent *n.* adversario
op-por-tune *adj.* oportuno
op-por-tun-ist *n.* oportunista
op-por-tu-ni-ty *n.* oportunidad
op-pose *v.* oponerse
op-po-site *adj.* opuesto
op-po-si-tion *n.* oposición
op-press *v.* oprimir
op-pres-sion *n.* opresión
op-pres-sive *adj.* opresivo
op-pres-sor *n.* opresor
opt *v.* optar
op-yic *adj.* optico
op-ti-cal *adj.* optico
op-ti-cian *n.* optico
op-ti-mal *adj.* optimo
op-ti-mism *n.* optmismo
op-ti-mist *n.* optimista
op-ti-mis-tic *adj.* optimista

op-tion *n.* opción

op-tion-al *adj.* opcional

op-tom-e-try *n.* optometria

op-u-lent *adj.* opulento

or *conj.* u; o

o-ral *adj.* oral

or-ange *adj.* anaranjado, *n.* naranja

o-ra-tion *n.* oración

or-ches-tra *n.* orquesta

or-der *n.* orden

or-di-nar-y *adj.* ordinario

or-gan-ism *n.* organismo

or-gan-i-za-tion *n.* organización

or-gan-ize *v.* organizar

o-rig-i-nal *adj.* original

o-rig-i-nate *v.* originar

os-ten-ta-tion *n.* ostentación

oth-er *prep.* el otro, *adj.* otro

ounce *n.* onza

our *adj.* nuestro

our-selves *pron.* nosotros

out *prep.* fuera de, *adv.* fuera

out-er *adj.* externo

out-fit *n.* traje

out-line *v.* bosquejar, *n.* bosquejo

out-side *adv.* fuera, *n.* exterior

out-ward *adj.* exterior

o-va-ry *n.* ovario

o-va-tion *n.* ovación

ov-en *n.* horno

o-ver *adj.* otra vez, *prep.* sobre; encima de

o-ver-lap *v.* solapar

o-ver-night *adj.* de noche

o-ver-sight *n.* olvido

o-vert *a.* publico

o-ver-turn *v.* volcar

o-ver-weight *adj.* gordo

o-vum *n.* ovulo

owe *v.* tener deudas

owl *n.* buho

own *v.* reconocer

ox-ide *n.* oxido

ox-i-dize *v.* oxidar(se)

ox-y-gen *n.* oxigeno

ox-y-gen-ate *v.* oxigenar

oys-ter *n.* ostra

o-zone *n.* ozono

pa *n.* papá

pace *n.* paso

pa-cif-ic *adj.* pacifico

pac-i-fism *n.* pacifismo

pac-i-fy *v.* pacificar

pack *n.* fardo

pack-age *n.* paquete

pact *n.* pacto

pad *n.* almohadilla

pad-dle *n.* canalete

pad-lock *n.* candado

pa-gan *n.* pagano

page *n.* página

pag-eant *n.* espectaculo

pa-go-da *n.* pagoda

pail *n.* cubo

pain *v.* doler; *n.* dolor

pain-ful *adj.* doloroso

pains-tak-ing *a.* laborioso; esmerado

paint *n.* pintura, *v.* pintar

paint-ing *n.* pintura

pair *n.* pareja; par

pa-jam-as *n.* pijama

pal-ace *n.* palacio

pal-ate *n.* paladar

pale *a.* palido; claro

pa-le-on-tol-o-gy *n.* paleontologia

pal-ette *n.* paleta

pal-i-sade *n.* palizada

pall *v.* perder su sabor

pal-lid palido

pal-lor *n.* palidez

palm *n.* palma

palm-is-try *n.* quiromancia

pal-pa-ble *adj.* palpable

pal-pi-ta-tion *n.* palpitación

pal-try *a.* miserable

pam-per *v.* mimar

pam-phlet *n.* folleto

pan *n.* cazuela

pan-a-ce-a *n.* panacea

pan-cake *n.* hojuela

pan-cre-as *n.* pancreas

pan-de-mo-ni-um *n.* pandemonium

pane *n.* hoja de vidrio

pan-el *n.* panel

pang *n.* punzada; dolor

pan-han-dle *v.* mendigar

pan-ic *n.* terror

pan-o-ram-a *n.* panorama

pan-sy *n.* pensamiento

pant *n., pl.* pantalones

pan-the-ism *n.* panteismo

pan-ther *n.* pantera

pan-to-mime *n.* pantomima

pan-try *n.* despensa

pa-pa *n.* papa

pa-pa-cy *n.* papado; pontificado

pa-per *n.* papel

pa-pier-ma-che *n.* carton piedra

pa-poose *n.* crio

pa-py-rus *n.* papiro

par *n.* par

par-a-ble *n.* parábola

par-a-chute *n.* paracaídas

pa-rade *n.* parada

par-a-dise *n.* paraiso

par-a-dox *n.* paradoja

par-af-fin *n.* paraffin

par-a-graph *n.* parrafo

par-al-lel *a.* paralelo

pa-ral-y-sis *n.* parálisis

par-a-lyze *v.* paralizar

par-ram-e-ter *n.* parametro; limite

par-a-noi-a *n.* paranoia

par-a-pher-nal-ia *n.* arreos

par-a-phrase *n.* parafrasis

par-a-site *n.* parásito

par-a-troop-er *n.* paracaidista

parcel *n.* paquete; bulto

parch *v.* secar

parch-ment *n.* pergamino

par-don *n.* perdón, *v.* perdonar

pare *v.* cortar

par-ent *n.* madre; padre

par-ren-the-sis *n.* parentesis

pa-ri-ah *n.* paria

par-ish *n.* parroquia

park *v.* aparcar, *n.* parque

par-ley *v.* parlamentar

par-lia-ment *n.* parlamento

par-lor *n.* sala de recibo

pa-ro-chi-al *a.* parroquial; estrecho

par-o-dy *n.* parodia

pa-role *n.* libertad bajo palabra

par-ox-ysm *n.* paroxismo

par-rot *n.* loro

par-ry *v.* parar

par-sley *n.* perejil

par-son *n.* clérigo

part *v.* separar(se); partir(se), *n.* parte

par-take *v.* tomar parte

par-tial *adj.* parcial

par-tial-i-ty *n.* parcialidad

par-tic-i-pant *a.* participe

par-tic-i-pate *v.* participar

par-tic-i-pa-tion *n.* participación

par-ti-ci-ple *n.* participio

par-ti-cle *n.* partículo

par-tic-u-lar *adj.* particular

par-tic-u-lar-i-ty *n.* particion; tabique

part-ing *a.* despendida

par-ti-san *n.* partidario

par-ti-tion *n.* partición; tabique

part-ner *n.* socio

par-tridge *n.* perdiz

par-ty *n.* fiesta

pass *v.* aprobar; pasar

pas-sage *n.* pasaje; travesia; pasadizo

pas-sen-ger *n.* pasajero; viajero

pas-sion *n.* pasión

pas-sion-ate *a.* apasionado

pas-sive *adj.* pasivo

pass-port *n.* pasaporte

pass-word *n.* santo y sena

past *n., adj.* pasado

paste *n.* enguido; pasta

paste-board *n.* carton

pas-teur-i-za-tion *n.* pasteurización

pas-teur-ize *v.* pasteurizar

pas-time *n.* pasatiempo

pas-tor *n.* pastor

pas-try *n.* pasteles

pas-ture *n.* pasto

pat *n.* golpecito; pastelillo

patch *n.* pedazo

pat-ent *n.* patente

pa-ter-nal *adj.* paterno

pa-ter-ni-ty *n.* paternidad

path *n.* senda

pa-thet-ic *a.* patético

pa-thol-o-gy *n.* patología

pa-tience *n.* paciencia
pa-tient *a.* paciente
pa-ti-o *n.* patio
pa-tri-ar-chy *n.* patriarcado
pat-ri-mo-ny *n.* patrimonio
pa-tri-ot *n.* patriota
pa-trol *v.* patrullar
pa-tron *n.* cliente
pat-tern *n.* patrón
pau-per *n.* pobre
pause *n.* pausa
pave *v.* empedrar; pavimentar
pave-ment *n.* pavimento
pa-vil-ion *n.* pabellon
paw *v.* manosear, *n.* pata
pawn *v.* empenar
pay *v.* pagar; ser provechoso
pay-roll *n.* nomina
pea *n.* guisante
peace *n.* paz
peace-ful *a.* tranquilo
peach *n.* melocoton
pea-cock *n.* pavo real; pavon
peak *n.* pico; cumbre
peal *v.* repicar
pea-nut *n.* cachuete
pear *n.* pera
pearl *n.* perla
peas-ant *n.* campesino
pab-ble *n.* guijarro
pec-ca-dil-lo *n.* pecadillo
pe-cu-liar *adj.* peculir
pe-cu-li-ar-i-ty *n.* peculiaridad
ped-al *n.* pedal
ped-dle *v.* vender por las calles
ped-dler *n.* buhonero
ped-es-tal *n.* pedestal
pe-des-tri-an *n.* peaton
ped-i-gree *n.* genealogia
peel *v.* pelar
peer *n.* par
peg *n.* clavija; estaca
pel-let *n.* bolita; pella
pelt *n.* piel
pel-vis *n.* pelvis
pen *n.* pluma
pe-nal *a.* penal
pen-al-ty *n.* pena; castigo
pen-cil *n.* lápiz

pend-ant *n.* pendiente
pend-ing *adj.* pendiente
pen-du-lum *n.* péndulo
pen-e-trate *v.* penetrar
pen-i-cil-in *n.* penicilina
pen-in-su-la *n.* península
pen-i-tent *n.* penitente
pen-i-ten-tia-ry *n.* presidio
pen-ny *n.* centavo
pen-sion *n.* pensión
pen-sive *adj.* pensativo
pen-ta-gon *n.* pentágono
pe-on *n.* peón
pe-o-ny *n.* peonía
peo-ple *n.* gente; pueblo
pep-per *n.* pimienta; pimiento
pep-per-mint *n.* menta
per *prep.* por
per-ceive *v.* percibir
per-cent *n.* por ciento
per-cent-age *n.* porcentaje
per-cep-tion *n.* percepción
perch *n.* percha; perca
per-di-tion *n.* perdición
per-en-ni-al *a.* perenne
per-fect *adj.* perfecto
per-fec-tion *n.* perfección
per-fo-rate *v.* perforar
per-form *v.* efectuar; hacer; representar
per-for-mance *n.* representación; función
per-fume *n.* perfume
per-il *n.* peligro
pe-rim-e-ter *n.* perimetro
pe-ri-od *n.* periodo
pe-ri-od-i-cal *n.* publicación periodica
pe-riph-er-y *n.* periferia
per-i-scope *n.* periscopia
per-ish *v.* perecer
per-jure *v.* perjurar(se)
per-ju-ry *n.* perjurio
per-ma-nent *a.* permanente
per-mis-sion *n.* permiso
per-mit *v.* permitir; tolerar
per-pen-dic-u-lar *adj.* perpendicular
per-pet-u-al *a.* perpetuo; continuo
per-plex *v.* confundir
per-se-cute *v.* perseguir

per-se-cu--tion *n.* persecución

per-sist *v.* persistir

per-son *n.* persona

per-son-al-i-ty *n.* personalidad

per-son-nel *n.* personal

per-spec-tive *n.* perspectiva

per-spi-ra-tion *n.* sudor

per-suade *v.* persuadi

per-spire *v.* sudar

per-ver-sion *n.* perversión

pe-ti-tion *n.* peticion

phar-ma-cy *n.* farmacia

phi-los-o-phy *n.* filosofía

pho-bi-a *n.* fobia

pho-to-cop-y *n.* fotocopia

pho-to-graph *n.* foto

pho-tog-ra-phy *n.* fotografia

phrase *n.* frase

phys-i-cal *adj.* fisico

phy-si-cian *n.* medico

pi-an-o *n.* piano

pick *v.* picar; elegir

pic-ture *n.* foto; cuadro; pelicula

pie *n.* pastel

piece *n.* pedazo

pig *n.* cerdo

pi-geon *n.* paloma

pil-lar *n.* pilar

pine *n.* piño

pink *adj.* rosado

pipe *n.* pipa

pis-tol *n.* pistola

pit-y *n.* lástima

place *v.* poner, *n.* posición; sitio

plac-id *adj.* placido

plague *n.* plaga

plain *adj., n.* llano

plan *v.* planear, *n.* plano

plane *n.* avion; plano

plan-et *n.* planeta

plant *v.* plantar, *n.* planta

plas-ma *n.* plasma

plas-tic *n., adj.* plastico

plate *n.* plato

play *v.* tocar; jugar, *n.* juego

plea *n.* defensa

plead *v.* suplicar; defender

pleas-ure *n.* placer

plen-ti-ful *adj.* abundante

plen-ty *n.* abundancia

plum *n.* ciruela

plum-age *n.* plumaje

plu-ral *n., adj.* plural

pock-et *n.* bolsillo

po-em *n.* poema

po-et *n.* poeta

po-et-ic *adj.* poético

point *n.* punto

po-lice *n.* policía

po-lit-i-cal *adj.* politico

pol-i-ti-cian *n.* politico

pol-i-tics *n.* politica

pol-lu-tion *n.* polución

pomp-ous *adj.* pomposo

pond *n.* estanque

po-ny *n.* jaca

pool *n.* piscina

poor *adj.* pobre

pop-u-lar *adj.* popular

pop-u-late *v.* poblar

pop-u-la-tion *n.* población

port *n.* puerto

por-tion *n.* parte

pose *v.* plantear

po-si-tion *n.* posición

pos-i-tive *adj.* positivo

pos-sess *v.* poseer

pos-ses-sion *n.* posesión

pos-si-bil-i-ty *n.* posibilidad

pos-si-ble *adj.* posible

post *n.* poste; puesto; correo

post-age *n.* porte; franqueo

post-card *n.* tarjeta

post-er *n.* cartel

pos-te-ri-or *adj.* posterior

post-man *n.* cartero

post-mark *n.* matasellos

post me-rid-i-em *a.* postmeridiano

post-mor-tem *n.* autopsia

post-pone *v.* alazar

post-script *v.* posdata

pos-ture *n.* postura

pot *n.* olla; tiesto

po-tas-si-um *n.* potasio

po-ta-to *n.* patata

po-tent *a.* potente; fuerte

po-ten-tial *adj.* potencial

po-tion *n.* posion

pot-ter-y *n.* alfareria

pouch *n.* bolsa

poul-try *n.* aves de corral

pound *n.* libra
pour *v.* diluviar
pout *v.* hace puncheros
pov-er-ty *n.* pobreza
pow-der *n.* polvo
pow-er *n.* fuerza; poder
pow-er-ful *a.* potente; poderoso
prac-ti-cal *adj.* práctico
practice *v.* practicar; ejercer
prag-mat-ic *a.* pragmatico
pari-rie *n.* pradera
praise *v.* alabar
prank *n.* travesura
pray *v.* rezar
prayer *n.* oración
preach *v.* predicar
pre-am-ble *n.* preambulo
pre-cau-tion *n.* precaución
pre-dede *v.* preceder
prec-e-dent *n.* precedente
pre-cint *n.* recinto; distrito electoral
pre-cious *adj.* precioso
prec-i-pice *n.* precipicio
pre-cip-i-ta-tion *n.* precipitacion
pre-cise *a.* preciso; exacto
pre-co-cious *a.* precoz
pre-cur-sor *n.* precursor
pred-e-ces-sor *n.* predecesor
pre-des-ti-na-tion *n.* predestinación.
pre-dic-a-ment *n.* apuro
pre-dict *v.* pronosticar
pre-dic-tion *n.* pronostico
pre-dom-i-nant *a.* predominante
pref-ace *n.* prologo; prefacio
pre-fer *v.* preferir
pref-er-ence *n.* preferencia
pre-fix *n.* prefijo
preg-nan-cy *n.* embarazo
preg-nant *adj.* embarazada
pre-his-tor-ic *adj.* prehistorico
prej-u-dice *n.* prejuicio
pre-lim-i-nar-y *n.* preliminar
pre-lude *n.* preludio
pre-med-i-tate *v.* premeditar
pre-miere *n.* estreno
pre-mi-um *n.* prima

pre-mo-ni-tion *n.* presentimiento
pre-oc-cu-pied *adj.* preocupado
prep-a-ra-tion *n.* preparación
pre-pare *v.* preparar(se)
prep-o-si-tion *n.* preposición
pre-pos-ter-ous *a.* absurdo
pre-req-ui-site *a.* requisito previo
pre-rog-a-tive *n.* prerrogativE
pre-scribe *v.* prescribir
pre-scrip-tion *n.* recenta
pres-ence *n.* presencia
pre-sent *adj.* presente, *v.* presentar, *n.* regalo
pres-en-ta-tion *n.* presentación
pre-serv-a-tive *a.* preservativo
pre-serve *v.* preservar; conservar
pre-side *v.* presidir
pres-i-dent *n.* presidente
press *n.* prensa; imprenta
pres-sure *n.* presión; urgencia
pres-ti-gid-i-ta-tion *n.* prestidigitación
pres-tige *n.* prestigio
pre0sume *v.* presumir; suponer
pre-tend *v.* pretender
pre-tense *n.* pretexto
pret-ty *a.* guapo; bonito; mono
pre-vail *v.* prevalecer; predominar
pre-vent *v.* impedir
pre-vi-ous *a.* previo
prey *n.* presa
price *n.* precio
price-less *a.* inapreciable
prick *v.* punzar
pride *n.* orgullo
priest *n.* sacerdote
prim *a.* estirado
pri-ma-ry *adj.* primario
prime *adj.* primero
prim-i-tive *adj.* primitivo
pri-mo-gen-i-ture *n.*

primogeniture
prince *n.* principe
prin-cess *n.* princesa
prin-ci-pal *n., adj.* principal
prin-ci-pal-i-ty *n.* principado
prin-ci-ple *n.* principio
print *v.* imprimir
print-ing *n.* imprenta
pri-or *a.* anterior
pri-or-i-ty *n.* prioridad
pri-or-y *n.* priorato
prism *n.* prism
pris-on *n.* carcel
pri-va-cy *n.* soledad
pri-vate *adj.* privado
priv-i-lege *n.* privilegio
prize *n.* premio
prob-a-bil-i-ty *n.* probabilidad
prob-a-ble *a.* probable
probe *n.* sonda
prob-lem *n.* problema
pro-ce-dure *n.* procedimiento
pro-ceed *v.* proceder
proc-ess *n.* proceso
pro-claim *v.* proclamar
pro-cliv-i-ty *n.* proclividad; inclinación
pro-cras-ti-nate *v.* dilatar; aplazar
pro-cure *v.* obtener; alcahuetear
prod *v.* ponzar
prod-i-gal *a.* prodigo
pro-d-i-gy *n.* prodigio
pro-duce *v.* producir
prod-uct *n.* producto
pro-fane *a.* profano
pro-fan-i-ty *n.* profanidad
pro-fes-sion *n.* profesión
pro-fes-sor *n.* profesora; profesor
pro-fi-cien-cy *n.* pericia
pro-file *n.* perfil
prof-it *n.* ganancia; beneficio
pro-found *a.* profundo
pro-fuse *a.* profuso
pro-fu-sion *n.* profusion
prog-e-ny *n.* progenie
prog-no-sis *n.* pronostico
pro-gram *n.* programa
prog-ress *n.* progreso;

desarrollo
pro-gres-sive *a.* progresivo
pro-hib-it *v.* prohibir
pro-hi-bi-tion *n.* prohibición
pro-ject *n.* proyecto, *v.* proyectar
pro-jec-tile *n.* proyectile
pro-lif-ic *adj.* prolifico
pro-logue *n.* prolongar
pro-long *v.* prolongar
prom-i-nent *a.* prominente
pro-mis-cu-ous *a.* promiscuo; libertino
prom-ise *v.* prometer, *n.* promesa
prom-on-to-ry *n.* promontorio
pro-mote *v.* promover; fomenter; ascender
pro-mo-tion *n.* promoción
prompt *a.* puntual; pronto
pro-noun *n.* pronombre
pro-nounce *v.* pronunciar(se)
pro-nounced *a.* marcado
pro-nun-ci-a-tion *n.* pronunciación
proof *n.* prueba
proof-read-er *n.* corrector de pruebas
prop *n.* apoyo
prop-a-gan-da *n.* propaganda
pro-pel *v.* propulsar
pro-pel-ler *n.* helice
pro-pen-si-ty *n.* propensión; inclinación
prop-er *a.* propio; apropiado; decente
prop-er-ty *n.* propiedad
proph-e-cy *n.* profeciz
proph-e-sy *v.* profetizar
proph-et *n.* profeta
pro-phy-lac-tic *a.* profilatico
pro-pi-tious *a.* propicio
pro-por-tion *n.* proporción
pro-pose *v.* proponer(se); declararse
prop-o-si-tion *n.* proposición; propuesta
pro-pri-e-tor *n.* propietario
pro-pri-e-ty *n.* corrección; decoro

pro-scribe v. proscribir

prose n. prosa

pros-e-cute v. proseguir

pros-pect n. perspectiva

pros-per v. prosperar

pros-per-i-ty n. prosperidad

pros-ti-tute n. prostituta; ramera

pros-trate v. postrar(se); derribar

pro-tag-o-nist n. protagonista

pro-tect v. proteger

pro-tein n. proteina

pro-test n. protesta, v. protestar

pro-to-col n. protocolo

pro-ton n. proton

pro-to-plasm n. protoplasma

pro-trude v. salir fuera

proud a. orgulloso; arrogante

prove v. probar

pro-verb n. proverbio

pro-vide v. proveer

prov-ince n. provincia

pro-vi-sion n. provision

pro-voc-a-tive a. provocativo; provocador

pro-voke v. provocar

prow n. proa

prox-y n. poder; apoderado

prude n. gasmona

prune n. ciruela pasa

pry v. meterse; fisgonear

psalm n. salmo

pseu-do-nym n. seudonimo

psych-e-del-ic a. psiquedelico

psy-chi-a-trist n. psiquiatra

psy-chi-a-try n. psiquiatria

psy-cho-a-nal-y-sis n. psicoanalisis

psy-cho-an-a-lyze v. psicoanalizar

psy-cho-log-i-cal adj. psicológico

psy-chol-o-gy n. psicología

psy-cho-sis n. psicosis

pto-maine n. ptomaina

pub n. taberna

pu-ber-ty n. pubertad

pub-lic n., adj. público

pub-li-ca-tion n. publicación

pub-lish v. publicar

pub-lish-er n. editor

puck-er v. arrugar

pud-ding n. pudin

pud-dle n. charco

puff v. soplar; inflar

pug-na-cious a. pugnaz

puke v. vomitar

pull v. tirar; arrastrar

pul-ley n. polea

pul-mo-nar-y a. pulmonar

pulp n. pulpa

pul-pit n. púlpito

pulse n. pulso

pul-ver-ize v. pulverizar

pum-ice n. piedra pómez

pump n. bomba

pump-kin n. calabaza

pun n. juego de palabras o vocablos

punch v. punzar

punc-tu-al adj. puntual

punc-tu-a-tion n. puntuación

punc-ture n. pinchazo

pun-ish v. castigar

pu-ny a. encanijado

pu-pa n. crisalida

pu-pil n. estudiante; pupila

pup-pet n. titere

pur-chase v. comprar

pure adj. puro

pur-ga-to-ry n. purgatorio

pu-ri-fy v. purificar

pu-ri-tan n. puritano

pur-ple adj. purpureo

pur-pose n. fin; proposito; resolucion

purr n. ronreneo

purse n. bolsa

pur-sue v. perseguir

pur-suit n. perseguimiento; busca; ocupación

pus n. pus

push v. empujar; apretar

puss-y n. gatito

put v. meter; poner(se)

pu-tre-fy v. pudrir

pu-trid a. odrido

put-ty n. masilla

pyr-a-mid n. piramide

pyre n. pira

py-thon n. pitón

quack v. graznar; n. graznido
quad-ran-gle n. cuadrangulo
quad-rant n. cuadrante
quad-rate adj. cuadrante
quad-rat-ic adj. cuadratico
quad-ri-ceps n. cuadriceps
quad-ri-lat-er-al n., adj. cuadrilátero
quad-ri-ple-gi-a n. cuadriplejia
quad-ri-ple-gic adj. cuadriplejico
quad-ru-ple v. cuadruplicar(se)
quag-mire n. pantano
quail n. codorniz
quake v. temblar
qual-i-fi-ca-tion n. calificacion
qual-i-fied adj. acreditado; capacitado
qual-i-fi-er n. calificativo
qual-i-fy v. habilitar
qual-i-fy-ing adj. eliminatoria
qual-i-ta-tive adj. cualitativo
qual-i-ty n. calidad
qualm n. duda
quan-ti-ta-tive adj. cuantitativo
quan-ti-ty n. cantidad
quar-an-tine n. cuarentena
quar-rel n. riña
quar-rel-er n. pendenciero
quar-rel-some adj. pendeciero
quar-ry n. cantera
quart n. cuarto
quar-ter n. cuarto
qua-ter-deck n. alcazar
quar-ter-ly adj. trimestral
quar-tet n. cuarteto
quartz n. cuarzo
qua-ver v. temblar
queen n. reina
quench v. matar; apagar
quench-a-ble adj. apagar
ques-tion n. pregunta
quick adj. listo; rapido
qui-et adj. silencioso
quit v. dejar; irse
quo-ta-tion n. cita
quote v. citar

rab-bi n. rabino
rab-bit n. conejo
rab-ble n. chusma
rab-id adj. rabioso
ra-bies n. rabia
rac-coon n. mapache
race v. correr de prisa, n. raza
rac-er n. corredor
race-track n. pista
ra-cial adj. racial
rac-ism n. racismo
ra-cist n. racista
rack n. potro
rack-et n. raqueta
rac-y adj. picante
ra-dar n. radar
ra-di-al adj. radial
ra-di-ance n. resplandor
ra-di-ant adj. radiante
ra-di-ate v. radiar; emitir; brillar
ra-di-a-tion n. radiación
ra-di-a-tor n. radiador
rad-i-cal n., adj. radical
rad-i-cle n. radícula
ra-di-o n. radio
ra-di-o-ac-tive adj. radiactivo
ra-di-o-ac-tiv-i-ty n. radiactividad
ra-di-o-broad-cast v. radiar
ra-di-o-gram n. radiograma
ra-di-o-graph n. radiografia
ra-di-ol-o-gist n. radiologo
ra-di-ol-o-gy n. radiologia
rad-ish n. rábano
ra-di-um n. radio
ra-di-us n. radio
ra-don n. radon
raff-ish adj. ostentoso
raf-fle n. rifa
raft n. balsa
raft-er n. cabrio
rag n. trapo
rage v. enfurecerse
rag-ged adj. desigual
raid v. atacar
rail n. carril
rail-ing n. baranda
rail-road n. ferrocarril
rail-way n. ferrocarril
rain v. llover, n. lluvia
rain-bow n. arco iris

rain-coat n. impereable
rain-drop n. gota de lluvia
rain-fall n. precipitación
rain-wear n. ropa impermeable
rain-y adj. lluvioso
raise v. criar; ;evantar
raised adj. repujado
rai-sin n. pasa
rake v. restrillar, n. rastro
ral-ly n. reunión, v. reunir(se)
ram n. carnero
ram-ble v. divagar
ram-bler n. vagabundo
ram-bunc-tious adj. alborotador
ram-i-fi-ca-tion n. ramificación
ramp n. rampa
ram-page n. alboroto
ramp-ant adj. destartalado
ranch n. hacienda
ranch-er n. hacendado
ran-cid adj. rancio
ran-cor n. rencor
ran-cor-ous adj. rencoroso
ran-dom adj. fortuito
range v. colocar; alinear
rang-er n. guardabosques
rank n. rango; fila
rank-ing adj. superior
ran-kle v. enconarse
ran-sack v. saquear
ran-som v. rescatar, n. rescate
rant v. vociferar
rap v. golpear
ra-pa-cious adj. rapaz
ra-pac-i-ty n. rapacidad
rape v. violar, n. violación
rap-id adj. rapido
ra-pid-i-ty n. rapidez
rap-ine n. rapiña
rap-ist n. violador
rap-port n. relación
rapt adj. absorto
rap-ture n. rapto
rap-tur-ous adj. extasiado
rare adj. poco; raro
rar-e-fied adj. refinado
rar-e-fy v. enrarecer(se)
rar-ing adj. impaciente

rar-i-ty n. rareza
ras-cal n. bribón
rash n. erupción
rash-er n. tocino
rasp-ber-ry n. frambuesa
rasp-y adj. aspero
rat n. rata
rate v. tasar, n. razón
rath-er adv. un poco
rat-i-fy v. ratificar
rat-ing n. popularidad; clasificación
ra-tio n. proporción
ra-ti-oc-i-nate v. raciocinar
ra-tion n. ración
ra-tion-al adj. racional
ra-tion-ale n. explicación; raxon
ra-tion-al-i-ty n. racionalidad
ra-tion-al-i-za-tion n. racionalización
ra-tion-al-ize v. racionalizar
ra-tion-ing n. racionamiento
rat-tle n. ruido
rat-trap n. ratonera
raun-chy adj. sucio
rav-age v. destruir, n. estrago
rave v. delirar
rav-el v. deshilar(se)
ra-ven n. cuervo
ra-ven-ous adj. coraz
ra-vine n. barranco
rav-ing adj. extraordinario
rav-ish v. raptar
rav-ish-ing adj. encantador
raw adj. novato; crudo
ray n. rayo
ray-on n. rayón
reach n. alcance, v. extenderse; alargar
re-act v. reaccionar
re-ac-tion n. reacción
re-ac-tion-ar-y n. reaccionario
re-ac-tor n. reactor
read v. decir; leer
read-ing n. lección
re-ad-just v. reajustar
read-y adj. pront; listo
re-al adj. real
re-al-i-ty n. realidad
re-al-ize v. realizar

re-al-ly adv. realmente
realm n. reino
ream n. resma
rea-son v. razonar, n. razon
rea-son-a-ble adj. razonable
reb-el adj., n. rebelde
re-bel-lion n. rebelión
re-buke n. reprimenda
re-call v. retirar; hacer
re-cant v. retractar(se)
re-cede v. retroceder
re-ceipt n. ingresos
re-ceive v. acoger; recibir
re-cent adj. reciente
re-cep-ta-cle n. receptaculo
re-cep-tion n. recepción
re-cess n. nicho
re-ces-sion n. retroceso
rec-i-pe n. receta
re-cip-ro-cal adj. reciproco
re-cit-al n. recital
rec-i-ta-tion n. recitación
re-cite v. recitar
reck-on v. considerar
re-claim v. reclamar
re-cline v. recostar(se)
rec-luse n. recluso
r e c - o g - n i - t i o n n.
reconocimiento
rec-om-pense n. recompensa
rec-on-cile v. reconcinar
re-con-struct v. reconstruir
re-cord n. disco, v. registrar
re-couse n. recurso
re-cov-er v. recobrar
re-cruit n. recluta
rec-tan-gle n. rectangulo
rec-ti-fy v. rectificar
re-cu-per-ate v. recuperar
r e - c u - p e r - a - t i o n n.
recuperación
red adj. rojo
red-dish adj. rojizo
re-deem v. redimir
re-demp-tion n. redención
re-do v. rehacer
re-duce v. disminuir; reducir
re-duc-tion n. reducción
reef n. escollo
reek n. olor
re-fer v. referir(se)
ref-er-ee n. arbitro

ref-er-ence n. referencia
re-fill v. rellenar
re-fine v. refinar
re-fin-er-y n. refinería
re-flect v. reflejar
re-flec-tion n. reflejo
re-flex adj. reflejo
re-flex-ive adj. reflexive
re-form n. reforma, v. reformarse
re-form-a-to-ry n. reformatorio
re-fract v. refractar
re-frain v. refrenar
re-fresh v. refrescar
re-fresh-ment n. refresco
re-frig-er-ate v. refrigerar
ref-uge n. refugio
ref-u-gee n. refugiado
re-fund n. reembolso
re-fuse v. rehusar
re-gain v. recobrar
re-gard v. considerar
re-gen-er-ate v. regenerar
re-gent n. regente
re-gime n. regimen
reg-i-men n. regimen
reg-i-ment n. regimiento
re-gion n. región
reg-is-ter v. registrar, n. registro
re-gret n. sentimiento
reg-u-lar adj. regular
reg-u-la-tion n. regulación
re-ha-bil-i-tate v. rehabilitar
r e - h a - b i l - i - t a - t i o n n.
rehabilitacion
re-hearse v. ensayar
reign v. reinar, n. reinado
re-im-burse v. reembolsar
rein n. rienda
re-in-car-na-tion n. reencarnacion
re-in-force v. reforzar
re-it-er-ate v. reiterar
re-ject v. rechazar
re-lapse n. recaida, v. reincidir
re-late v. relatar
re-lat-ed adj. afin
re-la-tion n. relación
re-lax v. relajar
re-lease n. descargo

re-lent v. ceder
re-li-a-ble adj. confiable
rel-ic n. reliquia
re-lief n. alivio
re-lieve v. aliviar
re-li-gion n. religión
re-li-gious adj. religioso
rel-ish n. apetencia, v. gustar
re-ly v. contar; confiar
re-main v. quedar(se)
rem-e-dy n. remedio
re-mem-ber v. acordarse de
re-mem-brance n. recuerdo
re-mind v. recordar
rem-i-nis-cence n. reminiscencia
re-miss adj. descuidado
re-mit v. remitir
re-mit-tance n. remesa
re-morse n. remordimiento
re-mote adj. remoto
re-move v. apartar(se); quitar(se)
ren-ais-sance n. renacimiento
rend v. hander
ren-der v. volver
red-dez-vous v. reunirse
ren-e-gade n. renegado
re-new v. renovar(se)
re-nounce v. renunciar
re-nown n. renombre
rent v. alquilar, n. alquiler
re-pair v. remendar; reparar
re-pay v. pagar; recompensar
re-peat v. repetir(se)
re-pel v. repeler
re-per-cus-sion n. repersución
rep-er-toire n. repertorio
re-place v. reponer
re-ply n. respuesta
re-port v. informar
rep-re-hen-si-ble adj. reprensible
rep-re-sen-ta-tion n. representación
re-press v. reprimir
rep-ri-mand v. reprender
re-proach n. reproche
re-pro-duce v. reproducir

rep-tile n. reptil
re-pub-lic n. república
re-pulse n. repulsa
rep-u-ta-tion n. reputación
re-quest v. rogar
re-quire v. necesitar; exigir
res-cue n. rescate
re-search v. investigar
re-sent v. resentirse de
res-er-va-tion n. reservación
re-serve v. reservar
re-side v. vivir; residir
res-i-dent n., adj. residente
re-sign v. resignarse
res-ig-na-tion n. resignación
res-in n. resina
re-sist v. resistir
re-sist-ance n. resistencia
res-o-lu-tion n. resolución
re-solve v. resolver(se)
re-sort n. recurso
re-source n. recurso
re-spect n. respeto
re-spect-a-ble adj. respetable
re-spect-ful adj. respetuoso
re-spect-ing prep. respecto
re-spec-tive adj. respectivo
res-pi-ra-tion n. respiración
res-pi-ra-tor n. respirador
res-pi-ra-to-ry adj. respiratorio
re-spire v. respirar
res-pite n. respiro
re-splen-dent adj. resplandeciente
re-spond v. responder
re-spon-dent adj. resplandeciente
re-sponse n. respuesta
re-spon-si-bil-i-ty n. responsabilidad
re-spon-si-ble adj. responsable
rest n. descansar
res-tau-rant n. restaurante
rest-ful adj. sosegado
res-ti-tute v. restituir
res-ti-tu-tion n. restitución
rest-less adj. inquieto
res-to-ra-tion n. restauración
re-store v. restaurar
re-strain v. refrenar

re-strict v. restringir
re-stric-tion n. restricción
re-sult n. resultado, v. resultar
re-sus-ci-tate v. resucitar
re-tain v. retener
re-tard v. retardar
ret-i-na n. retina
re-tire v. retirarse
re-tract v. retractar(se)
re-trieve v. recobrar
ret-ro-ac-tive adj. retroactivo
re-turn v. volver
re-un-ion n. reunión
re-veal v. revelar
rev-e-la-tion n. revelación
re-venge v. vengar(se)
re-verse adj. inverso
re-view n. resena
re-vise v. repasar; revisar
re-vi-sion n. revision
re-vive v. revivir
re-voke v. revocar
rev-o-lu-tion n. revolución
rev-o-lu-tion-ary n., adj. revolucionario
re-volve v. revolverse
re-volv-er n. revolver
re-ward n. recompensa
rhap-so-dy n. rapsodia
rhe-tor-i-cal adj. retorico
rheu-mat-ic adj. reumatico
rheu-ma-tism n. reumatismo
rhyme v. rimar, n. rima
rhythm n. ritmo
rib n. costilla
rib-bon n. cinta
rice n. arroz
rich adj. fertil; rico
rid v. librar(se)
rid-dle n. acertijo
ride v. montar
rid-i-cule v. ridiculizar
ri-dic-u-lous adj. ridículo
ri-fle n. rifle
right adj. exacto; derecho
rig-id adj. rigido
rig-or-ous adj. riguroso
rind n. piel
ring v. sonar, n. anillo
rink n. pista
rip v. arrancar; rasgar
ripe adj. maduro

rise v. subir; levantarse
risk n. riesgo
rite n. rito
rit-u-al n., adj. ritual
ri-val-ry n. rivalidad
riv-er n. rio
roach n. cucaracha
road n. camino
roar v. rugir
rob v. robar
robe n. bata
ro-bust adj. robusto
rock n. roca
ro-dent n. roedor
roll n. rollo; lista
ro-mance n. amorio
ro-man-tic adj. romántico
ro-man-ti-cism n. romanticismo
roof n. tejado
room n. sitio; cuarto
roost-er n. gallo
root n. raiz
rope n. cuerda
rose n. rosa
ros-y adj. rosado
ro-tate v. girar
rough adj. tosco; aspero
rou-lette n. ruleta
round prep. alrededor de, adj. redondo
route n. ruta
rou-tine n. rutina
roy-al-ty n. realeza
rub v. rozar; fregar
rub-bish n. basura
ru-by n. rubi
rud-der n. timón
rude adj. tosco; rudo
ru-di-ment n. rudimento
rug n. alfombra
ru-in v. arruinar, n. ruina
rule v. gobernar, n. regla
rul-er n. regla
rum n. ron
ru-mor n. rumor
run v. correr
run-ning adj. corriente
ru-ral adj. rural
rust n. orín
rus-tic adj. rustico
ruth-less adj. despiadado
rye n. centeno

Sab-bath *n.* domingo

sa-ber *n.* sable

sa-ble *n.* cabellina

sab-o-tage *v.* sabotear, *n.* sabotaje

sac-cha-rin *n.* sacrina

sack *n.* saco

sac-ra-ment *n.* sacramento

sacred *adj.* sagrado

sac-ri-fice *v.* sacrificar, *n.* sacrificio

sac-ri-lege *n.* sacrilegio

sad *adj.* triste

sad-den *v.* entristecer

sad-dle *v.* ensillar

sad-ism *n.* sadismo

sa-fa-ri *n.* safari

safe *adj.* seguro

safe-ty *n.* seguridad

sag *v.* combar(se)

sa-ga *n.* saga

sage *n., adj.* sabio

sail *v.* nevegar, *n.* vela

sail-or *n.* marinero

saint *n., adj.* santo

sake *n.* consideración; motivo

sal-ad *n.* ensalada

sal-a-man-der *n.* salamandra

sal-a-ry *n.* salario

sale *n.* venta

sa-line *n.* salino

sa-li-va *n.* saliva

sal-low *n.* cetrino

sal-ly *n.* salida

salm-on *n.* salmón

sa-lon *n.* salón

sa-loon *n.* salón

salt *n.* sal

sal-u-tar-y *adj.* saludable

sal-u-ta-tion *n.* saludo

sa-lute *v.* sakudar

sal-vage *n.* salvamento

sal-va-tion *n.* salvación

salve *n.* unguento

sal-vo *n.* salva

same *adj.* mismo

sam-ple *v.* probar

san-a-to-ri-um *n.* sanatorio

sanc-ti-fy *v.* santificar

sanc-tion *n.* sanción

sanc-ti-ty *n.* santidad

sanc-tu-ar-y *n.* santuario

sand *n.* arena

san-dal *n.* sandalia

sand-stone *n.* arenisca

sand-wich *n.* bocadillo

sand-y *adj.* arenoso

sane *adj.* sano

san-gui-nar-y *a.* sanguinario

san-i-tar-i-um *n.* sanatorio

san-i-tar-y *adj.* sanitario

san-i-ta-tion *n.* instalación sanitaria

san-i-ty *n.* juicio sano

sap *n.* savia

sa-pi-ent *a.* sabio

sap-phire *n.* zafiro

sar-casm *n.* sarcasmo

sar-cas-tic *adj.* sarcastico

sar-coph-a-gus *n.* sarcofago

sar-dine *n.* sardina

sa-ri, sa-ree *n.* sari

sash *n.* faja

sas-sy *adj.* descarado

sa-tan *n.* Satanas

sa-tan-ic *a.* satanico

sate *v.* saciar; dsatisfacer

sat-el-lite *n.* satelite

sa-ti-ate *v.* saciar

sat-in *n.* raso

sa-tire *n.* satira

sat-is-fac-tion *n.* satisfacción

sat-is-fy *v.* satisfacer

sat-u-rate *v.* saturar

Sat-ur-day *n.* sabado

sa-tyr *n.* satiro

sauce *n.* salsa

sau-cer *n.* platillo

sau-sage *n.* salchicha

sav-age *n., adj.* salvaje

save *v.* ahorrar; salvar

sav-ing *n.* economia

sav-ior *n.* salvador

sa-vor *n.* sabor

saw *n.* sierra

sax-o-phone *n.* saxofón

say *v.* decir

say-ing *n.* dicho

scab *n.* costra

scaf-fold *n.* andamio

scald *v.* escaldar

scale *n.* escala

scal-lop *n.* venera; feston

scalp *n.* pericraneo

scal-pel n. escalpelo
scan v. escundrinar
scan-dal n. escandalo
scan-dal-ize v. escandalizar
scant adj. escaso
scant-y adj. escaso
scape-goat n. cabeza de turco
scar n. cicatriz
scarce adj. escaso
scare v. asustar
scare-crow n. espantajo; espantapajaros
scarf n. bufanda
scar-let n. escarlata
scat-ter v. esparcir
scav-en-ger n. basurero
scene n. vista; escena
scen-er-y n. paisaje
scent n. pista; olor
sched-ule n. horario
scheme v. intrigar
schism n. cisma
schiz-o-phre-ni-a n. esquizofrenia
schol-ar n. erudito; alumno
schol-ar-ship n. erudición; beca
scho-las-tic adj. escolar
school n. escuela
sci-ence n. ciencia
sci-en-tist n. cientifico
scim-i-tar n. cimitarra
scis-sors n. tijeras
scoff v. mofarse
scold v. reganar
scoop n. paleta
scoot-er n. patinete
scope n. alcance
scorch v. chamuscar
score n. cuenta
scorn n. desden
scor-pi-on n. escorpión
scotch v. frustrar
scoun-drel n. canalla
scour v. fregar; recorrer
scout n. explorador
scowl v. poner mal gesto
scrag-gy a. escarnado
scram-ble v. revolver
scrap n. fragmento; sobras
scrape v. raer
scratch v. rayar; rasgunar; rascar

scrawl n. garrabatos; garrapatos
scream n. grito
screen n. biombo; pantalla
screw v. atornillar, n. tornillo
scrib-ble v. garrapatear
scrim-mage n. arrebatina
script n. letra cursiva; guion
scrip-ture n. Sagrada Escritura
scroll n. rollo de pergamino
scrub v. fregar
scru-ple n. escrupulo
scru-ti-nize v. escundrinar
scru-ti-ny n. escrutinio
scuf-fle v. pelear
sculp-tor n. escultor
sculp-ture v. esculpir, n. escultura
scum n. espuma
scur-ry v. darse prisa
scur-vy n. escorbuto
scut-tle v. echar a pique
scythe n. guadana
sea n. mar
seal n. foca
seal n. sello v. cerrar
seam n. costura
sea-man n. marinero
seam-stress n. costurera
seam-y a. asqueroso
se-ance n. sesión de espiritistas
sea-port n. puerto de mar
sear v. marchitar; chamuscar
search v. buscar
sea-shore n. orilla del rnar
sea-sick-ness n. mareo
sea-son n. estación
sea-son-ing n. condimento
seat v. sentar, n. asiento
sea-weed n. alga marina
se-clude v. aislar
se-clu-sion n. retiro
sec-ond n., adj. segundo
sec-ond-ar-y adj. secundario
sec-ond-hand a. de segunda mano
sec-ond-rate a. inferior
se-cre-cy n. secreto
se-cret n., adj. secreto
sec-re-tar-y n. secretario

se-crete v. secretar; ovultar
se-cre-tion n. secreción
sect n. secta
sec-tion n. sección
sec-tor n. sector
sec-u-lar adj. secular
se-cure adj. seguro
se-cu-ri-ty n. seguridad
se-date adj. sosegado
sed-a-tive n. sedativo
sed-en-tar-y a. sedentario
sed-i-ment n. sedimento
se-di-tion n. sedición
se-duce v. seducir
se-duc-tion n. seducción
see v. percibir; ver
seed n. semilla; simiente
seed-y a. desharrapado
seek v. buscar; solicitar
seem v. parecer
seem-ly a. decoroso; cor-
recto
seep v. rezumarse
se-er n. profeta
seg-ment n. segmento
seg-re-gate v. segregar
s e g - r e - g a - t i o n n.
segregación
s e i s - m o - g r a p h n. sis-
mografo
seize v. apoderarse de; asir
sei-zure n. asimiento
sel-dom adv. rarmente
se-lect adj. selecto, v. elegir
se-lec-tion n. selección
self n. See my-self, yourself
s e l f - c e n - t e r e d a.
egocentrico
self-com-mand n. dominio
de si mismo
self-con-fi-dence n. con-
fianza en si mismo
self con-scious a. timido
self-control n. dominio de si
mismo
self-ev-i-dent a. patente
s e l f - e x - p l a n - a - t o - r y a.
evidente; obvio
s e l f - g o v - e r n - m e n t n.
autonomia
self-im-por-tance n. presunción
self-ish a. egoista; inter-

esado
self-less a. desinteresado
self-re-li-ance n. confianza
en si mismo
self-same a. mismo
self-suf-fi-cient adj. independiente
self-will n. terquedad
sell v. vender
se-man-tics n. semantica
sem-blance n. parecido;
apariencia
se-men n. semen
se-mes-ter n. semestre
sem-i-cir-cle n. semicirculo
sem-i-co-lon n. punto y
coma
sem-i-fi-nal adj. semifinal
sem-i-nar n. seminario
sem-i-nar-y n. seminario
sem-i-of-fi-cial adj. semiofi-
cial
sem-i-pre-cious adj. semi-
precioso
sem-i-week-ly a. bisemanal
sen-ate n. senado
sen-a-tor n. senador
send v. mandar; enviar
se-nile adj. senil
sen-ior adj. superior
sen-ior-i-ty n. antiguedad
sen-sa-tion n. sensación
sense v. percibir, n. sentido
semse-less a. sin sentido;
insensato
sen-si-bil-i-ty n. sensibilidad
sen-si-ble adj. razonable
sen-si-tive adj. delicado
sen-si-tiv-i-ty n. delicadeza
sen-so-ry adj. sensorio
sen-su-al adj. sensual
sen-su-ous adj. sensorio
sen-tence n. frase
sen-ti-ment n. sentimiento
sen-ti-nel n. centinela
sen-try n. centinela
se-pal n. sepalo
sep-a-rate v. separar(se)
sep-a-ra-tion n. separación
Sep-tem-ber n. septiembre
sep-tic adj. septico
sep-ul-cher n. sepulcro
se-quel n. resultado

se-quence n. sucesión
sequestered a. aislado
se-ques-ter v. separar; aislar
se-quin n. lentejuela
ser-aph n. serafín
ser-e-nade n. serenata
se-rene n. sereno
se-ren-i-ty n. serenidad
serf n. siervo
ser-geant n. sargento
se-ri-al a. en serie
se-ries n. serie
se-ri-ous adj. serio
ser-mon n. sermon
ser-pent n. serpiente
se-rum n. suero
serv-ant n. serviente; ser-
   vidor
serve v. servir
serv-ice n. servicio
serv-ice-man n. militar
ser-vile a. servil
ses-sion n. sesion
set v. fijar; poner(se)
set-back n. revés
set-ting n. engaste
set-tle v. arreglar; resolver
set-tle-ment n. colonización
set-tler n. colono
seven adj., n. siete
sev-en-teen adj. diecisiete
sev-enth n., adj. séptimo
sev-en-ty n., adj. setenta
sev-er v. cortar
sev-er-al a. varios; diversos
se-vere adj. severo
se-ver-i-ty n. severidad
sew v. coser
sew-er n. albañal
sex n. sexo
sex-tet n. sexteto
sex-u-al adj. sexual
sex-y a. provocativo
shab-by a. raído; en mal estado
shack n. choza
shack-le n. grillete
shade v. sombrear, n.
   sombra
shad-ing n. degradación
shad-ow n. sombra
shadowy a. umbroso; vago
shad-y adj. sombreado

shaft n. eje; pozo
shag-gy adj. velludo
shake v. estrechar; temblar
shak-y a. poso profundo
sham v. fingir(se), adj. fin-
   gido
sham-bles n. desorden
shame n. verguenza
shame-less al desvergon-
   zado
sham-poo n. champú
shan-ty n. choza
shape v. formar, n. forma
shape-ly a. bien formado
share n. parte
shark n. tiburón
sharp adj. vivo; cortante
sharp-en v. afilar; sacar
   punta
shat-ter v. hacer(se)
   pedazos
shave v. afeitar(se)
shav-er n. maquina de
   afeitar
shawl n. chal
she pron. ella
shears n. tijeras grandes
shed v. quitarse; verter
sheen n. lustre
sheep n. oveja
sheep-ish a. timido
sheer adj. escarpado
sheet n. sábana; hoja;
   lamina
sheik, sheikh n. jeque
shelf n. estante
shell n. cascara
shel-lac, shel-lack n. goma
   laca
shell-fish n. marisco
shel-ter n. refugio
shep-herd n. pastor
sher-bet n. sorbete
sher-iff n. sheriff
sher-ry n. jerez
shield n. escudo
shift v. mover(se); cambiar
shil-ly-shal-ly v. vacilar
shim-mer v. rielar
shin n. espinilla
shine v. pulir; brillar
shin-gle n. ripia; tejamanil
shin-y adj. brillante

ship *n.* barco

ship-ment *n.* embarque; envio

ship-shape *a.* en buen orden

ship-wreck *n.* naufragio

shirk *v.* evitar; esquivar

shirt *n.* camisa

shiv-er *v.* temblar

shock *n.* susto; choque; postracion nerviosa

shod-dy *a.* de pacotilla; falso

shoe *n.* zapato

shoe-horn *n.* calzador

shoe-lace *n.* cordon

shoot *v.* espigar; disparar

shoot-ing *n.* tiro; caza con escopeta

shoot-ing star *n.* estrella fugaz

shop *n.* taller; tienda

shop-keep-er *n.* tendero

shore *n.* playa

short *adj.* breve; corto

short-age *n.* deficienca; escasez

short cir-cuit *n.* corto circuito

short-com-ing *n.* defecto

short-cut *n.* atajo

short-en *v.* acortar(se)

short-hand *n.* taquigrafia

short-lived *a.* de breve duración

short-tem-pered *a.* de mal genio

shot *n.* tiro; tirador

shot-gun *n.* escopeta

should *aux. v. past form of* **shall**

shoul-der *n.* hombro

shout *v.* gritar, *n.* grito

shov-el *n.* pala

show *v.* mostrar(se)

show-er *v.* ducharse, *n.* ducha

show-man *n.* director de espectaculos

shred *v.* hacer tiras

shrew *n.* arpia

shrewd *a.* sagaz; prudente

shriek *n.* chillar

shril *a.* estridente

shrimp *n.* camarón

shrine *n.* relicario

shrink *v.* encoger(se)

shriv-el *v.* encoger(se); secar(se)

shroud *n.* mortaja

shrub *n.* arbusto

shrub-ber-y *n.* arbustos

shrug *v.* encogerse de hombros

shud-der *v.* extremecerse

shuf-fle *v.* arrastrar los pies; *(cards)* barajar

shun *v.* evitar; apartarse de

shut *v.* cerrar(se)

shut-ter *n.* contraventana

shut-tle *n.* lanzadera

shy *adj.* timido

sic *v.* atacar

sick *adj.* enfermo

sick-en *v.* enfermar(se)

sick-le *n.* hoz

sick-ness *n.* enfermedad

side *n.* partido; lado

side-burns *n.* patillas

side-long *a.* lateral

side-track *v.* desviar

side-walk *n.* acera

side-ways *adv.* oblicuamente

siege *n.* sitio; cerco

sieve *n.* coladera; tamiz

sift *v.* tamizar

sigh *n.* suspiro, *v.* suspirar

sight *n.* visión; vista

sight-less *adj.* ciego

sight-see-ing *n.* visita de puntos de interes

sign *n.* signo; senal

sig-nal *n.* senal

sig-na-ture *n.* firma

sig-nif-i-cance *n.* significación

sig-ni-fy *v.* significar

si-lence *n.* silencio

si-lent *adj.* silencioso

sil-hou-ette *n.* silueta

sil-ic-a *n.* silice

sil-i-con *n.* silicio

silk *n.* seda

silk-y *adj.* sedoso

sil-ly *adj.* bobo

si-lo *n.* silo

silt *n.* sedimento
sil-ver *n.* plata
sil-ver-smith *n.* platero
sil-ver-ware *n.* vajilla de plata
sim-i-an *a.* simico
sim-i-lar *adj.* similar
sim-i-lar-i-ty *n.* semejanza
sim-mer *v.* hervir a fuego lento
sim-per *v.* sonreirse afectadamente
sim-ple *adj.* simple; facil
sim-pli-fy *v.* simplificar
sim-ply *adv.* sencillamente
sim-u-late *v.* simular
si-mul-ta-ne-ous *a.* simultaneo
sin *n.* pecado; transgresion
since *conj.* puesto que, *prep.* despues; desde
sin-cere *adj.* sincero
sin-cer-i-ty *n.* sinceridad
si-ne-cure *n.* sinecura
sin-ew *n.* tendón
sing *v.* cantar
sing-er *n.* cantante
sin-gle *adj.* único; soltero
sin-gle-hand-ed *a.* sin ayuda
sin-gu-lar *adj.* singular
sin-is-ter *adj.* siniestro
sink *v.* hundir(se)
sin-ner *n.* pecador
si-nus *n.* seno
sip *n.* sorbo, *v.* sorber
sir *n.* señor
sire *n.* padre
si-ren *n.* sirena
sir-loin *n.* solomillo
sis-ter *n.* hermana
sis-ter-in-law *n.* cuñada
sit *v.* sentar(se)
site *n.* sitio
sit-u-a-tion *n.* situacion
six *adj., n.* seis
six-teen *adj., n.* dieciséis
sixth *n., adj.* sexto
six-ty *adj., n.* sesenta
size *n.* talla
siz-zle *v.* chisporrotear
skate *v.* patinar
skel-e-ton *n.* esqueleto
skep-tic *n.* esceptico

skep-ti-cal *adj.* esceptico
sketch *n.* esbozo; bosquejo
skew-er *n.* broqueta
ski *v.* esquiar
skid *n.* patinazo
skill *n.* destreza; habilidad
skil-let *n.* sarten
skim *v.* expumar; desnatar; hojear
skin *n.* piel
skin-ny *adj.* flaco
skip *v.* saltar; pasar por alto
skir-mish *n.* escaramuza
skirt *n.* falda
skit *n.* parodia
skull *n.* cráneo
skunk *n.* mofeta
sky *n.* cielo
sky-rock-et *n.* cohete
sky-scrap-er *n.* rascacielos
slab *n.* table; plancha
slack *a.* flojo; negligente
slack-en *v.* aflojar
slacks *n.* pantalones
slag *n.* excoria
slam *v.* cerrarse de golpe
slan-der *v.* calumniar, *n.* calumnia
slang *n.* argot
slant *v.* inclinar(se); sesgar(se)
slap *v.* pegar
slash *v.* acuchillar
slat *n.* tabilla
slate *n.* pizarra; lista de candidatos
slaugh-ter *v.* matar
slave *n.* esclavo
slav-er-y *n.* esclavitud
slay *v.* matar
sled *n.* trineo
sleek *a.* liso; pulcro
sleep *v.* dormir
sleep-y *a.* sonoliento
sleet *n.* aguanieve
sleeve *n.* manga
sleigh *n.* trineo
slen-der *adj.* delgado
sleuth *n. inf.* detective
slice *v.* tajar, *n.* tajada
slide *v.* deslizarse
slight *a.* pequeño; de poco importancia

slim *adj.* delgado
slime *n.* legamo
sling *v.* tirar; suspender
slip *v.* introducir; deslizar(se); resbalar; escaparse
slip-knot *n.* nudo corredizo
slip-per *n.* zapatilla
slip-per-y *adj.* resbaladizo
slip-up *n. inf.* equivocación
slit *v.* cortar
sliv-er *n.* astilla
slob-ber *v.* babear; babosear
slo-gan *n.* mote
slop *v.* verter
slope *v.* inclinar(se), *n.* inclinación
slot *n.* ranura
slov-en-ly *a.* descuidado; desadeado
slow *adj.* torpe; lento
slow-ly *adv.* despacio
slung *n.* posta
slug-gish *a.* perezoso; lento
slum *n.* barrio bajo
slump *v.* hundires
slur *v.* comerse palabras; calumniar
slut *n.* pazpuerca; perra
sly *a.* astuto; disimulado
smack *v.* pegar
small *adj.* paqueño
small-pox *n.* viruelas
smart *adj.* listo; fresco
smash *v.* romper(se)
smear *v.* manchar; untar
smell *v.* oler
smile *n.* sonrisa, *v.* sonreir(se)
smirk *n.* sonrisa afectada
smith *n.* herrero
smock *n.* blusa de labrador
smog *n.* niebla y humo mezclados
smoke *v.* fumar, *n.* humo
smol-der *v.* arder sin llamas
smooch *v. inf.* besar
smooth *adj.* suave
smooth-er *v.* ahogar(se); sofocar(se)
smudge *n.* mancha
smug *a.* papado de si mismo

smug-gle *v.* pasar de (o hacer) contrabando
snack *n.* merienda
snag *n.* obstaculo; rasgon
snail *n.* caracol
snake *n.* culebra
snap-shot *n.* foto
snare *n.* trampa
snatch *n.* fragmento; trocito
sneak *v.* moverse a hurtadillas
sneer *v.* mofarse
sneeze *n.* estornudo, *v.* estornudar
sniff *v.* husmear; oler
snip *v.* tijeretear
snob *n.* esnob
snooze *v. inf.* dormitar
snore *n.* ronquido, *v.* roncar
snow *v.* nevar, *n.* nieve
snow-ball *n.* bola de nieve
snow-flake *n.* copo de nieve
snow-man *n.* figura de nieve
snub *v.* desairar
snug-gle *v.* arrimarse
so *conj.* por tanto, *adv.* así; tan
soak *v.* remojar
soap *n.* jabón
soar *v.* remontarse
sob *v.* sollozar
so-ber *adj.* sobrio
so-bri-quet, sou-bri-quet *n.* apodo
so-called *a.* llamado; supuesto
soc-cer *n.* fútbol
so-cia-ble *adj.* sociable
so-cial *adj.* social
so-cial-ism *n.* socialismo
so-cial-ize *v.* socializar
so-ci-e-ty *n.* sociedad
so-di-um *n.* sodio
so-fa *n.* sofa
soil *v.* manchar, *n.* tierra
so-lar *adj.* solar
sol-dier *n.* soldado
sole-ly *adv.* solamente
sol-emn *adj.* solemne
so-lic-it *v.* solicitar
sol-id *n., adj.* solido
sol-i-dar-i-ty *n.* solidaridad
sol-i-tar-y *adj.* solitario

sol-u-ble *adj.* soluble
so-lu-tion *n.* solución
solve *v.* resolver
sol-vent *adj.* solvente
som-ber *adj.* sombrio
some *pron.* algunos, *adj.* alguno
some-bo-dy *pron.* alguien
some-day *adv.* algun dia
some-one *pron.* alguién
some-thing *n.* algo
some-times *adv.* a veces
son *n.* hijo
song *n.* canción
son-in-law *n.* yerno
soon *adv.* pronto
soothe *v.* calmar
so-pran-o *n.* soprano
sor-did *adj.* vil
sor-ry *adj.* triste
so-so *adv.* así así
soul *n.* alma
sound *n.* ruido
soup *n.* sopa
sour *adj.* agrio
south *n.* sur
south-east *n.* sudeste
south-ern *adj.* del sur
south-west *n.* sudoeste
sov-er-eign *n., adj.* soberano
space *v.* espaciar, *n.* espacio
spa-cious *adj.* espacioso
spa-ghet-ti *n.* espagueti
spasm *n.* espasmo
spas-mod-ic *adj.* espasmodico
spas-tic *adj.* espastico
spat-u-la *n.* espatula
speak *v.* decir; hablar
spear *n.* lanza
spe-cial *adj.* especial
spe-cial-ist *n.* especialista
spe-cial-ize *v.* especializar(se)
spe-cial-ty *n.* especialidad
spe-cies *n.* especie
spe-cif-ic *adj.* especifico
spec-i-fy *v.* especificar
spec-ta-cle *n.* espectaculo
spec-tac-u-lar *adj.* espectacular
speech-less *adj.* mudo

speed *v.* apresurarse; acelerar
spell *v.* deletrear
spell-bind *v.* encantar
spell-ing *n.* ortografía
spend *v.* gastar
sperm *n.* esperma
sperm-whale *n.* cachalote
sphere *n.* esfera
spher-i-cal *adj.* esferico
spice *n.* especia
spic-y *adj.* picante
spi-der *n.* arana
spill *v.* verter(se)
spin-ach *n.* espinaca
spi-nal *adj.* espinal
spine *n.* espinazo
spi-ral *adj., n.* espiral
spir-it *n.* espiritu
spir-it-u-al *adj.* espiritual
spir-it-u-al-ism *n.* espiritismo
spit *v.* escupir
spite *n.* rencor
splin-ter *n.* astilla
split *v.* dividir; separarse
spoil *v.* echar(se); estropear(se)
spo-ken *adj.* hablado
sponge *n.* esponja
spon-gy *adj.* esponjoso
spon-ta-ne-i-ty *n.* espontaneidad
spon-ta-ne-ous *adj.* espontaneo
spoon *n.* cuchara
spoon-ful *n.* cucharada
spo-rad-ic *adj.* esporadico
spore *n.* espora
sport *n.* deporte
sports-man *n.* deportista
spot *n.* mancha
spot-ty *adj.* manchado
spouse *n.* esposa; esposo
spread *v.* diseminar
spring *n.* primavera, *v.* saltar
spring-time *n.* primavera
spruce *n.* picea
spu-ri-ous *adj.* espurio
spy *v.* espiar
squad-ron *n.* escuadron
squal-id *adj.* desalinado
square *adj., n.* cuadrado

squeak n. chirrido, v. chillar
sta-bil-i-ty n. estabilidad
sta-ble adj. estable
sta-di-um n. estadio
stage n. etapa
stain n. mancha
stair n. escalón
stair-way n. escalera
stamp n. sello
stam-pede n. estampida
stand v. colocar
stand-ing adj. derecho
sta-ple n. grapa
sta-pler n. grabadora
star n. estrella
star-less adj. sin estrellas
star-ry adj. estrellado
start v. comenzar; empezar
state n. estado
stat-ic adj. estatico
sta-tion n. estación
sta-tis-tic n. estadistico
stat-ue n. estatua
stay v. quedar(se)
steal v. robar
steam v. empanar, n. vapor
steam-y adj. vaporoso
stem n. tallo
step n. escalera
step-broth-er n. hermanastro
step-daugh-ter n. hijastra
step-fa-ther n. padrastro
step-moth-er n. madrastra
step-sis-ter n. hermanastra
step-son n. hijastro
ste-ril-i-ty n. esterilidad
stick n. palo
stick-y adj. viscoso
stiff adj. rigido
still adj. tranquilo
stim-u-lant n. estimulante
stim-u-late v. estimular
stink v. hedor
stip-u-late v. estipular
stip-u-la-tion n. estipulación
stock-ing n. media
sto-i-cal adj. estoico
stom-ach n. estomago
stone n. piedra
stop v. terminar
stop-light n. semaforo
store n. almacen; tienda

stork n. cigüeña
storm n. tempestad
sto-ry n. piso; historia
stove n. estufa
straight adj. directo
strange adj. extraño; raro
stra-te-gic adj. estrategico
strat-e-gy n. estrategia
straw n. pajilla
straw-ber-ry n. fresa
stream n. arroyo
street n. calle
strength n. vigor; fuerza
strict adj. estricto
strike v. atacar; golpear
string n. cordel
stripe n. raya
striped adj. rayado
strong adj. robusto; fuerte
struc-tur-al adj. estructural
stu-dent n. estudiante
stu-di-o n. estudio
stud-y v. estudiar
stu-pen-dous adj. estupendo
stu-pid adj. estupido
style n. modo; estilo
sub-di-vide v. subdividir
sub-ject adj., n. sujeto
sub-jec-tive adj. subjetivo
sub-lease v. subarrendar
sub-let v. subarrendar
sub-li-mate v. sublimar
sub-li-ma-tion n. sublimación
sub-lime a. sublime
sub-lim-i-ty n. sublimidad
sub-ma-rine n. submarino
sub-merge v. sumergir(se)
sub-mer-gence n. sumersión
sub-merse v. sumergir(se)
sub-mer-sion n. sumersión
sub-mis-sion n. sumisión
sub-mis-sive a. sumiso
sub-mit v. someter(se); presentar
sub-nor-mal adj. anormal
sub-or-di-nate a. subordinado; secundario; dependiente
sub-or-di-na-tion n. subordinacion

sub-poe-na, sub-pe-na *n.* citación; comparendo

sub-scribe *v.* subscribir(se)

sub-scrip-tion *n.* subscripción

sub-se-quent *a.* subsiguiente

sub-ser-vi-ent *a.* servil

sub-side *v.* bajar; calmarse

sub-sid-i-ar-y *a.* ubsidiario

sub-si-dize *v.* subvencional

sub-si-dy *n.* subvención; subsidio

sub-sist *v.* subsistir; existir

sub-sis-tence *n.* subsistencia

sub-stance *n.* esencia; substancia

sub-stan-tial *adj.* substancial

sub-stan-ti-a-tion *n.* comprobación; justificación

sub-stan-tive *n.* substantivo

sub-sti-tute *n.* substituto, *v.* substituir

sub-sti-tu-tion *n.* substitución; reemplazo

sub-ter-fuge *n.* subterfugio

sub-ter-ra-ne-an *a.* subterraneo

sub-ti-tle *n.* subtitulo

sub-tle *a.* sutil; ingenioso; delicado; astuto

sub-tle-ty *n.* sutileza

sub-tract *v.* substraer

sub-trac-tion *n.* substracción; resta

sub-urb *n.* suburbio

sub-ur-ban *a.* suburbano

sub-ver-sion *n.* subversión

sub-ver-sive *a.* sobversivo

sub-vert *v.* subvertir

sub-way *n.* metro

suc-ceed *v.* suceder

suc-cess *n.* exito

suc-cess-ful *a.* prospero; afortunado

suc-ces-sion *n.* sucesión

suc-ces-sor *n.* sucesor

suc-cinct *a.* sucinto

suc-cor *n.* soccorro; auxilio

suc-cu-lent *a.* suculento

suc-cumb *v.* sucumbir

such *adv.* tan, *pron., adj.* tal

suck *v.* chupar; mamar

suck-er *n.* piruli

suck-le *v.* lactar; amamantar

suc-tion *n.* succión

suf-fer *v.* sufrir

suf-fer-ance *n.* tolerancia

suf-fice *v.* bastar

suf-fi-cien-cy *n.* suficiencia

suf-fix *n.* sufijo

suf-fo-cate *v.* sofocar; asfixiar

suf-frage *n.* sufragio

suf-fuse *v.* extender; banar

suf-fu-sion *n.* difusión

sug-ar *n.* azucar

sug-ar-y *adj.* azucarado

sug-gest *v.* sugerir

sug-ges-tion *n.* sugestión

sug-ges-tive *a.* sugestivo

su-i-cide *n.* suicida

suit *n.* traje

suit-a-ble *a.* apropiado

suit-case *n.* maleta

suite *n.* juego; serie

sul-fur, sul-phur *n.* azufre

sul-fu-ric ac-id *n.* acido sulfurico

sulk *v.* estar de mal humor

sul-len *a.* hosco

sul-ly *v.* manchar

sul-tan *n.* sultan

sul-tan-ate *n.* sultanato

sul-try *a.* bochornoso

sum *v.* sumar, *n.* suma

sum-ma-ry *adj.* sumario

sum-mer *n.* verano

sun *n.* sol

Sun-day *n.* domingo

sun-down *n.* puesta del sol

sun-flow-er *n.* girasol

sun-glass-es *n.* gafas de sol

sun-light *n.* luz del sol

sun-rise *n.* salida del sol

su-per-fi-cial *adj.* superficial

su-per-in-tend *v.* superentender

su-pe-ri-or *n., adj.* superior

su-pe-ri-or-i-ty *n.* superioridad

su-per-mar-ket *n.* supermercado

su-per-sti-tion *n.* superstición

su-per-sti-tious *adj.* super-
sticioso

su-pine *adj.* supino

sup-per *n.* cena

sup-ple-ment *n.* suplemento

sup-pli-cate *v.* suplicar

sup-pose *v.* suponer

sup-pres-sion *n.* supresión

su-prem-a-cy *n.* supremacia

su-preme *adj.* supremo

sure *adj.* seguro

sure-ly *adv.* seguramente

sur-face *n.* superficie

sur-geon *n.* cirujano

sur-ger-y *n.* cirugía

sur-name *n.* apellido

sur-prise *v.* sorprender, *n.*
sorpresa

sur-vive *v.* sobrevivir

sus-cep-ti-ble *adj.* susceptible

sus-pend *v.* suspender

sus-pense *n.* incertidumbre

sus-pen-sion *adj.* suspen-
sión

sus-pi-cion *n.* sospecha;
sombra

sus-pi-cious *adj.*
sospechoso

sus-tain *v.* sustentar

sus-te-nance *n.* sustento

svelte *a.* esbelto

swab *n.* torunda

swan *n.* cisne

swap *v.* cambiar

swarm *n.* enjambre

swash-buck-ler *n.*
espadachin

swat *v.* matar

sway *v.* bambolearse; inclinar

swear *v.* jurar

swear-word *n.* palabrota

sweat *n.* sudor, *v.* sudar

sweat-y *adj.* sudoroso

sweet *adj.* dulce

sweet-en *v.* azucarar; endul-
zar

sweet-heart *n.* querida;
novia

sweet-meat *n.* dulce

swell *v.* hinchar(se)

swerve *v.* torcer(se);
desviar(se)

swift *a.* veloz

swig *v.* beber a grandes
tragos

swill *n.* bazofia

swim *n.* natación, *v.* nadar

swim-mer *n.* nadador

switch *v.* cambiar

swiv-el *n.* alacran,
torniquete; girar

swoon *n.* desmayo

sword *n.* espada

sword-belt *n.* talabarte

sword-fish *n.* pez espads

sword-play *n.* esgrima

swordsman *n.* espadachin

syc-a-more *n.* sicomoro

syc-o-phant *n.* adulador

syl-lab-i-cate *v.* silabear

syl-lab-i-ca-tion *n.* silabeo

syl-lab-i-fy *v.* silabear

syl-la-ble *n.* silaba

syl-la-bus *n.* resumen;
programa

syl-van *a.* silvestre

sym-bol *n.* simbolo

sym-bol-ic *adj.* simbolico

sym-bol-ism *n.* simbolismo

sym-bol-ize *v.* simbolizar

sym-me-try *n.* simetría

sym-pa-thet-ic *a.*
compasivo; sompatico

sym-pa-thy *n.* simpatia

sym-pho-ny *n.* sinfonía

symp-ton *n.* sintoma

syn-a-gogue *n.* sinagoga

syn-chro-nize *v.*
sincronizar(se)

syn-di-cate *v.* sindicar

syn-od *n.* sinodo

syn-o-nym *n.* sinonimo

syn-on-y-mous *adj.*
sinonimo

syn-op-sis *n.* sinopsis

syn-the-sis *n.* sintresis

syn-thet-ic *adj.* sintetico

syph-i-lis *n.* sifilis

sy-ringe *n.* jeringa

sy-rup *n.* jarabe; almibar

sys-tem *n.* sistema

sys-tem-at-ic *a.* sistemático

sys-tem-a-tize *v.* sis-
tematizar

tab *n.* cuenta
tab-er-nac-le *n.* tabernáculo
ta-ble *n.* mesa
ta-ble-spoon-ful *n.* cucharada
tab-let *n.* tableta
ta-boo, ta-bu *a.* tabú
tab-u-lar *adj.* tabular
tab-u-late *v.* tabular
tac-it *a.* tácito
tac-i-turn *adj.* taciturno
tack *n.* tachuela; virada
tack-le *n.* equipo; carga
tact *n.* tacto
tac-tics *n.* tactica
tad-pole *n.* renacuajo
taf-fe-ta *n.* tafetan
taf-fy *n.* caramelo
tag *n.* etiqueta; marbete
tail *n.* cola; rabo
tai-lor *n.* sastre
taint *v.* inficionar(se); corromper(se)
take *v.* coger; tomar; sacar
take-off *n.* despegue
tal-cum pow-der *n.* polvo de talco
tale *n.* cuenta
tal-ent *n.* talento
tal-ent-ed *adj.* talentoso
tal-is-man *n.* talismán
talk *v.* decir; hablar
talk-a-tive *adj.* hablador
tall *a.* alto
tal-low *n.* sebo
tal-ly *n.* cuenta
tal-on *n.* garra
tam-bou-rine *n.* pandereta
tame *a.* domesticado; manso; soso
tam-per *v.* estropear; falsificar
tan *v.* curtir; tostar
tan-dem *adv.* en tandem
tang *n.* sabor fuerte
tan-gent *n., adj.* alto
tan-ge-rine *n.* naranja mandarina o tangerina
tan-gi-ble *adj.* tangente
tan-gle *v.* enredar(se)
tan-go *n.* tango
tank *n.* tangible
tan-ta-lize *v.* atormentar

tan-ta-mount *a.* equivalente
tan-trum *n.* rabieta; berrinche
tap *n.* grifo; golpecito
tape *n.* tanque
ta-per *v.* afilar
tap-es-try *n.* tapiz
tape-worm *n.* cinta
tap-i-o-ca *n.* tenia
ta-pir *n.* tapir
tar *v.* alquitranar; embrear
ta-ran-tu-la *n.* tapioca
tar-dy *adj.* tarantula
tar-get *n.* blanco
tar-iff *n.* tardio
tar-nish *v.* deslustrar(se); empanar
tar-ry *v.* tardar; detenerse
tart *n.* tarifa
tar-tar *n.* tartaro
task *n.* tarea; labor
task-mas-ter *n.* capataz
tas-sel *n.* borla
taste *n.* sabor
tast-y *adj.* sabroso
tat-ter *n.* andrajo
tat-tered *a.* harapiento; andrajoso
tat-too *n.* tatuaje
taunt *n.* mofa; sarcasmo; escarnio
taut *a.* tieso; tirante
tav-ern *n.* taberna
taw-dry *a.* charro
taw-ny *a.* leonado
tax *n.* impuesto; contribución; carga
tax-i *n.* taxi
tax-i-cab *n.* taxi
tea *n.* té
tea-bag *n.* sobre de té; muneca de te
teach *v.* instruir
teach-er *n.* maestro; profesora; profesor
tea-cup *n.* taza para te
tea-ket-tle *n.* tetera
team *n.* equipo
team-mate *n.* compañero de equipo
team-ster *n.* camionero; camionista
team-work *n.* cooperación

tea-pot *n.* tetera
tear *n.* lágrima
tear *v.* rasgar(se); romper(se)
tease *v.* tomar el pelo; atormentar
tea-spoon *n.* cucharilla
tea-spoon-ful *n.* cucharadita
tech-ni-cal *adj.* técnico
tech-ni-cian *n.* tecnico
tech-nol-o-gy *n.* tecnología
te-di-ous *adj.* tedioso
tel-e-gram *n.* telegrama
tel-e-graph *n.* telegrafo
te-leg-ra-phy *n.* telegrafía
tel-e-phone *n.* telefono
tel-e-scope *n.* telescopio
tel-e-vi-sion *n.* televisión
tell *v.* mandar; decir
tem-per-a-ment-al *adj.* temperamental
tem-per-a-ture *n.* fiebre
tem-pes-tu-ous *adj.* tempestuoso
tem-pie *n.* templo
tem-po *n.* tiempo
tem-po-ral *adj.* temporal
temp-ta-tion *n.* tentación
ten *adj., n.* diez
tend *v.* tender
ten-den-cy *n.* tendencia
ten-der-ly *adv.* tiernamente
ten-don *n.* tendón
ten-nis *n.* tenis
tense *v.* tensar, *adj.* tenso
ten-sion *n.* tensión
ter-mi-nal *adj., n.* terminal
ter-mi-nate *v.* terminar
ter-mi-nol-o-gy *n.* terminología
ter-rain *n.* terreno
ter-res-tri-al *adj.* terrestre
ter-ri-ble *adj.* terrible
ter-rif-ic *adj.* terrifico
ter-ror *n.* terror
ter-ror-ism *n.* terrorismo
ter-ror-ist *n.* terrorista
test *v.* examinar, *n.* examen
tes-ti-fy *v.* testificar
text *n.* texto
tex-ture *n.* textura
than *conj.* de; que

thanks *n.* gracias
that *adj.* aquella; aquel; esa; ese
the *def. art.* la; le; las; los; lo
the-a-ter *n.* teatro
them *pron.* las; les; los; ellas; ellos
then *adv.* luego; entonces
the-ol-o-gy *n.* teologia
the-o-rize *v.* teorizar
the-o-ry *n.* teoria
there *adv.* ahí; allí; allá
ther-mal *adj.* termal
ther-mom-e-ter *n.* termometro
the-sau-rus *n.* tesauro
these *pron.* estas; estos
they *pron.* ellas; ellos
thick *adj.* denso
thief *n.* ladrón
thigh *n.* muslo
thin *adj.* escaso; delgado
thing *n.* cosa
think *v.* creer; pensar
third *adj.* tercero
thirst *n.* sed
thir-teen *n., adj.* trece
thir-ty *n., adj.* treinta
this *adj.* esta; este, *pron.* esto; esta; este
thorn *n.* espina
thorn-y *adj.* espinoso
thor-ough *adj.* completo
though *adv.* sin embargo, *conj.* aunque
thought-ful *adj.* pensativo
thou-sand *n., adj.* mil
threat-en *v.* amenazar
three *n., adj.* tres
throat *n.* garganta
throne *n.* trono
through *prep.* por
throw *v.* lanzar; echar
thumb *n.* pulgar
Thurs-day *n.* jueves
tib-i-a *n.* tibia
tick-le *v.* cosquillear
tide *n.* marea
ti-gar *n.* tigre
till *prep.* hasta
tim-ber *n.* madero
time *n.* hora; tiempo; vez
tim-id *adj.* timido

tim-id-i-ty *n.* timidez
tip *n.* propina
tire *v.* cansar(se)
tired *adj.* cansado
tire-some *a.* molesto
tis-sue *n.* tisu
ti-tan-ic *adj.* titanico
tithe *n.* diezmo
ti-tle *v.* titular, *n.* titulo
tit-ter *v.* reir a medias
tit-u-lar *a.* titular
TNT, T.N.T. *n.* explosívo
to *adv., prep.* hacía, *prep.* hasta; a
toad *n.* sapo
toad-stool *n.* hongo; hongo venenoso
toast *v.* tostar; brindar
to-bac-co *n.* tabaco
to-bog-gan *n.* tobogan
to-day *n., adv.* hoy
toe *n.* dedo del pie
tof-fee, tof-fy *n.* caramelo
to-ga *n.* toga
to-geth-er *adv.* juntos
toil *v.* trabajar asiduamente; afanarse
toi-let *n.* retrete; water; tacado
toi-let-ry *n.* articulo de tocador
to-ken *n.* indicio; prenda; señal
tol-er-a-ble *a.* tolerable; regular
tol-er-ance *n.* tolerancía
tol-er-ant *a.* tolerante
tol-er-ate *v.* permitir; tolerar
toll *n.* peaje
to-ma-to *n.* tomate
tomb *n.* tumba
tomb-stone *n.* lapida sepulcral
to-mor-row *adv., n.* mañana
ton *n.* tonelada
tone *n.* tono; tendencía
tongs *n.* tenazas
tongue *n.* lengua
ton-ic *n.* tonico
to-night *adv.* esta noche
ton-nage *n.* tonelaje
ton-sil *n.* amigdala; tonsila
ton-sil-li-tis *n.* amigdalitis

too *adv.* además; también
tool *n.* herramienta
tooth *n.* diente
tooth-ache *n.* dolor de muelas
tooth-brush *n.* cepillo de dientes
top *n.* tapa
to-paz *n.* topacio
top-coat *n.* sobretodo
top-hat *n.* chistera
top-ic *n.* tema
top-i-cal *adj.* topico
to-pop-ra-phy *n.* topografía
top-ple *v.* venirse abajo
top-sy-tur-vy *adv.* patas arriba
torch *n.* antorcha; hacha
tor-ment *v.* atormentar
tor-na-do *n.* tormento
tor-pe-do *n.* torpedo
tor-rent *n.* torrente
tor-rid *a.* torrido
tor-so *n.* torso
tor-toise *n.* tortuga
tor-tu-ous *a.* tortuoso
tor-ture *v.* torturar
toss *v.* echar
tot *n.* nene; nena
to-tal *n., adj.* total
to-tal-i-tar-i-an *a.* totalitario
to-tal-ly *adv.* totalmente
tote *v. inf.* llevar
to-tem *n.* tótem
tot-ter *v.* bambolearse
touch *v.* tocar(se)
touch-y *a.* irritable
tough *adj.* dificil
tough-en *v.* endurecer(se); hacer(se)
tour *n.* viaje; excursión
tour-ism *n.* turismo
tour-ist *n.* turista
tour-na-ment *n.* torneo
tour-ni-quet *n.* torniquete
tou-sle *v.* despeinar
tow *v.* llevar a remolque
to-ward *prep.* cerca de
tow-el *n.* toalla
tow-er *n.* torre
town *n.* pueblo; ciudad
tox-ic *a.* tóxico
tox-in *n.* toxina

toy *n.* juguete

trace *n.* indicio; huella; rastro

tra-che-a *n.* tráquea

track *n.* via; pista; senda

tract *n.* extensión; tratado

trac-tor *n.* tractor

trade *v.* comerciar

trade-mark *n.* marca de fabrica; marca registrado

trade un-ion *n.* sindicato

tra-di-tion *n.* tradición

tra-di-tion-al *adj.* tradicional

tra-duce *v.* calumniar

traf-fic *n.* tráfico

trag-e-dy *n.* tragedia

trag-ic *adj.* trágico

trail *v.* arrastrar(se); rastrear

trail-er *n.* remolque

train *n.* tren

trait *n.* caracteristica; rasgo

trai-tor *n.* traidor

tra-jec-to-ry *n.* trayectoria

tramp *v.* andar con pasos pesados

tram-ple *v.* pisotear

trance *n.* arrobamiento; estado hipnotico

tran-quil *adj.* tranquilo

tran-quil-li-ty *n.* tranquilidad

tran-quil-lize *v.* tranquilizar

tran-quil-iz-er *n.* tranquilizante

trans-act *v.* despachar

trans-ac-tion *n.* transacción

tran-scend *v.* sobresalir

tran-scribe *v.* transcribir

tran-script *n.* trasunto

tran-scrip-tion *n.* transcripción

trans-fer *v.* transferir; trasladar

trans-fer-ence *n.* transferencia

trans-form *v.* transformar

trans-for-ma-tion *n.* transcripción; copia

trans-form-er *n.* transformador

trans-fu-sion *n.* transfusión

trans-gress *v.* traspasar; pecar

trans-gres-sion *n.* transgresion

tran-sient *a.* transitorio; pasajero

tran-sis-tor *n.* transistor

trans-it *n.* transito

tran-si-tion *n.* transito

tran-si-tive *a.* transiotivo

tran-si-to-ry *adj.* transitorio

trans-late *v.* traducir

trans-la-tion *n.* traducción

trans-lu-cent *a.* translucido

trans-mis-sion *n.* transmisión

trans-mit *v.* transmitir

trans-mit-ter *n.* transmisor

tran-som *n.* travesano

trans-par-ent *a.* transparente; claro; obvio

tran-spire *v.* transpirar; suceder

trans-plant *v.* trasplantar

trans-port *n.* transporte, *v.* transportar

trans-por-ta-tion *n.* transporte

trans-pose *v.* transponer

trans-verse *a.* transversal

trap *v.* entrampar

tra-peze *n.* trapecio

trap-e-zoid *n.* trap-e-zoid

trash *n.* basura

trau-ma *n.* trauma

trau-mat-ic *adj.* traumatico

trav-el *v.* viajar

trea-son *n.* traición

treas-ure *n.* tesoro

treas-ur-er *n.* tesorero

treas-ur-y *n.* tesoro

treat *v.* tratar

trea-tise *n.n* tratado

treat-ment *n.* tratamiento

trea-ty *n.* tratado; pacto

tre-ble *a.* triple

tree *n.* arbol

trek *v.* caminar

trel-lis *n.* enrejado; espaldera

trem-ble *v.* temblar

tre-men-dous *a.* tremendo

trem-or *n.* temblor

trench *n.* foso; trinchera

tri-al *n.* prueba

tri-an-gle *n.* triángulo

tri-an-gu-lar *adj.* triangular

tri-bu-nal *n.* tribunal

trib-ute *n.* tributo

trick *n.* trucio; trampa; engano

trick-le *v.* gotear

tri-cy-cle *n.* triciclo

tried *adj.* probado

tri-fle *n.* bagatela

tri-fling *a.* sin importancia

trig-ger *n.* gatillo

trig-o-nom-e-try *n.* trigonometria

tril-lion *n.* billon

trim *v.* guarnecer

trin-ket *n.* dije

tri-o *n.* trio

trip *n.* viaje

tri-ple *v.* triplicar(se)

trip-let *n.* trillizo

trip-li-cate *v.* triplicar

tri-pod *n.* tripode

trite *a.* gastado

tri-umph *n.* triunfo

tri-um-phant *adj.* triunfante

triv-i-al *a.* trivial; frivolo

triv-i-al-i-ty *n.* trivialidad

trol-ley *n.* tranvia

trom-bone *n.* trombon

troop *n.* tropa; escuadron

troop-er *n.* soldado de caballeria

tro-phy *n.* trofeo

trop-ic *n.* tropico

trop-i-cal *adj.* tropical

trot *v.* ir al trote; hacer trotar

trou-ba-dour *n.* trovador

trou-ble *v.* molestar(se)

trou-ble-some *a.* molesto

trough *n.* abrevadero

troupe *n.* compania

trou-sers *n.* pantalones

trous-seau *n.* ajuar

trout *n.* trucha

trow-el *n.* paleta; desplantador

tru-ant *n.* novillero

truce *n.* tregua

truck *n.* camion

true *adj.* verdadero

tru-ly *adv.* verdaderamente; realmente

trump *n.* triumfo

trum-pet *n.* trompeta

trun-cate *v.* truncar

trunk *n.* tronco; baul

trus *v.* empaquetear

trust *v.* esperar, *n.* fideicomiso

trus-tee *n.* fideicomisario

trust-wor-thy *a.* fidedigno; confiable

trust-y *adj.* seguro

truth *n.* verdad

trugh-ful *a.* veraz

try *v.* probar

try-ing *a.* dificil; penoso

tryst *n.* cita

T-shirt *n.* camiseta

tub *n.* baño; tina

tu-ba *n.* tuba

tube *n.* tubo

tu-ber-cu-lo-sis *n.* tuberculosis

tuck *v.* alforzar

Tues-day *n.* martes

tuft *n.* copete

tug *v.* tirar con fuerza; remolcar

tug-boat *n.* remolcador

tu-i-tion *n.* ensenanza

tu-lip *n.* tulipan

tum-ble *v.* caer(se)

tum-bler *n.* volteador; vaso

tu-mor *n.* tumor

tu-mult *n.* tumulto

tu-mul-tu-ous *a.* tumultuoso

tu-na *n.* atun

tun-dra *n.* tundra

tune *n.* aire; afinacion

tu-nic *n.* tunica

tun-nel *n.* tunel

tur-ban *n.* turbante

tur-bid *adj.* turbido

tur-bine *n.* turbina

tur-bu-lence *n.* turbulencia; confusion

tur-bu-lent *adj.* turbulento

tu-reen *n.* sopera

turf *n.* cesped

tur-key *n.* pavo

tur-moil *n.* tumulto

turn *v.* volver(se); girar

turn-coat *n.* traidor

tur-nip *n.* nabo

turn-out *n.* ocncurrencia;

producción
turn-pike *n.* autopista de peaje
turn-stile *n.* torniquete
tur-pen-tin *n.* trementina
tur-quoise *n.* turquesa
tur-ret *n.* turrecilla
tur-tle *n.* tortuga
tusk *n.* colmillo
tus-sle *n.* agarrada
tu-te-lage *n.* tutela
tu-tor *n.* tutor
tux-e-do *n.* smoking
TV *n.* televisión
twang *n.* tanido; timbre nasal
tweed *n.* mezcla de lana
tweez-ers *n.* bruselas
twelfth *adj.* duodecimo
twelve *adj., n.* doce
twen-ty *adj., n.* veinte
twice *adv.* dos veces
twig *n.* ramita
twi-light *n.* crepusculo
twill *n.* tela cruzada
twin *adj., n.* gemelo
twine *n.* guita; bramante
twinge *n.* dolor agudo
twin-kle *v.* centellear
twirl *v.* girar; piruetear
twist *v.* torcer(se)
twitch *v.* crisparse
twit-ter *v.* gorjear
two *adj., n.* dos
two-faced *a.* falso; hipoocrita
ty-coon *n.* magnate
type *n.* tipo
type-write *v.* escribir a maquina
type-writ-er *n.* maquína de escribir
ty-phoid *n.* fiebre tifoidea
ty-phoon *n.* tifón
ty-phus *n.* tifus
typ-i-cal *adj.* típico
typ-i-fy *v.* simbolizar
typ-ist *n.* mecanografo
ty-pog-ra-phy *n.* tipografía
ty-ran-ni-cal *a.* tiránico; despotico
tyr-an-nize *v.* tiranizar
tyr-an-ny *n.* tirania

u-biq-ui-tous *adj.* ubicuo
u-biq-ui-ty *n.* ubicuidad
ud-der *n.* ubre
ug-li-ness *n.* fealdad
ug-ly *adj.* feo
u-ku-le-le *n.* ukelele
ul-cer *n.* úlcera
ul-cer-ate *v.* ulcerar(se)
ul-cer-ous *adj.* ulceroso
ul-na *n.* cúbito
ul-te-ri-or *adj.* ulterior
ul-ti-mate *adj.* último
ul-ti-ma-tum *n.* ultimatum
ul-tra *adj.* excesivo
ul-tra-mod-ern *adj.* ultramoderno
ul-tra-son-ic *adj.* ultrasonico
ul-tra-sound *n.* ultrasonido
ul-tra-vi-o-let *adj.* ultravioleta
ul-u-late *v.* ulular
um-bil-i-cal *adj.* umbilical
um-bil-i-cus *n.* ombligo
um-brel-la *n.* paraguas
um-pire *n.* arbitro
ump-teen *a.* muchos
un-a-bashed *a.* desvergonzado; descarado
un-a-ble *adj.* incapaz
un-a-bridged *adj.* no abreviado
un-ac-cent-ed *adj.* sin acento
un-ac-cept-a-ble *adj.* inaceptable
un-ac-count-a-ble *adj.* inexplicable
un-ac-cus-tomed *adj.* no acostumbrado
un-ac-knowl-edged *adj.* no econocido
un-a-dorned *adj.* sin adorno
un-a-dul-ter-at-ed *adj.* no adulterado
un-af-fect-ed *adj.* sin afectación
un-a-fraid *adj.* sin temor
un-aid-ed *adj.* sin ayuda
un-am-big-u-ous *adj.* sin ambiguedad
u-nan-i-mous *adj.* unanime
un-an-swer-a-ble *adj.* incontestable
un-ap-proach-a-ble *adj.* in-

accesible
un-armed *adj.* desarmado
un-as-sail-a-ble *adj.* inexpugnable
un-as-sist-ed *adj.* sin ayuda
un-as-sum-ing *a.* modesto; sencillo
un-at-tached *adj.* suelto
un-at-tend-ed *adj.* desatendido
un-at-trac-tive *adj.* inatractivo
un-au-thor-ized *adj.* sin autorización
un-a-void-a-ble *adj.* inevitable
un-a-ware *adj.* ignorante
un-a-wares *adv.* de improviso
un-bal-anced *adj.* desequilibrado
un-beat-a-ble *adj.* invencible
un-beat-en *adj.* invicto
un-be-com-ing *a.* que sienta mal
un-be-lief *n.* incredulidad
un-be-liev-a-ble *adj.* increible
un-be-liev-er *n.* descreido
un-be-liev-ing *adj.* incredulo
un-bend *v.* desencorvar; aflojar
un-bend-ing *adj.* inflexible
un-bi-ased *a.* imparcial
un-bind *v.* desatar
un-blem-ished *adj.* puro
un-born *a.* no nacido
un-bos-om *v.* revelar
un-bound-ed *adj.* ilimitado
un-bowed *adj.* recto
un-break-a-ble *adj.* irrompible
un-breath-a-ble *adj.* irrespirable
un-bri-dled *adj.* desenfrenado
un-bro-ken *adj.* inviolado; sin romper
un-buck-le *v.* deshebillar
un-bur-den *v.* descargar
un-bot-ton *v.* desabotonar(se)
un-caged *adj.* suelto

un-called-for *a.* inmerecido
un-can-ny *a.* extraño; misterioso
un-cap *v.* destapar
un-ceas-ing *adj.* incesante
un-cer-e-mo-ni-ous *a.* informal
un-cer-tain *adj.* indeciso
un-cer-tain-ty *n.* incertidumbre
un-change-a-ble *adj.* inalterable
un-changed *adj.* inalterado
un-chang-ing *adj.* invariable
un-chart-ed *adj.* desconocido
un-civ-il *adj.* incivil
un-civ-i-lized *adj.* incivilizado
un-clad *adj.* desnudo
un-clasp *v.* separar
un-cle *n.* tio
un-clean *adj.* sucio
un-clear *adj.* confuso
un-clog *v.* desatascar
un-com-fort-a-ble *adj.* incomodo
un-com-mon *adj.* raro
un-com-mu-ni-ca-tive *a.* poco comunicativo
un-com-pro-mis-ing *a.* inflexible
un-con-cern *n.* indiferencia
un-con-nect-ed *adj.* inconexo
un-con-scious *adj.* inconsciente
un-con-sid-ered *adj.* inconsiderado
un-con-trolled *adj.* desenfrenado
un-cooked *adj.* crudo
un-count-ed *adj.* innumerable
un-cross *v.* descruzar
un-de-cid-ed *adj.* indeciso
un-der-es-ti-mate *v.* subestimar
un-der-ground *adj.* subterráneo
un-der-line *v.* subrayar
un-der-neath *adv.* debajo, *prep.* bajo
un-der-wear *n.* ropa interior

un-do *v.* desatar
un-fin-ished *adj.* incompleto
unn-fold *v.* extender; abrir
u-ni-form *n.* uniforme
un-ion *n.* unión
u-ni-ted *adj.* unido
u-ni-ver-sal *adj.* universal
un-luck-y *adj.* desdichado
un-rest *n.* inquietud
un-sa-vor-y *adj.* desagradable
un-seem-ly *adj.* indecoroso
un-skilled *adj.* inexperto
un-so-phis-ti-cat-ed *adj.* candido
un-sta-ble *adj.* inestable
un-stead-y *adj.* inseguro
un-til *prep.* hasta
un-truth-ful *adj.* mentiroso
un-u-su-al *adj.* raro
un-wrap *v.* desenvolver
up *prep.* subiendo, *adj.* ascendente, *adv.* acabado; arriba
up-hill *adj.* ascendente
up-hol-ster-y *n.* tapiceria
up-on *prep.* sobre; encima de
up-per *adj.* alto
up-per-cut *n.* gancho
up-roar *n.* alboroto
up-set *n.* trastorno; *v.* volcar
up-stairs *adj.* arriba
u-ra-ni-um *n.* uranio
U-ra-nus *n.* Urano
ur-ban *adj.* urbano
urge *n.* impulso, *v.* incitar
ur-gent *adj.* urgente
u-rine *n.* orina
urn *n.* urna
us *pron.* nosotras; nosotros; nos
use *n.* uso, *v.* utilizar; usar
use-less *adj.* inútil
u-su-al *adj.* usual
u-ten-sil *n.* utensilio
utilitarian *n.* utilitario
u-til-i-ty *n.* utilidad
u-til-ize *v.t.* utilizar
ut-ter-ance *n.* expresion
u-ter-us *n.* útero
uxorious *a.* uxorio; gurromino

va-can-cy *n.* vacante
va-cant *adj.* vacío
va-ca-tion *n.* vacación
vac-ci-nate *v.* vacunar
vac-ci-na-tion *n.* vacunación
vac-cine *n.* vacuna
vac-il-late *n.* vacilar
vac-il-la-tion *n.* vacilacon; fluctuación
va-cu-i-ty *n.* vacuidad
vac-u-um *n.* vacio
va-gar-y *n.* capricho
va-grant *n.* vagabundo
vague *adj.* incierto; vago
vain *adj.* vano
vale *n.* valle
val-e-dic-to-ry *n.* discurso de despedida
val-en-tine *n.* novia o novio en el dia de San Valentine
val-id *adj.* valido
val-i-date *v.* validar
va-lid-i-ty *n.* validez
va-lise *n.* maleta
val-ley *n.* valle
val-or *n.* valor; valentia
val-u-a-ble *a.* valioso; costoso; precioso
val-u-a-tion *n.* valuación
val-ue *v.* valuar, *n.* valor
valve *n.* valvula
vam-pire *n.* vampiro
van *n.* vanguardia; camion de mudanzas
van-dal *n.* vandalo
van-dal-ism *n.* vandalismo
vane *n.* veleta
van-guard *n.* vanguardia
va-nil-la *n.* vainilla
van-ish *v.* desaparecer
van-i-ty *n.* vanidad
van-quish *v.* vencer; conquistar
van-tage *n.* ventaja; provecho
vap-id *a.* insipido
va-por *n.* vapor
va-por-ize *v.* vaporizar(se)
va-por-ous *adj.* vaporoso
var-i-a-bil-i-ty *n.* variabilidad
var-i-a-ble *n., adj.* variable
var-i-a-tion *n.* variación
var-i-cose *a.* varicoso

var-ied *adj.* variado
va-ri-e-ty *n.* variedad
var-i-ous *adj.* variado
var-nish *n.* barniz
var-si-ty *n.* equip principal de una universidad
var-y *v.* variar; desviarse; cambiar
vase *n.* jarrón
vast *adj.* vasto
veal *n.* ternera
veg-e-ta-ble *n.* legumbre
veg-e-tar-i-an *n.* vegetariano
veg-e-tate *v.* vegetar
veg-e-ta-tion *n.* vegetacion
ve-hi-cle *n.* vehiculo
vein *n.* vena
ve-loc-i-ty *n.* velocidad
ve-nal-i-ty *n.* venalidad
vend *v.* vender
ven-er-a-ble *adj.* venerable
ven-er-a-tion *n.* veneración
ve-ni-al *adj.* venial
ven-om *n.* veneno
ven-om-ous *adj.* venenoso
ven-ti-late *v.* ventilar
ven-tral *adj.* ventral
ven-tri-cle *n.* ventriculo
ven-ture-some *adj.* aventurero
Ve-nus *n.* Venus
ve-ra-cious *adj.* veraz
verb *n.* verbo
ver-bal *adj.* verbal
ver-bose *adj.* verboso
ver-bos-i-ty *n.* verbosidad
ver-dict *n.* veredicto
ver-i-fy *v.* verificar
ver-mouth *n.* vermut
ver-nal *adj.* vernal
ver-sa-til-i-ty *n.* adaptabilidad
verse *n.* versiculo
ver-sion *n.* versión
ver-te-bra *n.* vertebra
ver-te-brate *adj.* vertebrado
ver-ti-cal *adj.* vertical
ver-y *adj.* mismo, *adv.* muy
ves-sel *n.* vaso
vest *n.* chaleco
vet *n.* veterinario
vet-er-an *adj., n.* veterano
vet-er-i-nar-i-an *n.* veterinario
vet-er-i-nar-y *adj., n.* veterinario
vi-brant *adj.* vibrante
vi-brate *v.* oscilar
vi-bra-tion *n.* vibración
vic-ar *n.* vicario
vi-car-i-ous *a.* substituto
vice *n.* vicio
vice-pres-i-dent *n.* vicepresidente
vice-roy *n.* virrey
vice ver-sa *adv.* viceversa
vi-cin-i-ty *n.* vecindad
vi-cious *a.* depravado; vicioso; cruel
vic-tim *n.* victima
vic-tim-ize *v.* hacer victima
vic-to-ri-ous *adj.* victorioso
vic-to-ry *n.* victoria
view *v.* ver, *n.* escena
vig-i-lance *n.* vigilancia
vig-or *n.* vigor
vig-or-ous *adj.* vigoroso
vil-lage *n.* aldea
vin-di-cate *v.* vindicar
vine *n.* vid
vin-e-gar *n.* vinagre
vi-o-la *n.* viola
vi-o-la-tion *n.* violación
vi-o-lent *adj.* violento
vi-o-let *adj.* violado
vi-o-lin *n.* violin
vir-ile *adj.* viril
vi-ril-i-ty *n.* virilidad
vir-tu-al *adj.* virtual
vir-tu-al-ly *adv.* virtualmente
vir-u-lent *adj.* virulento
vi-rus *n.* virus
vis-cos-i-ty *n.* viscosidad
vis-count *n.* vizconde
vis-count-ess *n.* vizcondesa
vise *n.* tornillo
vis-i-bil-i-ty *n.* visibilidad
vis-i-ble *a.* visible; conspicuo
vi-sion *n.* visión
vi-sion-ar-y *n.* visionario
vis-it *n.* visita, *v.* visitar
vis-it-a-tion *n.* visitación
vi-sor *n.* visera
vis-u-al *adj.* visual
vis-u-al-ize *v.* representarse en la mente

vi-tal *adj.* vital
vi-tal-i-ty *n.* vitalidad
vi-ta-min *n.* vitamina
vit-re-ous *a.* vitreo
vit-ri-ol *n.* vitriolo
vi-tu-per-ate *v.* vituperar
vi-va-cious *a.* vivaz; animado; vivaracho
vi-vac-i-ty *n.* vivacidad; animacion
viv-id *adj.* intenso; vivo
vix-en *n.* arpia; zorra
vo-cab-u-lar-y *n.* vocabulario
vo-cal *adj.* vocal
vo-cal-ist *n.* cantante
vo-ca-tion *n.* vocación
vod-ka *n.* vodka
vogue *n.* moda; boga
voice *n.* voz
void *a.* nulo; vacio
vol-can-ic *adj.* volcanico
vol-ca-no *n.* volcan
vo-li-tion *n.* voluntad; volicion
vol-ley *n.* descarga; voleo
volt *n.* voltio
volt-age *n.* voltaje
vol-u-ble *a.* hablador
vol-ume *n.* cantidad; volumen
vol-un-tar-y *adj.* voluntario
vol-un-teer *n.* voluntario
vo-lup-tu-ar-y *n.* voluptuoso
vo-lup-tu-ous *a.* voluptuoso
vom-it *n.* vomito, *v.* vomitar
vom-it-ing *n.* vomito
voo-doo *n.* vodu
vo-ra-cious *a.* voraz
voracity *n.* voracidad
vor-tex *n.* vortice
votary *n.* devoto; partidario
vote *v.* votar, *n.* voto
vo-ter *n.* votante
vot-ing *n.* votacion
vo-tive *a.* votivo; exvoto
vouch *v.i.* afirmar
vouch-er *n.* comprobante
vow-el *n.* vocal
voy-age *v.* viajar, *n.* viaje
vul-gar *adj.* vulgar
vul-gar-ize *v.* vulgarizar
vul-ner-a-ble *a.* vulnerable
vul-ture *n.* buitre

wack-y *a.* loco; chiflado
wad *n.* fajo; taco; rollo; bolita
wad-dle *v.* anadear
wade *v.* vadear; pasar con dificultad
wag *v.* menear(se)
wage *n.* salario
wag-er *v.* apostar
wag-on *n.* carro
waif *n.* nino abandonado
wail *v.* lamentarse; sollozar
wain-scot *n.* friso de madera
waist *n.* cintura
waist-coat *n.* chaleco
waist-line *n.* talle
wait *n.* espera, *v.* esperar
wait-er *n.* camarero
wait-ress *n.* camarera
waive *v.* renunciar a; abandonar
waiv-er *n.* renuncia
wake *v.* despertar(se)
wake-ful *a.* vigilante
wak-en *v.* despertar(se)
walk *n.* caminata, *v.* caminar; andar
walk-out *n.* huelga
walk-o-ver *n.* triunfo facil
wall *n.* pared
wall-board *n.* carton de yeso
wal-let *n.* cartera
wal-lop *v.* zurrar
wal-low *v.* revp;carse
wall-pa-per *n.* papel pintado
wal-nut *n.* nogal
wal-rus *n.* morsa
waltz *n.* vals
wan *a.* palido
wan-der *v.* desviarse
wan-der-lust *n.* deseo de viajar
wane *v.* disminuir; menguar
want *v.* querer; requerir; desear
want-ing *a.* deficiente
wan-ton *a.* lascivo; desenfrenado
war *v.* guerrear, *n.* guerra
war-ble *v.* trinar
war-cry *n.* grito de guerra
ward *v.* desviar
war-den *n.* guardián; alsaide
ward-robe *n.* guardarropa;

vestuario

ware *n.* mercancias

ware-house *n.* almacén

war-fare *n.* guerra

war-lock *n.* hechicero

warm *v.* calentar(se), *adj.* caluroso; caliente

warm-heart-ed *a.* afectuoso

war-mong-er *n.* belicista

warmth *n.* calor

warn *v.* advertir

warn-ing *n.* advertencia; aviso

warp *v.* albearse; pervertir

war-rant *n.* autorizacion; garantia

war-ran-ty *n.* garantia

war-ren *n.* conejera

war-ri-or *n.* guerrero

wart *n.* verruga

war-y *a.* cauteloso

was *pret of* be

wash *v.* lavar(se)

wash-cloth *n.* paño para lavarse

wash-er *n.* lavadora

wash-ing *n.* lavado

wash-room *n.* lavabo

wash-stand *n.* lavamanos

wash-tub *n.* tin o cuba de lavar

wasp *n.* avispa

wast-age *n.* desgaste; merma

waste *n.* perdida, *v.* desperdiciar

wast-rel *n.* derrochador

watch *n.* reloj, *v.* mirar; observar

watch-ful *a.* vigilante; désvelado

watch-man *n.* vigilante

watch-word *n.* santo y sena

wa-ter *n.* agua

wa-ter-col-or *n.* acuarela

wa-ter-course *n.* corriente

wa-ter-fall *n.* cascada

wa-ter-fowl *n.* ave acuantica

wa-ter-front *n.* terreno rebereno

wa-ter lil-y *n.* nenufar

wa-ter-logged *a.* anegado

wa-ter-mark *n.* nivel de agua; filigrana

wa-ter-mel-on *n.* sandia

wa-ter-proof *a.* impermeable

wa-ter-side *n.* orilla del agua

wa-ter sof-ten-er *n.* ablandador quimico de agua

wa-ter-spout *n.* tromba marina; mangua

wa-ter-tight *a.* estanco; seguro

wa-ter-way *n.* canal

wa-ter-y *adj.* insipido

watt *n.* vatio

wave *v.* ondular, *n.* onda

wa-ver *v.* oscilar; vacilar

wav-y *a.* ondulado

wax *n.* cera

wax-en *a.* de cara; palido

wax-work *n.* figura de cera

way *n.* camino; modo; direccion

way-far-er *n.* viajero

way-lay *v.* asaltar

way-side *n.* borde del camino

way-ward *a.* voluntarioso; travieso

we *pron.* nosotras; nosotros

weak *adj.* débil

weak-en *v.* debilitar(se)

weak-ling *n.* alfenique

weak-ly *a.* achacoso

weak-mind-ed *a.* sin voluntad

weak-ness *n.* debilidad

wealth *n.* riqueza

wealth-y *adj.* rico

wean *v.* destetar

weap-on *n.* arma

weap-on-ry *n.* armas

wear *v.* desgastar(se); llevar

wear-ing *adj.* penoso

wea-ri-some *a.* fastidioso

wea-ry *a.* fatigado; aburrido

wea-sel *n.* comadreja

weath-er *n.* tiempo

weath-er-beat-en *a.* curtido pro la intemperie

weath-er-glass *n.* barometro

weath-er-man *n.* pronosticador de tiempo

weave *v.* tejido

web *n.* tela

web-bing n. cincha
wed v. casar(se)
wed-ding n. boda
wedge n. cuña
wed-lock n. matrimonio
Wednes-day n. miércoles
wee a. paqueñito
weed v. escardar
week n. semana
week-day n. dia laborable o de trabajo
week-end n. fin de la semana
week-ly a. semanal
weep v. llorar
wee-vil n. gorgojo
weigh v. pesar
weight n. pesa
weight-y adj. pesado
weird adj. extrano
wel-come adj. agradable
weld v. soldar
wel-fare n. bienestar
well adv. pues, n. fuente
well-be-ing n. bienestar
well-bred a. bien criado
well-dis-posed a. bien dispuesto
well-known adj. famoso
well-off a. adimerado
well-read a. leido
well-thought-of a. bien mirado
well-timed a. oportuno
well-to-do a. acaudalado
welt n. verdugon
wel-ter v. revolcar(se)
wench n. moza
were pret. of be
were-wolf n. hombre que puede transformarse en lobo
west n. oeste
west-ern adj. occidental
wet v. mojar(se)
whack v. golpear
whale n. ballena
whale-bone n. ballena
wharf n. muelle
what pron. qué; lo que; cual
what-ev-er pron. todo lo qué
what-not n. estante; juguetero

wheat n. trigo
whee-dle v. engatusar; halagar
wheel n. rueda
wheel-bar-row n. carretilla
wheel-chair n. silla de ruedas
wheeze v. respirar asmaticamente
when conj. cuando
whence adv. de donde; de que
when-ev-er adv. siempre que
where conj., adv. donde, adv. adonde
where-a-bouts n. paradero
where-as conj. visto que
where-up-on adv. con lo cual
wher-ev-er adv. dondequiera
wheth-er conj. si
whey n. suero de la leche
which pron. lo que; cual; la; le
which-ev-er pron. cualquiera
whiff n. olorcillo
while conj. mientras
whim v. lloriquear
whim-per v. lloriquear
whim-si-cal a. caprichoso
whine v. gimotear
whin-ny n. relincho
whip v. batir
whir v. zumbar; batir
whirl v. girar repidamente
whirl-pool n. remolino
whirl-wind n. torbellino
whisk-ers n. barbas; bigotes
whis-key n. whisky
whis-per n. cuchicheo, v. cuchichear
whis-tle v. silbar
white n., adj. blanco
white-col-lar a. oficinesco
whit-en v. blanquear
white-wash n. jalbeque
whith-er conj. adonde
whit-tle v. cortar poco a poco
whiz v. silbar; rehilar
who pron. la; el; lo; quién;

que

who-ev-er *pron.* quienquiere que

whole *n., adj.* todo

whole-heart-ed *a.* sincero; incondicional

whole-sale *n.* venta al por menor

whole-some *a.* saludable

whol-ly *adv.* completamente

whom *pron.* a quién

whom-ev-er *pron.* a quien-quiera

whoop *n.* alarido

whore *n.* puta; prostituta

whose *pron.* cuyo

why *adv.* ¿por qué?

wick *n.* mecha

wick-ed *adj.* malicioso

wick-er *a.* de mimbre

wide *adj.* ancho

wide-a-wake *a.* despabilado

wid-en *v.* ensanchar(se)

wide-spread *a.* extendido; difuso

wid-ow *n.* viuda

wid-ow-er *n.* viudo

width *n.* anchura

wield *v.* ejercer; mandar; manejar

wife *n.* esposa

wig *n.* peluca

wig-gle *v.* menear(se); cimbrearse

wild *adj.* descabellado

wild boar *n.* jabalí

wil-der-ness *n.* yermo; desierto

wile *n.* ardid

will *v.* querer

will-ful *a.* voluntarioso; terco; premeditado

will-ing *a.* dispuesto; com-placiente

wil-low *n.* sauce

wil-low-y *a.* esbelto

wil-ly-nil-ly *adv.* de grado o por fuerza

wilt *v.* marchitar(se)

win *n.* victoria, *v.* lograr; ganar

wince *v.* estremecerse; respingar

winch *n.* torno

wind *n.* viento

wind *v.* arrollar(se)

wind-fall *n.* ganacia in-esperada

wind-mill *n.* molino de viento

win-dow *n.* ventana

win-dow-pane *n.* cristal

wind-shield *n.* parabrisas

wind-y *adj.* ventoso

wine *n.* vino

win-er-y *n.* lagar; candiotera

wing *n.* ala

wink *v.* guinar; pestanear

win-ner *n.* ganador

win-ning *n.* ganancias

win-now *v.* aventar

win-some *a.* atractivo; alegre

win-ter *n.* invierno

win-try *adj.* invernal

wipe *v.* enjugar; secar; borrar

wire *n.* alambre

wire-tap *v.* intervenir

wir-ing *n.* instalación de alambres

wir-y *a.* nervudo

wis-dom *n.* sabiduria

wise *adj.* acertado; sabio

wise-crack *n.* cuchufleta; pulla

wish *n.* deseo, *v.* desear

wish-ful *adj.* deseoso

wit *n.* sal

witch *n.* bruja

witch-craft *n.* brujeria

with *prep.* con

with-draw-al *n.* retirada

with-drawn *a.* ensimismado

with-er *v.* marchitar(se); secarse

with-hold *v.* retener

with-in *adv.* dentro

with-out *adv.* por fuera

with-stand *v.* resistir

wit-less *a.* tonto

wit-ness *n.* testigo

wi-ti-cism *n.* dicho gracioso

wit-ty *a.* salado; ingenioso

wiz-ard *n.* hechicero

wob-ble *v.* bambolear; bailar

woe *n.* afliccion; infortunio

wolf *n.* lobo

wom-an *n.* mujer

wom-an-kind n. sexo femenino

womb n. matriz

wom-en's rights n. derechos de la mujer

won-der v. asombrarse

won-der-ful adj. maravilloso

woo v. cortejar

wood n. madera

wood-en a. de madera; sin expresión

wood-land n. monte

w o o d - p e c k - e r n. picamaderos

wood-y adj. lenoso

wool n. lana

wool-ly adj. lanudo

word n. palabra

work v. trabajar, n. obra; trabajo

work-book n. cuaderno

work-er n. trabajador

work-shop n. taller

world n. mundo

world-ly adj. mundano

world-wide a. mundial

worm n. gusano

worm-eaten a. carcomido

wormwood n. ajenjo

worn adj. usado

w o r r i e r n. aprensivo; pesimista

wor-ry v. inquietar(se)

wors-en v. empeorar

wor-ship v. venerar

worth n. valor

worth-less adj. despreciable

wound v. herir

wrap v. envolver

wreck v. naufragar, n. ruina

wrin-kle v. arrugar(se), n. arruga

wrist n. muñeca

write v. escribir

writ-er n. escritora; escritor

writ-ing n. escrito

wrong adj. equivocado

wrong-ful a. injusto; falso

wrong-head-ed a. terco

w r o u g h t a. forjado; trabajado

wry a. torcido; ironico; mueca

x-ray v. radiografiar, n. radiografia

yank v. sacar de un tirón

Yan-kee n. yanqui

yard n. yarda

yard-goods n. tejidos

yard-stick n. vara de medir

yarn n. hilaza

yar-row n. milenrama

yawn n. bostezo, v. bostezar

ye pron. vosotros

yea adv. sí

year n. año

year-ling n. primal

year-ly adv. anualmente

yearn v. suspirar; anhelar

yearn-ing n. anhelo

yeast n. levadura

yell n. grito, v. gritar

yel-low n., adj. amarillo

yes adv. sí

yes-ter-day n. ayer

yet adv. todavía

yew n. tejo

yield v. rendir(se)

yolk n. yema

yon-der adv. allí; allá

yore n. antaño

you pron. vosotras; vosotros; tu

young adj. joven

young-ster n. jovencito

your adj. sus; tus; vuestras; vuestros

yours pron. tu; vos; vosotros; vosotras

your-self pron. usted mismo; tu mismo

youth n. jovenes

youth-ful adj. juvenil

zeal n. ardor

zeal-ous adj. celoso

ze-bra n. cebra

ze-nith n. cenit

ze-ro n. cero

ze-ro hour n. hora de ataque

zest n. gusto

zone n. zona

zoo n. jardin zoologico

zo-o-log-i-cal adj. zoologico

zuc-chi-ni n. cidracayote de verano